N

FINE ARTS

Library of Congress Classification

1996 EDITION

Prepared by the
Cataloging Policy
and Support Office,
Library Services

Library of Congress, Cataloging Distribution Service, Washington, D.C.

The additions and changes in Class N adopted while this work was in press will be cumulated and printed in List 265 of *LC Classification--Additions and Changes*

Library of Congress Cataloging-in-Publication Data

Library of Congress. Cataloging Policy and Support Office.
Library of Congress classification. Class N. Fine arts / prepared by the Cataloging Policy and Support Office. Collections Services. — 1996 ed.
p. cm.
Rev. ed. of: Classification. Class N, fine arts. 4th ed. 1970.
ISBN 0-8444-0907-3
—— Copy 3 Z663.78.C5N 1996
1. Classification—Books—Art. 2. Classification, Library of Congress. I. United States. Library of Congress. Subject Cataloging Division. Classification. Class N, fine arts. II. Title.
Z696.U5N 1996
025.4'67—dc20 96-23211
CIP

For sale by the Library of Congress,
Cataloging Distribution Service,
Washington, D.C. 20541

PREFACE

The first edition of Class N, Art, was published in 1910, the second in 1917, the third in 1922, and the fourth in 1970. This 1996 edition has been produced using a new automated system developed at the Library of Congress for this purpose. The system will allow for the production of new editions on a regular and frequent basis.

In 1992, Rebecca Guenther, Network Development and MARC Standards Office, began overseeing the conversion of Library of Congress Classification data to machine-readable form using the provisionally approved USMARC format for classification data. In 1993-1994, the Cataloging Distribution Service developed programs for producing printed classification schedules from the MARC records in cooperation with Lawrence Buzard, editor of classification schedules, Paul Weiss, senior cataloging policy specialist, and Rebecca Guenther. The Cataloging Distribution Service also coordinated the layout and design of the new schedules.

The classification data were converted to the MARC format by Harriet Harrison, senior cataloging policy specialist, who simplified the use of the schedules by expanding many areas previously covered by "Divide like" notes and who also created the index. Mary K.D. Pietris, senior cataloging policy specialist, proofread the converted data and deleted some unneeded or outdated examples and Cf. notes, updated some notes and captions, including captions for geographic names, and edited the index.

New or revised numbers and captions are added to the L.C. Classification schedules as a result of development proposals made by the cataloging staff of the Library of Congress and cooperating institutions. Upon approval of these proposals by the weekly editorial meeting of the Cataloging Policy and Support Office, new classification records are created or existing records are revised in the master classification database. The Classification Editorial Team, consisting of Lawrence Buzard, editor, and Barry Bellinger, Kent Griffiths, Nancy Jones, and Dorothy Thomas, assistant editors, is responsible for creating new classification records, maintaining the master database, and creating index terms for the captions.

Barbara B. Tillett, Chief
Cataloging Policy and Support Office

May 1996

OUTLINE

N	1-(9211)	Visual arts
	1-58	General
	61-72	Theory. Philosophy. Aesthetics of the visual arts
	81-390	Study and teaching. Research
	400-3990	Art museums, galleries, etc.
	4390-5098	Exhibitions
	5198-5299	Private collections and collectors
	5300-7418	History
	7420-7525.8	General works
	7560-8266	Special subjects of art
	8350-8356	Art as a profession. Artists
	8510-8553	Art studios, materials, etc.
	8554-8585	Examination and conservation of works of art
	8600-8675	Economics of art
	8700-9165	Art and the state. Public art
NA	1-9428	Architecture
	1-60	General
	100-130	Architecture and the state
	190-1555.5	History
	1995	Architecture as a profession
	2000-2320	Study and teaching. Research
	2335-2360	Competitions
	2400-2460	Museums. Exhibitions
	2500-2599	General works
	2599.5-2599.9	Architectural criticism
	2695-2793	Architectural drawing and design
	2835-4050	Details and decoration
	4100-8480	Special classes of buildings
	4100-4145	Classed by material
	4150-4160	Classed by form
	4170-8480	Classed by use
	4170-(7020)	Public buildings
	4590-5621	Religious architecture
	7100-7884	Domestic architecture. Houses. Dwellings
	7910-8125	Clubhouses, guild houses, etc.
	8200-8260	Farm architecture
	8300-8480	Outbuildings, gates, fences, etc.
	9000-9428	Aesthetics of cities. City planning and beautifying

OUTLINE

NB	1-1952	Sculpture
	1-50	General
	60-1115	History Including collective biography
	1120-1133	Study and teaching
	1134-1134.4	Competitions
	1135-1150	General works
	1160-1195	Designs and technique
	1199-1200	Restoration of sculptures
	1203-1270	Special materials
	1272-1291	Mobiles, color, sculpture gardens, etc.
	1293-1895	Special forms
	1293-1310	Portrait sculpture
	1312-1313	Equestrian statues
	1330-1685	Sculptural monuments
	1750-1793	Religious monuments and shrines
	1800-1880	Sepulchral monuments
	1910-1952	Special subjects
NC	1-1940	Drawing. Design. Illustration
	1-45	General Including collective biography
	50-266	History of drawing
	390-670	Study and teaching
	673-677	Competitions
	703-725	General works
	730-758	Technique
	760-825	Special subjects
	845-915	Graphic art materials
	930	Conservation and restoration of drawings
	950-(996)	Illustration
	997-1003	Commercial art. Advertising art
	1280-1284	Printed ephemera. Imagerie populaire
	1300-1766	Pictorial humor, caricature, etc.
	1800-1850	Posters
	1860-1896	Greeting cards, postcards, invitations, book jackets, etc.
	1920-1940	Copying, enlarging, and reduction of drawings
ND	25-3416	Painting
	25-(48)	General
	49-813	History

OUTLINE

ND		Painting - Continued
	1115-1120	Study and teaching
	1130-1156	General works
	1288-1460	Special subjects
	1290-1293	Human figure
	1300-1337	Portraits
	1340-1367	Landscape painting
	1370-1375	Marine painting
	1380-1383	Animals. Birds
	1385-1388	Sports. Hunting, fishing, etc.
	1390-1393	Still life
	1400-1403	Flowers. Fruit. Trees
	1410-1460	Other subjects
	1470-1625	Technique and materials
	1630-1662	Examination and conservation of paintings
	1700-2495	Watercolor painting
	2550-2733	Mural painting
	2889-3416	Illuminating of manuscripts and books
NE	1-3002	Print media
	1-978	Printmaking and engraving
	1-90	General
	218-(330)	Engraved portraits. Self-portraits
	380	Conservation and restoration of prints
	390-395	Collected works
	400-773	History of printmaking
	830-898	General works
	951-962	Special subjects
	965-965.3	Tradesmen's cards
	970-973	Study and teaching
	975-975.4	Competitions
	977-978	Equipment
	1000-1352	Wood engraving
	1000-1027	General
	1030-1196.3	History
	1220-1233	General works
	1310-1326.5	Japanese prints
	1330-1336	Linoleum block prints
	1340	Fish prints
	1344-1345	Potato prints
	1350-1352	Other materials used in relief printing
	1400-1879	Metal engraving
	1400-1422	General

OUTLINE

NE		Print media
		Metal engraving - Continued
	1620-1630	General works
	1634-1749	History
	1750-1775	Copper engraving
	1850-1879	Color prints
	1940-2232.5	Etching and aquatint
	1940-1975	General
	1980-2055.5	History
	2120-2140	General works
	2141-2149	Special subjects
	2220-2225	Dry point
	2236-2240.6	Serigraphy
	2242-2246	Monotype (Printmaking)
	2250-2570	Lithography
	2685-2685.8	Lumiprints
	2690	Engraving on glass
	2800-2880	Printing of engravings
	3000-3002	Copying art. Copying machine art
NK	1-(9990)	Decorative arts
	1-570	General
	600-806	History
	1135-1149.5	Arts and crafts movement
	1160-1590	Decoration and ornament. Design
	1160-1174	General
	1175-(1498)	History
	1505-1535	General works
	1548-1590	Special subjects for design
	1648-1678	Religious art
	1700-2195	Interior decoration. House decoration
	1700-2138	General. History, etc. Including special rooms
	2140-2180	Decorative painting
	2190-2192	Church decoration
	2200-2750	Furniture
	2775-2898	Rugs and carpets
	2975-3049	Tapestries
	3175-3296.3	Upholstery. Drapery
	3375-3496.3	Wallpapers
	3600-(9990)	Other arts and art industries
	3700-4695	Ceramics
	4700-4890	Costume

OUTLINE

NK		Decorative arts
		Other arts and art industries - Continued
	5100-5440	Glass
	5500-6060	Glyptic arts
	6400-8459	Metalwork
	8800-9505.5	Textiles
	9600-9955	Woodwork
NX	1-820	Arts in general
	1-260	General
	280-410	Study and teaching. Research
	411-415	Competitions
	420-430	Exhibitions
	440-632	History of the arts
	650-694	Special subjects, characters, persons, religious arts, etc.
	700-750	Patronage of the arts
	760-770	Administration of the arts
	775-777	Voluntarism in the arts
	798-820	Arts centers and facilities

	Visual arts
	Including architecture, decorative arts, drawing, painting, prints, and sculpture
	Cf. TR1+, Photography
	Periodicals
1.A1	Polyglot
1.A12-Z	American and English
2	French
3	German
4	Italian
5	Dutch and Flemish
6	Russian. Slavic
6.5	Scandinavian
7	Spanish and Portuguese
8.A-Z	Other (including Oriental), A-Z
	Yearbooks
9.A1	Polyglot
9.A12-Z	American and English
9.2	French
9.3	German
9.4	Italian
9.5	Dutch
9.6	Slavic
9.65	Scandinavian
9.7	Spanish and Portuguese
	Oriental
9.8	Arabic
9.82	Chinese
9.83	Hebrew
9.84	Indic
9.85	Japanese
9.88.A-Z	Other Oriental, A-Z
9.9.A-Z	Other, A-Z
	Societies
10	General
11	American
12	English
13	French and Belgian
14	German, Austrian, and Swiss
15	Italian
16	Spanish and Portuguese
17.A-Z	Other, A-Z
21	Congresses

Collected writings (Serial)
Including monographs in series classified together, and bound volumes of miscellaneous pamphlets by several authors
Class bound volumes of miscellaneous pamphlets by one author with collected writings of the author, as in N7445
For collected writings of artists, see N7452+
For Festschriften, see N7442+
For single volumes of collected writings, including addresses, essays, lectures, see N7442+
25 Several authors
(27) Individual authors
see N7445-N7445.8
31 Encyclopedias
33 Dictionaries
34 Terminology
Biography
Collective
Class collective biography of special countries in N6501-N7414
For collective biography of artists in special media, see the medium, e.g. painting, sculpture, etc.
40 General
42 Juvenile works
43 Women artists (Collective)
Cf. N8354, Women as artists
Cf. ND38, Women painters
(44.A-Z) Individual artists, A-Z
Class with medium and nationality
45 Artists' marks and monograms
For artists' marks in a particular genre, see the genre
Directories
50 General
United States
51 General
52.A-W By state, A-W
55.A-Z Other countries, A-Z
Communication of information
57 General works
58 Information services
Theory. Philosophy. Aesthetics of the visual arts
For general works on visual arts, see N7420+
Cf. BH, Aesthetics (General)
61 History
Theories of the visual arts. By language
For translations, see the original language
Works written before 1870
62 English
63 French
64 German

Theory. Philosophy. Aesthetics of the visual arts
Theories of the visual arts. By language
Works written before 1870 -- Continued
65.A-Z Other languages, A-Z
Recent writings, 1870-
66 English
67 French
68 German
68.3 Italian
68.6 Spanish
69.A-Z Other European languages, A-Z
69.3.A-Z Oriental languages, A-Z
69.6.A-Z Other languages, A-Z
70 General special
Special topics
71 Psychology of art and the artist
Optical illusions, see N7430.5
(71.3) Physically handicapped artists
see N8355
71.5 Mental illness and art
Cf. N7432.5.A78, Art brut
Cf. RC455.4.A77, Psychiatry
71.8 Visual disorders and art
72.A-Z Art in relation to other subjects, A-Z
Class here general works on the topics as well as works on the topics in a particular region, country, etc.
Cf. NX170+, Interrelationships among the arts
Cf. NX, Arts in general
72.A33 Aged
Cf. N8356.A43, Aged as artists
72.A34 AIDS (Disease)
72.A56 Anthropology
72.A75 Artist-architect collaboration
72.A76 Artists and community
72.A77 Artists and museums
72.B5 Biology
72.C36 Camouflage
(72.C62) Communism
see HX321
(72.C8) Culture
see N72.S6
72.E53 Electronics
72.E8 Ethics. Morals
Cf. BJ46, Ethics in relation to aesthetics
72.F45 Feminism
72.H58 History
72.H64 Homosexuality
72.I53 Industry
72.L36 Language
(72.L5) Literature
see PN53
72.M28 Mass media

Theory. Philosophy. Aesthetics of the visual arts
Special topics
Art in relation to other subjects, A-Z -- Continued
72.M3 Mathematics
72.M48 Meteorology
Morals, see N72.E8
72.M6 Motion pictures
72.M85 Mysticism
72.P5 Photography. Paintings from photographs
72.P6 Politics
72.P74 Psychoanalysis
72.R4 Religion
Cf. BM538.A7, Judaism and art
Cf. BP190.5.A7, Islam and art
Cf. BR115.A8, Christianity and art
Cf. BX1795.A78, Catholic church and art
72.S3 Science
Seals, see CD5033
72.S6 Society. Culture
72.T4 Technology
72.T45 Telecommunication
72.5 Artistic masterpieces
(73) Nude in art
see N7572+
(74) Style
see N7432-N7432.5
75 Taste in the visual arts
Cf. NX210, Taste in the arts
(76) Symmetry. Proportion. Rhythm
see N7431-N7431.5
(78) Beautiful in nature
see BH301.L3, Landscape; BH301.N3, Nature
(79) Miscellaneous. Essays, etc.
see N61+; N7420+
Study and teaching. Research
Class here works on art education which include the study of the history and appreciation of art and training in studio techniques
Cf. N7433.83, Study of computer art
For works specifically on art appreciation, see N7477
For works specifically on the study of the history of art, see N380+
81 Periodicals and societies
82 Congresses
84 Theory. Philosophy
Including semiotics
85 General works
87 General special
For outlines, syllabi, chronologies, see N5305+
Art teacher training, recruiting, etc.
88 General works
By region or country
United States

	Study and teaching. Research
	Art teacher training, recruiting, etc.
	By region or country
	United States -- Continued
88.3	General works
88.4.A-Z	By region or state, A-Z
88.5.A-Z	Other regions or countries, A-Z
	Biography of art teachers
89	Collective
89.2A-Z	Individual, A-Z
	History
90	General works
101-285	Special regions or countries (Table N2)
	Art schools
325	General works
	Special countries
	United States
328.A-W	By state, A-W
330.A-Z	Special schools. By city, A-Z
	Under each city:
	.x *General*
	.x2A-.x2Z *Individual schools, A-Z*
331.A-Z	Other American countries, A-Z
	Under each country:
	.x *General*
	.x2A-.x2Z *By state, region, etc., A-Z*
	.x3A-.x3Z *By city, town, etc., A-Z*
	Europe
332.A1	General works
332.A2-Z	By country, A-Z
	Apply table at N331.A-Z
333.A-Z	Other countries, A-Z
	Apply table at N331.A-Z
	Correspondence schools
335.A1	General works
335.A2-Z7	United States. By school, A-Z
335.Z9A-Z	Other regions or countries, A-Z
340	Examinations, questions, etc.
	For examination papers on history of art, see N382
	Art study in universities and colleges
345	General works
	By region or country
	United States
346.A1	General works
346.A2-Z	By region or state, A-Z
	Under each state:
	.x *General works*
	.x2A-.x2Z *Special institutions. By place, A-Z*

Study and teaching. Research
Art study in universities and colleges
By region or country -- Continued
346.5.A-Z Other regions or countries, A-Z
Under each country:
.x General works
.x2A-.x2Z Special institutions. By place, A-Z
347 Art scholarships, fellowships, etc.
Art study in elementary and secondary schools
Cf. LB1187, Art for the kindergarten
Cf. LC4075, Art study for socially handicapped children
Cf. NC610+, Study of drawing
Cf. NK70, Art crafts for children
350 General works
351 Children as artists
Cf. BF723.D7, Drawing (Child psychology)
Cf. LB1139.D7, Drawing (Education)
Children's art
Class here art produced by children under fifteen years of age
352 General works
352.2.A-Z By region or country, A-Z
Special countries
United States
353 General works
354.A-W By state, A-W
355.A-Z By city, A-Z
357.A-Z Special systems, A-Z
Prefer classification by grade
Under each:
.x Teacher's manuals
.x2 Textbooks
Special grades
361 Primary
362 Elementary
363 Secondary
365.A-Z Other regions or countries, A-Z
Picture study in the school and the home
366 General works
Audiovisual materials
Including films on art, filmstrips, phonodiscs, etc.
Cf. N4040.A+, Catalogs of lantern slides
367 General works
368 Select lists
369.A-Z Dealers' catalogs. By dealer, A-Z
Still picture study (especially reproductions)
Including picture study by adults in the home
Cf. N7477, Art appreciation
370 General works
373 Select lists of pictures for schools

Study and teaching. Research
Picture study in the school and the home
Still picture study (especially reproductions)
Select lists of
pictures for schools -- Continued
(375) Dealers' catalogs of reproductions
see N4035
377 Supplies, materials, etc.
Art rental and lending services
Including reproductions and original works of art
378 General works
379.A-Z Catalogs of picture lending collections. By collection, A-Z
Study of the history of art
380 General works
Cf. N5305+, Art history outlines, syllabi
382 Examinations, questions, etc.
Special countries
United States
385 General works
386.A-Z Special universities, schools, etc., A-Z
390.A-Z Other countries, A-Z
Under each country:
.x General works
.x2A-.x2Z Special universities, schools, etc. By name or place, A-Z
Prefer classification by place
Competitions
Including individual awards, prizes, etc.
393 General and international
394 United States
395.A-Z Other American. By country, A-Z
396.A-Z Europe. By country, A-Z
397.A-Z Other countries. By country, A-Z
Art museums, galleries, etc.
400 Periodicals and societies
Prefer the special museum
405 Collections of catalogs, handbooks, etc.
Biography of museum personnel
406.A1 Collective
406.A2-Z Individual, A-Z
For biography of a person associated with only a single museum, see the museum
408 Museum work as a profession
410 General works
420 Organization
Cf. NE60, Engraving museums
430 Aim, utility, etc.
435 Museum visitors and museum public
Class here general works only
For works on museums in a specific location or works on an individual museum, see N510+

Art museums, galleries, etc. -- Continued

440 Accessioning, cataloging, and classification of works of art

Buildings. Art museum architecture, see NA6695

460 Equipment, heating, lighting, etc.

463 Security measures

470 Administration

490 Relations to the public (Hours, etc.)

Special countries and special museums

Including catalogs

For histories, treatises, catalogs, etc. of special collections prefer classification by medium, subject, period, or nationality

United States

Collective

510 General

510.5.A-Z By region, A-Z

511.A-W By state, A-W

512 A - Ann Arbor

512.A4 Akron, O. Art Institute (Table N9)

512.A5 Albuquerque, N. Mex. University. Art Museum (Table N9)

512.A54 Allentown, Pa. Art Museum (Table N9)

512.A6 Andover, Mass. Phillips Academy. Addison Gallery of American Art (Table N9)

513 Ann Arbor, Mich. Michigan. University. Museum of Art (Table N9)

514 Ann Arbor - Baltimore

514.A66 Annapolis, Md. U.S. Naval Academy. Museum (Table N9)

514.A8 Athens, Ga. Georgia Museum of Art (Table N9)

514.A85 Atlanta. High Museum of Art (Table N9)

Baltimore, Md.

515 Baltimore. Museum of Art (Table N9)

516.B3 Maryland Historical Society (Table N9)

516.B4 Municipal Museum (Table N9)

516.B42 Walters Art Gallery (Table N9)

516.B45-B49 Baltimore - Berkeley

516.B5 Baton Rouge, La. Anglo-American Art Museum (Table N9)

516.B8 Bennington, Vt. Historical Museum and Art Gallery (Table N9)

517 Berkeley, Calif. Bacon Art Gallery (Table N9)

518 Berkeley - Boston

518.B36 Birmingham, Ala. Museum of Art (Table N9)

518.B4 Bloomington, Ind. Indiana. University. Museum of Art (Table N9)

Boston, Mass.

520 Museum of Fine Arts (Table N9)

521.A-Z Other public collections, A-Z

521.A8 Athenaeum Gallery (Table N9)

521.I7 Isabella Stewart Gardner Museum (Table N9)

522-523 Boston - Brunswick

Art museums, galleries, etc.
Special countries and special museums
United States -- Continued
524 Brunswick, Me. Bowdoin College. Museum of Fine Arts (Table N9)
525 Buffalo, N.Y. Fine Arts Academy (Table N9)
525.7 Burlington, Vt. Vermont University. Robert Hull Fleming Museum (Table N9)
Cambridge, Mass. Harvard University. Art Museums
526 Collective
527 William Hayes Fogg Art Museum (Table N9)
Formerly Fogg Art Museum
528 Busch-Reisinger Museum (Table N9)
Formerly known as Germanic Museum, and Busch-Reisinger Museum of Germanic Culture
529 Cambridge - Chicago
529.C15 Canajoharie, N.Y. Canajoharie Library and Art Gallery (Table N9)
529.C17 Cedar Rapids. Cedar Rapids Museum of Art (Table N9)
529.C2 Chapel Hill, N.C. Ackland Art Museum (Table N9)
Formerly known as William Hayes Ackland Memorial Art Center
Charleston, S.C.
529.C27 Carolina Art Association (Table N9)
529.C3 Municipal Art Gallery (Table N9)
529.C35 Charlotte, N.C. Mint Museum of Art (Table N9)
529.C38 Charlottesville, Va. Bayly Art Museum (Table N9)
529.C42 Chattanooga, Tenn. Hunter Museum of Art (Table N9)
Chicago, Ill.
530 Art Institute (Table N9)
531.A-Z Other public collections, A-Z
531.C5 Čiurlionio vardo galerija (Table N9)
531.D38 David and Alfred Smart Gallery (Table N9)
531.M37 Martin D'Arcy Gallery of Art (Table N9)
531.U6 Union League Club (Table N9)
Cincinnati, O.
550 Art Museum (Table N9)
550.5 Institute of Fine Arts. Taft Museum (Table N9)
552 Cleveland, O. Museum of Art (Table N9)
552.5 Colorado Springs, Colo. Fine Arts Center (Table N9)
552.8 Columbia, Mo. Missouri. University. Museum of Art and Archaeology (Table N9)
553 Columbia, S.C. Museum of Art (Table N9)
554 Columbus, O. Columbus Museum of Art (Table N9)
Formerly Columbus Gallery of Fine Arts
554.7 Coral Gables (Fla.) Lowe Art Museum (Table N9)

Art museums, galleries, etc.
Special countries and special museums
United States -- Continued
Dallas, Tex.
557 Meadows Museum (Table N9)
558 Museum of Fine Arts (Public Art Gallery) (Table N9)
559 Dallas - Detroit
559.D3 Dayton, O. Art Institute (Table N9)
559.D4 Denver, Colo. Art Museum (Table N9)
560 Detroit, Mich. Institute of Arts (Museum of Art) (Table N9)
563 Duluth, Minn. Tweed Gallery (Table N9)
Formerly Minnesota University. Tweed Memorial Art Collection
567 East Lansing, Mich. Kresge Art Museum (Table N9)
Formerly Kresge Art Center
567.4 Elmira, N.Y. Arnot Art Museum (Table N9)
568 El Paso, Tex. Museum of Art (Table N9)
569 Farmington, Conn. Hill-Stead Museum (Table N9)
Fitchburg, Mass.
570 Art Center (Table N9)
570.2 Public Library (Table N9)
570.28 Flint, Mich. Flint Institute of Art (Table N9)
570.29 Fort Dodge, Ia. Blanden Memorial Art Museum (Table N9)
Fort Worth, Tex.
570.7 Amon Carter Museum (Table N9)
570.73 Fort Worth Art Museum (Table N9)
570.8 Kimbell Art Museum (Table N9)
570.88 Gainesville (Fla.) University of Florida. University Gallery (Table N9)
570.9 Greensboro, N.C. Weatherspoon Art Gallery (Table N9)
571 Greenville, S.C. Bob Jones University. Art Gallery and Museum (Table N9)
573 Greenville - Hanover
573.G75 Grosse Point Shores, Mich. Edsel & Eleanor Ford House (Table N9)
573.H3 Hagerstown, Md. Washington County Museum of Fine Arts (Table N9)
575 Hanover, N.H. Dartmouth College. Hood Museum of Art (Table N9)
Formerly Dartmouth College Museum and Galleries
576 Hanover - Indianapolis
576.H3 Hartford, Conn. Wadsworth Atheneum (Table N9)
576.H45 Hempstead, N.Y. Emily Lowe Gallery (Table N9)
576.H6 Honolulu, Hawaii. Academy of Arts (Table N9)
Houston, Tex.
576.H68 Menil Collection (Table N9)

Art museums, galleries, etc.
Special countries and special museums
United States
Hanover - Indianapolis
Houston, Tex. -- Continued

576.H7 Museum of Fine Arts (Table N9)

576.H8 Huntington, N.Y. Heckscher Art Museum (Table N9)

576.H83 Huntington, W. Va. Huntington Galleries (Table N9)

577 Indianapolis, Ind. Indianapolis Museum of Art (Table N9)
Formerly Art Association of Indianapolis. John Herron Art Institute

582 Indianapolis - Minneapolis

582.I58 Iowa City. University of Iowa. Museum of Art (Table N9)

582.I8 Ithica, N.Y. Herbert F. Johnson Museum of Art (Table N9)

582.J34 Jackson, Miss. Mississippi Museum of Art (Table N9)

582.J36 Jacksonville (Fla.) Alexander Brest Museum and Gallery (Table N9)

582.J47 Jersey City. Museum of Soviet Unofficial Art (Table N9)

582.K24 Kalamazoo. Kalamazoo Institute of Arts (Table N9)

Kansas City, Mo.

582.K25 Art Institute (Table N9)

582.K3 Nelson-Atkins Museum of Art (Table N9)
Formerly William Rockholl Nelson Gallery of Art and Mary Atkins Museum of Fine Arts

582.L23 Laurel, Miss. Lauren Rogers Museum of Art (Table N9)

Lawrence, Kans.

582.L24 Helen Foresman Spencer Museum of Art (Table N9)

582.L25 Kansas. University. Museum of Art (Table N9)

582.L4 Lexington, Ky. Kentucky. University (Table N9)

582.L5 Lincoln, Nebr. Nebraska. University. Sheldon Memorial Art Gallery (Table N9)

582.L53 Little Rock, Ark. Arkansas Arts Center Foundation (Table N9)

Los Angeles, Calif.

582.L6 General

582.L65 California. University. University at Los Angeles. Willitts J. Hole Art Collection (Table N9)

582.L7 Los Angeles Co., Calif. Museum of Art (Table N9)
Including Robert O. Anderson Building

Art museums, galleries, etc.
Special countries and special museums
United States
Indianapolis - Minneapolis
Los Angeles -- Continued

582.L75 Los Angeles Co., Calif. Otis Art Institute (Table N9)
582.L8 Louisville, Ky. Speed Art Museum (Table N9)
582.M22 Madison. Elvehjem Museum of Art (Table N9)
Until 1978 known as Elvehjem Art Center
582.M25 Malibu, Calif. Getty (J. Paul) Museum (Table N9)
582.M3 Manchester, N.H. Currier Gallery of Art (Table N9)
Memphis, Tenn.
582.M4 Memphis Brooks Museum of Art (Table N9)
Formerly Brooks Memorial Art Gallery
582.M42 Dixon Gallery and Gardens (Table N9)
Milwaukee, Wis.
582.M5 Art Museum (Table N9)
Formerly Art Center
582.M6 Marquette University (Table N9)
Minneapolis, Minn.
582.6 Institute of Arts (Table N9)
582.8 Public Library (Table N9)
583 Walker Art Center (Table N9)
584 Minneapolis - Muskegon
584.M654 Montclair, N.J. Art Museum (Table N9)
584.M7 Montgomery, Ala. Montgomery Museum of Fine Arts (Table N9)
585 Muskegon, Mich. Hackley Art Gallery (Table N9)
588 New Brunswick, N.J. Rutgers University. University Art Gallery (Table N9)
590 New Haven, Conn. Yale University. Art Gallery (Table N9)
594 New London, Conn. Lyman Allyn Museum (Table N9)
598 New Orleans. Museum of Art (Table N9)
Until 1968 known as Isaac Delgado Museum of Art
New York City
600 General
601 Municipal collections
605 Lenox Library. New York Public Library (Table N9)
610 Metropolitan Museum of Art (Table N9)
Special collections. By name, A-Z
611.A5 Benjamin Altman collection (Table N9)
611.A6 American wing (Table N9)
611.B58 George Blumenthal collection (Table N9)
611.B7 Crosby Brown collection (Table N9)
611.C6 The Cloisters (Table N9)
611.H15 H.O. Havemeyer collection (Table N9)
611.H2 George A. Hearn collection (Table N9)

Art museums, galleries, etc.
Special countries and special museums
United States
New York City
Metropolitan Museum of Art
Special collections.
By name, A-Z -- Continued

611.L4 Adele and Arthur Lehman collection (Table N9)

611.L43 Robert Lehman collection (Table N9)

611.L55 Jack and Belle Linsky collection (Table N9)

611.M7 Morgan collection (Table N9)

612 Loan exhibitions. By date

613 New York Historical Scoeity (Table N9)

618 Whitney Museum of American Art

620.A-Z Other, A-Z

620.A6 American Academy of Arts and Letters. Museum (Table N9)

620.B6 Brooklyn Museum (Table N9)
Formerly Brooklyn Institute of Arts and Sciences. Museum

620.C4 Century Association (Table N9)

620.F6 Frick Collection (Table N9)

620.G3 Gallery of Modern Art. Huntington Hartford Collection (Table N9)

620.G7 Grolier Club (Table N9)

620.H5 Hispanic Society of America (Table N9)

620.J48 Jewish Museum (Table N9)

620.M8 Municipal Art Gallery (Table N9)

620.M9 Museum of Modern Art (Table N9)

620.M94 Museum of Primitive Art (Table N9)

620.N4 New York University. Gallery of Living Art (Table N9)

620.P6 The Players (Table N9)

620.Q4 Queens College, Flushing, N.Y. Art Collection (Table N9)

620.S63 Solomon R. Guggenheim Museum (Table N9)

620.U5 United Nations (Table N9)

620.V3 Van Cortlandt Mansion (Table N9)

624 Newark, Del. University of Delaware (Table N9)

625 Newark, N.J. Newark Museum Association (Table N9)

Norfolk, Va.

626.5 Chrysler Museum (Table N9)
Formerly Chrysler Museum at Norfolk

627 Museum of Arts and Sciences (Table N9)

628 Northampton, Mass. Smith College. Museum of Art (Table N9)

630 Norwich, Conn. Slater Memorial Museum (Table N9)

Art museums, galleries, etc.
Special countries and special museums
United States -- Continued

635 Notre Dame, Ind. University. Art Gallery (Table N9)
Until 1952 known as Wightman Memorial Art Gallery

645 Oakland, Calif. Center for the Visual Arts (Table N9)

650 Oberlin, O. Oberlin College. Dudley Peter Allen Memorial Art Museum (Table N9)

654 Oklahoma City. National Cowboy Hall of Fame and Western Heritage Center (Table N9)

Omaha, Nebr.

657 Art Institute (Table N9)

658 Joslyn Art Museum (Table N9)

660 Lininger Art Gallery (Table N9)

661 Oshkosh, Wis. Paine Art Center and Arboretum (Table N9)

663 Palm Beach, Fla. Henry Morrison Flagler Museum (Table N9)

665 Pasadena, Calif. Norton Simon Museum of Art at Pasadena (Table N9)

Philadelphia, Pa.

675 Collective

677 LaSalle College. Art Museum (Table N9)

678 Makler Gallery (Table N9)

680 Pennsylvania Academy of the Fine Arts (Table N9)

683 Pennsylvania Historical Society (Table N9)

685 Philadelphia Museum of Art (Table N9)

690 Memorial Hall (Table N9)

692 Union League (Table N9)

696 Phoenix, Ariz. Art Museum (Table N9)

Pittsburgh

710 Carnegie Institute. Museum of Art (Table N9)
Until April 1963 known as the Institute's Dept. of Fine Arts

710.3 Clayton Museum (Pittsburgh, Pa.) (Table N9)

710.5 Frick Art Museum (Table N9)

711 Pittsfield, Mass. Berkshire Museum (Table N9)

711.5 Portland, Me. Joan Whitney Payson Gallery of Art (Table N9)

712 Portland, Oreg. Art Museum (Table N9)

713 Poughkeepsie, N.Y. Vassar College. Art Gallery (Table N9)

714 Poughkeepsie, N.Y. - Q

714.P65 Princeton, N.J. Princeton University. Art Museum (Table N9)

714.P7 Providence, R.I. Rhode Island School of Design. Museum of Art (Table N9)

714.P74 Provincetown, Mass. Provincetown Art Association and Museum (Table N9)

Art museums, galleries, etc.
Special countries and special museums
United States
Poughkeepsie, N.Y. - Q -- Continued
714.P8 Purchase, N.Y. Neuberger Museum (Table N9)
715 R - Richmond
715.R2 Raleigh, N.C. North Carolina. Museum of Art (Table N9)
715.R4 Reading, Pa. Public Museum and Art Gallery (Table N9)
Richmond, Va.
716.H5 Virginia Historical Society (Table N9)
716.L5 Virginia. State Library (Table N9)
716.M8 Virginia Museum of Fine Arts (Table N9)
Rochester, N.Y.
718 Margaret Woodbury Strong Museum (Table N9)
719 University. Memorial Art Gallery (Table N9)
Formerly Memorial Art Gallery
720 Power's Art Gallery (Table N9)
720.5 Roslyn, N.Y. Nassau County Museum of Fine Art (Table N9)
721 Roswell, N.Mex. Museum and Art Center (Table N9)
726 Sacramento, Calif. Crocker Art Gallery (Table N9)
Saint Louis, Mo.
729 City Art Museum (Table N9)
730 Washington University. Saint Louis Museum of Fine Arts (Table N9)
735 Salem, Mass. Peabody Museum of Salem (Table N9)
735.5 Salt Lake City, Utah. Utah Museum of Fine Arts (Table N9)
736 San Antonio, Tex. Marion Koogler McNay Art Institute (Table N9)
San Diego, Calif.
737 Fine Arts Gallery (Table N9)
737.5 Timken Art Gallery (Table N9)
San Francisco, Calif.
738 General
739 California Palace of the Legion of Honor (Table N9)
739.5 De Young Memorial Museum (Table N9)
740 California. University. San Francisco Institute of Art (Table N9)
Formerly Mark Hopkins Institute of Art
740.3 Fine Arts Museums of San Francisco (Table N9)
Formed 1972 by the merger of California Palace of the Legion of Honor (1924) and De Young Memorial Museum (1844)
740.5 Museum of Modern Art (Table N9)
Until 1976 known as Museum of Art

Art museums, galleries, etc.
Special countries and special museums
United States -- Continued
741 San Marino, Calif. Henry E. Huntington Library and Art Gallery (Table N9)
742 San Marino - Savannah
742.S13 Santa Ana, Calif. Charles W. Bowers Memorial Museum (Table N9)
742.S15 Santa Barbara, Calif. Museum of Art (Table N9)
742.S3 Santa Fe, N. Mex. Museum of New Mexico. Museum of Fine Arts (Table N9)
742.S5 Sarasota, Fla. Ringling Museums (Table N9)
743 Savannah, Ga. Telfair Academy of Arts and Sciences (Table N9)
Seattle, Wash.
745 Art Museum (Table N9)
745.5 Charles and Emma Frye Free Public Art Museum (Table N9)
745.7 Henry Art Gallery (Table N9)
746 Washington (State) University (Table N9)
748 Sharon, Mass. Kendall Whaling Museum (Table N9)
749 Shelburne, Vt. Museum (Table N9)
749.5 South Hadley, Mass. Mount Holyoke College Art Museum (Table N9)
750 Southampton, N.Y. Art Museum (Table N9)
Springfield, Mass.
772 George Walter Vincent Smith Art Museum (Table N9)
773 Museum of Fine Arts (Table N9)
775 Springfield, Ohio. Springfield Art Center (Table N9)
778 St. Petersburg, Fla. Museum of Fine Arts (Table N9)
Stanford, Calif. Stanford University
781 Art Museum (Table N9)
783 Thomas Welton Stanford Art Gallery (Table N9)
790 Swarthmore, Pa. Swarthmore College (Table N9)
Syracuse, N.Y.
800 Everson Museum of Art of Syracuse and Onondaga County (Table N9)
Formed 1959 by the merger of the Syracuse Museum of Fine Arts (founded 1896) and the Everson Museum of Art (incorporated 1945)
802 Syracuse University. Art Collections (Table N9)
804 Tampa, Fla. Museum of African-American Art (Table N9)
805 Taos, N. Mex. Harwood Foundation (Table N9)
818 Terre Haute, Ind. Sheldon Swope Art Gallery (Table N9)
820 Toledo, O. Museum of Art (Table N9)

Art museums, galleries, etc.
Special countries and special museums
United States -- Continued
Tucson, Ariz.
829 Dinnerware Artists' Cooperative Gallery (Table N9)
830 University of Arizona. Museum of Art (Table N9)
Formerly Art Gallery of the University
835 Tulsa, Okla. Philbrook Art Center (Table N9)
838 Urbana, Ill. Illinois. University. Krannert Art Museum (Table N9)
840 Wakefield, R.I. Hera Gallery (Table N9)
Washington, D.C.
845 General
850 Corcoran Gallery of Art (Table N9)
851.A-Z Special collections, A-Z
851.C6 Clark Collection
853 United States Capitol (Table N9)
855 Library of Congress (Table N9)
855.8 Smithsonian Institution (Table N9)
856 National Gallery of Art (Established 1937) (Table N9)
Original collection and building given by Andrew Mellon
857 National Museum of American Art (Table N9)
Formerly National Collection of Fine Arts. 1920-1937 called the National Gallery of Art
857.2 National Museum of African Art (Table N9)
Formerly Museum of African Art
857.3 Arthur M. Sackler Gallery (Table N9)
857.5 Freer Art Gallery (Table N9)
857.6 Joseph H. Hirschorn Museum and Sculpture Garden (Table N9)
857.8 National Portrait Gallery (Table N9)
858 Other special, A-Z
858.D8 Dumbarton Oaks (Table N9)
858.H54 Hillwood (Table N9)
858.N36 National Museum of Women in the Arts (U.S.) (Table N9)
858.P4 Phillips Collection (Table N9)
858.W3 White House Collection (Table N9)
Wellesley, Mass.
859.5 Davis Museum and Cultural Center (Table N9)
860 Wellesley College. Farnsworth Museum of Art (Table N9)
862 West Palm Beach, Fla. Norton Gallery and School of Art (Table N9)
863 Westerly, R.I. Westerly Memorial and Library Association (Table N9)
863.5 Wichita, Kan. Wichita Art Museum (Table N9)

Art museums, galleries, etc.
Special countries and special museums
United States -- Continued
865 Williamsburg, Va. William and Mary College (Table N9)
Williamstown, Mass.
867 Sterling and Francine Clark Art Institute (Table N9)
867.3 Williams College. Museum of Art (Table N9)
868 Winter Park, Fla. George D. and Harriet W. Cornell Fine Arts Museum (Table N9)
Worchester, Mass.
870 Art Museum (Table N9)
871 Clark University (Table N9)
880 Youngstown, O. Butler Institute of American Art (Table N9)
908.A-Z Other American countries, A-Z
910.A-Z Special cities, A-Z
910.A38 Aguascalientes (Mexico). Museo de Aguascalientes (Table N9)
910.A57 Antigua. Museo de Arte Colonial (Table N9)
910.A8 Asunción. Museo Nacional de Bellas Artes (Table N9)
Bogotá
910.B52 Colegio Mayor de Nuestra Señora del Rosario (Table N9)
910.B53 Museo de Arte Colonial (Table N9)
910.B55 Museo de Arte Moderno (Table N9)
910.B6 Museo Nacional (Table N9)
910.B62 Seminario Conciliar. Museo (Table N9)
910.B7 Brampton, Ont. Perkins Bull Collection (Table N9)
910.B72 Brasília. Palácio Itamaraty (Table N9)
Buenos Aires
910.B75 Collective
910.B78 Instituto Torcuato di Tella. Centro de Artes Visuales (Table N9)
910.B79 Museo Nacional de Arte Decorativo (Argentina) (Table N9)
910.B8 Museo Nacional de Bellas Artes (Table N9)
Caracas
910.C22 Galería de Arte Nacional (Venezuela) (Table N9)
910.C25 Museo de Arte Colonial de Caracas (Table N9)
910.C3 Museo de Bellas Artes (Table N9)
910.C35 Museo de Caracas (Table N9)
910.C57 Ciudad Bolívar. Museo de Arte Moderno Jesús Soto (Table N9)
910.C6 Coimbra. Museu Machado de Castro (Table N9)
910.C8 Cuenca, Ecuador. Museo de Arte Abstracto Español (Table N9)

Art museums, galleries, etc.
Special countries and special museums
Other American countries, A-Z
Special cities, A-Z -- Continued

910.C83 Culiacán (Sinaloa, Mexico). Museo de Arte de Sinaloa (Table N9)
910.C86 Curaçao. Curaçaosch Museum (Table N9)
910.C88 Curitiba. Museu Paranaense (Table N9)
910.E4 Edmonton, Alta. Edmonton Art Gallery (Table N9)
910.F7 Fredericton, N.B. Beaverbrook Art Gallery (Table N9)
910.G8 Guatemala (City). Museo Nacional/Sección de Historia y Bellas Artes (Table N9)
910.G84 Guelph (Ont.) University of Guelph (Table N9)
910.H255 Hamilton, Ont. McMaster University. Art Gallery (Table N9)
910.H3 Havana. Museo Nacional (Table N9)
910.J6 Joliette, Quebec. Musée d'art de Joliette (Table N9)

Kingston, Ont.
910.K45 Agnes Etherington Art Center (Table N9)
910.K5 Queen's University. Art Foundation (Table N9)
910.K57 Kleinburg, Ont. McMichael Canadian Collection (Table N9)
Formerly McMichael Conservation Collection of Art
910.L25 La Malbaie, Que. Manoir Richelieu (Table N9)
Formerly Murray Bay, Que. Manoir Richelieu
910.L3 La Paz, Bolivia. Museo Nacional (Table N9)
910.L5 Lima. Museo de Arte (Table N9)
910.M28 Medellín. Museo de Arte de Medellín Francisco Antonio Zea (Table N9)

Mexico (City)
910.M34 Galería de Arte Mexicano (Table N9)
910.M35 Instituto Nacional de Bellas Artes (Table N9)
910.M37 Museo de las Culturas (Table N9)
910.M4 Museo Nacional de Artes Plásticas (Table N9)
910.M44 Pinacoteca Virreinal de San Diego (Table N9)

Montevideo
910.M66 Museo de Historia del Arte (Table N9)
Formerly Galerías de Historia del Arte
910.M68 Museo Nacional de Bellas Artes (Table N9)

Montreal
910.M7 Château de Ramezay (Table N9)
910.M712 Musée d'art contemporain de Montreal (Table N9)
910.M714 Museum of Fine Arts (Table N9)

Art museums, galleries, etc.
Special countries and special museums
Other American countries, A-Z
Special cities, A-Z
Montreal -- Continued
910.M715 Notre Dame Museum (Table N9)
Ottawa
910.O43 Carlton University. Art Collection (Table N9)
910.O45 Firestone Art Collection (Table N9)
910.O7 National Gallery of Canada (Table N9)
910.O72 Canada. Public Archives (Table N9)
910.O9 Owen Sound, Ont. Tom Thomson Memorial Gallery and Museum of Fine Art (Table N9)
910.P4 Petropolis, Brazil. Museu Imperial (Table N9)
910.P6 Ponce, P.R. Museo de Arte (Table N9)
910.P83 Puerta, Mexico (City). Museo Bello (Table N9)
Quebec (City)
910.Q73 Hôtel Dieu (Table N9)
910.Q75 Musée du Québec (Table N9)
Formerly Musée de la Province de Québec
910.Q8 Université Laval (Table N9)
910.R36 Regina (Saskatchewan). Mackenzie Art Gallery (Table N9)
Rio de Janeiro
910.R42 Academia Imperial das Belas Artes (Brazil) (Table N9)
910.R5 Escola Nacional de Belas Artes (Table N9)
910.R52 Museu de Arte Moderna (Table N9)
910.R53 Museu Nacional de Belas Artes (Table N9)
910.R58 Roldanillo, Colombia. Museo Rayo (Table N9)
910.R6 Rosario, Argentine Republic (Santa Fé). Museo Municipal de Bellas Artes "Juan B. Castagnino" (Table N9)
910.S3 St. John, N.B. New Brunswick Museum (Table N9)
Salvador, Brazil
910.S31 Museu do Estado (Table N9)
910.S312 Museu de Arte (Table N9)
910.S314 Santa Casa da Misericordia (Table N9)
Santa Fé, Argentina
910.S32 Museo Municipal de Bellas Artes (Table N9)
910.S33 Museo Provincial de Bellas Artes "Rosa Galisteo de Rodríguez" (Table N9)
Santiago de Chile
910.S34 Museo Colonial de San Francisco (Table N9)
910.S35 Museo de Bellas Artes (Table N9)
São Paulo, Brazil
910.S356 Fundacão Maria Luisa e Oscar Americano (Table N9)

Art museums, galleries, etc.
Special countries and special museums
Other American countries, A-Z
Special cities, A-Z
São Paulo, Brazil -- Continued
910.S36 Museu de Arte de São Paulo Assis Chateaubriand (Table N9)
Formerly Museu de Arte
910.S363 Museu de Arte Moderna (Table N9)
910.S37 Pinacoteca (Table N9)
910.S4 Universidade. Museu de Arte Contemporânea (Table N9)
910.S42 Universidade. Museu de Arte e Arqueologia (Table N9)
Sucre, Bolivia
910.S77 Museo Religiosa Charcas (Table N9)
910.S8 Universidad Mayor de San Francisco Xavier. Museo Colonial "Charcas." (Table N9)
910.S92 Surrey, B.C. Surrey Art Gallery (Table N9)
910.T3 Tandil, Argentine Republic (Partido). Museo y Academia Municipal de Bellas Artes de Tandil (Table N9)
910.T4 Tepotzotlán, Mexico. Museo Nacional del Virreinato (Table N9)
Toronto
910.T6 Art Gallery of Ontario (Table N9)
Formerly Art Gallery
910.T65 Royal Ontario Museum (Table N9)
910.T8 Tucumán, Argentine Republic. Museo Provincial. Museo de Bellas Artes (Table N9)
910.V3 Vancouver, B.C. Art Gallery (Table N9)
910.V52 Victoria. Art Gallery of Greater Victoria (Table N9)
910.W5 Windsor, Ont. Art Gallery of Windsor (Table N9)
910.W55 Winnipeg. Winnipeg Art Gallery (Table N9)
910.X62 Xochimilco (District Federal, Mexico). Fundación Dolores Olmedo (Table N9)
910.Z32 Zacatecas. Museo Pedro Coronel (Table N9)
Europe
1010 Collective
Great Britain
1020 Collective
1025 Royal collections
1027 Ireland (Collective)
1027.5 Scotland (Collective)
1028 Wales (Collective)
London
1030 Collective
1033 Collections of the Corporation of London (Table N9)
1040 British Museum (Table N9)

Art museums, galleries, etc.
Special countries and special museums
Europe
Great Britain
London -- Continued
1045 Dulwich College. Dulwich Gallery (Table N9)
1047 Clore Gallery (Table N9)
1050 Grosvenor Gallery (Table N9)
1060 Kenwood House (Table N9)
National Gallery
1070 General works
1070.2 Sainsbury Wing
1080 National Gallery of British Art. Tate Gallery (Table N9)
1090 National Portrait Gallery (Table N9)
1100 Royal Academy of Arts (Permanent collections) (Table N9)
Cf. N12, English societies
Cf. N5054, Royal Academy of Arts exhibition
1110 Sir John Soane's Museum and Library (Table N9)
1150 Victoria and Albert Museum (Table N9)
Formerly South Kensington Museum
1151.A-Z Special collections, A-Z
1151.F7 Forster Collection
1151.I7 Constantine Alexander Ionides Collection
1151.J7 Jones Collection
1151.P3 Lord Francis Pelham Clint-Hope Collection
1151.S3 Salting Collection
1152 Bethnal Green Branch (Table N9)
1158 Wellington Museum (Table N9)
1160 Wallace Collection, Hertford House (Table N9)
1165.A-Z Other London, A-Z
1165.B3 Bank of London (Table N9)
1165.F7 Freemasons (Table N9)
1165.G76 Grosvenor Gallery (London: 1877-1890) (Table N9)
1165.I6 India Office (Table N9)
1165.L5 Livery companies (Table N9)
1165.M8 Museum (Table N9)
1165.P3 Parliament (Table N9)
1165.R5 Robert Noortman Gallery (Table N9)
1165.R6 Royal College of Surgeons of England (Table N9)
1165.U45 University. Courtauld Institute of Art (Table N9)
1165.U5 University. University College (Table N9)
Places other than London
1185 Aberdeen. Art Gallery (Table N9)

Art museums, galleries, etc.
Special countries and special museums
Europe
Great Britain
Places other than London -- Continued
1190 Barnard Castle. Bowes Museum (Table N9)
1195 Bath. Holburne Art Museum (Table N9)
1198 Belfast (Northern Ireland). Ulster Museum (Table N9)
Birmingham
1210 Museum and Art Gallery (Table N9)
1212 University. Barber Institute of Fine Arts (Table N9)
1214 Blackburn. Public Library, Museum and Art Gallery (Table N9)
1214.5 Bournemouth. Russell-Cotes Art Gallery and Museum (Table N9)
1214.7 Brighton. Royal Pavilion, Art Gallery and Museums (Table N9)
Bristol
1215.C5 City Art Gallery (Table N9)
1215.M8 Bristol Museum and Art Gallery (Table N9)
1216 Burnley. Towneley Hall Art Gallery and Museums (Table N9)
Cambridge
1216.95 Kettle's Yard Gallery (Table N9)
1217 University. Fitzwilliam Museum (Table N9)
1217.3 Cardiff. National Museum of Wales (Table N9)
Cardiff - Doncaster
1219.C7 Coniston. Coniston Institute. Ruskin Museum (Table N9)
1219.C75 Cork. Crawford Municipal Art Gallery (Table N9)
1219.5 Doncaster. Museum and Art Gallery (Table N9)
Dublin
1220 Collective
1245 Municipal Gallery of Modern Art (Table N9)
1250 National Gallery of Ireland (Table N9)
1260 National Museum of Ireland (Table N9)
1265 Dundee, Scot. Museum and Art Galleries Dept. (Table N9)
1272 Eastbourne, England. Towner Art Gallery (Table N9)
Edinburgh
1279 Collective
1280 National Gallery of Scotland (Table N9)
1282 Scottish National Gallery of Modern Art (Table N9)

Art museums, galleries, etc.
Special countries and special museums
Europe
Great Britain
Places other than London
Edinburgh -- Continued
1285 Scottish National Portrait Gallery (Table N9)
Glasgow
1310 Collective
1315 Glasgow Museums and Art Galleries (Table N9)
Formerly Glasgow Art Gallery and Museums
1316.A-Z Special collections. By name, A-Z
1316.B87 Burrell collection
1317 Hunterian Art Gallery (University of Glasgow) (Table N9)
1320 Greenwich
1320.3 National Maritime Museum (Table N9)
1349 Hampstead. Iveagh Bequest (Table N9)
Hampstead. Kenwood House, see N1060
1350 Hampton. Hampton Court (Table N9)
1403 Leeds (Collective)
1405 Leicester. Museums and Art Gallery (Table N9)
1406 Limerick. Hunt Museum (Table N9)
Liverpool
1407 Public Libraries, Museums and Art Gallery. Museum (Table N9)
1408 Royal Institution. Gallery of Art (Table N9)
1409 Sudley Art Gallery and Museum (Table N9)
1410 Walker Art Gallery (Table N9)
Manchester
1430 Art Gallery (Table N9)
1434 Victoria University of Manchester. Whitworth Art Gallery (Table N9)
Formerly Whitworth Art Gallery
1438 Newcastle-upon-Tyne. Tyne and Wear County Council Museum and Art Galleries (Table N9)
1439 Norwich. Castle Museum (Table N9)
1440 Nottingham. Museum and Art Gallery (Table N9)
Oxford
1449 University. Ashmolean Museum (Table N9)
1450 University. Galleries (Table N9)
1455 Port Sunlight. Lady Lever Art Gallery (Table N9)
1457 Preston. Harris Museum and Art Gallery (Table N9)
1480 Salford
Sheffield

Art museums, galleries, etc.
Special countries and special museums
Europe
Great Britain
Places other than London
Sheffield -- Continued
1490 Mappin Art Gallery (Table N9)
1491 Ruskin Museum (Table N9)
Originally St. George's Museum, offshoot of St. George's Guild; name changed to Ruskin Museum in 1890
1493 Southampton. Southampton Art Gallery (Table N9)
1495 Twickenham. Marble Hill House (Table N9)
1510 Warrington
1550 Windsor. Windsor Castle (Table N9)
1557 Wolverhampton. Wolverhampton Art Gallery (Table N9)
1560 York. Art Gallery (Table N9)
Austria, Hungary, Czech Republic and Slovakia
1610 Collective
1610.5.A-Z By region, state, etc., A-Z
1610.5.S75 Středoslovenský kraj (Slovakia)
1611 Bratislava (Slovakia). Slovenská národná galéria (Table N9)
1612 Brünn. Moravská galerie (Table N9)
Budapest
1614 Collective
1614.5 Magyar Nemzeti Galéria (Table N9)
1615 Magyar Nemzeti Múzeum (Table N9)
1617 Hopp Ferenc Keletázsiai Müvészeti Múzeum (Table N9)
Országos Képtár, see N1619
1618 Országos Ráth György Múzeum (Table N9)
1619 Régi Képtár (Table N9)
Formerly Országos Képtár
1620 Szépmüvészeti Múzeum (Table N9)
1621 Debrecen. Déri Múzeum (Table N9)
1621.3 Eger (Hungary). Egri Képtár (Table N9)
1621.4 Eisenstadt. Burgenländisches Landesmuseum (Table N9)
1623 Esztergom. Keresztény Múzeum (Table N9)
1623.3 Gottwaldov. Oblastní galerie výtvarného umění v Gottwaldove (Table N9)
1623.5 Graz. Neue Galerie am Landesmuseum Johanneum (Table N9)
Innsbruck
1624 Ferdinandeum (Table N9)
1624.4 Kunsthistorisches Museum, Sammlungen Schloss Ambras (Table N9)
1624.43 Kaposvár, Hungary. Rippl-Rónai Múzeum (Table N9)
1625.5 Krems an der Donau (City). Museum (Table N9)

Art museums, galleries, etc.
Special countries and special museums
Europe
Austria, Hungary, Czech Republic and Slovakia -- Continued
Kroměříž
1626 Arcibiskupská Obrazárna (Table N9)
1626.3 Uměleckonistorické muzeum v Kroměříži (Table N9)
1627 Lienz. Osttiroler Heimatmuseum Schloss Bruck (Table N9)
Linz
1627.2 Neue Gallerie (Table N9)
1627.3 Oberösterreichisches Landesmuseum (Table N9)
Formerly Schlossmuseum
1627.5 Stadtmuseum (Table N9)
1627.8 Markt St. Florian (Table N9)
Prague
1628 Hrad (Table N9)
1628.5 Jizdárna Pražského hradu (Table N9)
1629 Národní galerie (Table N9)
1630 Státní sbírka starého umění (Table N9)
1630.4 Středočeská galerie v Praze (Table N9)
1635 Rájec (Kraj Brnenský). Zámecká obrazárna v Rájci nad Svitzvou (Table N9)
1637 Rychnov nad Kněžnou. Rychnovská zámecká obrazárna (Table N9)
Salzburg
1638.5 Dommuseum zu Salzburg (Table N9)
1639 Residenzgalerie (Table N9)
1639.5 Salzburger Landessammlungen Rupertinum (Table N9)
1640 Museum Carolino Augusteum (Table N9)
Formerly Städtisches Museum Carolino-Augusteum
Vienna
1650 Collective
1660 Akademie der Bildenden Künste. Gemäldegalerie (Table N9)
1670 Albertina (Table N9)
Belvedere collections to 1891, see N1680
1673 Gräflich Harrachsche gemälde-galerie (Table N9)
Hofburg. Hausschat, see NK7415.A8
1675 Künstlerhaus (Table N9)
1677 Kunsthistorisches Museum (Table N9)
1680 Gemälde Galerie (Table N9)
1681 Neue Galerie (Table N9)
1682.A-Z Special collections, A-Z
1682.A4 Ambraser Sammlung
1682.E8 Estensische Sammlung

Art museums, galleries, etc.
Special countries and special museums
Europe
Austria, Hungary, Czech Republic and Slovakia
Vienna -- Continued

1685 Fürstlich Liechtensteinsche gemäldegalerie (Table N9)
1688 Museum des 20. Jahrhunderts (Table N9)
1700 Nationalbibliothek (Table N9)
1702 Niederösterreischisches Landesmuseum Kunstabteilung (Table N9)
1708 Österreichische Galerie (Table N9)
1710 Österreichisches Museum für Angewandte Kunst (Table N9)

Belgium
1750 Collective
Antwerp
1760 Collective
1768 Musée Mayer van den Bergh (Table N9)
1770 Koninklijk Museum voor Schone Kunsten (Belgium) (Table N9)
Formerly Musée royal des beaux-arts
1775 Museum Ridder Smidt van Gelder (Table N9)

Bruges
1810 Collective
1812 Gruuthusemuseum (Table N9)
1815 Stedelijk Museum van Schone Kunsten (Table N9)

Brussels
1830 Collective
1832 Musée Communal (Table N9)
1835 Musées royaux d'art et d'histoire (Musées royaux des arts décoratifs at industriels. Musées royaux du Cinquantenaire, etc.) (Table N9)
1836 Musées royaux ... Musées de Ravestein (Table N9)
For arms and armor, see NK6602.5.B4B8
1840 Musées royaux des beaux-arts de Belgique (Musées royaux de peinture et de sculpture de Belgique) (Table N9)
1841.A-Z Other museums, A-Z
1841.P3 Palais des beaux-arts (Table N9)

Charleroi
1845 Collective
1845.2.A-Z Other, A-Z

1850.A-Z Other Belgian cities, A-Z
1850.D3 Damme. Musée Van Maerlant (Table N9)
1850.D44 Deinze. Museum van Deinze en Leiestreek (Table N9)
1850.G2 Gaasbeek. Château-Musée de Gaasbeek (Table N9)
Ghent

Art museums, galleries, etc.
Special countries and special museums
Europe
Belgium
Other Belgian cities, A-Z
Ghent -- Continued

1850.G5 Museum van Oudheden der Byloke (Table N9)
1850.G55 Museum voor Schone Kunsten (Table N9)
1850.I9 Ixelles. Musée d'Ixelles (Table N9)
Formerly Musée des beaux-arts
1850.J3 Jabbeke. Provinciaal Museum Constant Permeke (Table N9)
Liège
1850.L5 Musée Curtius (Table N9)
1850.L53 Musée en pleinair du Sart Tilman (Table N9)
1850.L6 Louvain. Université catholique. Musée (Table N9)
1850.M6 Morlanwelz. Musée de Mariemont (Table N9)
Denmark
1880 Collective
Copenhagen
1910 Collective
1915 Statens museum for kunst (Table N9)
1920 Ny Carlsberg glyptotek (Table N9)
1925 Thorvaldsens museum (Table N9)
1930.A-Z Other, A-Z
1930.D3 Danske kongers kronologiske samling (Table N9)
1930.H55 Hirschsprungske samling af danske kunstneres arbejder (Copenhagen, Denmark) (Table N9)
1930.K84 Kunstkammeret (Table N9)
1930.M3 Maleri- og skulptursamling (Table N9)
1930.N3 Nationalmuseet (Table N9)
1930.O7 Ordrupgaardsamlingen (Table N9)
1935.A-Z Other museums, A-Z
1935.A3 Aarhus. Aarhus kunstmuseum (Table N9)
1935.F33 Fåborg museum (Table N9)
1935.H45 Herning Kunstmuseum (Table N9)
1935.H5 Hillerød. Nationalhistoriske museum, paa Frederiksborg slot (Table N9)
1935.H85 Humlebæk. Louisiana (Museum) (Table N9)
1935.K6 Kolding. Musset på Koldinghus (Table N9)
1935.L6 Lolland-Falster. Reventlowmuseet (Table N9)
1935.N58 Nivaagaards malerisamling (Table N9)
1935.S48 Silkeborg kunstmuseum (Table N9)
1935.S55 Skagens museum (Table N9)
1935.V4 Vejen Kunstmuseum (Table N9)
France
2010 Collective

Art museums, galleries, etc.
Special countries and special museums
Europe
France -- Continued

2010.5.A-Z By region, A-Z
e.g.
2010.5.F74 French Riviera
Paris
2020 Collective
2025 Bibliothèque nationale (Table N9)
Louvre (Musée national, royal, impérial, etc.)
2030.A1-A4 Reports
2030.A5-A7 Catalogs
Subarranged by title
History and description
Including biographies of individual museum personnel associated with only a single museum
2030.A8-A89 Cataloged under name of museum
2030.A9-Z9 Cataloged under author other than then museum
2031 Folios
2032.A-Z Special collections. By name, A-Z
2032.C5 Chauchard
2032.D3 Davillier
2032.R6 Rothschild
2032.S6 Société des amis du Louve
2032.T5 Timbal
2040 Musée national du Luxembourg (Table N9)
2045 Musée de Cluny (Table N9)
Formerly Musée des Thermes et de l'Hôtel de Cluny
2048 Palais des beaux-arts (Table N9)
2049.A-Z Special collections, A-Z
2049.D8 Dutuit
2050.A-Z Other Parisian, A-Z
2050.A6 Musée d'art moderne de la ville de Paris (Table N9)
2050.A7 Musée des arts décoratifs (Table N9)
2050.B6 Musée Bourdelle (Table N9)
2050.C2 Musée Carnavalet (Table N9)
2050.C5 Chat noir (Table N9)
2050.C6 Musée Cognacq-Jay (Table N9)
2050.G7 Musée Grévin (Table N9)
2050.J3 Musée Jacquemart-André (Table N9)
2050.J4 Musée de jeu de paume (Table N9)
2050.M7 Musée des monuments francais (Table N9)
2050.N3 Musée national d'art moderne (Table N9)
2050.O77 Musée d'Orsay (Table N9)
2050.P3 Palais-Royal (Table N9)
2050.P48 Musée du Petit Palais (Table N9)
2050.R6 Musée Rodin (Table N9)

Art museums, galleries, etc.
Special countries and special museums
Europe
France
Paris
Other Parisian, A-Z -- Continued
2050.S4 Galerie Séraphine (Table N9)
2050.U53 Unesco (Table N9)
Other French galleries
2052 A - Albi
2052.A2 Abbeville (Table N9)
2052.A5 Aix. Musée (Table N9)
2053 Albi. Musée (Table N9)
2053.2 Angers. Musée des beaux-arts (Table N9)
Formerly Musée de peinture et de sculpture et galerie David
2053.5 Arras. Musée (Table N9)
2053.7 Aurillac. Musée Hippolyte de Parieu (Table N9)
2053.8 Autun. Musée Rolin (Table N9)
2054 Avignon. Musée Calvet (Table N9)
2057 Bagnères-de-Bigorre. Musée (Table N9)
2058 Bagnères - Cagnes
2058.B35 Bayonne. Musée Bonnat (Table N9)
2058.B4 Beauvais. Musée (Table N9)
Besançon
2058.B44 Musée des beaux-arts (Table N9)
2058.B45 Musée historique de la Franche-Comté (Table N9)
2058.B5 Blérancourt. Musée national de la coopération franco-américaine (Table N9)
2058.B55 Bollène. Musée du Belvédère Louis Pasteur (Table N9)
2058.B6 Bordeaux. Musée des beaux-arts (Table N9)
2058.B7 Bourg-en-Bresse. Musée de l'Ain (Table N9)
2058.C33 Caen (France). Musée des beaux-arts (Table N9)
2059 Cagnes - Compiègne
2059.C14 Cagnes-sur-Mer. Château-Musée de Cagnes-sur-Mer (Table N9)
2059.C2 Castres. Musée Goya, Musée Juarès (Table N9)
2059.C3 Chaalis (Cistercian abbey). Musée Jacquemart-André (Table N9)
2059.C4 Chambéry. Musée (Table N9)
2059.C5 Chantilly. Musée Condé (Table N9)
2059.C54 Châteauroux. Musée (Table N9)
2059.C58 Clermont-Ferrand. Musée Bargoin (Table N9)

Art museums, galleries, etc.
Special countries and special museums
Europe
France
Other French galleries
Cagnes - Compiègne -- Continued
2059.C6 Colmar. Musée des Unterlinden (Table N9)
2060 Compiègne. Palais (Table N9)
2060.5 Courbevoie. Musée Roybet-Fould (Table N9)
2061 Dijon (France). Musée des beaux-arts (Table N9)
Formerly known as Musée municipal
2062 Douai. Musée (Table N9)
2063 Dunkerque. Musée de Dunkerque (Table N9)
2064 Gray. Musee du Baron-Martin (Table N9)
2065 Grenoble. Musée de Grenoble (Table N9)
Formerly known as Musée de peinture et de sculpture
2065.8 Honfleur. Musée (Table N9)
2068 Langres. Musées de Langres (Table N9)
2069 Laon. Musée municipal (Table N9)
2069.3 La Rochelle. Musée des beaux-arts (Table N9)
2070 Lille. Musée des beaux-arts (Table N9)
Limoges
2071.5 Musée Adrien-Dubouché (Table N9)
2072 Musée municipal (Table N9)
Lyons
2080 Musée des beaux-arts (Musée de la ville) (Table N9)
2080.3 Musée des Hospices civils (Table N9)
2081 Musée des Guimet (Table N9)
2108 Marcigny-sur-Loire. Musée de la Tour du moulin (Table N9)
Marseille
2110 Musée Borély (Table N9)
Formerly Musée d'archéologie
2112 Musée Grobet-Labadié (Table N9)
2116 Melun. Musée de Melun (Table N9)
2118 Metz. Musée central (Table N9)
2119 Montauban. Musée Ingres (Table N9)
2120 Montpellier. Musée Fabre (Table N9)
2140 Nancy. Musée des beaux arts (Table N9)
Nantes
2143 Musée des beaux-arts (Table N9)
2143.5 Musées départementaux de Loire-Atlantique (Table N9)
2144 Nantes - Poitiers
2144.N53 Nice. Musée international d'art naïf Anatole Jakovsky (Table N9)
2144.P3 Pau. Musée des beaux-arts (Table N9)
2144.P47 Perpignan. Musée Rigaud (Table N9)

Art museums, galleries, etc.
Special countries and special museums
Europe
France
Other French galleries -- Continued
2145 Poitiers. Musée des beaux-arts (Table N9)
2145.5 Port-Royal des Champs. Musée national des Granges (Table N9)
2146 Puy. Musée Crozatier (Table N9)
2155 Quimper. Musée Breton (Table N9)
2157 Reims. Collective
Rouen
2160 Musée départemental des antiquités (Table N9)
2161 Musée des beaux-arts (Table N9)
2165 Saint-Germaine-en-Laye. Château (Table N9)
2165.5 Saint-Omer. Musée de l'Hôtel Sandelin (Table N9)
Strasbourg
2167.A1 General
2167.B4 Musée des beaux-arts de la ville de Strasbourg (Table N9)
2168 Toulon (France). Musée (Table N9)
2169 Toulouse. Musée des Augustins (Table N9)
2170 Tours. Musée des beaux-arts (Table N9)
2173 Troyes. Musée (Table N9)
2175 Valence. Musée (Table N9)
Versailles. Musée national (Table N9)
2180 General works
2180.2.A-Z Special galleries, A-Z
2180.2.G34 Galerie des batailles
Germany
Collective
Including West Germany; East Germany; East and West Germany; Germany before 1949
2210 General
2210.5.A-Z By region or state, A-Z
e.g.
2210.5.B3 Bavaria
Aachen
2210.8 Ludwig Forum für Internationale Kunst (Table N9)
2211 Suermondt-Museum (Table N9)
2211.8 Altena. Museum der Grafschaft Mark (Table N9)
2212 Altenburg. Staatliches Lindenau-Museum (Table N9)
Aschaffenburg
2213 Museum (Table N9)
2213.4 Schlossmuseum (Table N9)
2213.5 Staatsgalerie (Table N9)
Augsburg

Art museums, galleries, etc.
Special countries and special museums
Europe
Germany
Augsburg -- Continued
2214 K. Gemälde-galerie (Table N9)
2214.3 Staatsgalerie (Table N9)
2216 Baden-Baden. Staatliche Kunsthalle (Table N9)
2217 Bamberg. Staatliche bibliothek (Table N9)
Berlin (General and West Berlin)
2220 Collective
Including K. Museen and Staatliche Museen in general
2222 East Berlin (Collective)
Special
2230 Gemäldegalerie (Table N9)
The pre-1945 museum and/or that portion now in West Berlin
2230.5 East Berlin (Table N9)
2231 Altes Museum (Table N9)
2231.5 Neues Museum (Table N9)
2232 Kaiser Friedrich-Museum (Table N9)
For Gemäldegalerie, see N2230
Kunstgewerbemuseum, see NK480.B5
2233 National-Galerie (Table N9)
The pre-1945 museum and/or that portion now in West Berlin
2233.5 East Berlin (Table N9)
2250.A-Z Other special, A-Z
2250.B47 Berliner Jüdisches Museum (Table N9)
2250.D4 Deutsche Staatsbibliothek (Table N9)
2250.E4 Electoral collections (Table N9)
2250.G25 Galerie des 20. Jahrhunderts (Table N9)
2250.G3 Galerie Haberstock (Table N9)
2250.I2 Ibero-Amerikanisches Institut (Table N9)
2250.J83 Jüdische Ableitung (Table N9)
2250.K86 Kunstbibliothek (Table N9)
2250.K87 Kupferstichkabinett (Table N9)
2250.M87 Museum für Indische Kunst (Germany) (Table N9)
2250.P4 Pergamon-Museum (Table N9)
2250.R2 Rauch Museum (Table N9)
2250.S48 Schinkelmuseum Friedrichwerdersche Kirche (Table N9)
2250.S7 Stiftung Preussischer Kulturbesitz (Table N9)
2250.V6 Vorderasiatisches Museum (Table N9)
Biberach an der Riss
2251 General works
2251.5 Braith-Mali-Museum (Table N9)
Bielefeld

Art museums, galleries, etc.
Special countries and special museums
Europe
Germany
Bielefeld -- Continued
2252 Collective
2253 Historisches Museum (Table N9)
2253.5 Richard Kaselowsky Haus, Kunsthalle der Stadt Bielefeld (Table N9)
Bonn
2255.K85 Kunst- und Asustellungshalle der Bundesrepbulik Deutschland (Table N9)
2255.R5 Rheinisches Landesmuseum (Table N9)
2255.S8 Städtische Kunstsammlungen (Table N9)
2255.S83 Städtische Kunstmuseum Bonn (Table N9)
2255.U6 Universität. Akademisches Kunstmuseum (Table N9)
Bremen
2256 Collective
2257.8 Focke-Museum (Table N9)
2258 Kunsthalle (Table N9)
2258.5 Roselius-Haus (Table N9)
Brunswick
2260 Herzog Anton-Ulrich-Museum (Table N9)
2260.8 Städtisches Museum (Table N9)
2260.9 Burg. Bergisches Museum (Table N9)
2262 Celle. Schlossmuseum (Table N9)
2263.5 Coburg (City). Kunstsammlungen der Veste Coburg (Table N9)
Colmar. Musée des Unterlinden, see N2059.C6
Cologne
2264.2 Collective
2264.4 Gemälde-Galerie Abels (Table N9)
2264.5 Kölnisches Stadtmuseum im Zeughaus (Table N9)
2264.6 Kunstgewerbemuseum (Table N9)
2264.7 Museum Ludwig (Table N9)
2264.8 Museum für Ostasiatische Kunst (Table N9)
2264.85 Römisch-Germanisches Museum (Table N9)
2264.9 Schnütgen Museum (Table N9)
2265 Wallraf-Richartz-Museum (Table N9)
2266 Constance. Rosgartenmuseum (Table N9)
2266.5 Cottbus. Bezirksmuseum (Table N9)
Darmstadt
2267 Hessisches Landesmuseum (Table N9)
Until 1918 known as Grossherzogliches Hessisches Museum
2267.3 Hessisches Landesmuseum. Gemäldegalerie (Table N9)
2268 Darmstadt - Dortmund
Dessau
2268.D77 Staatliche Galerie Dessau (Table N9)

Art museums, galleries, etc.
Special countries and special museums
Europe
Germany
Darmstadt - Dortmund
Dessau -- Continued
2268.D8 Staatliches Museum Schloss Mosigkau (Table N9)
2269 Dortmund - Dresden
2269.D6 Dortmund. Museum für Kunst und Kulturgeschichte (Table N9)
Dresden
2270 Collective
2275 Albertinum (Table N9)
2280 Gemäldegalerie Alte Meister (Table N9)
Formerly known as Gemälde-Galerie. In 1959 divided into Gemäldegalerie Alte Meister and Gemäldegalerie Neue Meister
2280.5 Gemäldegalerie Neue Meister (Table N9)
Grünes Gewölbe, see NK480.D8
2285 Sächsischer Altertumsverein Museum (Table N9)
2287 Düren. Leopold-Hoesch-Museum der Stadt Düren (Table N9)
Düsseldorf
2292 Collective
2294 Electoral gallery (Table N9)
2295 Staatliche Kunstakademie (Table N9)
Formerly Kunst-Akademie
2296 Kunstmuseum (Table N9)
2296.6 North Rhine-Westphalia. Kunstsammlung (Table N9)
2297 Duisburg. Wilhelm-Lehmbruck-Museum der Stadt Duisburg (Table N9)
2298 Duisburg - Essen
2298.E7 Erlangen. Universität (Table N9)
2299 Essen. Museum Folkwang (Table N9)
Frankfurt am Main
2300 Collective
2301 Freies Deutsches Hochstift (Table N9)
2302 Historisches Museum (Table N9)
2303 Städelsches Kunstinstitut (Table N9)
2304 Städtische galerie (Table N9)
2304.28 Frankfurt an der Oder. Galerie Junge Kunst (Table N9)
2304.29 Freiburg im Breisgau. Augustinermuseum (Table N9)
2304.3 Friedrichshafen. Städtisches Bodensee-Museum Friedrichshafen (Table N9)
2305 Fulda - Hildescheim
2305.F8 Fulda. Dom-Museum (Table N9)
2305.G66 Gotha. Schlossmuseum (Table N9)

Art museums, galleries, etc.
Special countries and special museums
Europe
Germany
Fulda - Hildescheim -- Continued

2305.H2 Hagen. Karl-Ernst-Osthaus Museum (Table N9)
2305.H25 Halle. Staatliche Galerie Moritzburg (Table N9)
Hamburg
2305.H26 Collective
2305.H27 Altonaer Museum in Hamburg. Landeschaftsgalerie (Table N9)
2305.H28 Helms-Museum (Table N9)
2305.H3 Kunsthalle (Table N9)
2305.H315 Kunsthalle. Gemälde-Galerie (Table N9)
2305.H32 Hamm. Städtisches Gustav-Lübcke-Museum (Table N9)
2305.H34 Hanau. Historisches Museum (Table N9)
Hanover
2305.H36 Collective
2305.H37 Kestner-Museum (Table N9)
2305.H4 Landesmuseum (Table N9)
2305.H42 Niedersächsische Landesgalerie (Table N9)
2305.H43 Niedersächsisches Heimatmuseum (Table N9)
2305.H45 Heidelberg. Kurpfälzisches Museum (Table N9)
2305.H5 Hildescheim. Roemer-Pelizaeus Museum (Table N9)
Formerly Pelizaeus-Museum
2307 Hildesheim - Kassel
2307.J4 Jena. Stadtmuseum und Kunstsammlung (Table N9)
Karlsruhe
2307.K5 Badisches Landesmuseum (Table N9)
2307.K6 Grossherzogliche Sammlungen für Altertums- und Völkerkunde (Table N9)
2307.K65 Pfinzgau-Museum (Table N9)
2307.K7 Staatliche Kunsthalle (Table N9)
Kassel
2307.8 Hessisches Landesmuseum (Table N9)
2307.9 Neue Gallerie (Table N9)
2308 Staatliche Gemäldegalerie (Table N9)
2308.4 Städtische Kunstsammlungen (Table N9)
2308.5 Kasseler Museumverein (Table N9)
2309 Kasseler - Leipzig
2309.K5 Kiel. Kunsthalle (Table N9)
2309.K55 Kleve. Städtisches Museum Haus Koekkoek (Table N9)
2309.K6 Koblenz. Mittelrhein-Museum Koblenz (Table N9)

Art museums, galleries, etc.
Special countries and special museums
Europe
Germany
Kasseler - Leipzig -- Continued

2309.K7 Krefeld. Kaiser-Wilhelm-Museum (Table N9)

2309.K75 Kronach. Fränkische Galerie. (Branch of Bayerisches National Museum, Munich) (Table N9)

2309.L27 Landsberg am Lech. Neues Stadtmuseum (Table N9)

2309.L3 Landshut. Stadtresidenz (Table N9)

2310 Leipzig. Museum der Bildenden Künste (Table N9)

2311 Leverkusen. Städtisches Museum, Schloss Morsbroich (Table N9)

Lübeck

2312 Collective

2312.22 Behnhaus (Table N9)

2312.7 St. Annen-Museum (Table N9)

2314 Mainz. Städische gemäldegalerie (Table N9)

Mannheim

2315 Kunsthalle (Table N9)

2315.3 Reiss-Museum (Table N9)

2316 Mannheim - Munich

2316.M36 Marburg. Marburger Universitätsmuseum für Kunst und Kulturgeschichte (Table N9)

Mönchen-Gladbach

2316.M6 Städtisches Museum (Table N9)

2316.M67 Städtisches Museum Schloss Rheydt (Table N9)

2316.M69 Moritzburg (Bezirk Dresden). Barockmuseum Schloss Moritzburg (Table N9)

2316.M8 Mülheim an der Ruhr. Städtsiches Museum (Table N9)

Münster

2316.M82 Landesmuseum der Provinz Westfalen (Table N9)

2316.M83 Westfälischen Landesmuseums für Kunst und Kulturgeschichte (Table N9)

Munich

2317 Collective

2318 Antiquarium (Table N9)

2319 Bayerisches Nationalmuseum (Table N9)

2319.5 Galerie Caspari (Table N9)

2320 Glyptothek (Table N9)

2321 Haus der Kunst (Table N9)

2325 Pinakothek, Alte (Table N9)

2330 Pinakothek, Neue (Table N9)

2333 Residenzmuseum (Table N9)

2335 Schackgalerie (Table N9)

2339.A-Z Other special, A-Z

2339.K3 Kameradschaft der Künstler (Table N9)

Art museums, galleries, etc.
Special countries and special museums
Europe
Germany
Munich
Other special, A-Z -- Continued
2339.N9 Nymphenburg (Castle). Amalienburg (Table N9)
2339.S7 Städtische Galerie im Lenbachhaus (Table N9)
Formerly Städische Galerie
2348 Nördlingen. Stadtmuseum (Table N9)
Nuremburg
2350 Germanisches Nationalmuseum (Table N9)
2355 St. Morizkapelle (Table N9)
2358 Oberhausen. Städtische Galerie Schloss Oberhausen (Table N9)
Oldenburg
2360 Grossherzogliche Kunstsammlungen. Gemäldesammlung (Table N9)
2361 Landesmuseum für Kunst und Kulturgeschichte (Table N9)
2363 Potsdam. Staatliche Schlösser und Gärten Potsdam-Sanssouci. Bildergalerie (Table N9)
2364 Recklinghausen. Collective
2365 Rheydt. Städisches Museum Schloss Rheydt (Table N9)
2370 Saarbrücken. Moderne Galerie Saarbrücken (Table N9)
2375 Schleissheim. K. Gemäldegalerie (Table N9)
2378 Schleswig (City). Schleswig-Holsteinisches Landesmuseum für Vor- und Frühgeschichte in Schleswig (Table N9)
2379 Schwabmünchen. Museum und Galerie der Stadt Schwabmünchen (Table N9)
Schwerin
2380 Grossherzogliches Museum und grossherzogliche Kunstsammlungen (Table N9)
2380.5 Staatliches Museum (Table N9)
2382 Sigmaringen. Fürstlich Hohenzollernsches Museum (Table N9)
Stuttgart
2390 Kunst- und altertümer-kabinet (Table N9)
2390.5 Linden-Museum Stuttgart (Table N9)
2392 Staatsgalerie (Table N9)
2392.8 Württembergisches Landesmuseum (Table N9)
Trier
2394 Rheinisches Landesmuseum (Table N9)
2394.5 Städtisches Museum (Table N9)
2398 Ulm. Museum der Stadt Ulm (Table N9)
2399 Weimer. Kunstsammlungen (Table N9)

N

Art museums, galleries, etc.
Special countries and special museums
Europe
Germany -- Continued
2401 Wernigerode. Feudalmuseum Schloss Wernigerode (Table N9)
Wiesbaden
2402 Nassauisches Landesmuseum. Städtische Kunstsammlung (Table N9)
2402.3 Städtisches Museum. Gemäldegalerie (Table N9)
2402.5 Witten. Märkisches Museum (Table N9)
2403.7 Wolfsburg. Kunstmuseum (Table N9)
2404 Wörlitz. Schlossmuseum (Table N9)
2404.5 Worms. Kunsthaus Heylshof (Table N9)
Würzburg
2404.8 Mainfränkisches Museum (Table N9)
2405 Universität. Martin von Wagner-Museum (Table N9)
2405.5 Wuppertal. Von der Heydt-Museum (Table N9)
2406 Xanten. Dommuseum (Table N9)
Greece
2410 Collective
Athens
2420 Collective
2422 Byzantinon Mouseion (Table N9)
2422.5 Ethnikē Pinakothēkē, Mouseion Alexandrou Soutsou (Table N9)
2425 Mouseion Mpenakē (Table N9)
2430 Paul and Alexandra Canellopoulos Museum (Table N9)
Netherlands
2450 Collective
2450.5.A-Z By region, province, etc., A-Z
Amsterdam
2458 Museum Fodor (Table N9)
2460 Rijks-Museum (Table N9)
2463 Stedelijk Museum (Table N9)
2465 Antwerp. Musée Plantin-Moretus (Table N9)
2467 Arnhem. Gemeentemuseum (Table N9)
2467.2 Delft. Rijksmuseum Huis Lambert van Meerten (Table N9)
2467.3 Eindhoven. Stedelijk Van Abbe-Museum (Table N9)
2467.5 Enschede. Rijksmuseum Twenthe (Table N9)
2468 Gorinchem. Kunstcentrum Badhuis (Table N9)
Haarlem
2469 Bisschoppelijk Museum (Table N9)
2470 Frans Hals-Museum der Gemeente Haarlem (Table N9)
2475 Stedelijk Museum van Schilderijen en Oudheden (Table N9)
2477 Teyler's Stichting. Museum (Table N9)

Art museums, galleries, etc.
Special countries and special museums
Europe
Netherlands -- Continued
Hague
2480 Kabinet van Schilderijen (Table N9)
2480.5 Koninklijke Bibliotheek (Table N9)
2482 Gemeentemuseum (Table N9)
2483 Mauritshuis (Table N9)
2484 Museum Mesdag (Table N9)
2490 Leyden. Rijksmuseum van Oudheden (Table N9)
2490.4 Maastricht. Bonnefantenmuseum (Table N9)
2492 Nijmegen. Rijksmuseum G.M. Kam (Table N9)
2500 Otterlo. Rijksmuseum Kröller-Müller (Table N9)
2502 Overijssel. Stichting Hannema-De Stuers Fundatie (Table N9)
Rotterdam
2504.5 Lijnbaan Kunstcentrum Rotterdam (Table N9)
2505 Museum Boymans-Van Beuningen (Table N9)
2505.5 's Hertogenbosch. Noordbrabants Museum (Table N9)
2506 Utrecht. Centraal Museum (Table N9)
Italy
2510 Collective
Ancona
2513 Museo nazionale (Table N9)
2513.5 Pinacoteca comunale Francesco Podesti (Table N9)
2515 Aquileia. Museo archeologico (Table N9)
2515.2 Arezzo. Museo (Table N9)
2515.4 Bari (Province). Pinacoteca provinciale (Table N9)
2515.5 Bassano del Grappa. Museo civico (Table N9)
2516 Benevento. Museo del Sannio (Table N9)
2517 Bergamo. Accademia Carrara (Table N9)
Bologna
2519.5 Cassa di risparmio in Bologna (Table N9)
2519.8 Museo civico d'arte industriale e galleria Davia Bargellini (Table N9)
2520 Pinacoteca nazionale (Table N9)
Bolzano (City)
2521.7 Museo civico (Table N9)
2522 Museo dell'Alto Adige (Table N9)
2523 Breno. Museo camuno (Table N9)
Brescia
2524.5 Collective
2525 Museo civico (Table N9)
2526 Cagliari. Museo nazionale (Table N9)
2526.5 Campobasso. Museo di Baranello (Table N9)
2528 Catania. Museo comunale (Table N9)
In 1932 acquired the collections of the Museo Biscari

Art museums, galleries, etc.
Special countries and special museums
Europe
Italy -- Continued
Cento (City)
2529 Galleria d'arte moderna Aroldo Bonzagni (Table N9)
2529.5 Pinacoteca Civica di Centro (Table N9)
2529.7 Chiari. Pinacoteca Repossi (Table N9)
2530 Crema. Museo civico di Crema e del Cremasco (Table N9)
2532 Cremona. Museo civico (Table N9)
2537 Este. Museo nazionale atestino (Table N9)
2539 Feltre. Museo civico (Table N9)
Ferrara
2539.2 Museo civico l'arte antica di Palazzo Schifanoia (Table N9)
2539.3 Pinacoteca nazionale (Table N9)
Fiesole
2539.45 Museo Bandini (Table N9)
2539.5 Museo fiesolano (Table N9)
Florence
2540 Collective
Fondazione Horne, see N2554.5
2545 Fondazione Roberto Longhi (Table N9)
2550 R. Galleria antica e moderna (Accademia di belle arti) (Table N9)
2550.5 Galleria Buonarroti (Table N9)
2552 Museo archaeologico (Table N9)
2552.4 Museo Bardini (Table N9)
2553.6 Museo del Bigallo (Table N9)
2553.8 Museo dell'antica casa fiorentina (Table N9)
2554 Museo di San Marco (Table N9)
2554.5 Museo Horne (Table N9)
Name changed to Fondazione Horne
2555 Museo nazionale del Bergello (Table N9)
Formerly Museo nazionale
2555.5 Museo Stibbert (Table N9)
2557 Opera del Duomo. Museo (Table N9)
2560 Palazzo Pitti (Table N9)
2560.5.A-Z Special galleries. By name, A-Z
2560.5.P34 Galleria Palatina
2570 Galleria degli Uffizi (Table N9)
Formerly Real Galleria di Firenze
2571 Folios
2610 Forli. Pinacoteca (Table N9)
2612 Fucecchio. Museo (Table N9)
2620 Genoa
2623 Galleria di Palazzo Bianco (Table N9)
2625 Galleria Durazzo Pallavicini (Table N9)
2626 Galleria nazionale di Palazzo Spinola (Table N9)

Art museums, galleries, etc.
Special countries and special museums
Europe
Italy
Genoa -- Continued
2627 Museo d'arte orientale E. Chiossone (Table N9)
2627.4 Museo Luxoro (Table N9)
2627.5 Museo di S. Agostino (Table N9)
2628 Ospedale di San Martino. Museo (Table N9)
2630 Palazzo Bianco. Museo civico di storia e d'arte (Table N9)
2640 Palazzo Rosso (Table N9)
2645 Gualdo Tadino. Pinacoteca comunale (Table N9)
2647 Istrana. Villa Lattes (Table N9)
2649 L'Aquila. Museo nazionale abruzzese (Table N9)
2650 Lecce. Museo provinciale Castromediano (Table N9)
2650.5 Legnano, Italy. Museo d'arte moderna Fondazione Pagani (Table N9)
2650.8 Lodi. Museo civico (Table N9)
2650.85 Loreto. Palazzo apostolico (Table N9)
2651 Lovere. Accademia Tadini (Table N9)
Lucca
2651.5 Museo nazionale Villa Guinigi (Table N9)
2651.7 Pinacoteca di Lucca (Table N9)
2654 Mantua. Galleria e museo di Palazzo ducale (Table N9)
Messina
(2655) Museo nazionale di Messina
See N2656
2656 Museo regionale di Messina (Table N9)
Formerly Museo nazionale di Messina
Milan
2660 Collective
2661 Castello sforzesco (Table N9)
2661.3 Duomo. Museo (Table N9)
2661.7 Galleria Melzi (Table N9)
2662 Museo archeologico (Table N9)
2663 Museo Poldi-Pezzoli (Table N9)
2665 Palazzo reale (Table N9)
2668 Pinacoteca ambrosiana (Table N9)
2670 Pinacoteca di Brera (Table N9)
Modena
2690 Galleria, museo e medagliere estense (Table N9)
2693 Museo civico di storia e arte medievale e moderna (Table N9)
2700 Montalcino. Collective
2705 Monza. Collective

Art museums, galleries, etc.
Special countries and special museums
Europe
Italy -- Continued

2706 Mozzo. Pinacoteca alla Crocetta di Mozzo (Table N9)

Naples

2720 Collective

2721 Accademia de belle arti e liceo artistico. Galleria (Table N9)

2724 Museo archeologico nazionale (Table N9)

2726 Museo civico Gaetano Filangieri (Table N9)

2727 Museo e gallerie nazionale di Capodimonte (Table N9)

2730 Museo nazionale (Museo borbonico) (Table N9)

2731 Museo nazionale di S. Martino (Table N9)

2732 Museo principe Diego Aragona Pignatelli Cortes (Table N9)

2734 Novara. Civica galleria Gianonni (Table N9)

2735.5 Olivone. Museo di San Martino (Table N9)

2735.7 Orvieto. Opera del Duomo. Museo (Table N9)

2736 Padua. Museo del Liviano (Table N9)

2737 Paestum. Museo (Table N9)

Palermo

2737.6 Galleria nazionale della Sicilia (Table N9)

2738 Museo nazionale archeologico (Table N9)
Formerly Museo nazionale

Parma

2740 Galleria nazionale (Table N9)

2740.4 Museo bodoniano (Table N9)

2740.5 Museo d'arte cinese (Table N9)

2740.7 Museo Glauco Lombardi (Table N9)

2741 Museo nazionale di antichità (Table N9)

2741.5 Pavia. Musei civici (Table N9)

Perugia

2741.8 Collegio del Cambio (Table N9)

2743 Galleria nazionale dell'Umbria Pinacoteca Vannucci, 1863-1918 (Table N9)

2743.4 Pesaro. Pinacoteca civica di Pesaro (Table N9)

2744 Piacenza. Museo civico (Table N9)

2745 Pisa. Campo santo

2746 Pisa. Campo santo to Prato

2746.P6 Pisa. Museo civico (Table N9)

2746.P66 Pistoia. Museo civico (Table N9)

2746.P8 Potenza. Museo archeologico provinciale (Table N9)

Prato

2746.7 Collective

2747 Museo Comunale (Table N9)

2748 Randazzo. Museo Vagliasindi (Table N9)

Ravenna

Art museums, galleries, etc.
Special countries and special museums
Europe
Italy
Ravenna -- Continued
2749 Accademia di belle arti. Galleria (Table N9)
2750 Museo nazionale (Table N9)
2755 Pinacoteca comunale di Ravenna (Table N9)
2765 Reggio Calabria. Museo nazionale (Table N9)
2775 Rieti. Museo civico (Table N9)
2778 Rimini. Museo civico (Table N9)
Rome
2810 Collective
Including such groups as the Musei Capitolini
2812 Accademia nazionale di San Luca (Table N9)
2813 Albani, Villa (Table N9)
2815 Palazzo Barberini (Table N9)
2818 Ludovisi, Villa (Table N9)
2820 Borghese, Villa. Galleria e museo Borghese (Table N9)
2830 Museo capitolino (Table N9)
2840 Galleria Colonna (Table N9)
2850 Conservatori, Palazzo dei (Table N9)
2860 Corsini gallery (Table N9)
Diocletian's baths (National museum), see N2934
2875 Dodwell gallery (Table N9)
2878 Galleria comunale d'arte moderna e contemporanea (Table N9)
2880 Galleria Doria-Pamphili (Table N9)
2910 Galleria nazionale d'arte antica (Table N9)
Formerly Galleria Nazionale d'arte antica e Gabinetto delle stampe
2915 Galleria nazionale d'arte moderna (Table N9)
2920 Galleria nazionale e gabinetto delle stampe (Table N9)
2922 Galleria Pallavicine (Table N9)
2923 Galleria Spada (Table N9)
2925 Museo Kircheriano (Table N9)
2930 Lateran collections (Table N9)
2931 Museo di Palazzo Venezia (Table N9)
2931.5 Museo di Roma (Table N9)
2932 Museo nazionale di Villa Giulia (Table N9)
2934 Museo nazionale romano (Table N9)
2934.5 Museo ostiense (Table N9)
2937 Galleria Sciarra (Table N9)
Vatican collections (Table N9)
2940 Collective
2941 Biblioteca vaticana. Museo sacro
2943 Museo Chiaramonti

Art museums, galleries, etc.
Special countries and special museums
Europe
Italy
Rome
Vatican collections -- Continued
(2944) Museo etrusco gregoriano
see N5750-N5751
2945 Museo Pio-Clementino
2945.5 Museo profano lateranense
2947 Pinacoteca (1932-)
2950 Cappella sistina
2955 Rovigo. Accademia dei Concordi di Rovigo. Pinacoteca (Table N9)
2959 Saluzzo. Museo civico di Casa Cavassa (Table N9)
2963 Sassari. Museo G. A. Sanna (Table N9)
2963.5 Senigallia. Museo Pio IX (Table N9)
2964 Sestri Levante. Galleria Rizzi (Table N9)
Siena
2966 Collective
2967 Duomo. Museo (Table N9)
2969 Museo civico di Siena (Table N9)
2970 Pinacoteca (Table N9)
2975 Sorrento. Museo Correale (Table N9)
2975.8 Syracuse. Museo archeologico (Table N9)
2976 Taranto. Museo nazionale (Table N9)
2977 Trapani. Museo nazionale Pepoli (Table N9)
2977.6 Trieste. Civico museo Revoltella-Galleria d'arte moderna (Table N9)
Turin
2979 Galleria d'arte moderna (Table N9)
2980 Galleria sabauda (Table N9)
2983 Museo civico (Table N9)
2985 Museo di antichità (Table N9)
2987.A-Z Other, A-Z
2987.A4 Accademia Albertina di belle arti. Regia galleria (Table N9)
2987.M8 Museo civico d'arte antica (Table N9)
2987.R43 Regia Pinacoteca di Torino (Table N9)
3005 Urbino. Galleria nazionale delle Marche (Table N9)
Venice
3010 Collective
3020 Galleria dell'Accademia (Table N9)
Formerly Accademia di belle arti (R.R. Galleria)
3025 Galleria Giorgio Franchetti alla Ca' d'oro (Table N9)
3030 Museo civico Correr (Table N9)
3032 Museo d'arte moderna Ca' Pesaro (Table N9)
3040 Palazzo ducale (Table N9)
3042.A-Z Other, A-Z

Art museums, galleries, etc.
Special countries and special museums
Europe
Italy
Venice
Other, A-Z -- Continued
3042.S4 Seminario patriarcale di Santa Maria della salute (Table N9)
3055 Vercelli. Civico museo Francesco Borgogna (Table N9)
Verona
3060 Museo civico (Table N9)
3062 Museo di Castelvecchio (Table N9)
3063 Museo lapidario (Table N9)
3064 Vicenza. Museo civico. Pinacoteca (Table N9)
3065 Viterbo. Museo civico (Table N9)
(3070) Zara. Museo nazionale
See N3690.Y8Z2
3080 Monaco. Palais (Table N9)
Norway
3110 Collective
3120 Bergen. Billedgalleriet (Table N9)
Oslo
3124 Collective
3125 Bymuseet (Table N9)
3128 Museet far samtidskunst (Oslo, Norway) (Table N9)
3130 Nasjonalgalleriet (Table N9)
3135.A-Z Other cities, A-Z
3135.L5 Lillehammer bys malerisamling (Table N9)
3135.L97 Lysaker. Riksgalleriet (Table N9)
3135.M6 Molde. Romsdalsmuseet (Table N9)
3135.S76 Stavanger faste galleri (Table N9)
Poland
3150 Collective
3150.5 Danzig. Muzeum Pomorskiew Gdansku (Table N9)
3152 Koszalin. Muzeum (Table N9)
Krakow
3152.2 Galeria Malarstwa Polskiego wieku XIX (Table N9)
3152.3 Muzeum Narodowe (Table N9)
3152.32.A-Z Special collections. By name, A-Z
3152.32.C92 Czartoryski collection
3152.35 Uniwersytet Jagielloński. Muzeum (Table N9)
3153 Łódź. Muzeum Sztuki (Table N9)
3154 Nieborow. Muzeum Narodowe (Table N9)
3157 Posen. Muzeum Narodowe (Table N9)
3157.4 Rogalin. Pałac w Rogalinie (Table N9)
Warsaw
3159 Muzeum imienia Mathiasa Bersohne (Table N9)
3160 Muzeum Narodowe (Table N9)

Art museums, galleries, etc.
Special countries and special museums
Europe
Poland -- Continued
Wilanow
3163 Galeria Malarstwa Stanisława Kostki Potockiego (Table N9)
3163.5 Muzeum w Wilanowie (Table N9)
3165 Pałac (Table N9)
Wrocław
3165.7 Collective
3165.8 Muzeum Narodowe we Wrocławiu (Table N9)
3166 Muzeum Narodowe we Wrocławiu. Galeria Malarstwa Polskiego (Table N9)
Portugal
3210 Collective
3212 Beja. Museu Regional (Table N9)
3213 Bilbao. Museo Guggenheim Bilbao (Table N9)
3215 Caramulo. Museu (Table N9)
3219 Evora. Biblioteca Publica (Table N9)
3219.5 Funchal. (Madeira: Autonomous District). Museu da Quinta das Cruzes (Table N9)
3221 Guimarães. Museu de Alberto Sampaio (Table N9)
Lisbon
3228 Collective
3230 Museu Nacional das Bellas Artes (Table N9)
3231.A-Z Other, A-Z
3231.A3 Academia de Bellas-Artes de Lisboa (Table N9)
3231.C36 Casa-Museu Dr. Anastácio Gonçalves (Table N9)
3231.M76 Museu Calouste Gulbenkian (Table N9)
3231.M8 Museu Nacional de Arte Antiga (Table N9)
3231.P3 Palacio da Ajuda. Galeria de Pintura (Table N9)
Oporto
3235 Collective
3236.A-Z Special museums, A-Z
3236.M8 Museu Nacional de Soares dos Reis (Table N9)
Russia
Including Russia in Asia
3310 Collective
3310.15.A-Z By region, province, etc., A-Z
3310.2 Abramt͡sevo. Muzeĭ "Abramt͡sevo" (Table N9)
Alma-Ata (Kazakhstan)
3310.7 Kazakhskai͡a gosudarstvennai͡a khudozhestvennai͡a galerei͡a (Table N9)
3310.8 Qazaq SSR Memlekettik òner muzeĭi (Table N9)
3311 Alupka. Dvoret͡s-muzeĭ (Table N9)

Art museums, galleries, etc.
Special countries and special museums
Europe
Russia -- Continued

3311.3 Arkhangel'skiĭ muzeĭ-zapovednik dereviannogo zodchestva (Table N9)

3311.5 Baku. Azerbaĭdzhanskiĭ gosudarstvennyĭ muzeĭ iskusstv (Table N9)

3312.5 Dnipropetrovsk (Ukraine). Dnipropetrovs'kyĭ khudozhnii muzeĭ (Table N9)

3313 Donetsk. Oblasna kartynna halereia (Table N9)

3313.5 Dushanbe (Tajikistan). Respublikanskiĭ ob"edinennyĭ muzeĭ istoriko-kraevedcheskiĭ i izobrazitel'nykh iskusstv (Tajikistan) (Table N9)

3314 Feodosia. Feodosiĭaskaia kartinnaia gallereia (Table N9)

3315 Gorki. Gosudarstvennyĭ khudozhestvennyĭ muzeĭ (Table N9)

3315.3 Irkutsk. Irkutskiĭ oblastnoĭ khudozhestvennyĭ muzeĭ (Table N9)

3315.42 Kalininskaia oblastnaia kartinnaia galereia (Table N9)

3315.43 Kaluga (City). Kaluzhskiĭ oblastnoĭ khudozhestvennyĭ muzeĭ (Table N9)

3315.45 Kaunas. Valstybinis M. K. Čiurlionio vardo dailės muziejus (Table N9)

3315.47 Kazan. Muzeĭ izobrazitel'nykh iskusstv Tatarskoĭ ASSR (Table N9)

3315.49 Kemerovo (City). Kamerovskaia oblastnaia kartinnaia galereia (Table N9)

Kharkov

3315.5 Derzhavnyĭ muzeĭ obrazotvorchoho mystetstva (Table N9)

3315.52 Imperatorskiĭ khar'kovskiĭ universitet. Muzeĭ iziashchnykh iskusstv (Table N9)

3315.53 Kharkivs'kyĭ khudozhniĭ muzeĭ (Table N9)

3315.6 Muzeĭ iziashchnykh iskusstv i drevnosteĭ (Table N9)

Kiev

3315.9 Collective

3316 Akademiia nauk URSR. Muzeĭ mystetstva (Table N9)

3317 Derzhavnyĭ muzeĭ imeni Khanenko (Table N9)

3317.25 Derzhavnyĭ muzeĭ rosiĭs'koho mystetstva (Table N9)

3317.3 Derzhavnyĭ muzeĭ T. H. Shevchenka (Table N9)

3317.4 Derzhavnyĭ muzeĭ ukraïns'koho mystetstva (Table N9)

Art museums, galleries, etc.
Special countries and special museums
Europe
Russia
Kiev -- Continued
3317.45 Derzhavnyĭ muzeĭ ukraïns'koho obrazotvorchoho mystetstva (Table N9)
3317.5 Kyïvs'kyĭ muzeĭ zakhidnoho ta skhidnoho mystetstva (Table N9)
Formerly Derzhavnyĭ muzeĭ zakhidnoho ta skhidnoho mystetstva
3317.9 Kirov. Oblastnoĭ khudozhestvennyĭ muzeĭ (Table N9)
3317.915 Kishinev. Muzeul Artistik de Stat din RSS Moldoveniaske (Table N9)
3317.92 Kizhi Island. Gosudarstvennyĭ istoriko-arkhitekturnyĭ i ėthnograficheskiĭ muzeĭ-zapovednik "Kizhi" (Table N9)
Formerly known as Arkhitekturno-bytovoĭ muzeĭ-zapovednik pod otkrytm nebom; Kizhskiĭ muzeĭ-zapovednik narodnogo dereviannogo zodchestva i ėtnografii Karel'skoĭ ASSR. Gosudarstvennyĭ istoriko-arkhitekturnyĭ muzeĭ "Kizhi"
3317.95 Krasnodar. Krasnodarskiĭ kraevoĭ khudozhestvennyĭ muzeĭ (Table N9)
3318 Kuybyshev. Khudozhestvennyĭ muzeĭ (Table N9)
Leningrad, see N3340+
3318.4 Lutsk (Ukraine). Volyns'kyĭ kraienznavchyĭ muzeĭ Khudozhniĭ viddil (Table N9)
Lvov
3318.9 Collective
3319 L'vivs'ka kartynna halereia (Table N9)
Formerly Derzhavna kartnyya halereia
3319.2 Derzhavnyĭ muzeĭ ukraïns'koho mystetstva (Table N9)
3319.8 Minsk. Dziarzhaŭny mastatski muzeĭ BSSR (Table N9)
Moscow
3320 Collective
3320.14 Golitsynskiĭ muzeĭ (Table N9)
3320.15 Gosudarstvennye muzeĭ Moskovskogo Kremlia (Table N9)
3320.2 Gosudarstvennyĭ muzeĭ iskusstva narodov Vostoka (Table N9)
3320.3 Gosudarstvennyĭ muzeĭ iskusstva narodov Vostoka. Otdel Sovetskogo Vostoka (Table N9)
3321 Gosudarstvennyĭ muzeĭ izobrazitel'nykh iskusstv imeni A.S. Pushkina (Table N9)
3322 Gosudarstvennyĭ muzeĭ novogo zapadnogo iskusstva (Table N9)

Art museums, galleries, etc.
Special countries and special museums
Europe
Russia
Moscow -- Continued
3322.5 Gosudarstvennyĭ muzeĭ vostochnykh kul'tur (Table N9)
3322.7 Kolomenskoe. Gosudarstvennyĭ muzeĭ-zapovednik "Kolomenskoe" (Table N9)
3323 Moskovskiĭ i Rumi͡antsovskiĭ muzeĭ (Rumiantsov museum) (Table N9)
3323.2 Muzeĭ izi͡ashchnykh iskusstv imeni Imperatora Aleksandra III (Table N9)
3323.8 Ostankinskiĭ dvoret͡s-muzeĭ (Table N9)
3323.9 Pervyĭ muzeĭ novoĭ zapadnoĭ zhivopisi (Table N9)
3324 Studii͡a voennykh khudozhnikov imeni Grekova (Table N9)
3325 Gosudarstvennai͡a Tret'i͡akovskai͡a gallerei͡a (Tretyakov gallery) (Table N9)
3327 Nikolaev (Nikolaevskai͡a oblast'). Mykolaïvs'kyĭ khudozhniĭ muzeĭ imenii V.V. Vereshchahina (Table N9)
Formerly Derzhavnyĭ khudozhniĭ muzeĭ
3327.5 Nukus. Gosudarstvennyĭ muzeĭ iskusstv Karakalpakskoĭ ASSR (Table N9)
Odessa
3328.5 Collective
3329 Derzhavna kartynna halerei͡a (Table N9)
3329.3 Derzhavnyĭ khudozhniĭ muzeĭ (Table N9)
3329.6 Odes'kyĭ derzhavnyĭ muzeĭ zakhidnoho ta skhidnoho mystet͡stva (Table N9)
3330 Omsk. Muzeĭ izobrazitel'nykh iskusstv (Table N9)
3331 Penza. Penzenskai͡a kartinnai͡a galerei͡a (Table N9)
3332.5 Perm' (City). Khudozhestvannai͡a gallerei͡a (Table N9)
3333 Petrodvorets. Ėrmitazh (Table N9)
3335 Polenovo. Gosudarstvennyĭ muzeĭ-usad'ba V. D. Polenova (Table N9)
Poltava
3336 Derzhavnyĭ muzeĭ (Table N9)
3336.3 Poltavs'kyi khudozhnii muzeĭ (Table N9)
3336.4 Riazan' (City). Riazanskiĭ oblastnoĭ khudozhestvennyĭ muzeĭ (Table N9)
3337 Riga. Latvijas PRS Aizrobeiu mākslas muzejs (Table N9)
St. Petersburg. Petrograd. Leningrad
3340 Collective

Art museums, galleries, etc.
Special countries and special museums
Europe
Russia
St. Petersburg.
Petrograd. Leningrad -- Continued

3342 Akademii͡a khudozhestv. Muzeĭ (Table N9)
3344 Gosudarstvennyĭ russkiĭ muzeĭ (Table N9)
3350 Ėrmitazh (Hermitage) (Table N9)
3350.2.A-Z Special galleries. By name, A-Z
3350.2.O73 Otdel zapadnoevropeĭskogo iskusstva
3350.5 ĬUsupovskai͡a gallereia (Table N9)
3351.2 Saratov (City). Gosudarstvennyĭ khudozhestvennyĭ muzeĭ imeni A.N. Radishcheva (Table N9)
3351.5 Serpukhov (City). Serpukhovskiĭ istoriko-khudozhestvennyĭ muzeĭ (Table N9)
3352 Sevastopol. Sevastopol's'kyĭ khudozhniĭ muzeĭ (Table N9)
Simferopol
3355 Kryms'ka oblasna kartynna halerei͡a (Table N9)
3355.5 Simferopol's'kyi khudozhniĭ muzeĭ (Table N9)
3359 Sumy. Derzhavnyĭ khudozhniĭ muzeĭ (Table N9)
3360 Sverdlovsk. Kartinnai͡a galerei͡a (Table N9)
3361.7 Tallinn. Eesti NSV Riiklik Kunstimuuseum (Table N9)
3362 Tashkend. Gosudarstvennyĭ muzeĭ iskusstv Uzbekskoĭ SSR (Table N9)
3362.2 Tblisi. Sak'art'velos xelovnebis muzeumi (Table N9)
3362.7 Tuk'skiĭ oblastnoĭ khudozhestvennyĭ muzeĭ (Table N9)
3364 Ufa. Bashkirskiĭ gosudarstvennyĭ khudozhestvennyĭ muzeĭ (Table N9)
Uzhgorod
3365 Zakarpats'ka oblasna kartynna halerei͡a (Table N9)
3365.5 Zakarpats'kyĭ khudozhniĭ muzeĭ (Table N9)
3368 Vilna. Valstybinis dailės muziejus (Table N9)
3368.5 Voronezh. Voronezhskiĭ oblastnoĭ muzeĭ izobrazitel'nykh iskusstv (Table N9)
3371 Yakutsk. Respubliakanskiĭ muzeĭ izobrazitel'nykh iskusstv (Table N9)

Art museums, galleries, etc.
Special countries and special museums
Europe
Russia -- Continued
3375 Yerevan. Hayastani Petakan Patkerasrah (Table N9)
Formerly Gosudarstvennaia kartinnaia gallereia Armenii
3380 Zagorsk. Gosudarstvennyĭ istoriko-khudozhestvennyĭ muzeĭ (Table N9)
3382 Zaporozh'e (Ukraine). Zaporiz'kyĭ khudozhniĭ muzeĭ (Table N9)
Spain
Collective
3410 General
3410.2.A-Z By region, province, etc., A-Z
3410.25 Badalona. Museu municipal de Badalona (Table N9)
Barcelona
3410.3 Collective
3410.5 Museo de Arte de Cataluña (Table N9)
Formerly Museo de Bellas Artes
3410.7 Museo de Arte Moderno (Table N9)
3411 Museo Marés (Table N9)
Formerly Museo Federico Marés
3412 Bilbao. Museo de Bellas Artes (Table N9)
3413 Burgos. Museo Arqueológico Provincial (Table N9)
3415 Cadiz. Museo de Bellas Artes (Table N9)
3415.23 Castelló (Spain). Museo de Bellas Artes (Table N9)
3415.3 Coruña. Museo Provincial de Bellas Artes de La Coruña (Table N9)
3416 Cuenca. Museo municipal de arte (Table N9)
3418 Escorial (Table N9)
3425 Granada. Museo Provincial de Bellas Artes (Table N9)
3427 Huesca. Museo Provincial (Table N9)
Madrid
3430 Collective
3440 Biblioteca Nacional (Table N9)
3442 Cortes (Table N9)
3442.5 Museo del Palacio de El Pardo (Table N9)
3444 Museo Lázaro Galdiano (Table N9)
3445 Museo Nacional de Arte Moderno (Table N9)
3450 Museo Nacional de Pintura y Escultura (Museo del Prado) (Table N9)
3455.A-Z Other museums, A-Z
3455.A3 Academia de Bellas Artes de San Fernando (Table N9)
3455.D4 Descalzas Reales (Franciscan convent) Museo (Table N9)

Art museums, galleries, etc.
Special countries and special museums
Europe
Spain
Madrid
Other museums, A-Z -- Continued

3455.I5 Instituto de Valencia de Don Juan (Table N9)
3455.M78 Museo Cerralbo (Table N9)
3455.M79 Museo de América (Table N9)
3455.M8 Museo de Reproducciones Artísticas (Table N9)
3455.M83 Museo Romántico (Table N9)
3455.M86 Museo Sorolla (Table N9)
3457 Martorell. Museu Santacana (Table N9)
3457.4 Medina de Ríoseco. Museo de Santa María de Mediavilla (Table N9)
Murcia
3458 Collective
3458.8 Museo Arqueológico (Table N9)
3458.82 Museo de Murcia (Table N9)
3459 Museo Salzillo (Table N9)
3463 Orihuela. Museo (Table N9)
3463.2 Oviedo. Universidad de Oviedo (Table N9)
3463.4 Pamplona. Museo de Navarra (Table N9)
3464 Pontevedra. Museo (Table N9)
Salamanca
3464.5 Museo Municipal de Béjar (Table N9)
3464.7 Museo Provincial de Bellas Artes (Table N9)
3464.85 Santander. Museo de Bellas Artes (Table N9)
Saragossa (Zaragoza)
3464.864 Académia Aragonesa de Nobles y Bellas Artes de San Luis (Table N9)
3464.87 Museo e Instituto "Camon Aznar" (Table N9)
3465 Museo Provincial de Bellas Artes (Table N9)
Seville
3470 Museo Provincial de Bellas Artes (Table N9)
3471.A-Z Other, A-Z
3471.C8 Catedral (Table N9)
3471.M8 Museo Arqueológico Provincial (Table N9)
3472 Sitges. Museo del Cau Ferrat (Table N9)
Toledo
3474 Collective
3475 Catedral. Museo (Table N9)
3476 Museo de Santa Cruz (Table N9)
Valencia
3485 Collective
3486.A-Z Special, A-Z
3486.C6 Colegio del Santíssimo Corpus Christi (Table N9)
3486.M8 Museo Provincial de Bellas Artes (Table N9)

Art museums, galleries, etc.
Special countries and special museums
Europe
Spain -- Continued
3490 Valladolid. Museo Nacional de Escultura (Table N9)
3495 Vich. Museo Episcopal (Table N9)
3497 Villafranca de Panadés. Collective
3499 Zamora. Disputación de Zamora
Sweden
3510 Collective
3520 Falun (Table N9)
Gothenburg
3525 Museum (Art collections only) (Table N9)
3527 Röhsska konstslöjdmuseet (Table N9)
3531 Leksand. Konstgalleriet (Table N9)
3532 Malmö. Museum (Table N9)
3533 Mora. Zornmuseet (Table N9)
3534 Norrköping. Museet (Table N9)
Stockholm
3538 Collective
3540 Nationalmuseum (Table N9)
3545.A-Z Other, A-Z
3545.H3 Hallwylska museet (Table N9)
3545.M43 Medelhavsmuseet (Table N9)
3545.M5 Millesgården (Table N9)
3545.M62 Moderna museet (Table N9)
3545.S8 Stadsmuseet (Table N9)
3545.S83 Statens historiska museum (Table N9)
3545.U5 Universitetet (Table N9)
3570 Uppsala. Universitet (Table N9)
Switzerland
3610 Collective
3610.5.A-Z By region, A-Z
Basel
3617 Antikenmuseum Basel (Table N9)
3618 Museum für Gegenwartskunst Basel (Table N9)
3620 Öffentliche Kunstammlung (Table N9)
3625 Universität. Historisches Museum (Table N9)
3627 Bellinzona. Museo civico di Bellinzona (Table N9)
Bern
3629 Kunsthalle (Table N9)
3630 Kunstmuseum (Table N9)
Geneva
3640 Musée Ariana (Table N9)
3641 Musée d'art et d'historie (Table N9)
3642 Musée Rath (Table N9)
Zürich
3645 Collective
3646 Kunstgewerbemuseum (Table N9)

Art museums, galleries, etc.
Special countries and special museums
Europe
Switzerland
Zürich -- Continued

3647.5	Kunsthaus (Table N9)
3648	Museum Rietberg (Table N9)
3650	Schweizerisches Landesmuseum (Table N9)
3655.A-Z	Other Swiss museums. By city, A-Z
3655.A17	Aarau. Aargauer Kunsthaus (Table N9)
3655.C58	Chur. Rätisches Museum Chur (Table N9)
	Lausanne
3655.L28	Galerie Paul Vallotton (Table N9)
3655.L3	Musée de beaux-arts (Table N9)
3655.L82	Lucerne. Kunstmuseum Luzern (Table N9)
3655.O47	Olten. Kunstmuseum Olten (Table N9)
3655.R5	Riggisberg. Abegg-Stiftung Bern (Table N9)
	St. Gall
3655.S3	Historisches Museum (Table N9)
3655.S35	Natur- und Kunstmuseum (Table N9)
	Solothurn
3655.S55	Kunstmuseum (Table N9)
3655.S6	Museum der Stadt (Table N9)
	Winterthur
3655.W5	Kunstmuseum (Table N9)
3655.W54	Museum Lindengut (Table N9)
3655.W58	Sammlung Oskar Reinhart "Am Römerholz" (Table N9)
3655.W586	Stiftung Oskar Reinhart (Table N9)
3690.A-Z	Other European countries. By country and city, A-Z Each museum further subarranged only by author
3690.B6J3	Jajce, Bosnia. Spomen-muzej II zasedanja AVNOJ-a (Table N9)
3690.B8K58-B8K589	Ki͡ustendil, Bulgaria. Khudozhestvena galerii͡a "Vladimir Dimitrov-Maĭstora" (Table N9)
3690.B8P43	Pleven, Bulgaria. Khudozhestvena galerii͡a "Ilii͡a Beshkov" (Table N9)
	Plovdiv, Bulgaria
3690.B8P45-B8P49	Collective
3690.B8P5	Dŭrzhavna khudozhestvena galerii͡a (Table N9)
3690.B8S5	Silistra, Bulgaria. Khudozhestvena galerii͡a (Table N9)
3690.B8S64-B8S649	Sofia, Bulgaria. Collective
3690.B8T87	Tŭrgovishte, Bulgaria. Khudozhestvena galerii͡a Nikola Marinov (Table N9)
	Varna, Bulgaria
3690.B8V3	Arkheologicheski muzeĭ (Table N9)
3690.B8V34	Naroden muzei (Table N9)
	Helsinki, Finland
3690.F5H4	Ateneumin Taidemuseo (Table N9)
3690.F5H45	Sinebrychoffin taidemuseo (Table N9)

Art museums, galleries, etc.
Special countries and special museums
Europe
Other European countries.
By country and city, A-Z
Helsinki, Finland -- Continued

3690.F5H46 Suomen Kansallismuseo (Table N9)
3690.F5H48 Valtion taidemuseo (Table N9)
3690.F5K457 Kemin, Finland. Taidemuseo (Table N9)
3690.F5M36 Mänttä. Gösta Serlachiuksen Taidesäätio Museo (Table N9)
3690.F5T8 Turku, Finland. Taidemuseo (Table N9)
3690.I2R49 Reykjavík, Iceland. Listasafn Íslands
3690.L8L8 Luxembourg (City). Musée d'histoire (Table N9)
3690.M3V3 Valetta, Malta. Palace (Table N9)

Bucharest, Romania

3690.R9B75-R9B759 Collective
3690.R9B8 Muzeul de Artă al Republicii Populare Române (Table N9)

Formerly Muzeul de Artă al Republicii Socialiste România

3690.R9B85 Galeria de Artă Natională
3690.R9B86 Galeria de Artă Universală
3690.R9B89 Muzeul Zambaccian (Table N9)
3690.R9C72 Craiova (Romania). Muzeul de Artă din Craiova (Table N9)
3690.R9M6 Mogoşoaia, Romania. Muzeul de Artă Brîncovenească (Table N9)
3690.R9S52 Sibiu, Romania. Muzeul Bruckenthal (Table N9)
3690.R9S54 Sinaia, Romania. Muzeul Peleş (Table N9)
3690.R9T55 Timişoara. Muzeul Banatului (Table N9)
3690.T7C5 Cluj, Transylvania. Muzeul de Artă (Table N9)

Istanbul, Turkey

3690.T8I6-T8I65 Collective
3690.T8I7 Arkeoloji Müzeleri (Table N9)
3690.T8I75 Resim ve Heykel Müzesi (Table N9)
3690.T8I77 Topkapi Sarayi Müzesi (Table N9)
3690.T8I82 Türk ve Islâm Eserleri Müzesi (Table N9)
3690.T8I9 Izmir, Turkey. Resim ve Heykel Galerisi (Table N9)

Yugoslavia

3690.Y8A1-Y8A5 Collective

Beograd

3690.Y8B4-Y8B419 Collective
3690.Y8B45 Muzej kneza Pavla (Table N9)
3690.Y8B5 Narodni muzej (Table N9)
3690.Y8C4 Celje. Mestni muzej (Table N9)

Ljubljana

3690.Y8L5 Moderna galerija (Table N9)
3690.Y8L6 Narodna galerija (Table N9)

Art museums, galleries, etc.
Special countries and special museums
Europe
Other European countries.
By country and city, A-Z
Yugoslavia -- Continued

3690.Y8N6 Novi Sad. Matica srpska. Galerija (Table N9)

3690.Y8O84 Osijek. Galerija likovnih umjetnotnosti "Osijek" (Table N9)

3690.Y8S4 Skopje. Muzej na sovremena umetnost (Table N9)

Split

3690.Y8S6 Galerija umjetnina (Table N9)

3690.Y8S67 Muzej grada (Table N9)

3690.Y8S75 Sremska Mitrovica. Umetnička galerija Sremska Mitrovica (Table N9)

3690.Y8Z2 Zadar. Arheološki muzej (Table N9)

3690.Y8Z23 Zagreb. Jugoslavenska akademija znanosti i umjetnosti. Galerija (Table N9)
Formerly Strossmayerova galerija

3690.Y8Z48 Zagreb. Muzej Zbirka umjetnina Ante i Wiltrud Topic Mimara (Table N9)

Asia

3700 Collective

3710.A-Z By region, A-Z

3720 India. Collective

3735 Japan. Collective

3740.A-Z Other Asian countries, A-Z

3750.A-Z Special museums of Asia. By city, etc., A-Z
For museums of Russia, see N3310+

3750.A3 Ajmer. Rajputana Museum (Table N9)

(3750.A4) Alma-Ata, Kazakhstan. Kazakhskaia͡ gosudarstvennaia͡ khudozhestvennaia͡ galereia͡
See N3310.7

3750.A5 Antioch. Hatay Müzesi (Table N9)

Baroda

3750.B27 Maharaja Fatesingh Museum (Table N9)

3750.B3 State Museum and Picture Gallery (Table N9)

3750.B65 Bombay. St. Xavier's College. Heras Institute of Indian History and Culture (Table N9)

Calcutta

3750.C27 Collective

3750.C3 Asiatic Society (Table N9)

3750.C32 Indian Museum (Table N9)

3750.C34 Canton, China. Wên wu kuan li wei yüan hui (Table N9)

3750.C5 Chandigarh, India. Museum and Art Gallery (Table N9)

3750.C54 Chiba-shi (Japan). Chiba Kenritsu Bijutsukan (Table N9)

3750.D25 Dacca, Pakistan. Museum (Table N9)

Art museums, galleries, etc.
Special countries and special museums
Asia
Special museums of
Asia. By city, etc., A-Z -- Continued

3750.D3 Damascus. Matḥaf Dimashq (Table N9)
3750.D4 Delhi. National Museum of India (Table N9)
(3750.D87) Dushanbe (Tajikistan). Respublikanskiĭ ob"edinennyĭ muzeĭ istorikokraevedcheskiĭ i izobrazitélnykh iskusstv (Tajikistan)
See N3313.5
3750.E5 'En Harod, Israel. Mishkan le-omanut 'al shem Ḥayim Atar (Table N9)
(3750.E7) Erivan. Gosudarstvennai͡a kartinnai͡a gallerei͡a Armenii
See N3375
3750.F7 Frunze, Kirghizistan. Kirgizskiĭ gosudarstvennyĭ muzeĭ isobrazitel'nykh iskusstv (Table N9)
3750.F79 Fujinomiya-shi (Japan). Fuji Bijutsukan (Table N9)
3750.F84 Fukuoka-shi (Japan). Fukuoka-shi Bijutsukan (Table N9)
3750.H34 Haifa. Muze'ou Ḥefah (Table N9)
3750.H37 Hanoi (Vietnam). Bâ0 tàng mỹ thuât Viêt Nam (Table N9)
3750.H57 Hiroshima. Hiroshima Bijutsukan (Table N9)
3750.H59 Hiroshima. Hiroshima Kenritsu Bijutsukan (Table N9)
3750.H9 Hyderabad. Salar Jung Museum (Table N9)
3750.J35 Jakarta, Indonesia. Museum Purna Bhakti Pertiwi (Table N9)
Jerusalem
3750.J4 Bet ha-nekhot ha-le' umi le-oumanut Betsat'el (Table N9)
Formerly Bezalal Museum
3750.J5 Israel Museum (Table N9)
3750.J55 Stadium Biblicum Franciscanum. Museum (Table N9)
3750.K3 Kabul, Afghanistan. Mūzah (Table N9)
3750.K35 Kamakura-shi (Japan). Kanagawa Kenritsu Kindai Bijutsukan (Table N9)
3750.K58 Kitakyūshū, Japan. Kitakyūshū Shiritsu Bitjutsukan (Table N9)
3750.K63 Kōfu-shi (Japan). Yamanashi Kenritsu Bijutsukan (Table N9)
3750.K8 Kuala Lumpur, Malasia. Balai Seni Lukis Negara (Table N9)
3750.K85 Kumamoto. Kumamoto Kenritsu Bijutsukan (Table N9)
3750.K87 Kurashiki-shi (Japan). Ōhara Bijutsukan (Table N9)
Kyōto

Art museums, galleries, etc.
Special countries and special museums
Asia
Special museums of Asia. By city, etc., A-Z
Kyōto -- Continued

3750.K93 Kyōto Kokuritsu Kindai Bijutsukan (Table N9)
3750.K94 Kyōto-shi Bijutsukan (Table N9)
3750.K95 Kyōto Shiritsu Geijutsu Daigaku. Geijutsu Shiryōkan (Table N9)
3750.L3 Lahore. Central Museum (Table N9)
Madras
3750.M25 Government Museum (Table N9)
3750.M27 National Art Gallery (Table N9)
Manila
3750.M28 National Library. Gallery of Art and History (Table N9)
3750.M3 Philippine Art Gallery (Table N9)
3750.M4 Meshed, Iran. Āstāne-ye Qods-e Rasavī. Mūzeh (Table N9)
Nagoya, Japan
3750.N27 Nagoya-shi Bijutsukan (Table N9)
3750.N3 Tokugawa Bijutsukan (Table N9)
3750.N36 Nara, Japan. Shōsōin (Table N9)
3750.N48 New Delhi (India). National Museum of India (Table N9)
3750.N54 Nigata-shi (Japan). Nigata Kenritsu Kindai Bijutsukan (Table N9)
3750.O25 Obihiro-shi (Japan). Hokkaidōritsu Obihiro Bijutsukan (Table N9)
3750.O8 Ōsaka Shiritsu Bijutsukan (Table N9)
3750.P3 Peking. Ku kung po wu yüan (Table N9)
3750.P35 Peshawar. Peshawar Museum (Table N9)
3750.P6 Port Arthur. Ryojun Hakubutsukan (Table N9)
3750.P96 Pyongyang (Korea). Chosŏn Misul Pangmulgwan (Table N9)
3750.R5 Rhodes. Museo archeologico (Table N9)
3750.S2 Saigon. Musée Blanchard de la Brosse (Table N9)
3750.S24 Sakata-shi (Japan). Honma Bijutsukan (Table N9)
Seoul
3750.S38 Kungnip Kyŏngju Pangmulgwan (Table N9)
3750.S4 Kungnip Pangmulgwan (Table N9)
3750.S45 Shanghai. Shang-hai po wu kuan (Table N9)
3750.S93 Suita-shi. Kokuritsu Kokusai Bijutsukan (Japan) (Table N9)
3750.T32 T'ai-pei. Kuo li ku kung po wu yüan (Table N9)
3750.T37 T'ai-pei. T'ai-pei shih li mei shu kuan (Table N9)
Tokyo
3750.T6 Burijisuton Bijutsukan (Table N9)

Art museums, galleries, etc.
Special countries and special museums
Asia
Special museums of Asia. By city, etc., A-Z
Tokyo -- Continued

3750.T618 Tōkyō Geijutsu Daigaku. Geijutsu Shiryōkan (Table N9)

3750.T62 Idemitsu Bijutsukan (Table N9)

3750.T63 Tōkyō Kokuritsu Hakubutsukan (Table N9)
Formerly Tōkyō Teishitsu Hakubutsukan

3750.T635 Kokuritsu Kindai Bijutsukan (Table N9)

3750.T637 Kokuritsu Seiyō Bijutsukan (Table N9)

3750.T64 Nichidō Garō (Table N9)

3750.T648 Shibuya Kuritsu Shōtō Bijutsukan (Table N9)

3750.T649 Shiseidō. Gyararī (Table N9)

3750.T65 Tokyo-to Bijutsukan (Table N9)

Trivandrum, India

3750.T7 Sri Chitralayam (Table N9)

3750.T73 Trivandrum Museum (Table N9)

3750.T77 Tsu-shi (Japan). Mie Kenritsu Bijutsukan (Table N9)

3750.U2 Ubud, Indonesia. Puri Lukisan (Table N9)

3750.V3 Vārānasi, India. Bharat Kala Bhavan (Table N9)

3750.Y38 Yasugi, Japan. Adachi Bijutsukan (Table N9)

3750.Y63 Yogyakarta (Indonesia). Museum Sonobudyo Yogyakarta (Table N9)

3750.Y66 Yonago-shi. Yonago-shi Bitjutsukan (Table N9)

Africa

3800 Collective

3810.A-Z Special countries, A-Z

Special museums. By city, etc.

3815 Alexandria. al-Mathaf al-Yūnānī al-Rūmāī (Table N9)

3825 Cairo. al-Mathaf al-Qibṭī (Table N9)

Cape Town, South Africa

3828 Irma Stern Museum (Table N9)

3830 South African National Gallery (Table N9)

3885.A-Z Other museums of Africa. By city, etc., A-Z

3885.D8 Durban, Natal. Art Gallery (Table N9)

3885.G3 Gaborone (Botswana). National Museum and Art Gallery, Botswana (Table N9)

3885.H37 Harare (Zimbabwe). National Gallery of Zimbabwe (Table N9)
Formerly Rhodes National Gallery

3885.J6 Johannesburg. Africana Museum (Table N9)

3885.K5 Kimberley. William Humphreys Art Gallery (Table N9)

3885.L4 Le Bardo, Tunisia. al-Mathaf al- 'Alawī (Table N9)

Art museums, galleries, etc.
Special countries and special museums
Africa
Special museums. By city, etc.
Other museums of Africa.
By city, etc., A-Z -- Continued
Salisbury. Rhodes National Gallery, see N3885.H37
3885.T8 Tunis. Bardo Museum (Table N9)
Australia
Collective
3910 General
3911.A-W By state, A-W
Adelaide
3913 National Gallery (Table N9)
3913.5 South Australia. Art Gallery (Table N9)
3915 Brisbane. Queensland Art Gallery (Table N9)
3916 Canberra. Australian National Gallery (Table N9)
3920 Castelmaine. Caltlemaine Art Gallery and Historical Museum (Table N9)
Melbourne
3948 National Gallery of Victoria (Table N9)
3950 State Library of Victoria (Gallery) (Table N9)
3952 University of Melbourne. University Gallery (Table N9)
3965 Perth. Western Australian Art Gallery (Table N9)
Sydney
3970 Art Gallery of New South Wales (Table N9)
3975 University. Nicholson Museum of Antiquities (Table N9)
New Zealand
3976 Collective
3977 Auckland. Art Gallery (Table N9)
3978 Christchurch. Robert McDougall Art Gallery (Table N9)
3978.4 Dunedin. Theomin Gallery (Table N9)
3979 Nelson. Bishop Suter Art Gallery (Table N9)
3980 Wanganui. Sarjeant Gallery (Table N9)
3982 Wellington. National Art Gallery (Table N9)
3990.A-Z Pacific islands. By city, A-Z
3990.P3 Papeari, Tahiti. Musée Gauguin (Table N9)
3990.P6 Port Moresby. Papua New Guinea Public Museum and Art Gallery (Table N9)
3998 Art documentation

Catalogs of photographs and picture collections in art museums, libraries, etc.
Prefer classification of photographs of a museum's collection under number for that museum
Classify by subject when possible
Cf. N370+, Picture study in school and home
Cf. N378+, Art lending or rental collections
Cf. Z695.718, Cataloging of photographs and pictures in libraries
4000 General
Public collections
4010.A-Z United States. By city and institution, A-Z
4015.A-Z Other countries. By country and city, A-Z
Private
4020.A-Z United States. By collector, A-Z
4025.A-Z Other countries. By collector, A-Z
4030 Select lists for libraries, etc.
e.g. California Library Association Picture list
Cf. N373, Select lists of pictures for schools
4035.A-Z Trade catalogs. Catalogs of reproductions. By firm, A-Z
Including general and reproductions of paintings
For catalogs limited to a particular subject, see the subject
Cf. NE75, Catalogs of prints
Catalogs of slides of works of art
4039 General
4040.A-Z Trade catalogs. By firm, A-Z
4042.A-Z Catalogs of public and private collections. By name of institution or collector, A-Z
Exhibitions
Including all general exhibitions and general exhibitions of paintings.
Prefer classification of exhibition catalogs by medium, subject, or nationality in NA, NB, NC, etc.
Exhibitions of special artists are classed with biography in N6537, ND237, etc.
For paintings of a specific country, see ND201+
4390 Periodicals. Societies. Collections
4392.A-Z Documents. By country, A-Z
4395 General works. History. Organization, etc.
4396 General special
e.g. traveling exhibitions
4396.5 Art exhibition audiences
4397 Miscellaneous. Essays, etc.

Exhibitions -- Continued
International exhibitions
Class here only general exhibitions that are internationally sponsored, e.g. world's fairs
Each class subarranged by date unless otherwise specified
Prefer classification by medium, subject, period, or nationality
For exhibitions which include the art of several nations but are not associated with an international exposition (i.e., exhibitions sponsored by one museum or institution), see N5010+

4402 Aberdeen (Table N10)
4405 Agra (Table N10)
Agram, see N4992
4407 Alexandria (Table N10)
4410 Algiers (Table N10)
Amsterdam
4414 1859 (Table N10)
4415 1869 (Table N10)
4416 1883 (Table N10)
Antwerp
4420 Before 1930 (Table N10)
4421 Later (by date) (Table N10)
4424 Athens (Table N10)
Atlanta
4426 1881 (Table N10)
4427 1895 (Table N10)
4427.5 Later (by date) (Table N10)
4429 Bahia (Table N10)
4430 Baltimore (Table N10)
4433 Barcelona (Table N10)
4436 Basel (Table N10)
4439 Batavia (Table N10)
4440 Berlin (Table N10)
4442 Bern (Table N10)
4450 Birmingham (Table N10)
4452 Bogotá (Table N10)
4453 Bombay (Table N10)
4456 Bordeaux (Table N10)
4460 Boston (Table N10)
4463 Brisbane (Table N10)
4465 Brussels (Table N10)
4475 Bucharest (Table N10)
4478 Budapest (Table N10)
4482 Buenos Aires (Table N10)
4485 Buffalo (Table N10)
4486 Burgos (Table N10)
4488 Calcutta (Table N10)
4491 Canton (Table N10)
4494 Cape Town (Table N10)
4495 Caracas (Table N10)

Exhibitions
International exhibitions -- Continued
4497 Charleston (Table N10)
Chicago
4499 1873 (Table N10)
4500 1893 (Table N10)
4501 1933-1934 (Table N10)
4502 Later (by date) (Table N10)
(4511) Christiania
See N4797
Cincinnati
4515 1879 (Table N10)
4516 1888 (Table N10)
4517 Later (by date) (Table N10)
4520 Cleveland (Table N10)
4525 Constantinople (Table N10)
4535 Copenhagen (Table N10)
4536 Cordova (Table N10)
4537 Cork (Table N10)
4540 Curitiba (Table N10)
4543 Dallas (Table N10)
4545 Denver (Table N10)
4550 Detroit (Table N10)
4555 Dresden (Table N10)
4560 Dublin (Table N10)
4561 Duluth (Table N10)
4565 Dunedin (Table N10)
4570 Edinburgh (Table N10)
4590 Florence (Table N10)
4606 Geneva (Table N10)
4610 Genoa (Table N10)
4614 Ghent (Table N10)
4618 Glasgow (Table N10)
4619 Gratz (Table N10)
4620 Guatemala (Table N10)
4621 Haarlem (Table N10)
4624 Hague (Table N10)
4631 Hamburg (Table N10)
4633 Hanoi (Table N10)
4635 Havana (Table N10)
4640 Hong Kong (Table N10)
4645 Indianapolis (Table N10)
4648 Jamestown (Table N10)
4650 Johannesburg (Table N10)
4655 Klagenfurt (Table N10)
4660 Leeds (Table N10)
4665 Leipzig (Table N10)
Liège
4670 1905 (Table N10)
4672 1939 (Table N10)
4673 Later (by date) (Table N10)
4675 Lima (Table N10)
4681 Lisbon (Table N10)

Exhibitions
International exhibitions -- Continued
4684 Liverpool (Table N10)
London
4690 1851 (Table N10)
4691 1862 (Table N10)
4695 1871 (Table N10)
4697 1887 (Table N10)
4700 Later (by date) (Table N10)
4710 Lyons (Table N10)
4715 Madrid (Table N10)
4719 Manchester (Table N10)
4723 Manila (Table N10)
4727 Marseilles (Table N10)
Melbourne
4730 1861 (Table N10)
4731 1880-1881 (Table N10)
4732 1888-1889 (Table N10)
4733 Later (by date) (Table N10)
4739 Memphis (Table N10)
4742 Mexico (Table N10)
4745 Milwaukee (Table N10)
4748 Minneapolis (Table N10)
4752 Montreal (Table N10)
4757 Moscow (Table N10)
4762 Munich (Table N10)
4766 Nagasaki (Table N10)
4770 Nanking (Table N10)
4773 Naples (Table N10)
4775 Nashville (Table N10)
4777 New Orleans (Table N10)
New York
4783 1853-1854 (Table N10)
4784 Later (by date) (Table N10)
4793 Odessa (Table N10)
4796 Omaha (Table N10)
4796.5 Osaka (Table N10)
4797 Oslo (Christiania) (Table N10)
Paris
4799 Before 1855 (Table N10)
4800 1855 (Table N10)
4801 1867 (Table N10)
4802 1878 (Table N10)
4803 1889 (Table N10)
4804 1900 (Table N10)
4805 1937 (Table N10)
4806 Later (by date) (Table N10)
4820 Peking (Table N10)
Petrograd, see N4868
4825 Philadelphia, 1876 (Table N10)
4828 Pisa (Table N10)
4830 Pittsburgh (Table N10)
4834 Portland, Oreg. (Table N10)

Exhibitions
International exhibitions -- Continued
4836 Prague (Table N10)
4840 Rio de Janeiro (Table N10)
4850 Rome (Table N10)
4860 St. Louis (Table N10)
4865 St. Paul (Table N10)
4868 St. Petersburg (Table N10)
San Diego
4873 1915 (Table N10)
4873.2 1935 (Table N10)
4873.3 Later (by date) (Table N10)
San Francisco
4874 1915 (Table N10)
4875 1939 (Table N10)
4875.5 Later (by date) (Table N10)
4877 San Jose (Table N10)
Santiago de Chile
4879 1873 (Table N10)
4880 1875 (Table N10)
4883 1910 (Table N10)
4883.2 Later (by date) (Table N10)
4883.5 São Paulo (Table N10)
4884 Saragossa (Table N10)
4885 Schwerin (Table N10)
4888 Seattle (Table N10)
4892 Seoul (Table N10)
4894 Seville (Table N10)
4896 Shanghai (Table N10)
4910 Stockholm (Table N10)
4920 Sydney (Table N10)
4937 Tokyo (Table N10)
4940 Toronto (Table N10)
4944 Trieste (Table N10)
4947 Turin (Table N10)
4949 Valladolid (Table N10)
4951 Valparaiso (Table N10)
4955 Venice (Table N10)
Vienna
4960 1873 (Table N10)
4961 Later (by date) (Table N10)
4975 Warsaw (Table N10)
4983 Washington (Table N10)
4990 Yokohama (Table N10)
4992 Zagreb (Agram) (Table N10)
4995 Zurich (Table N10)
Other general exhibitions. By place held
Including those that are international in scope but sponsored by one institution (or jointly by several institutions within one country)
Prefer classification by medium, subject, period, or nationality

Exhibitions
Other general exhibitions.
By place held -- Continued
(5010) General
See N4390-N4397
America
United States
5015.A-Z Societies not limited to one city. By name, A-Z
5020.A-Z Exhibitions in special cities. By city and by museum or other place of exhibition, A-Z
5030.A-Z Other American exhibitions. By city, A-Z
Europe
5050 Collective
Including general histories of exhibitions held locally, e.g. Council of Europe. Record of European art exhibitions. Do not use for individual exhibitions, or recurring exhibitions sponsored by one organization, such as annual or biennial exhibitions
Great Britain
5051 Collective
Including general histories of exhibitions held locally. Do not use for individual exhibitions, or recurring exhibitions sponsored by one organization, such as annual or biennial exhibitions
London
5053 Collective
Including general histories of exhibitions held locally. Do not use for individual exhibitions, or recurring exhibitions sponsored by one organization, such as annual or biennial exhibitions
5054 Royal Academy
5055.A-Z Other London exhibitions. By museum, A-Z
5056.A-Z Other British cities. By city, A-Z
5060.A-Z Austria. By city or other place of exhibition, A-Z
5061.A-Z Belgium. By city or other place of exhibition, A-Z
5062.A-Z Denmark. By city or other place of exhibition, A-Z
France
5063 Collective
Including general histories of exhibitions held locally. Do not use for individual exhibitions, or recurring exhibitions sponsored by one organization such as annual or biennial exhibitions
Paris
5064 Collective
Including general histories of exhibitions held locally. Do not use for individual exhibitions, or recurring exhibitions sponsored by one organization such as annual or biennial exhibitions

Exhibitions
Other general exhibitions. By place held
Europe
France
Paris -- Continued
5065 The two salons
5066 Salon of the Société des artistes français
5067 Salon of the Société nationale des beaux-arts
Salons des refusés, see N6850
Société des artistes indépendants, see N6850
5068.A-Z Other Paris exhibitions. By museum, A-Z
5069.A-Z Other French cities. By city, A-Z
5070.A-Z Germany. By city or other place of exhibition, A-Z
5071.A-Z Greece. By city or other place of exhibition, A-Z
5072.A-Z Holland. By city or other place of exhibition, A-Z
5073.A-Z Italy. By city or other place of exhibition, A-Z
5074.A-Z Norway. By city or other place of exhibition, A-Z
5075.A-Z Portugal. By city or other place of exhibition, A-Z
5076.A-Z Russia. By city or other place of exhibition, A-Z
Spain
5076.5 Collective
Including general histories of exhibitions held locally. Do not use for individual exhibitions, or recurring exhibitions sponsored by one organization such as annual or biennial exhibitions
5077.A-Z Individual exhibitions. By city or other place of exhibition, A-Z
5078.A-Z Sweden. By city or other place of exhibition, A-Z
5079.A-Z Switzerland. By city or other place of exhibition, A-Z
5080.A-Z Other European. By city or other place of exhibition, A-Z
5085.A-Z Asia. By city or other place of exhibition, A-Z
5090.A-Z Africa. By city or other place of exhibition, A-Z
5095.A-Z Australia. By city or other place of exhibition, A-Z
5097.A-Z New Zealand. By city or other place of exhibition, A-Z
5098.A-Z Pacific islands. By city or other place of exhibition, A-Z
For Hawaiian islands, see N5015+

Private collections and collectors
Including exhibition catalogs and catalogs of auctions devoted to single private collections.
Prefer classification by subject, medium, period or nationality.
Cf. AM200+, Collectors and collecting
Cf. N4020+, Catalogs of photographs and picture collections
Cf. NB30.A+, Sculpture collections
Cf. NC30+, Drawing collections
Cf. NE57+, Print collections
Cf. NK530+, Collections of decorative arts
Cf. Z987+, Book collecting
For general art auction catalogs, see N8650.A+
Art collectors and collecting
5198 Periodicals
Biography, see N5213+
5200 General works
By region or country
United States
5201 General works
5201.5.A-Z By region or state, A-Z
5202.A-Z Other regions or countries, A-Z
5203 Collectors' marks
Art patronage
Cf. NX700+, Patronage of the arts
5205 General works
Commissioning of art
5205.5 General works
5205.7.A-Z By region or country, A-Z
Government patronage and protection of art, see N8825+
Corporate patrons of art (especially, business and industry)
Including collections
5206 General works
United States
5207 General works
5207.5.A-Z Special. By collector or patron, A-Z
5208.A-Z Other countries, A-Z
Under each country:
.x General works
.x2A-.x2Z Special. By collector or patron, A-Z
Private patronage and collections
For collections owned by schools, see N510+
5210 General works
American
5213 General works
United States
5215 General works
5216.A-Z By region or state, A-Z
5220.A-Z Special. By collector, A-Z
Lehman, Robert, 1892, see N611.L43

Private collections and collectors
Private patronage and collections
American -- Continued
5230.A-Z Other American. By country, A-Z
Under each country:
.x General works
.x2A-.x2Z Special. By collector, A-Z
European
5240 General works
Great Britain
5245 General works
5247.A-Z Special. By collector, A-Z
Austria
5250 General works
5252.A-Z Special. By collector, A-Z
Belgium
5255 General works
5255.2.A-Z Special. By collector, A-Z
Czechoslovakia
5256 General works
5256.2.A-Z Special. By collector, A-Z
Denmark
5257 General works
5258.A-Z Special. By collector, A-Z
France
5260 General works
5262.A-Z Special. By collector, A-Z
Germany
5265 General works
5267.A-Z Special. By collector, A-Z
Greece
5270 General works
5271.A-Z Special. By collector, A-Z
Netherlands
5272 General works
5272.2.A-Z Special. By collector, A-Z
Italy
5273 General works
5273.2.A-Z Special. By collector, A-Z
Norway
5274 General works
5274.2.A-Z Special. By collector, A-Z
Portugal
5275 General works
5275.2.A-Z Special. By collector, A-Z
Russia
5276 General works
5276.2.A-Z Special. By collector, A-Z
Spain
5277 General works
5277.2.A-Z Special. By collector, A-Z
Sweden
5278 General works

Private collections and collectors
Private patronage and collections
European
Sweden -- Continued
5278.2.A-Z Special. By collector, A-Z
Switzerland
5279 General works
5279.2.A-Z Special. By collector, A-Z
5280.A-Z Other European countries. By country, A-Z
Apply table at N5230.A-Z
Asia
5284 General works
5285.A-Z By country, A-Z
Apply table at N5230.A-Z
Africa
5289 General works
5290.A-Z By country, A-Z
Apply table at N5230.A-Z
Australia
5295 General works
5296.A-Z Special. By collector, A-Z
New Zealand
5297 General works
5298.A-Z Special. By collector, A-Z
5299.A-Z Pacific islands. By collector, A-Z
History
5300 General works
5301 Illustrations
Including "University prints."
Cf. N7510+, Miscellaneous collections of pictures
5302 Compends
Historiography, see N7480
5303 General special
Including collections of historical essays
Cf. N7428.5, Comparative art
Outlines, syllabi
5305 General works
5306 Chronological lists
Cf. ND55, Chronologies of history of painting
(5307) Examinations, questions, etc.
see N382
5308 Juvenile works
Prehistoric art. Origins of art
Including art of the Paleolithic, Mesolithic, and Neolithic ages
Cf. GN700+, Prehistoric archaeology
Cf. NB61.5, Prehistoric sculpture
5310 General works
5310.5.A-5Z Special continents, regions, countries, etc., A-Z

History -- Continued
Primitive art
Used here to denote art produced outside the traditions of the art of Europe, the Mediterranean area, and Asia. That is, the art of the Negro peoples of sub-Saharan Africa; of the inhabitants of the islands of the Pacific Ocean, Australia and some areas off the coast of Southeast Asia
Does not include "primitive" or "naive" artists who, while seemingly untutored, work in the traditions of European folk art or easel painting
Cf. GN429+, Primitive arts and crafts
Cf. N7432.5.P7, Primitivism
Cf. NB62+, Primitive sculpture
Cf. NC54, Primitive drawing
Cf. ND1482.P7, Primitive painting, naive painting
Cf. NK1177, Primitive ornament
Cf. E-F, American Indian art
5310.7 Periodicals. Societies. Congresses
Museums. Collections. Exhibitions
5310.75.A-Z United States. By city and museum, A-Z
5310.8.A-Z Other countries. By country and city, A-Z
5310.9.A-Z Private collections. By collector, A-Z
5311 General works
Special countries, see N6501+
Folk art
Cf. NC1280+, Imagerie populaire
Cf. TT385, Decorative painting. Tole painting
5312 Periodicals. Societies. Congresses. Collections
5313 General works
Special countries, see NK801+
Art of minority ethnic groups in particular places, see N6501+
5315 Ancient and medieval art
Old Germanic art, see N5930
Ancient art. Artistic archaeology
Cf. CC73+, Methods and aims of archaeology
Cf. CN120+, Inscriptions
Cf. D1+, Local antiquities
Cf. NA210+, Ancient architecture
Cf. NB69+, Ancient sculpture
Cf. E-F, American Indian art and archaeology
5320 Periodicals
5325 Societies
5327 Congresses
5329 History and method of artistic archaeology
5330 General works
5331 Folios
5333 General special
Including Seven wonders of the world
5334 Pictorial works

History
Ancient art. Artistic archaeology -- Continued
Museums. Collections. Exhibitions
5335.A-Z United States. By city and museum, A-Z
5336.A-Z Other countries. By country and city, A-Z
5337.A-Z Private collections. By collector, A-Z
5340 Miscellaneous groups of countries
5343 Ancient Oriental art (General)
Including India, etc.
5345 Classic Orient (Egypt and southwestern Asia)
Including Cyprus, Syria, and Egypt
Special countries and groups of countries
5350 Egypt
For museums and collections, see N5335+
5351 Folios
5360 Bactria
5370 Chaldea. Babylonia. Assyria. Mesopotamia. Elam. Sumer
5380 Ninevah
5385 Hittite art
5390 Persia. Media
Phoenicia and its colonies
5410 General works
5420 Carthage
5430 Cyprus
5440 Sardinia
5460 Judea. Syria
Cf. N7414.75+, Jewish art
5470 Arabia
Asia Minor
5480 General works
5490 Cappadocia
5510 Galatia
5520 Gordion
5530 Lycia
5540 Mysia
5545 Pergamum
5550 Phrygia
5560 Troy (Ilium)
Classical art
For congresses, see N5327
For periodicals, see N5320
For societies, see N5325
Museums. Collections. Exhibitions
5603.A-Z United States. By city and museum, A-Z
5604.A-Z Other countries. By country and city, A-Z
5605 Collected works
5610 Treatises
5613 General special
5615 Pictorial works
Special countries
Greece
Cf. DF130+, Antiquities

History
Ancient art. Artistic archaeology
Classical art
Special countries
Greece -- Continued

5630 General works
5633 General special
5634.A-Z Catalogs of collections. By collection, A-Z
5635.A-Z Catalogs of exhibitions. By place, A-Z
5640 Aegina
5645 Argos
5650 Athens
5653 Boeotia
5654 Corfu
5655 Corinth
5660 Crete
5670 Delos
5672 Delphi
5680 Dordona
5683 Ephesus
5687 Macedonia
5688 Megara
5690 Melos
5700 Mycenae
5702 Olynthus
5704 Peloponnesus
5706 Rhodes (Island)
5708 Sicyon. Sicyonia
5710 Tanagra
5720 Tiryns

Ancient Italy

5740 General works
5750 Etruria
5751 Folios
5752 Friuli (Province)
5753 Magna Grecia
5755 Campania

Rome

5760 General works
5761 Folios
5763 General special

Pompeii and Herculaneum

5769 General works
5770 Pompeii
5771 Folios
5775 Herculaneum
5790.A-Z Other cities, A-Z
5790.K45 Khalchaian
5790.P3 Paestum
5790.P7 Praeneste
5790.T8 Tusculum
5790.V4 Velleia

History
Ancient art. Artistic archaeology
Classical art -- Continued
5801-5896.3 Classical art in other countries (Table N1)
Add country number in table to N5800
Under each (1-number or decimal countries):
.A1 General works
.A3A-.A3Z Special regions, provinces, etc., A-Z
.A5-.Z Special cities, A-Z
Under each (Cutter-number countries):
.x General
.x2A-.x2Z Special cities, A-Z
5899.A-Z Other ancient, A-Z
Limited to Mediterranean world and Near East
For other areas, see appropriate period in N6501-N7413
5899.A4 Amlash
5899.C39 Caucasian Albania
5899.C5 Cimmerian Bosporus (Kingdom)
5899.C9 Cycladic
5899.D23 Dacian
5899.I2 Iberian
5899.I4 Illyrian
5899.K8 Kushan
5899.P36 Parthian
5899.S3 Scythian
5899.T5 Thracian
5899.U72 Urartian
5925 Celtic art
Cf. N6782+, Ancient Irish art
For special countries, see N6501+
5930 Old Germanic art
5940 Medieval and modern art
5941 Folios
Medieval art
Prefer classification by subject or country
General works
5950 Periodicals
5960 Societies
5961 Congresses
Museums. Collections. Exhibitions
5963.A-Z United States. By city and museum, A-Z
5964.A-Z Other countries. By country and city, A-Z
5965 Dictionaries
5970 Treatises
5971 Folios
5975 General special
Special types
(6240) Celtic art
see N5925
6242 Visigothic art
6243 Merovingian art
6245 Carolingian art

History
Medieval art
Special types -- Continued
6246 Albigensian art
6250 Byzantine art
Islamic. Moorish. Arabic
Cf. NA380+, Islamic architecture
Cf. NK720+, Islamic applied arts
Cf. NK1270+, Islamic decoration
Cf. NK1820, Islamic interior decoration
6260 General works
6261 Folios
Museums. Collections. Exhibitions
6263.A-Z United States. By city and museum, A-Z
6264.A-Z Other countries. By country and city, A-Z
6270 Moors in Spain
6271 Folios
Other special countries, see N6501+
6275 Viking art
For special countries, see N6501+
6280 Romanesque art
For special countries, see N6501+
6300 Crusader art
For special countries, see N6501+
Gothic art. 12th-16th centuries
For special countries, see N6501+
6310 General works
6311 Folios
Catalogs of collections. Public
6313.A-Z United States. By city and institution, A-Z
6314.A-Z Other countries. By country and city, A-Z
By period
6316 Early Gothic
6318 High Gothic
For Bohemian School, see N6828.5.B64
6320 Late Gothic
Modern art
Prefer classification by subject or country
6350 General works
6351 Folios
6351.2.A-Z Special aspects or movements, A-Z
6351.2.E39 Egyptian Revival (Art)
By century
Under each century is provided a "General" number, followed by a number for "Special aspects or movements." The latter is used for historical movements, etc. that are considered international
Class special movements identified with one country and largely one century under the country in N6501-N7413
Renaissance art. 15th and 16th centuries
6370 General works

History
Modern art
By century
Renaissance art.
15th and 16th centuries -- Continued
15th century
6371 General works
6372.A-Z Special aspects or movements, A-Z
16th century
6374 General works
6375.A-Z Special aspects or movements, A-Z
For Donauschule (Austrian), see N6805.5.D6
For Donauschule (German), see N6865.5.D6
6375.M3 Mannerism
Cf. N7432.5.M3, Mannerism as a style in art
17th and 18th centuries
17th century
6410 General works
6415.A-Z Special aspects or movements, A-Z
6415.B3 Baroque
6415.C55 Classicism
6415.N3 Naturalism
18th century
6420 General works
6425.A-Z Special aspects or movements, A-Z
6425.N4 Neoclassicism (General, and Early)
Cf. N7432.5.C6, Classicism as a style in art
6425.R6 Rococo
6425.R64 Romanticism (Early)
19th and 20th centuries
6447 General works
6448.A-Z Special exhibitions, etc., A-Z
6448.A74 Armory Show, New York, 1913
19th century
6450 General works
6460 Special. By year
Subarranged by author
6465.A-Z Special aspects or movements, A-Z
6465.A25 Abstract art
Aesthetic movement (British), see N6767.5.A3
6465.A7 Art nouveau. Jugendstil
Arts and crafts movement, see NK1135+
Barbizon school (French), see N6847.5.B3
Beuroner Kunstschule (German), see N6867.5.B47
6465.B5 Biedermeier
Divisionism, see N6465.N44
Düsseldorfer Malerschule (German), see N6867.5.D8
6465.E25 Eclecticism
6465.E35 Edwardian art
Cf. N6767+, English 19th century art

History
Modern art
By century
19th and 20th centuries
19th century
Special aspects or movements, A-Z -- Continued

6465.E48 Egyptian Revival (Art)

Gödöllői Múvésztelep (Hungarian), see N6819.5.G63

6465.G68 Gothic revival

Grötzinger Malerkolonie (German), see N6867.5.G7

Group do Leão (Group of artists), see N7127.5.L4

Haagse school (Dutch), see N6948.5.H2

Hamburgische Künstlerclub (Germany), see N6867.5.H36

6465.I4 Impressionism

Cf. N7432.5.I4, Impressionism as a style in art

Intimism, see N6847.5.N3

Jugendstil, see N6465.A7

6465.K5 Kitsch

Cf. BH301.K5, Theory and philosophy of kitsch

Leibl-Kreis, see N6867.5.L45

Machiaioli, see N6917.5.M3

6465.M63 Modernism

Munich school of painting, see N6867.5.M85

Nabis, Symbolists, Intimists (French), see N6847.5.N3

Nazarenes, see N6465.P7

6465.N4 Neoclassicism (Late)

Cf. N7432.5.C6, Classicism as a style in art

6465.N44 Neo-impressionism

Pointillism, see N6465.N44

Pont-Aven school (French), see N6847.5.P58

6465.P6 Post-impressionism

6465.P7 Pre-Raphaelites

General works, including Purism and the Nazarenes

Cf. N6847.5.P8, Purism (19th century French movement)

Cf. N6867.5.N3, Nazarenes (German)

6465.P74 Primitivism

Purism, see N6465.P7

History
Modern art
By century
19th and 20th centuries
19th century
Special aspects
or movements, A-Z -- Continued
6465.R4 Realism in 19th century art. The "Academicians"
Cf. N6987.5.R4, Russian realism. Peredvizhniki (Group of painters)
Cf. N7432.5.R4, Realism as a style in art
6465.R45 Renaissance revival
6465.R6 Romantic movement
Saint-Siméon school of painting (French), see N6847.5.S24
Sint-Martens-Latem (Group of artists), see N6967.5.S56
6465.S9 Symbolism
Szolnoki Múvésztelep (Hungarian), see N6819.5.S95
6465.V5 Victorian art
Cf. N6767+, English 19th century art
Worpsweder Künstlervereinigung (German), see N6867.5.W67
20th century
6480 Periodicals
6485 Congresses
6485.3 Directories
Museums. Collections. Exhibitions
6486 Collective
6487.A-Z United States. By city and museum, A-Z
6488.A-Z Other countries. By country and city, A-Z
6488.5.A-Z Private collections. By collector, A-Z
6489 Collective biography
For subarrangement by country, see N6501
6490 General works
6490.3 Film catalogs
(6491) Art and World War I
See N9150-N9155
(6492) Exhibitions
See N9152
(6492.2) Art and World War II
See N9160-N9165
6493 Special, by year or brief span of years
Subarranged by author
For span of years subdivide by first year of span, e.g., 1914 Baltimore Museum's "1914; an exhibition ..."; 1925 "Lo stile 1925"; 1930 Joslyn Museum's "The thirties decade"

History
Modern art
By century
19th and 20th centuries
20th century -- Continued

6494.A-Z Special aspects or movements, A-Z
AKKU Gruppe, see N6868.5.A16
6494.A2 Abstract art
Including general works on non-objective art, and the "International Style" of the 1920s
Cf. N6848.5.P8, Purism (French)
Cf. N6868.5.A15, Abstrakten Hannover (German)
Cf. N6948.5.D42, De Stijl (Dutch)
Cf. N6988.5.R3, Rayonism (Russian)
Cf. N6988.5.S9, Suprematism (Russian)
6494.A25 Abstract expressionism. Abstract impressionism. Tachism. Action painting
Cf. ND196.A25, Abstract expressionist painting
Abstrakten Hannover (Association), see N6868.5.A15
6494.A35 Air art
Aktual (Group), see N6831.5.A38
American Abstract Artists, see N6512.5.A2
Amsterdamse Joffers (Women artists), see N6948.5.A57
Anonima group, see N6512.5.A5
6494.A66 Appropriation
Arme og ben (Group) (Denmark), see NE683.6.A74
Art & Language (Group), see N6848.5.C66
Art Club (Austria), see N6808.5.A77
6494.A7 Art deco
Art nouveau, see N6465.A7
Artim Groep, see N6948.5.A77
Artist Placement Group, see N6768.5.A75
Ashcan school (American), see N6512.5.E4
Aspekt, Gruppe, see N6868.5.A85
6494.A8 Assemblage
Cf. N6494.C6, Collage
Cf. TT910, Handicraft
Bauhaus, see N6868.5.E9
Bergense school of painting, see N6948.5.B47
Berliner Secession, see N6868.5.B3
Bieler Künstlergruppe Alibi, see N7148.5.B53
Blaue Reiter, see N6868.5.E9
Blaue Vier (Group of artists), see N6868.5.E9
Blaues Quadrat, see N6868.5.B59
De Bloedschuit (Engravers' Group), see NE671.6.B5
Bloomsbury group, see N6768.5.B55
6494.B63 Body art

History
Modern art
By century
19th and 20th centuries
20th century
Special aspects
or movements, A-Z -- Continued
Bonner Künstlergruppe, see N6868.5.B64
Die Brücke, see N6868.5.E9
CAYC Group, see N6635.5.C38
Camden Town Group, see N6768.5.C53
Cent-Neuf (Association). 109
(Association), see N6848.5.C46
6494.C45 Cercle et carré (Group)
6494.C47 Chenal (Group)
6494.C5 CoBrA
6494.C6 Collage. Papiers collés
Cf. N6494.A8, Assemblage
Cf. TT910, Handicraft
Color-field painting (American), see
N6512.5.C6
6494.C63 Conceptual art
6494.C635 Concrete art
6494.C64 Constructivism
6494.C8 Cubism
Cf. N6512.5.S9, Synchromism
Cf. N6768.5.V6, Vorticism
Cf. N6848.5.O7, Orphism
Cf. N6848.5.P8, Purism (20th century)
Cf. N6918.5.F8, Futurism
6494.D3 Dadaism
Dau al set (Group of artists), see N7108.5.D38
De Stijl. Neoplasticism (Dutch), see
N6948.5.D42
Decembristerne (Society), see N7018.5.D43
6494.E27 Earthworks (Art)
École de Paris, see N6850
Eight, The (American), see N6512.5.E4
Einmal Sechs (Group), see N6868.5.E37
6494.E43 Electricity. Electronics
Electronics, see N6494.E43
6494.E6 Environment (Art)
Equipo/57, see N7108.5.E68
6494.E87 Experiments in Art and Technology
6494.E9 Expressionism
Cf. N6848.5.F3, Fauvism
Cf. N7432.5.E9, Expressionism
(General as a style in art)
6494.F28 Fascism
6494.F3 Fauvism
For Fauvism (French), see N6848.5.F3
Fiatal Képzómúvészek Stúdiója, see
N6820.5.F5

History
Modern art
By century
19th and 20th centuries
20th century
Special aspects
or movements, A-Z -- Continued

6494.F47 Fiberwork
6494.F5 Figurative art
6494.F55 Fluxus (Group of artists)
6494.F6 Found objects
Frauenwörther (Society), see N6868.5.F73
6494.F7 Functionalism
6494.F8 Futurism
Fynske forårsudstilling (Artists' group), see N7018.5.F94
Geometria e ricerca (Group of artists), see N6918.5.G45
Germinalen (Group of artists), see N7018.5.G4
Groep Vlaams Brabant, see N6968.5.V55
Group Zero, see N6868.5.Z4
6494.G72 Groupe de recherche d'art visuel. GRAV
Groupe des Corps-Saints, see N7148.5.C67
Groupe Henri Rousseau, see N6494.P7
Groupe Montpellier-Sète, see N6848.5.M65
Grupo de Bagé, see N6655.5.B34
Grupo Quince, see N7108.5.Q5
Grupo Santa Helena, see N6655.5.S25
Gruppe AKKU, see N6868.5.A16
Gruppe Aspekt, see N6868.5.A85
Gruppe Die Spur, see N6868.5.S8
Gruppe Geflecht, see N6868.5.G4
Gruppe Gyrr, see N7018.5.G78
Gruppe Kilo, see N6868.5.K5
Gruppe Plus, see N6868.5.P58
Gruppe Progressiver Künstler, see N6868.5.P7
Gruppe Realismus im BBK, see N6868.5.R42
Gruppe 33, see N7148.5.T45
Gruppe WeibsBilder, see N6868.5.W43
Gruppe Zebra, see N6868.5.Z37
Gruppe ZEN 49, see N6868.5.Z38
Gruppe Zink, see N7068.5.Z55
Gruppo Enne, see N6918.5.E55
Gruppo Forma uno, see N6918.5.F6
Halmstadgruppen, see N7088.5.H3
Hamburgische Sezession (Germany), see N6868.5.H357
Happenings, see PN3203+
Haus-Rucker-Co, see N6808.5.H3
Hyperrealism, see N6494.P42
6494.I55 Impressionism (Late)
6494.I56 Installations (Art)
6494.I58 Internationale situationniste

History
Modern art
By century
19th and 20th centuries
20th century
Special aspects
or movements, A-Z -- Continued

Jeune peinture (Association). Salon de la Jeune peinture, see N6848.5.J47

6494.K5 Kinetic art
Cf. N6494.O6, Op art

6494.K54 Kitsch
Cf. BH301.K5, Theory and philosophy of kitsch

Københavnstrup, see N7018.5.K62

Kooperative Kunst, see N6868.5.K66

Künstlergruppe (Galerie Elefant), see N6808.5.K84

Künstlergruppe Burgenland, see N6808.5.B8

Künstlergruppe "Der Kreis", see N6808.5.K8

Künstlergruppe Semikolon, see N6868.5.S46

Künstlergruppe Tendenzen, see N6868.5.T4

Künstlergruppe Winterthur (Switzerland), see N7148.5.W55

Kunstnergruppen M59, see N7018.5.K8

6494.L3 Lasers

Leipziger Asso, see N6868.5.L45

6494.L4 Lettrism. Letter-pictures
Cf. N8219.L4, Lettering in art
Cf. NK3600+, Alphabets, Calligraphy. Initials
Cf. PN6110.C77, Concrete poetry

Linie (Group), see N6831.5.L54

Lücke (Group of artists), see N6868.5.L83

6494.M3 Magic realism
Cf. N6494.S8, Surrealism

6494.M35 Mail art

Malassis, Coopérative des, see N6848.5.M34

Metaphysical school, see N6918.5.M48

6494.M5 Minimal art

6494.M64 Modernism

6494.M8 Multiple art

6494.N3 Narrative art

National socialism, see N6868.5.N37

6494.N34 Naturalism

Neodadaism, see N6494.P6

Neoplasticism. De Stijl (Dutch), see N6948.5.D42

Neoromanticism (British), see N6768.5.N46

Neue Sachlichkeit (German); New objectivity (German), see N6868.5.E9

New realism, see N6494.P42

New York School (American), see N6512.5.N4

History
Modern art
By century
19th and 20th centuries
20th century
Special aspects
or movements, A-Z -- Continued
Nio-gruppen, see N7088.5.N5
Non-objective art, see N6494.A2
Novecento italiano (Group of artists), see N6918.5.N68
Novembergruppe, see N6868.5.N6
Núcleo Bernardelli, see N6655.5.N83
Nul-groep (Netherlands), see N6948.5.N85
Ny Saklighet (Swedish); New objectivity (Swedish), see N7088.5.E95
6494.O6 Op art. Optical art. Perceptual art
Cf. N6494.K5, Kinetic art
Orphism (French), see N6848.5.O7
6494.P34 Paper art
Paris, School of (French), see N6850
(6494.P38) Performance art
See NX600.P47
Pfälzische Sezession, see N6868.5.P55
6494.P42 Photo-realism. New realism. Hyperrealism
Les Plasticiens, see N6545.5.P55
De Ploeg (Association), see N6948.5.P55
6494.P6 Pop art. Neodadaism. Neo-realism
Postimpressionism, see N6465.P6
6494.P66 Postmodernism
6494.P7 Primitivism. Groupe Henri Rousseau
6494.P72 Process art
6494.P74 Projection art
6494.P79 Psychedelic art
Purism (20th century French), see N6848.5.P8
Quadriga (Group of artists), see N6868.5.Q3
6494.R3 Ratilly (Artists' colony)
Rayonism (Russian), see N6988.5.R3
6494.R4 Realism
Cf. N6494.S65, Socialist realism
6494.R44 Relief art
Rhino Horn (Group of painters), see N6512.5.R48
6494.R65 Romanticism
Rousseau Group, see N6494.P7
6494.S24 Salon des réalités nouvelles
Schlossstrasse Acht (Group of artists), see N6868.5.S43
Sensibilizar (Group), see N6655.5.S45
6494.S47 Serial art
Sezession Oberschwaben Bodensee, see N6868.5.O34

History
Modern art
By century
19th and 20th centuries
20th century
Special aspects
or movements, A-Z -- Continued

6494.S65 Socialist realism
Cf. N6988+, Russia
Sound sculpture, see NB198.5.S68
6494.S7 Spatialism
Stieglitz Group, see N6512.5.S75
Stijl, De. Neoplasticism (Dutch), see N6948.5.D42
Styrian Artline (Art group), see N6808.5.S76
Superstudio (Group of architects), see NA1118.5.S96
Suprematism (Russian), see N6988.5.S9
6494.S8 Surrealism
Cf. N6494.D3, Dadaism
Cf. N6494.M3, Magic realism
Sursum (Group), see N6831.5.S82
Synchromism (American), see N6512.5.S9
Systems Group, see N6768.5.S9
Tachism, see N6494.A25
Taller de Gráfica Popular (Mexico City, Mexico), see NE544.6.T34
Témoignage (Group of artists), see N6848.5.T44
Trinadt͡sat' (Group of artists), see N6988.5.T74
6494.T94 Typewriter art
Veinte Pintores y Escultores, see N6635.5.V45
6494.V53 Video art
Vorticism (British), see N6768.5.V6
Wiener Schule des phantastischen Realismus, see N6808.5.M3
6494.W5 Wiener Secession
6494.Z42 Zebra (Group of artists)
Zero, Group, see N6868.5.Z4
De Zwarte Panter (Group of artists), see N6968.5.Z85

6501-7414 Special countries (Table N5 modified)
Establish special movements identified with one country and largely one century by adding .5 to the appropriate century number where possible and subdividing it alphabetically by movement
Add country number in table to N6500
For ancient art prefer N5350-N5896, when applicable
For guidebooks to the galleries and collections, see N400+
America

History
Special countries
America -- Continued
(6501.5) Primitive American art
See E59.A7, E98.A7, F1219.3.A7, etc.
Latin America
6502 General works
6502.2 Colonial period (16th-18th centuries)
6502.3.A-Z Special aspects or movements, A-Z
6502.3.M36 Mannerism
20th century
6502.5 General works
6502.57.A-Z Special aspects or movements, A-Z
6502.57.D48 Desde la Tierra (Artists' group)
6502.57.M63 Modernism
6502.57.P64 Pop art
6502.57.P67 Postmodernism
6502.57.S87 Surrealism
United States
Cf. N6538.N5, Afro-American artists
6505 General works
6505.5.A-Z Special aspects or movements, A-Z
6505.5.P74 Primitivism
6505.5.R42 Realism
Colonial period (18th and early 19th centuries)
6507 General works
6507.5.A-Z Special aspects or movements, A-Z
6507.5.N44 Neoclassicism
6507.5.P7 Primitivism
19th century
6510 General works
6510.5.A-Z Special aspects or movements, A-Z
6510.5.A77 Art nouveau
6510.5.B67 Boston school of painting. Classical realism
Classical realism, see N6510.5.B67
6510.5.E25 Eclecticism
6510.5.E48 Egyptian Revival (Art)
6510.5.I4 Impressionism. Ten American Painters
6510.5.M63 Modernism
6510.5.N4 Neoclassicism (Late)
6510.5.P67 Preraphaelites. Preraphaelitism
6510.5.P7 Primitivism
6510.5.R4 Realism
6510.5.R6 Romanticism
6510.5.S93 Symbolism
Ten American Painters, see N6510.5.I4
6510.5.T6 Tonalism
6510.5.V5 Victorian art
20th century
6512 General works
6512.5.A-Z Special aspects or movements, A-Z
6512.5.A2 Abstract art. American Abstract Artists

History
Special countries
America
United States
20th century
Special aspects
or movements, A-Z -- Continued

6512.5.A25 Abstract expressionism. Abstract impressionism. Tachism. Action painting
6512.5.A5 Anonima group
6512.5.A7 Art deco
6512.5.B64 Body art
6512.5.C55 Collage. Papiers collés
6512.5.C6 Color-field painting
6512.5.C64 Conceptual art
6512.5.E4 The Eight. Ashcan school
6512.5.E58 Environment (Art)
6512.5.F48 Fiberwork
6512.5.F5 Figurative art
6512.5.F68 Found objects
6512.5.G83 Guerrilla Girls (Group of artists)
6512.5.I45 Impressionism
6512.5.I56 Installations (Art)
6512.5.L85 Luminism
6512.5.M3 Magic realism
6512.5.M5 Minimal art
6512.5.M63 Modernism
6512.5.N3 Narrative art
6512.5.N37 Neoplasticism
6512.5.N4 New York School
6512.5.P34 Paper art
6512.5.P45 Photo-realism
6512.5.P6 Pop art
6512.5.P64 Post-impressionism
6512.5.P67 Precisionism
6512.5.P7 Primitivism
6512.5.P72 Process art
6512.5.P74 Projection art
6512.5.P79 Psychedelic art
6512.5.R4 Realism
6512.5.R43 Relief art
6512.5.R48 Rhino Horn (Group of painters)
6512.5.R65 Romanticism
6512.5.S34 Salons of America, Inc.
6512.5.S43 Serial art
6512.5.S57 Social realism
6512.5.S6 Spatialism
6512.5.S75 Stieglitz Group
6512.5.S87 Surrealism
6512.5.S9 Synchromism
Cf. N6848.5.O7, Orphism
6512.5.T34 Taos school. Taos Society of Artists
6512.5.T7 Transcendental Painting Group

History
Special countries
America
United States
20th century
Special aspects
or movements, A-Z -- Continued
6512.5.V53 Video art
6538.A-Z Special races or ethnic groups, A-Z
6538.N5 Negroes. Afro-Americans. Blacks
Canada
6540 General works
6540.5.A-Z Special aspects or movements, A-Z
6540.5.P7 Primitivism
6544 19th century
6544.5.A-Z Special aspects or movements, A-Z
6544.5.I4 Impressionism
6544.5.N45 Neoclassicism (Late)
6545 20th century
6545.5.A-Z Special aspects or movements, A-Z
6545.5.A28 Abstract art
6545.5.C66 Conceptual art
6545.5.C83 Cubism
6545.5.K56 Kinetic art
6545.5.P55 Les Plasticiens
6545.5.P7 Primitivism
6545.5.R33 Radio art
6545.5.R4 Realism
6545.5.S4 Group of Seven
6545.5.S97 Surrealism
Mexico
6555 20th century
6555.5.A-Z Special aspects or movements, A-Z
6555.5.A28 Abstract art
6555.5.C66 Concrete art
6555.5.H45 Grupo Hermes
6555.5.I58 Installations (Art)
6555.5.N83 Nueva Presencia (Group of artists)
6555.5.P55 Grupo de Pintores 30-30!
6555.5.P74 Primitivism
6555.5.S8 Surrealism
Central America
Costa Rica
6573.2 20th century
6573.5.A-Z Special aspects or movements, A-Z
6573.5.C64 Cofradía (Group)
Guatemala
6576.2 20th century
6576.5.A-Z Special aspects or movements, A-Z
6576.5.P75 Primitivism
Nicaragua
6582.2 20th century
6582.5.A-Z Special aspects or movements, A-Z

History
  Special countries
    America
      Central America
        Nicaragua
          20th century
            Special aspects
                or movements, A-Z -- Continued
6582.5.P74 Primitivism
      West Indies
        Haiti
6606.2 20th century
6606.5.A-Z Special aspects or movements, A-Z
6606.5.P74 Primitivism
      South America
        Argentina
6635 20th century
6635.5.A-Z Special aspects or movements, A-Z
6635.5.C38 CAYC Group. Grupo Babel
6635.5.C64 Concrete art
Grupo Babel, see N6635.5.C38
6635.5.O6 Op art. Optical art. Perceptual art
6635.5.V45 Veinte Pintores y Escultores (Group of artists)
        Brazil
6655 20th century
6655.5.A-Z Special aspects or movements, A-Z
6655.5.A28 Abstract art
6655.5.A75 Art deco
6655.5.B34 Grupo de Bagé
6655.5.C62 Conceptual art
6655.5.C63 Concrete art
6655.5.C65 Constructivism
6655.5.E85 Expressionism
6655.5.M63 Modernism
6655.5.N83 Núcleo Bernardelli
6655.5.P7 Primitivism
6655.5.S25 Grupo Santa Helena
6655.5.S45 Sensibilizar (Group)
        Chile
          20th century
6665 General works
6665.5.A-Z Special aspects or movements, A-Z
6665.5.M67 Grupo Montparnasse
        Colombia
6675 20th century
6675.5.A-Z Special aspects or movements, A-Z
6675.5.A27 Abstract art
        Ecuador
6685 20th century
6685.5.A-Z Special aspects or movements, A-Z
6685.5.A26 Abstract art
        Peru

	History
	Special countries
	America
	South America
	Peru -- Continued
6713	Through 1800
6713.5.A-Z	Special aspects or movements, A-Z
6713.5.C95	Cuzco school of painting
	Venezuela
6730	General works
6730.5.A-Z	Special aspects or movements, A-Z
6730.5.P75	Primitivism
6734	19th century
6734.5.A-Z	Special aspects or movements, A-Z
6734.5.R6	Romanticism
6735	20th century
6735.5.A-Z	Special aspects or movements, A-Z
6735.5.C55	Círculo de Bellas Artes
6735.5.P7	Primitivism
	Europe
	Modern
	19th century
6757	General works
6757.5.A-Z	Special aspects or movements, A-Z
6757.5.A78	Art nouveau
6757.5.M63	Modernism
6757.5.R65	Romanticism
6757.5.S94	Symbolism
	20th century
6758	General works
6758.5.A-Z	Special aspects or movements, A-Z
6758.5.F53	Figurative expressionism
6758.5.M63	Modernism
6758.5.P74	Primitivism
	Special countries
	Great Britain. England
	Modern
	17th-18th centuries
6766	General works
6766.5.A-Z	Special aspects or movements, A-Z
6766.5.N4	Neoclassicism
6766.5.P74	Primitivism
	19th century
6767	General works
6767.5.A-Z	Special aspects or movements, A-Z
6767.5.A3	Aesthetic movement
6767.5.B7	Bristol School of Artists
6767.5.E48	Egyptian Revival (Art)
6767.5.I46	Impressionism
6767.5.N45	Neoclassicism (Late)
6767.5.N48	Newlyn school of painting
	Norfolk & Norwich Art Circle, see N6767.5.N65

History
Special countries
Europe
Special countries
Great Britain. England
Modern
19th century
Special aspects or movements, A-Z -- Continued

6767.5.N65 Norwich school of painting. Norfolk & Norwich Art Circle
6767.5.P7 Preraphaelites. Preraphaelitism
6767.5.P74 Primitivism
6767.5.R6 Romanticism
6767.5.V52 Victorian art

20th century
6768 General works
6768.5.A-Z Special aspects or movements, A-Z
6768.5.A2 Abstract art
6768.5.A75 Artist Placement Group
6768.5.B55 Bloomsbury group
6768.5.C53 Camden Town Group
6768.5.C63 Conceptual art
6768.5.C65 Constructivism (Art)
6768.5.E87 Euston Road School of Painting
6768.5.F53 Fiberwork
6768.5.F55 Figurative art
6768.5.I53 Independent Group (Association : Great Britain)
6768.5.I58 Installations (Art)
6768.5.L65 London Group
6768.5.M63 Modernism (Art)
6768.5.N37 Narrative art (Art movement)
6768.5.N46 Neoromanticism
6768.5.P65 Pop art
6768.5.P67 Post-impressionism
6768.5.P74 Primitivism
6768.5.R85 Brotherhood of Ruralists
6768.5.S87 Surrealism
6768.5.S9 Systems Group
6768.5.V6 Vorticism

Ireland
Modern
19th century
6788 General works
6788.5.A-Z Special aspects or movements, A-Z
6788.5.I46 Impressionism

20th century
6789 General works
6789.5.A-Z Special aspects or movements, A-Z
6789.5.M63 Modernism

Austria
Modern

History
Special countries
Europe
Special countries
Austria
Modern -- Continued
14th-16th centuries. Renaissance
6805 General works
6805.5.A-Z Special aspects or movements, A-Z
6805.5.B8 Künstlergruppe Burgenland
6805.5.D6 Donauschule
17th-18th centuries
6806 General works
6806.5.A-Z Special aspects or movements, A-Z
6806.5.R6 Rococo
19th century
6807 General works
6807.5.A-Z Special aspects or movements, A-Z
6807.5.A7 Art nouveau
6807.5.B53 Biedermeier
6807.5.E24 Eclecticism
6807.5.R42 Realism
20th century
6808 General works
6808.5.A-Z Special aspects or movements, A-Z
6808.5.A23 Abstract art
6808.5.A25 Abstract expressionism. Abstract impressionism. Tachism. Action painting
6808.5.A77 Art Club (Austria)
6808.5.B8 Künstlergruppe Burgenland
6808.5.C65 Conceptual art
6808.5.E9 Expressionism
6808.5.H3 Haus-Rucker-Co
6808.5.K78 Künstlerbund Hagen
6808.5.K8 Künstlergruppe "Der Kreis"
6808.5.K84 Künstlergruppe (Galerie Elefant)
6808.5.M3 Magic realism
6808.5.M64 Modernism
6808.5.R42 Realism
6808.5.S76 Styrian Artline (Art group)
6808.5.W53 Wiener Secession
Hungary
Modern
19th century
6819 General works
6819.5.A-Z Special aspects or movements, A-Z
6819.5.A75 Art nouveau
6819.5.E25 Eclecticism
6819.5.G63 Gödöllői Múvésztelep
6819.5.I58 Impressionism
6819.5.N4 Neoclassicism (Late)
6819.5.R4 Realism

History
Special countries
Europe
Special countries
Hungary
Modern
19th century
Special aspects
or movements, A-Z -- Continued

6819.5.R6 Romanticism
6819.5.S95 Szolnoki Múvésztelep (Hungarian)

20th century
6820 General works
6820.5.A-Z Special aspects or movements, A-Z
6820.5.A35 Aktivisták (Group of artists)
6820.5.C64 Constructivism
6820.5.F5 Fiatal Képzómúvészek Stúdiója
6820.5.F52 Fiberwork
6820.5.N93 Nyolcak (Group of artists)
6820.5.P42 Pécsi Múhely (Art group)
6820.5.P7 Primitivism
6820.5.S93 Szocialista Képzómúvészek Csoportja
6820.5.S95 Szolnoki Múvésztelep

Czechoslovakia
Modern
14th-16th centuries
6828 General works
6828.5.A-Z Special aspects or movements, A-Z
6828.5.B64 Bohemian School

19th century
6830 General works
6830.5.A-Z Special aspects or movements, A-Z
6830.5.A7 Art nouveau
6830.5.M63 Modernism
6830.5.P7 Primitivism

20th century
6831 General works
6831.5.A-Z Special aspects or movements, A-Z
6831.5.A38 Aktual (Group)
6831.5.C6 Concrete art
6831.5.C8 Cubism
6831.5.D48 Devětsil (Society)
6831.5.E95 Expressionism
6831.5.F86 Functionalism
6831.5.L54 Linie (Group)
6831.5.M5 Minimal art
6831.5.N46 Neoclassicism (Late)
6831.5.R43 Realism
6831.5.S35 Sdružení Q (Organzation)
6831.5.S63 Socialist realism
6831.5.S818 Surrealism
6831.5.S82 Sursum (Group)

France

History
Special countries
Europe
Special countries
France -- Continued
Modern
14th-16th centuries
6845 General works
6845.5.A-Z Special aspects, A-Z
6845.5.M3 Mannerism. School of Fontainebleau
17th-18th centuries
6846 General works
6846.5.A-Z Special aspects or movements, A-Z
6846.5.B35 Baroque
6846.5.C55 Classicism
6846.5.N4 Neoclassicism
6846.5.R6 Rococo
19th century
6847 General works
6847.5.A-Z Special aspects or movements, A-Z
6847.5.A78 Art nouveau. Art Nouveau Bing (Firm). Modern style
6847.5.B3 Barbizon School
6847.5.E34 Eclecticism
6847.5.I4 Impressionism
6847.5.N3 Nabis. Intimism. Symbolism
6847.5.N35 Neoclassicism (Late)
6847.5.N37 Neo-impressionism. Pointillism
6847.5.P58 Pont-Aven school
6847.5.P6 Post-impressionism
6847.5.P68 Primitivism
6847.5.P8 Purism (related to Pre-Raphaelites)
6847.5.R4 Realism
6847.5.R6 Romanticism
6847.5.R65 Rouen school of painting
6847.5.S24 Saint-Siméon school of painting
20th century
6848 General works
6848.5.A-Z Special aspects or movements, A-Z
6848.5.A35 Abstract art
6848.5.C46 Cent-Neuf (Association). 109 (Association)
6848.5.C66 Conceptual art
Including Art & Language (Group)
6848.5.C82 Cubism
6848.5.F3 Fauvism
6848.5.F53 Figurative art
6848.5.F56 Groupe Finistère
6848.5.F67 Forces nouvelles
6848.5.F85 Functionalism
6848.5.J47 Jeune peinture (Association). Salon de la Jeune peinture
6848.5.M34 Malassis, Coopérative des

History
Special countries
Europe
Special countries
France
Modern
20th century
Special aspects
or movements, A-Z -- Continued
6848.5.M65 Groupe Montpellier-Sète
6848.5.O7 Orphism
Cf. N6512.5.S9, Synchromism
6848.5.P7 Primitivism
6848.5.P8 Purism (related to Cubism). Esprit nouveau
6848.5.S95 Supports-Surfaces (Group)
6848.5.S96 Surrealism
6848.5.T44 Témoignage (Group of artists)
6850 Paris
Including Salons des refusés, Société des artistes indépendants, École de Paris
6853.A-Z Special artists, A-Z
e.g.
6853.J4 Jeanneret-Gris, Charles Edouard, 1887-1965
Le Corbusier, 1887-1965, see N6853.J4
Germany
Modern
14th-16th centuries
6865 General works
6865.5.A-Z Special aspects or movements, A-Z
6865.5.D6 Donauschule
6865.5.M3 Mannerism
17th-18th centuries
6866 General works
6866.5.A-Z Special aspects or movements, A-Z
6866.5.B3 Baroque
6866.5.C55 Classicism
6866.5.N45 Neoclassicism
19th century
6867 General works
6867.5.A-Z Special aspects or movements, A-Z
6867.5.A7 Art nouveau
6867.5.B47 Beuroner Kunstschule
6867.5.B5 Biedermeier
6867.5.D8 Düsseldorfer Malerschule
6867.5.E35 Eclecticism
6867.5.G68 Gothic revival
6867.5.G7 Grötzinger Malerkolonie
6867.5.H36 Hamburgische Künstlerclub (Germany)
6867.5.I4 Impressionism
6867.5.K7 Kronberger Malerkolonie
6867.5.L45 Leibl-Kreis
6867.5.M83 Münchener Secession

History
Special countries
Europe
Special countries
Germany
Modern
19th century
Special aspects
or movements, A-Z -- Continued

6867.5.M85 Munich school of painting
6867.5.N3 Nazarenes
6867.5.R4 Realism. The "Academicians"
6867.5.R6 Romantic movement
6867.5.W67 Worpsweder Künstlervereinigung

20th century
6868 General works
6868.5.A-Z Special aspects or movements, A-Z
6868.5.A13 Abstract art
6868.5.A14 Abstract expressionism. Abstract impressionism. Tachism. Action painting
Abstract impressionism, see N6868.5.A14
Action painting, see N6868.5.A14
6868.5.A15 Abstrakten Hannover (Association)
6868.5.A16 Gruppe AKKU
6868.5.A54 Anker (Artists' organization)
6868.5.A85 Gruppe Aspekt
6868.5.B3 Berliner Secession
6868.5.B59 Blaues Quadrat (Group of artists)
6868.5.B64 Bonner Künstlergruppe
6868.5.C63 Conceptual art
6868.5.C64 Constructivism
6868.5.D67 Dortmunder Gruppe. Dortmunder Künstlerbund (1956-)
6868.5.E37 Einmal Sechs (Group)
6868.5.E58 Environment (Art)
6868.5.E9 Expressionism. Blaue Reiter. Die Brücke. Neue Sachlichkeit. New objectivity. Blaue Vier (Group of artists)
6868.5.F54 Figurative art
6868.5.F73 Frauenwörther (Society)
6868.5.G4 Gruppe Geflecht
6868.5.H357 Hamburgische Sezession (Germany)
6868.5.I56 Installations
6868.5.K5 Gruppe Kilo
6868.5.K53 Kinetic art
6868.5.K66 Kooperative Kunst
Künstlersonderbund in Deutschland, see N6868.5.R4
6868.5.K84 Künstlervereinigung Der Kreis
6868.5.L45 Leipziger Asso
6868.5.L83 Lücke (Group of artists)

History
Special countries
Europe
Special countries
Germany
Modern
20th century
Special aspects
or movements, A-Z -- Continued

6868.5.M3 Magic realism
6868.5.M33 Mail art
6868.5.M5 Minimal art
6868.5.M63 Modernism
6868.5.M78 Mülheimer Freiheit (Group)
6868.5.M8 Multiple art
6868.5.N37 National socialism
6868.5.N4 Neue Darmstädter Sezession
6868.5.N6 Novembergruppe
6868.5.O34 Sezession Oberschwaben-Bodensee
6868.5.O38 Gruppe Odious
6868.5.P55 Pfälzische Sezession
6868.5.P58 Gruppe Plus
6868.5.P67 Primitivism
6868.5.P7 Gruppe Progressiver Künstler
6868.5.Q3 Quadriga (Group of artists)
6868.5.R4 Realism. Künstlersonderbund in Deutschland
6868.5.R42 Gruppe Realismus im BBK
6868.5.S43 Schlossstrasse Acht (Group of artists)
6868.5.S44 Seerose (Group)
6868.5.S46 Künstlergruppe Semikolon
6868.5.S8 Gruppe Die Spur
Tachism, see N6868.5.A14
6868.5.T4 Künstlergruppe Tendenzen
6868.5.W35 Wandmalgruppe
6868.5.W43 Gruppe WeibsBilder
6868.5.Z37 Gruppe Zebra
6868.5.Z38 Gruppe ZEN 49
6868.5.Z4 Group Zero

Greece
Modern
19th century
6897 General works
6897.5.A-Z Special aspects or movements, A-Z
6897.5.N4 Neoclassicism (Late)
20th century
6898 General works
6898.5.A-Z Special aspects or movements, A-Z
6898.5.P7 Primitivism

Italy
Modern
14th-16th centuries
6915 General works

History
Special countries
Europe
Special countries
Italy
Modern
14th-16th centuries -- Continued
6915.5.A-Z Special aspects or movements, A-Z
6915.5.M3 Mannerism
17th-18th centuries
6916 General works
6916.5.A-Z Special aspects or movements, A-Z
6916.5.B25 Bamboccianti (Group of artists)
6916.5.B3 Baroque
6916.5.E35 Egyptian Revival (Art)
6916.5.N45 Neoclassicism
19th century
6917 General works
6917.5.A-Z Special aspects or movements, A-Z
6917.5.A7 Art nouveau
6917.5.M3 Macchiaioli
6917.5.N37 Naturalism
6917.5.N44 Neo-impressionism
6917.5.P7 Pre-Raphaelites
6917.5.R6 Romanticism
6917.5.S63 Socialism
6917.5.S96 Symbolism
20th century
6918 General works
6918.5.A-Z Special aspects or movements, A-Z
6918.5.A2 Abstract art
6918.5.A25 Abstract expressionism
6918.5.A7 Art deco
6918.5.C63 Conceptual art
6918.5.C65 Concrete art. Movement arte concreta
6918.5.C67 Corrente
6918.5.C73 Cracking Art (Group)
6918.5.E55 Gruppo Enne
6918.5.E94 Expressionism
6918.5.F28 Fascism
6918.5.F47 Fiberwork
6918.5.F5 Figurative art
6918.5.F6 Gruppo Forma uno
6918.5.F7 Functionalism
6918.5.F8 Futurism
6918.5.G45 Geometria e ricerca (Group of artists)
6918.5.M33 Magic realism
6918.5.M48 Metaphysical school
6918.5.N68 Novecento italiano (Group of artists)
6918.5.P6 Pop art
6918.5.P7 Primitivism
6918.5.R4 Realism
6918.5.S37 Scuola romana

History
Special countries
Europe
Special countries
Italy
Modern
20th century
Special aspects
or movements, A-Z -- Continued
6918.5.S6 Spatialism
6918.5.S8 Surrealism
6918.5.V34 Gruppo Valvoline
6923.A-Z Special artists, A-Z
e.g.
6923.B283 Barbieri, Giovanni Francesco, 1591-1666
6923.B9 Buonarroti, Michel Angelo, 1475-1564
6923.C324 Canal, Antonio, 1697-1768
Canaletto, 1697-1768, see N6923.C324
6923.C5 Chirico, Giorgio de, 1888-
De Chirico, Giorgio, 1888- , see N6923.C5
Guercino, 1591-1666, see N6923.B283
Michelangelo Buonarroti, 1475-1564, see N6923.B9
Low countries
Netherlands (Holland)
Modern
14th-16th centuries
6945 General works
6945.5.A-Z Special aspects or movements, A-Z
6945.5.M37 Mannerism
17th-18th centuries
6946 General works
6946.5.A-Z Special aspects or movements, A-Z
6946.5.T7 Trompe l'oeil
19th century
6947 General works
6947.5.A-Z Special aspects or movements, A-Z
6947.5.H3 Haagse school
6947.5.N46 Neo-impressionism
6947.5.R65 Romanticism
6947.5.S93 Symbolism
20th century
6948 General works
6948.5.A-Z Special aspects or movements, A-Z
6948.5.A28 Abstract art
6948.5.A57 Amsterdamse Joffers (Women painters)
6948.5.A77 Artim Groep
6948.5.B47 Bergense school of painting
CoBrA, see N6494.C5
6948.5.C58 Conceptual art
6948.5.C6 Constructivism
6948.5.D42 De Stijl. Neoplasticism
6948.5.E27 Earthworks (Art)

History
Special countries
Europe
Special countries
Low countries
Netherlands (Holland)
Modern
20th century
Special aspects
or movements, A-Z -- Continued
6948.5.E96 Expressionism
6948.5.H2 Haagse Kunstkring
6948.5.I35 IJmuider Kring
6948.5.M3 Magic realism
Neoplasticism, see N6948.5.D42
6948.5.N85 Nul-groep
6948.5.P45 Photo-realism
6948.5.P55 De Ploeg (Association)
6948.5.P74 Primitivism
6948.5.R4 Realism
Stijl, De, see N6948.5.D42
6948.5.S86 Surrealism
6953.A-Z Special artists, A-Z
e.g.
6953.G3 Gogh, Vincent van, 1853-1890
Van Gogh, Vincent, 1853-1890, see N6953.G3
Belgium
Modern
19th century
6967 General works
6967.5.A-Z Special aspects or movements, A-Z
6967.5.A48 Als Ik Kan (Society)
6967.5.A75 Art nouveau
6967.5.G67 Gothic revival
6967.5.I46 Impressionism
6967.5.N46 Neoclassicism (Late)
6967.5.R4 Realism
6967.5.R6 Romanticism
6967.5.S56 Sint-Martens-Latem (Group of artists)
6967.5.S9 Symbolism
20th century
6968 General works
6968.5.A-Z Special aspects or movements, A-Z
6968.5.A2 Abstract art
6968.5.A77 Art deco
6968.5.C64 Conceptual art
6968.5.E9 Expressionism
6968.5.J35 Association "Jeune peinture belge"
6968.5.M34 Magic realism
6968.5.P42 Photo-realism
6968.5.P6 Pop art
6968.5.P74 Primitivism
6968.5.S93 Surrealism

History
Special countries
Europe
Special countries
Low countries
Belgium
Modern
20th century
Special aspects
or movements, A-Z -- Continued
6968.5.V55 Groep Vlaams Brabant
6968.5.Z85 De Zwarte Panter (Group of artists)
6973.A-Z Special artists, A-Z
e. g.
6973.D9 Dyck, Anthony van, Sir, 1599-1641
Van Dyck, Anthony, Sir, 1599-1641, see N6973.D9
Russia
Modern
17th-18th centuries
6986 General works
6986.5.A-Z Special aspects or movements, A-Z
6986.5.B37 Baroque
6986.5.N44 Neoclassicism
6986.5.P74 Primitivism
19th century
6987 General works
6987.5.A-Z Special aspects or movements, A-Z
6987.5.A77 Art nouveau
6987.5.R4 Realism. Peredvizhniki (Group of painters)
6987.5.R65 Romanticism
6987.5.V45 Venet͡sianov School
20th century
6988 General works
6988.5.A-Z Special aspects or movements, A-Z
6988.5.A24 Abstract art
6988.5.C62 Conceptual art
6988.5.C64 Constructivism
6988.5.D85 Dvizhenie (Group of artists)
6988.5.I57 Installations
6988.5.M55 Mir iskusstva (Association)
6988.5.O25 Obshchestvo khudozhnikov-stankovistov
6988.5.P7 Primitivism
6988.5.R3 Rayonism
Socialist realism, see N6988+
6988.5.S9 Suprematism
6988.5.T74 Trinadt͡sat′ (Group of artists)
Scandinavia
Modern
19th century
7007 General works
7007.5.A-Z Special aspects or movements, A-Z

History
Special countries
Europe
Special countries
Scandinavia
Modern
19th century
Special aspects
or movements, A-Z -- Continued
7007.5.R43 Realism
7007.5.S9 Symbolism
20th century
7008 General works
7008.5.A-Z Special aspects or movements, A-Z
7008.5.M64 Modernism
Denmark
Modern
17th-18th centuries
7016 General works
7016.5.A-Z Special aspects or movements, A-Z
7016.5.N46 Neoclassicism
19th century
7017 General works
7017.5.A-Z Special aspects or movements, A-Z
7017.5.R65 Romanticism
7017.5.S96 Symbolism
20th century
7018 General works
7018.5.A-Z Special aspects or movements, A-Z
7018.5.A97 Azuda 40 (Group)
7018.5.C6 Corner (Group of artists)
7018.5.D43 Decembristerne (Society)
7018.5.F94 Fynske forårsudstilling (Artists' group)
7018.5.G4 Germinalen (Group of artists)
7018.5.G78 Gruppe Gyrr
7018.5.K35 Kammeraterne (Group)
7018.5.K62 Københavnstrup
7018.5.K8 Kunstnergruppen
7018.5.S87 Surrealism
Norway
Modern
19th century
7067 General works
7067.5.A-Z Special aspects or movements, A-Z
7067.5.A75 Art nouveau
20th century
7068 General works
7068.5.A-Z Special aspects or movements, A-Z
7068.5.Z55 Gruppe Zink
Sweden
Modern
17th-18th centuries

History
Special countries
Europe
Special countries
Scandinavia
Sweden
Modern
17th-18th centuries -- Continued

7086 General works
7086.5.A-Z Special aspects or movements, A-Z
7086.5.N45 Neoclassicism

20th century
7088 General works
7088.5.A-Z Special aspects or movements, A-Z
7088.5.A73 Arbetsgruppen ARARAT
7088.5.C6 Constructivism
7088.5.E95 Expressionism. New objectivity. Ny Saklighet (Swedish)
7088.5.F85 Functionalism
7088.5.G76 Grodingegruppen
7088.5.H3 Halmstadgruppen
7088.5.N5 Nio-gruppen
7088.5.P46 Photo-realism
7088.5.P7 Primitivism
7088.5.R4 Realism
7088.5.S8 Surrealism

Spain
Modern
14th-16th centuries
7105 General works
7105.5.A-Z Special aspects or movements, A-Z
7105.5.M36 Mannerism

17th-18th centuries
7106 General works
7106.5.A-Z Special aspects or movements, A-Z
7106.5.N3 Naturalism
7106.5.N46 Neoclassicism

19th century
7107 General works
7107.5.A-Z Special aspects or movements, A-Z
7107.5.A7 Art nouveau
7107.5.I66 Impressionism
7107.5.N45 Neoclassicism (Late)
7107.5.R64 Romanticism

20th century
7108 General works
7108.5.A-7107.8.Z Special aspects or movements, A-Z
7108.5.A2 Abstract art
7108.5.A25 Abstract expressionism
7108.5.A97 Azuda 40 (Group)
7108.5.D38 Dau al set (Group of artists)
7108.5.E53 Grupo Endesa
7108.5.E66 Equipo Crónica

History
Special countries
Europe
Special countries
Spain
Modern
20th century
Special aspects
or movements, A-Z -- Continued

7108.5.E68 Equipo/57
7108.5.E72 Equipo Realidad
7108.5.E94 Expressionism
7108.5.F38 Fascism
7108.5.F5 Figurative art
7108.5.K55 Kinetic art
7108.5.M28 Madrid school of painting
7108.5.M3 Magic realism
7108.5.M63 Modernism
7108.5.P37 Grupo Parpalló
7108.5.P65 Grupo Pórtico
7108.5.P67 Postmodernism
7108.5.P74 Primitivism
7108.5.Q45 Quatre Gats
7108.5.Q5 Grupo Quince
7108.5.R4 Realism
7108.5.S87 Surrealism
7108.5.V3 Vallecas school

Portugal
Modern
14th-16th centuries
7125 General works
7125.5.A-Z Special aspects or movements, A-Z
7125.5.M34 Mannerism
17th-18th centuries
7126 General works
7126.5.A-Z Special aspects or movements, A-Z
7126.5.B37 Baroque
19th century
7127 General works
7127.5.A-Z Special aspects or movements, A-Z
7127.5.L4 Grupo do Leão
20th century
7128 General works
7128.5.A-Z Special aspects or movements, A-Z
7128.5.A27 Abstract art
7128.5.R4 Realism
7128.5.S96 Surrealism

Switzerland
Modern
17th-18th centuries
7146 General works
7146.5.A-Z Special aspects or movements, A-Z
7146.5.R65 Romanticism

History
Special countries
Europe
Special countries
Switzerland
Modern -- Continued
19th century
7147 General works
7147.5.A-Z Special aspects or movements, A-Z
7147.5.R65 Romanticism
20th century
7148 General works
7148.5.A-Z Special aspects or movements, A-Z
7148.5.A44 Allianz (Association: Switzerland)
7148.5.B53 Bieler Künstlergruppe Alibi
7148.5.C63 Concrete art
7148.5.C65 Constructivism
7148.5.C67 Groupe des Corps-Saints
7148.5.E94 Expressionism
7148.5.F53 Figurative art
7148.5.G78 Gruppe 7/84 Basel
7148.5.M8 Multiple art
7148.5.T45 Gruppe 33
7148.5.W55 Künstlergruppe Winterthur
7153.A-Z Special artists, A-Z
e.g.
Arp, Sophie Taeuber-, 1889-1943, see N7153.T33
7153.T33 Taeuber-Arp, Sophie, 1889-1943
Turkey
Modern
17th-18th centuries
7166 General works
7166.5.A-Z Special aspects or movements, A-Z
7166.5.B3 Baroque
Bulgaria
Modern
20th century
7188 General works
7188.5.A-Z Special aspects or movements, A-Z
7188.5.P74 Primitivism
Romania
Modern
19th century
7227 General works
7227.5.A-Z Special aspects or movements, A-Z
7227.5.A7 Art nouveau. Jugendstil
7227.5.I45 Impressionism
7227.5.N46 Neoclassicism (Late)
20th century
7228 General works
7228.5.A-Z Special aspects or movements, A-Z
7228.5.P7 Primitivism

History
Special countries
Europe
Special countries -- Continued
Yugoslavia
Modern
19th century
7247 General works
7247.5.A-Z Special aspects or movements, A-Z
7247.5.K5 Kitsch
20th century
7248 General works
7248.5.A-Z Special aspects or movements, A-Z
7248.5.C6 Conceptual art
7248.5.C64 Constructivism
7248.5.J84 Grupa Junij
7248.5.P7 Primitivism. Hlebinski krug
Asia. The Orient
Southwestern Asia. Middle East
7277-7279 Israel
Class here the secular art of Israel
For Jewish art, see N7414.75+
Southern Asia
India
20th century
7304 General works
7304.5.A-Z Special aspects or movements
7304.5.B46 Bengal School
7304.5.E94 Expressionism
7304.5.S9 Surrealism
Philippines
7327 General works
19th century
7327.15 General works
7327.17.A-Z Special aspects, A-Z
7327.17.R43 Realism
20th century
7327.2 General works
7327.5.A-Z Special aspects or movements, A-Z
7327.5.A25 Abstract art
Eastern Asia
China
Ming-Ch'ing dynasties, 1368-1912
7343.5 General works
7343.53.A-Z Special aspects or movements, A-Z
7343.53.E35 Eight Eccentrics of Yang-chou
7343.53.L55 Ling-nan school of painting
7343.53.O8 Orthodox school of painting
7343.53.W8 Wu school of painting
20th century
7345 General works
7345.5.A-Z Special aspects or movements, A-Z
7345.5.Y84 Yunnan school of painting

History
Special countries
Asia. The Orient
Eastern Asia -- Continued
Japan
Fujiwara (Heian) period (794-1185)
7353.3 General works
7353.35.A-Z Special aspects or movements, A-Z
7353.35.Y34 Yamatoe
Kamakura-Momoyama periods (1185-1600)
7353.4 General works
7353.44.A-Z Special aspects or movements, A-Z
7353.44.K35 Kanō School
7353.44.T67 Tosa School
Tokugawa (Edo) period (1600-1868)
7353.5 General works
7353.6.A-Z Special aspects or movements, A-Z
7353.6.A35 Akita Ranga School
Hokusai School, see N7353.6.K37
7353.6.K36 Kanō school of painting
7353.6.K37 Katsushika School
7353.6.M37 Maruyama School
7353.6.R4 Realism
7353.6.S54 Shijō School
7353.6.S64 Sōtatsu-Kōrin School
7353.6.U35 Ukiyoe
7353.6.U82 Utagawa School
19th century
7354 General works
Meiji period (1868-1912)
7354.5 General works
7354.6.A-Z Special aspects or movements, A-Z
7354.6.A76 Art nouveau
7354.6.I46 Impressionism
7354.6.R43 Realism
20th century
7355 General works
Taishō period (1912-1926)
7355.3 General works
7355.35.A-Z Special aspects or movements, A-Z
7355.35.R65 Romanticism
7355.5.A-Z Special aspects or movements, A-Z
7355.5.A19 Abstract art
7355.5.A2 Abstract expressionism. Abstract impressionism. Tachism. Action painting
7355.5.A83 Avant-garde
7355.5.C6 Conceptual art
7355.5.C65 Concrete art
7355.5.F53 Fiberwork
7355.5.F55 Figurative art
7355.5.G87 Gutai Bijutsu Kyokai
7355.5.I58 Installations (Art)

History
Special countries
Asia. The Orient
Eastern Asia
Japan
20th century
Special aspects or movements, A-Z -- Continued

7355.5.M64 Modernism
7355.5.R4 Realism
7355.5.V53 Video art

Africa
Egypt
20th century
7381.7 General works
7381.75.A-Z Special aspects or movements, A-Z
7381.75.S97 Surrealism
7382 Coptic art
Southern Africa
Republic of South Africa
7392 General works
20th century
7392.2 General works
7392.5.A-Z Special aspects or movements, A-Z
7392.5.N47 New Group
Australasia. Oceania
Australia
7400 General works
19th century
7400.15 General works
7400.17.A-Z Special aspects or movements, A-Z
Heidelberg School, see N7400.17.I45
7400.17.I45 Impressionism. Heidelberg School
20th century
7400.2 General works
7400.5.A-Z Special aspects or movements, A-Z
7400.5.A37 Abstract art
7400.5.C64 Collage. Papiers collés
7400.5.F53 Figurative art
7400.5.M54 Minimal art
7400.5.P74 Primitivism
New Zealand
20th century
7406.5 General works
7406.6.A-Z Special aspects or movements, A-Z
7406.6.F53 Figurative art
7414.5 Carmelite art
Including secular and religious art by Carmelites from various countries
For Carmelite art from special countries, see N6501+
Islamic art, see N6260+

History -- Continued
Jewish art
Cf. ND199, Jewish painting
Cf. NK1672, Jewish ceremonial art
Cf. NK3636, Decorative Hebrew alphabets and lettering
For secular art of Israel, see N7277+
For special countries, see N6501+
Museums. Collections. Exhibitions
7414.75.A-Z United States. By city and museum, A-Z
7414.8.A-Z Other countries. By country and city, A-Z
7414.9.A-Z Private collections. By collector, A-Z
7415 General works
7416 General special
By period
Ancient, see N5460
7417 Medieval and modern
7417.3 Middle ages
7417.5 16th-18th centuries
7417.6 19th-20th centuries
7418 Jewish artists (Collective biography)
For individual artists, see medium and nationality
General works
For philosophy of aesthetics of the visual arts, see N61+
7420 Early works to 1800
1800-
Class by language; class translations with the original language
7424 Polyglot
7425 English
7425.3 French
7425.4 German
7425.5 Italian
7425.55 Russian
7425.6 Spanish and Portuguese
7425.8.A-Z Other languages, A-Z
7428 General special
7428.5 Comparative art
Including influences and relationships between cultures, e.g., comparisons of ancient and modern art; comparisons of primitive and modern art
7429 Influences of Oriental, or Islamic art on Western art, and vice versa
Including chinoiserie, influence of Japanese prints
For such influences in particular countries, see N6501+
7429.2 Extraterrestrial influences
7429.3 Dissident art (General)
For dissident art in particular countries, see N6501+

General special -- Continued
7429.4 Ethnic art (General)
For art of minority ethnic groups in particular places, see N6501+
7429.5 Popular culture
Class here general works on visual arts about popular culture
Technique, composition, etc.
Including general studies or comparisons of techniques, and practical application of principles of composition
Cf. N8510+, Art studios and materials
Cf. NB1170, Sculpture techniques
Cf. NC730+, Drawing techniques
Cf. ND1470+, Painting techniques
Cf. ND1500+, Painting materials and methods
General works
7429.7 Early works through 1800
7430 1801-
7430.5 General special
Including optical illusion and visual perception
7430.7 Space as an element in visual art
Symmetry. Proportion. Rhythm
7431 General works
7431.5 General special
Including dynamic symmetry and golden section
Styles
Cf. ND1480+, Styles in painting
Cf. NX200, Styles in the arts
7432 General works
7432.3 General special
7432.5.A-Z Special styles, A-Z
Class here material not limited to one century
7432.5.A2 Abstraction
Prefer N6494.A2 where applicable
7432.5.A78 Art brut. Naive art. Outsider art
7432.5.C6 Classicism
Prefer N5603 N5896 or N6425.N4 where applicable
7432.5.E9 Expressionism
Prefer N6494.E9 where applicable
7432.5.F5 Figurative art
7432.5.I4 Impressionism
Prefer N6465.I4 where applicable
7432.5.M3 Mannerism
Prefer N6375.M3 where applicable
Naive art, see N7432.5.A78
Naturalism, see N7432.5.R4
Outsider art, see N7432.5.A78
7432.5.P7 Primitivism
Cf. N5312+, Folk art
Cf. N6494.P7, 20th century
Cf. N7432.5.A78, Art brut, naive art
7432.5.R4 Realism. Naturalism

Technique, composition, etc.
Styles
Special styles, A-Z -- Continued
7432.5.R6 Romanticism
Cf. N6465.R6, 19th century Romantic movement
7432.7 Color
Including use of specific colors
Cf. NA2795, Color in architecture
Cf. NB1275, Color in sculpture
Cf. NE1850+, Color prints
7433 Popular manuals
Including "how-to" books
Cf. ND1473, Popular painting manuals
Miscellaneous genres and media, not limited by time period, style, place, or subject matter
Artists' books
Class here works about books which are produced by artists and intended as visual art objects as well as such books themselves
7433.3 General works
7433.35.A-Z Special regions or countries, A-Z
7433.38.A-Z Special aspects or movements, A-Z
7433.38.C65 Comediants (Group)
7433.4.A-Z Special artists, A-Z
Under each artist:
.xA2 *Autobiography. By date*
.xA3 *Letters. By date*
.xA35 *Speeches, essays, interviews, etc. of the artist. By date*
.xA4 *Exhibition catalogs. By date*
.xA7-.xZ6 *Individual artists' books. By title, A-Z*
.xZ7-.xZ99 *Biography and criticism*
7433.5 Artists' preparatory studies
e.g. studies or sketches preparatory to executing works of art
For studies of individual artists, see the artist under special media and countries, N-NK
7433.6 Anamorphic art
7433.7 Assemblage. Collage. Found objects
Class here works of general interest on assemblage, collage and found objects
Cf. N6494.A8, Assemblage (20th century movement)
Cf. N6494.C6, Collage (20th century movement)
Cf. N6494.F6, Found objects (20th century movement)
Computer art
7433.8 General works
7433.83 Study and teaching
7433.84.A-Z Special regions or countries, A-Z
7433.85.A-Z Special artists, A-Z

Miscellaneous genres and media, not limited by time period, style, place, or subject matter -- Continued

7433.9 Fiberwork

Class here works of general interest on fiberwork

Cf. N6494.F47, 20th century movement

Cf. NK8475.F53, Miniature fiberwork

7433.93 Narrative art

Class here works of general interest on narrative art

Cf. N6494.N3, Narrative art (20th century movement)

Panoramas, see N7436.5+

7433.95 Plastic art

7433.96 Screens

7433.97 Tableaux

7433.98 Triptychs

(7434) Artists' models

See N7574

For models and model making, see TT154+

(7435) Art criticism

See N7475-N7485

(7436) Technical examination; expertise, X-rays, etc.

See N8558

Panoramas

Here are entered works in a variety of media and formats

For works on painted panoramas, see ND2880+

7436.5 General works

7436.52.A-Z By region or country, A-Z

7436.53.A-Z By special artists, A-Z

7437 Small art works

Including works on special regions or countries

7438 Popular works

7440 Juvenile works

Cf. N42, Biography for juveniles

Cf. N5308, History for juveniles

Collected writings (nonserial)

Prefer N25 for miscellaenous pamphlets bound together, or monographs in series

Festschriften

Class by language; class translations with the original language

Subarranged by honoree, A-Z

7442 Polyglot

7442.2 English

7442.3 French

7442.4 German

7442.5 Italian

7442.6 Spanish

7442.8.A-Z Other languages, A-Z

Addresses, essays, lectures, thoughts, and sayings (Collective)

Collected writings (nonserial)
Addresses, essays, lectures, thoughts, and sayings (Collective) -- Continued
Several authors
Class by language; class translations with the original language
7443 Polyglot
7443.2 English
7443.3 French
7443.4 German
7443.5 Italian
7443.6 Spanish
7443.8.A-Z Other languages, A-Z
Individual authors
Class by language; class translations with the original language
7445 Polyglot
7445.2 English
7445.3 French
7445.4 German
7445.5 Italian
7445.6 Spanish
7445.8.A-Z Other languages, A-Z
Writings by artists (General)
Prefer classification by subject where applicable
7452 Several authors
Individual authors
See individual artist in Tables 1-4, Table 5 subdivided by Table 6, .xA35 or Table 7, .x
7460 Anecdotes and curiosities of art and artists
7470 Facetiae
Art criticism
Including the history of art criticism
7475 General works
7476 General special
7477 Popular works on art appreciation
Cf. N345+, Art study in school
Cf. N366+, Picture study in the school and home
Cf. N7428.5, Comparative art
Cf. NB1142.5, Appreciation of sculpture
Cf. ND1143, Appreciation of painting
7479 Book reviews
7480 Historiography
Biography and criticism of art critics and historians
Collective
7482 General
7482.5 Women
7483.A-Z Individual, A-Z
7485.A-Z By region or country, A-Z
Collected writings of art critics and historians, see N7442+

Atlases. Iconographies (i.e., Miscellaneous collections of pictures)
Cf. N5301, Art history (Illustrations)
Cf. N7565, Iconographies. Iconology
7510 Periodicals
7511 Folios
7520 General collections
7521 Folios
Special periods and countries, see N5310+
7525 Indexes to illustrations (General). Repertoires
Including indexes to photographic illustrations of all subjects as well as works of art, such as Vance, "Illustration index"
Cf. N7620, Portrait indexes
Cf. ND45, Indexes to paintings
Special subjects of art
7560 Choice of subject. Titles. Themes and motives
7565 Iconography. Iconology
Descriptive and classificatory study of images with the aim of understanding the meaning of the subject matter represented
Prefer classification under specific subject, country, artist, or religion, where applicable; e.g., Buddhist iconography, see N8193; Christian iconography, see N8010 N8012
For icons of the Eastern Church, see N8185.5+
Human figures
Class here works on the techniques of depicting the human body in art
Cf. NC760, Drawing, art anatomy
For works on the representation of human beings in art, see N7625.5+
7570 General works
7572 Nude in art
Including general works and male nude in art
7573 Female nude in art
Cf. N7629+, Women in art
7573.3 Faces in art. Heads in art
7574 Artists' models
Cf. N8217.A67, Artists' models as a subject in art
Special countries
7574.4 United States
7574.5.A-Z Other countries, A-Z

Special subjects of art -- Continued
Portraits
Prefer CT and D-F for works with historical rather than aesthetic emphasis
Cf. NC773, Drawing
Cf. NC1300+, Caricatures
Cf. ND1300+, Painting
Cf. ND2200+, Watercolor
Cf. NE218+, Engravings
Cf. NK4659, Portraits in pottery
Cf. NK9580+, Wax portraits

7575 General works
Ancient
Cf. NB164, Ancient sculpture
7580 General works
7582 Egyptian
Greek and Roman
7585 General works
Greek iconographies
7586 General works
7587.A-Z Special, A-Z
7587.A4 Alexander, the Great
7587.A7 Aristoteles
7587.P6 Plato
7587.S2 Sappho
Roman iconographies
7588 General works
7589.A-Z Special, A-Z
7589.A8 Augustus, Emperor of Rome
7589.C2 Julius Caesar
7589.S26 Scipio Africanus the Elder
7589.S3 Severi family
7591.A-Z Other, A-Z
7591.P5 Phoenician
Medieval and modern
7592 General works
By period
7592.2 16th century
7592.3 17th century
7592.4 18th century
7592.5 19th century
7592.6 20th century
By country
For museums and collections, see N7621+
7592.8 America
United States
7593 General works
7593.1 17th-18th centuries
7593.2 19th century
7593.3 20th century
7593.5 New England
7593.6 South
7593.65 Central

Special subjects of art
Portraits
Medieval and modern
By country
America
United States
General works -- Continued
7593.7 West
7593.75 Pacific States
7593.8.A-Z States, A-W
7593.9.A-Z Cities, A-Z
Canada
7594 General works
7595.A-Z Special, A-Z
Latin America
7595.5 General works
7596 Mexico
7596.7 Central America
7596.8 South America
7597.A-Z Special countries, A-Z
Europe
Great Britain
7598 General works
7598.2 England
7598.4 Wales
7600 Ireland
7602 Austria
7603 Belgium
7604 France
7605 Germany
7606 Italy
7607 Netherlands
7608 Russia
Scandinavia
7609 General works
7610.A-Z Special countries, A-Z
7610.D5 Denmark
7610.S9 Sweden
Spain and Portugal
7611 General works
7611.2 Spain
7612 Portugal
7613 Switzerland
7613.5 Yugoslavia
7614.A-Z Other European countries, A-Z
Asia
7614.5 General works
7615.A-Z Special countries, A-Z
Africa
7615.2 General works
7615.25 Sub-Saharan Africa
7615.3.A-Z Special countries, A-Z
7615.4 Australia

Special subjects of art
Portraits
Medieval and modern
By country -- Continued
7615.5 New Zealand
7615.9.A-Z Other countries, A-Z
7616 Portrait miniatures
Cf. ND1329.8+, Painted miniatures
Self-portraits
7618 General works
By region or country
United States
7619 General works
7619.2.A-Z Local, A-Z
7619.5.A-Z Other regions or countries, A-Z
7620 Indexes of portraits (General)
Catalogs of collections
Including portrait miniatures and self-portraits
Public
7621.A-Z United States. By city and institution, A-Z
7621.2.A-Z Other countries. By country and city, A-Z
Private
7622.A-Z United States. By collector, A-Z
7622.2.A-Z Other countries. By country and collector, A-Z
Exhibitions
Prefer classification by nationality or sitter
7623.A-Z United States. By city and museum or other place of exhibition, A-Z
7623.2.A-Z Other countries. By country and city, A-Z
7624.A-Z Dealers' catalogs. By dealer, A-Z
Cf. NE250.A+, Engraved portraits
7624.5.A-Z Auction catalogs. By firm, A-Z
(7625) Special classes of persons
See subject in classes B-Z, e.g., Cardinals, BX4663-BX4665, Musicians ML140, Physicians, R153.5
Humans in art. Human life cycle in art
Class here works on the representation of human beings in art
For works on the techniques of depicting the human body in art, see N7570+
7625.5 General works
Men in art
Cf. N7572, Male nude in art
Cf. N8217.C75, Cowboys in art
Cf. N8219.K5, Kings and rulers in art
7626 General works
Portraits
For national collections, see N7575+
7627 General works
7628.A-Z Individual, A-Z
Cf. N7586+, Ancient Greek iconographies
Cf. N7588+, Ancient Roman iconographies

Special subjects of art
Humans in art. Human life cycle in art
Men in art
Portraits
Individual, A-Z -- Continued
7628.G44 George III, King of Great Britain
Women in art. Feminine beauty (Aesthetics)
Cf. N7573, Female nude in art
Cf. N8070, Madonna (Virgin Mary) in art
Cf. N8219.K5, Queens in art
Exhibitions
7629.A-Z United States. By city and museum or other place of exhibition, A-Z
7629.2.A-Z Other countries. By country and city, A-Z
7630 General works
Including mother-and-child as subject of secular art
7632 Minor collections, picture books, etc.
Portraits
7633 General works
7634 American
7635 English
7638.A-Z Other countries, A-Z
7639.A-Z Individual, A-Z
e.g.
7639.E4 Elizabeth I, Queen of England
7639.H3 Hamilton, Emma, Lady
7639.I78 Isabel de Borbon
7639.I8 Isabel I, la Católica, Queen of Spain
7639.L8 Luise, Queen Consort of Frederick William III, King of Prussia
7639.M2 Marie Antoinette
7639.M3 Mary, Queen of Scots
7639.M5 Medici, House of
7639.S5 Sforza-Riario, Caterina
7639.V5 Victoria, Queen of Great Britain
Children
Cf. N8266, Youth in art
7640 General works
7642 Minor collections, picture books, etc.
Portraits
7643 General works
7644 American
7645 English
7648.A-Z Other countries, A-Z
7649.A-Z Individual, A-Z

Special subjects of art -- Continued
Animals. Wildlife
Class here general works on the topics as well as works on the topics in a particular region, country, etc.
Cf. NB1940+, Animals in sculpture
Cf. NC780+, Animal anatomy and drawing
Cf. ND1380+, Animals and birds in painting
Cf. NK1555, Animal forms in design
7660 General works
7662 Minor collections, picture books, etc.
Birds
7665 General works
7666.A-Z Special birds, A-Z
7666.E33 Eagles
7666.O94 Owls
7666.P43 Peafowl
7668.A-Z Other animals, A-Z
7668.B84 Bulls
7668.C3 Cats
7668.D6 Dogs
7668.F57 Fishes
For fishing, see N8250
7668.F76 Frogs
7668.H6 Horses. Race horses
7668.I56 Insects
7668.K36 Kangaroos
7668.L56 Lions
Race horses, see N7668.H6
7668.R46 Reptiles
7668.S95 Swine
7668.T53 Tigers
7668.W48 Whales
7680 Plants. Trees. Flowers
Class here general works on the topics as well as works on the topics in a particular region, country, etc.
Cf. NB1950, Plants in sculpture
Cf. NC805, Trees, plants, flowers in drawing
Cf. ND1400+, Flowers, fruit in painting
Cf. NK1560+, Plant forms in design
7690 Devices
Allegories
Cf. NX650.A44, Allegories in the arts
7710 General works
Dance of death
Cf. NX650.D34, Dance of death in the arts
7720.A1A-Z General works, by author or editor
7720.A5-Z Special, by artist, A-Z, or if artist unknown, by place, A-Z
7725.A-Z Other, A-Z
7725.G66 Good and evil
7725.R58 Rivers

Special subjects of art
Allegories
Other, A-Z -- Continued
7725.W3 War
Symbolism. Emblematic art
Cf. PN6349+, Emblems (Literature)
7740 General works
7742.A-Z Special artists, A-Z
7745.A-Z Special, A-Z
7745.A4 Alchemy
7745.A5 Animals, Mythical
7745.A7 Apotheosis
7745.A85 Astrology
7745.C3 Carnations
7745.C5 Chinese imperial ritual robes
7745.D73 Dragons
7745.J87 Justice
7745.L5 Lions
7745.L6 Love
7745.M6 Months
Mythical animals, see N7745.A5
7745.O55 Occultism
7745.S4 Serpents
7745.S73 Stags (Deer)
7745.U54 Unicorns
7745.V57 Visions
7750 Fables
Mythology. Heroes. Legends
Cf. N8079.5+, Saints
7760 General works
7763.A-Z Special subjects, A-Z
7763.A23 Achelous
7763.A24 Achilles
7763.A35 Adonis
7763.A63 Apis
7763.A66 Apollo (Greek deity)
7763.A88 Assembly of gods
7763.A886 Athena (Greek deity)
7763.A89 Attis
Bacchanalia, see N7763.B23
7763.B23 Bacchantes. Bacchanalia
7763.C46 Centaurs
7763.C47 Cerberus
7763.C86 Cupid
7763.D56 Dionysus (Greek deity)
7763.E87 Europa
7763.F37 Fates
7763.F38 Faust
7763.G36 Ganymede
7763.G67 Gorgons
7763.H43 Hector
7763.H46 Hephaestus
7763.H47 Heracles. Hercules

Special subjects of art
Mythology. Heroes. Legends
Special subjects, A-Z -- Continued

7763.I75 Isis
7763.L36 Laocoon
7763.M35 Marsyas (Greek deity)
7763.O74 Orestes
7763.O76 Orpheus
7763.P36 Pandora
7763.P37 Paris (Trojan hero)
7763.P47 Perseus
7763.P53 Phaethon
7763.P65 Polyphemus
7763.P74 Prometheus
7763.P78 Psyche (Greek deity)
7763.S27 Satyrs
7763.S47 Serapis (Egyptian deity)
7763.S55 Sirens
7763.T45 Telephus
7763.V46 Venus (Roman deity)
7763.Y94 Ywain

Religious art
7790 General works
7793.A-Z Special subjects, A-Z
For special subjects in a particular religious art, see the religious art, e.g. N8020-N8180, Christian art
7793.A53 Angels
7793.H4 Heaven. Hell
Hell, see N7793.H4
7793.L35 Landscape
7793.V66 Votive offerings

Christian art
For Christian symbolism, see N8010+
7810 Periodicals
7820 Societies
7820.5 Congresses
7821 Catalogs (General)
Including catalogues raisonnés, etc.
Museums. Collections
Public
7822.A-Z United States. By institution, A-Z
7823.A-Z Other countries. By country and city, A-Z
Private
7824.A-Z United States. By collector, A-Z
7824.2.A-Z Other countries. By country and collector, A-Z
Exhibitions
Prefer classification by country or special subject
7824.4.A-Z United States. By city and museum or other place of exhibition, A-Z
7824.5.A-Z Other countries. By country and city, A-Z
7825 Dictionaries

Special subjects of art
Religious art
Christian art -- Continued
7826.A-Z Special firms, A-Z
Class here history or biography of special firms
7828.A-Z Dealers' catalogs. By dealer, A-Z
7829 Sources
e.g. Mitralis of Sicardus
7829.5 Study and teaching
7830 General works
7831 General special
History
7832 Early Christian
7840 Art of the catacombs
Cf. DG807.4, Roman antiquities
Medieval
7850 General works
7852.5 Byzantine
7853 Romanesque
7853.5 Cistercian
7857 Gothic
Modern
7860 General works
7862 Renaissance. Reformation. 15th and 16th centuries
7865 17th century
7870 18th century
7875 19th century
7880 20th century
7901-7996.3 Special countries (Table N1)
Add country number in table to N7900
Apply table at N5801-5896.3
Coptic art, see N7382
Christian symbolism
8010 General works
8012.A-Z Special, A-Z
8012.A66 Aquilegia (Columbine)
8012.C45 Church
8012.C57 Cosmology
8012.C6 Councils and Synods
8012.H35 Hand
8012.M66 Moon
8012.N8 Numbers
8012.P3 Papacy
8012.P43 Peace
8012.T45 Throne
8012.T74 Tree of life
Vices, see N8012.V57
8012.V52 Victory
8012.V57 Virtues. Vices
Special subjects
Bible illustrations
Including works by one artist

Special subjects of art
Religious art
Christian art
Special subjects
Bible illustrations -- Continued

8020 General works
8023 Before 1700
Cf. NE1070, Bible woodcuts
8025 1701-1820
8026 1820-1875
8027 1875-1965
8028 1965-
New Testament
8030 General works
8033 Before 1700
8035 1701-1820
8036 1820-1875
8037 1875-1965
8038 1965-
8038.3 Creation in art
8038.5 Apocalyptic art
8040 God in art
8045 Trinity in art
Christ in art
8050 General works
8052 The Good Shepherd and similar figures in ancient art
Passion
8052.4 General works
8052.5 Mount of Olives
8053 The crucifixion and the crucifix
8053.2 Descent from the cross
8053.5 Entombment. Holy Sepulcher in art
8053.7 Descent into hell. Resurrection
8054 Lord's Supper. Eucharist
8055 Holy Spirit
8060 Nativity. Holy Family
8061 Star of Bethlehem
8063 Adoration of the magi
8065 Crèches. Christmas crib
Cf. GT4989.5, Christmas customs
8070 Madonna. Mary, Blessed Virgin
Apostles. Saints
8079.5 General works
8080.A-Z Special apostles or saints, A-Z
8090 Angels
8110 Bible characters
8120 Last Judgment. Second Advent
8140 Devil
8150 Heaven. Hell. Purgatory
8160 Nimbus, aureola, etc.
8180 Other (not A-Z)

Special subjects of art
Religious art
Christian art -- Continued
8185 Special works
e.g. Speculum humanae salvationis
Icons (Eastern Church)
8185.5 Periodicals
8186.A-Z Exhibitions. Collections. Museums. By country and collector or place of exhibition, A-Z
8187 General works
Including history
8187.5 General special
8188 Technique of icon painting
8188.5 Study and teaching
Including special institutions (not A-Z)
8189.A-Z Special countries, A-Z
Under each country:
.x General works
.x2A-.x2Z Local, A-Z
8189.3.A-Z Special subjects, A-Z
8189.3.J47 Jesus Christ
8189.3.M35 Mary, Blessed Virgin
8189.5.A-Z Special icon painters, A-Z
e.g.
8189.5.R8 Rublev, Andreĭ
8189.6.A-Z Special icons. By name, A-Z
8189.6.A7 Arkhangel Mikhail s dei͡anii͡ami
8189.6.B6 Bogomater' Bogoli͡ubskai͡a s zhitii͡ami Zosimy i Savvatii͡a
8189.6.B62 Bogomater' Donskai͡a
8189.6.E54 Eikona tēs Agriōtissas
8189.6.K6 Konevskai͡a Bogorodit͡sa
8189.6.M3 Madonna di San Luca
8189.6.N4 Nedremannoe oko
8189.6.N45 Neopalimai͡a kupina
8189.6.N6 Novgorodskiĭ Svi͡atoĭ Ḟeodor Stratilat
8189.6.S85 Svi͡atai͡a Troit͡sa
8189.6.S87 Svi͡atye Boris i Gli͡eb v di͡ei͡anii͡akh
8189.6.T54 Tikhvinskai͡a Bogomater'
8189.6.V5 Vladimirskai͡a Bogomater'
Non-Christian art
Cf. NK1670+, Non-Christian religious applied arts
8190 General works
8191.A-Z By region or country, A-Z
Apply table at N8189.A-Z
Special
8193 Buddhist (Table N11)
Special subjects, characters, etc.
8193.2 Gautama Buddha in art
8193.3.A-Z Other, A-Z
8193.3.A3 Acala
8193.3.A54 Angels

Special subjects of art
Religious art
Non-Christian art
Special
Buddhist
Special subjects, characters, etc.
Other, A-Z -- Continued

8193.3.A82 Avalokiteśvara
8193.3.B53 Bhaiṣajyaguru
8193.3.B64 Bodhiṣattvas
8193.3.G36 Gandharvas
8193.3.H44 Hell
8193.3.H47 Heruka (Buddhist deity)
8193.3.L35 Lamaism in art
8193.3.L68 Lotus
8193.3.M27 Mahayana Buddhism
8193.3.M3 Mandala
8193.3.N54 Nimbus
8193.3.P33 Padma Sambhava, ca. 717-ca. 762
8193.3.P8 Pure Land Buddhism
8193.3.S75 Stars
8193.3.T3 Tantra
8193.3.T45 Tendai Sect
8193.3.Z4 Zen
8194 Shinto (Table N11)
8195 Hindu (Table N11)
8195.3.A-Z Special subjects or topics, A-Z
8195.3.B35 Balarāma (Hindu deity)
8195.3.D87 Durgā (Hindu deity)
8195.3.G35 Gaṅgā (Hindu deity)
8195.3.H35 Hanumān (Hindu deity)
8195.3.J33 Jaganātha (Hindu deity)
8195.3.K7 Krishna (Hindu deity)
8195.3.L34 Lakshmi (Hindu deity)
8195.3.M34 Mahiṣāsuramardinī (Hindu deity)
8195.3.S24 Saptamātṛkāṣ (Hindu deities)
8195.3.S48 Shaktism. Śakti (Hindu deity)
8195.3.S5 Sivaism
8195.3.S9 Sūrya (Hindu deity)
8195.3.V3 Vaishavism

Islamic art (General), see N6260+
Special countries, see N6501+
Jewish art (General), see N7414.75+
Special countries, see N6501+
Ancient Egyptian religious art, see N5350

8199.A-Z Other religions, A-Z
8199.J3 Jainism (Table N12)
8199.M36 Manichaeism (Table N12)
8199.S54 Sikhism (Table N12)
8199.T3 Taoism (Table N12)
8205 Pastoral art
8210 Historical subjects

Special subjects of art -- Continued

8212 Humorous art. Wit and humor in art

Cf. NC1300+, Caricature. Pictorial humor and satire

8213 Landscapes, views, mountains, etc. Places in art

8214 Indexes of views, etc.

8214.5.A-Z By region or country, A-Z

8215 Literary subjects. Scenes from the works of great authors

Illustrations by several artists, accompanying the text, are to be classed preferably in PA-PT; when text is secondary in importance, illustrations are to be classed in N-NK

Illustrations after the drawings or paintings of special artists are to be classed under the artist in NC, ND, or NE, as the case may be or in PA-PT under the author illustrated. In the case of authors such as Shakespeare, Dante, and Goethe classification in literature is to be preferred

Other special subjects (alphabetically)

Class here general works on the topics as well as works on the topics in a particular region, country, etc.

8217 A - Industry

8217.A3 Acrobats. Acrobatics

8217.A35 Advertising

8217.A4 Aeronautics

Afro-Americans, see N8232

8217.A47 Age groups

8217.A52 Anarchists

8217.A53 Androgyny

8217.A62 Apartheid

Architecture, see N8217.B85

8217.A67 Artists and models

Astrology, see N7745.A85

Athletics, see N8250

8217.A94 Automobiles

8217.B35 Ballet

8217.B356 Barbie dolls

8217.B36 Baseball

Battles, see N8260

8217.B37 Beard

8217.B38 Beds and bedsteads

8217.B39 Beer

8217.B4 Beggars

8217.B53 Bicycles

Blacks, see N8232

8217.B58 Bookkeeping

8217.B6 Books

8217.B7 Bread

8217.B75 Breast

8217.B85 Buildings. Architecture

8217.B86 Bullfights

Special subjects of art
Other special subjects (alphabetically)
A - Industry -- Continued

8217.B87 Butchers
8217.C24 Carriages, carts, coaches, etc. Coaching
8217.C26 Castles
Including individually named castles
8217.C28 Chess
8217.C3 Circus
8217.C35 Cities and towns
8217.C4 Clocks and watches
Clothing and dress, see N8217.C63
8217.C462 Coca Cola (Registered trademark)
see N8217.C24
8217.C464 Coffeehouses
8217.C47 Comets
8217.C475 Comic books, strips, etc.
8217.C478 Commedia dell'arte
8217.C48 Commercial products
8217.C5 Commercial travelers
8217.C6 Cookery
8217.C63 Costume. Clothing and dress
8217.C65 Country life
8217.C7 Courage
8217.C75 Cowboys
8217.C76 Cows
8217.C78 Cricket
8217.C8 Cube
8217.D3 Dance (General)
Cf. N8217.B35, Ballet
Cf. N8239.S37, Sardana
8217.D48 Deadly sins
8217.D5 Death
8217.D57 Demoniac possession
8217.D6 Dentistry
8217.D63 Deserts
8217.D67 Dinners and dining
8217.D69 Donald Duck (Cartoon character)
8217.D73 Drapery
8217.D74 Dreams
Dress, see N8217.C63
8217.D9 Dwarfs
Eagles, see N7666.E33
8217.E3 Education. Schools
Cf. N8251.S4, Students
8217.E53 Emotions
8217.E55 Entertainers
8217.E6 Erotic
8217.E75 Eskimos
8217.E88 Exoticism
8217.E9 Eye
Eyeglasses, see N8248.S7
Fabrics, see N8251.T4

Special subjects of art
Other special subjects (alphabetically)
A - Industry -- Continued

8217.F27 Family
8217.F28 Fantasy
8217.F3 Farm life
8217.F33 Fashion
8217.F4 Fencing
8217.F5 Fire
Fishing, see N8250
8217.F55 Flags
8217.F6 Flight
8217.F63 Folly
8217.F64 Food
8217.F66 Fools and jesters
8217.F67 Forge shops
8217.F68 Four elements (Philosophy)
8217.F8 Fur garments
8217.G34 Games
8217.G36 Gardens
Including individual gardens
8217.G38 Gauchos
8217.G43 Generosity
8217.G44 Geometry
8217.G6 Gold
8217.G8 Grotesque
8217.H27 Hair
8217.H3 Hand
8217.H34 Hats
8217.H5 Head
8217.H53 Heart
8217.H65 Holidays
8217.H68 Horror
8217.H78 Humanism
8217.H8 Hunger
Hunting, see N8250
8217.I5 Indians
8218 Industry
8219 Industry - Love
8219.I47 Interiors
8219.J6 Joy and sorrow
8219.K34 Kalmyks
8219.K5 Kings and rulers. Queens
8219.K57 Kissing
8219.L2 Labor. Laboring classes. Working class
8219.L26 Laughter
8219.L27 Laundresses
8219.L3 Law
Letter writing, see N8219.L43

Special subjects of art
Other special subjects (alphabetically)
Industry - Love -- Continued

8219.L4 Lettering in art
Cf. N6494.L4, Lettrism
Cf. ND1454+, Calligraphy as painting
Cf. NK3600+, Alphabets, calligraphy, initials, etc.
Cf. PN6110.C77, Concrete poetry

8219.L43 Letters. Letter writing

8219.L47 Liberty

8219.L5 Light

Lines (Drawing), see NC754

Lines (Decorative element), see NK1570

8220 Love

8222 M - Med

8222.M27 Machinery

8222.M3 Magic

8222.M35 Man, Prehistoric

8222.M37 Maoris

8222.M375 Maps

8222.M38 Masculinity

8222.M39 Masks

8222.M4 Mate (Tea)

8223 Medicine

8224 Med - Mi

8224.M44 Melancholy

8224.M47 Mickey Mouse (Cartoon character)

8224.M5 Mines and mineral resources

8224.M54 Minorities

8224.M6 Mirrors

8225 Mo - Mur

Models and artists, see N8217.A67

8225.M56 Money

Mothers, see N7630

(8225.M6) Mountains
See N8213-N8214.5

8225.M65 Mourning customs

(8226) Music and musical instruments
See ML85

8230 Naval and marine. Ships in art
Cf. VM307, Ship illustrations

8232 Negroes. Afro-Americans. Blacks

8233 Neh - Nz

8233.N48 Newspapers

8233.N6 Notaries

8234 O - Pear

8234.O24 Occupations

8234.O4 Old age

Olympic games, see N8250

8234.O8 Outer space

Owls, see N7666.O94

Parasols, see N8256

Special subjects of art
Other special subjects (alphabetically)
O - Pear -- Continued
8234.P3 Parks
Peafowl, see N7666.P43
8235 Peasants
8236 Peat - Pray
8236.P4 Physically handicapped
Including congenital abnormalities, etc.
8236.P45 Pinocchio (Fictitious character)
8236.P5 Politics
8236.P6 Potatoes
8237 Prayer
8237.5 Psychiatry
8237.53 Punchinello (Fictitious character)
8237.8 Q - R
Queens, see N8219.K5
8237.8.R3 Railroads
8237.8.R6 Rocks
8237.8.R8 Ruins
8239 S - Sc
8239.S37 Sardana
8239.S6 Scales (Weighing instruments)
Schools, see N8217.E3
8240 Sea and seaside
8241 Seasons
8241.5 Sex role
8243 Sh - So
8243.S36 Shades and shadows
8243.S4 Shells
Ships, see N8230
8243.S5 Sick
8243.S53 Skating
8243.S55 Skies
8243.S57 Skull
8243.S58 Sleep
8243.S6 Smile
Smoking, see N8253.T6
8243.S64 Soap bubbles
8243.S65 Social problems
Soldiers, see N8260
8248 Spe - Spo
8248.S7 Spectacles. Eyeglasses
8248.S74 Sphinxes
8248.S76 Spirals
8248.S77 Spirituality
8250 Sports. Hunting, fishing, etc.
Including Olympic games
Cf. NE960+, Sporting prints
8251 St - Te
8251.S25 Statue of Liberty
8251.S3 Still life
8251.S37 Streets

Special subjects of art
Other special subjects (alphabetically)
St - Te -- Continued
8251.S4 Students
8251.S57 Sugar
8251.S6 Sun
8251.T3 Tanning
8251.T37 Terezín (Czech Republic: Concentration camp)
8251.T4 Textile fabrics. Textile industry
8252 Theater
8253 Th - Tr
8253.T3 The Thinker
8253.T5 Time
8253.T6 Tobacco. Smoking
8253.T65 Tools
8253.T67 Tourist trade
8253.T68 Transportation
8253.T7 Tree of life
8254 Triumphs
8256 Umbrellas and parasols
8256.5 Underground movements
8257 Violence
8258 Voyages and travels
8260 War. Battles
Including art about specific wars or battles
Cf. N9100+, Art and war
8261 Wara - Wind
8261.W27 Water
8261.W3 Waterfronts
8261.W34 Wayang
8261.W42 Weather
8261.W5 Windmills
8261.W56 Windows
8262 Wine
8262.5 Winter
8262.7 Witchcraft
Work, working class, workers, see N8219.L2
8262.85 World
8265 Writing
8266 Youth
Art as a profession. Artists
For special countries, including special races and ethnic groups of special countries, see N6501+
8350 General works
8351 General special
8353 Economic aspects of the artist's profession
Cf. N8600, Economics of art
Psychology of the artist, see N71
Special classes of persons as artists
8354 Women
Children, see N351
Soldiers, see N8260
8355 Physically handicapped

Art as a profession
Special classes of persons as artists -- Continued
8356.A-Z Other classes, A-Z
8356.A43 Aged
8356.A9 Authors
8356.B55 Blacks
8356.M4 Mentally handicapped
Negroes, see N8356.B55
(8370-8375) Art critics and historians; historiography
See N7480-N7483
(8380-8410) Art collectors, patrons, etc.
See N5200-N5299
Art and the state, see N8700+
Art studios, materials, etc.
Cf. NB1202, Sculpture materials
Cf. NC845+, Graphic art materials
Cf. ND1500+, Painting materials
8510 General works
8520 Studios
8530 Materials
8540 Catalogs
8543 Tools
Framing of pictures
Including history of picture frames
Cf. TT380, Gilding
8550 General works
8551.A-Z By region or country, A-Z
8553 Tables, etc.
Examination and conservation of works of art
Cf. NB1199, Sculpture
Cf. NC930, Drawings
Cf. ND1630+, Paintings
Cf. NE380, Prints
8554 Periodicals. Societies
8554.5 Congresses
8554.6 Directories
8555 General works
8557 Mutilation or defacement of works of art
Cf. N8795+, Theft of art works
For works on the mutilation, defacement, etc. of art found in particular places, see N6501+
8558 Technical examination: Expertising, X-ray, micrography
8558.5 Deterioration of art works
Preservation. Cleaning. Restoration
For works on the conservation and restoration of art found in particular places, see N6501+
8560 General works
8560.5 Training of art restorers
8561.A-Z Exhibitions. Collections. By country and place of exhibition, A-Z
8563.A-Z Special. By restorer, A-Z (Table N6)

Examination and conservation of works of art -- Continued
8580 Copying and reproducing
Cf. TR657+, Photography of art objects
For forgery of works of art, see N8790+
8585 Handling
Including crating, packing, shipping, inspection, etc.
8600 Economics of art
Cf. N8353, Economic aspects of the artist's profession
8601 Art previews
Art auctions. Auctioneers
8602 General works
By region or country
United States
8603 General works
8603.5.A-Z Local, A-Z
8604.A-Z Individual auctioneers, firms, families, A-Z
8605.A-Z Other regions or countries, A-Z
Under each country:
.x *General works*
.x2A-.x2Z *Individual auctioneers, firms, families, A-Z*
Art dealers
8610 Periodicals and societies
8620 General works
8630 Directories
Catalogs
8640.A-Z General. By dealer, A-Z
8650.A-Z Special auction sales. By dealer, A-Z
Prefer classification of catalogs of auctions of single private collections in N5210-N5299
Exhibitions (by place held)
8655.A-Z United States. By city and museum or other place of exhibition, A-Z
8655.5.A-Z Other countries. By country and city, A-Z
Biography of art dealers
8659 Collective
8660.A-Z Individual, A-Z
8665 Sidewalk art exhibitions
Prices of paintings, prints, etc.
Prefer classification by medium, subject, period, or nationality
Cf. ND46+, Paintings
Cf. NE85, Prints
8670 Periodicals. Annuals, etc.
8675 General works

Art and the state. Public art
Cf. GT3980+, Public rejoicing, pageants, etc.
Cf. GT5010+, Ceremonies of royalty, etc.
Cf. N7429.3, Dissident art
Cf. NA100+, Architecture and the state
Cf. NX720+, Governmental patronage of the arts
Cf. SB469+, Landscape gardening, parks
Art and the state
8700 Periodicals
8710 Societies. Commissions
8720 Congresses
8725 General works
8740 Art censorship
Protection and cultivation of art
8750 General works
Legal protection of art
(8770) Legislation and tariffs
See class K
Copyright
See class K
Forgeries
8790 General works
8791.A-Z Special, by forger or work of art, A-Z
Theft of works of art
Cf. N8557, Mutilation of works of art
8795 General works
8795.3.A-Z By region or country, A-Z
8795.5.A-Z Special. By thief or detective, A-Z
For theft of individual works of art, see the work of art
Corporate and private patronage of art, see N5205+
8798 Cooperation between private and government agencies in the support of art
Government support of art. Public art
8825 General works
8830 General special
Special countries
United States
8835 General works
8836.A-Z By region or state, A-Z
Federal aid to art
8837 General works
For texts of specific bills, See class K
8838 Special programs
e.g. the Federal Art Project
State aid to art
8840 General works
8842.A-W Special projects. By state, A-W
Municipal (or other local) projects
8844 General works
8845.A-Z Special. By city (or place), A-Z
8846.A-Z Other countries, A-Z

Art and the state. Public art
Protection and cultivation of art -- Continued
Preservation of monuments. Conservation of artistic resources
Prefer CC135 CC137 for historic monuments, landmarks
Cf. N9100+, Preservation of monuments in wartime
Cf. NA105+, Preservation and restoration of architectural monuments
Cf. NA9000+, City planning

8849 Periodicals. Societies. Congresses. Collections
8850 General works
8860 General special
8901-9085 Special countries (Table N2)
Add country number in table to N8900

Art and war. Protection of monuments and art works during wartime. Lost works of art
For war as a subject of art, see N8260

9100 General works
9103 General special
Biography
9110.A1 Collective
9110.A2-Z Individual, A-Z
Special
Wars before 1900
9111 General works
9114 Antiquity, through 5th century A.D.
9115 6th-10th centuries
9120 11th-15th centuries
9125 16th century
9130 17th century
9135 18th century
9140 19th century
20th century
9145 General works
World War I, 1914-1918
9150 General works
9152.A-Z Exhibitions. By country and city, A-Z
9155.A-Z Special countries, A-Z
Prefer N5312 N7413 where emphasis is on indigenous art of the country
World War II, 1939-1945
9160 General works
9162.A-Z Exhibitions. By country and city, A-Z
9165.A-Z Special countries, A-Z
Prefer N5312 N7413 where emphasis is on indigenous art of the country

Folk art, see N5312+
(9201) Periodicals. Societies. Congresses. Collections
see N5312
(9211) General works
see N5313

	Architecture
	Periodicals
1.A1	Polyglot
1.A12-Z	American and English
2	French
3	German
4	Italian
4.5	Slavic
5	Spanish and Portuguese
6.A-Z	Other, A-Z
9	Yearbooks
	Societies
10	General works
11	American
12	English
13	French and Belgian
14	German, Austrian, and Swiss
15	Italian
16	Spanish and Portuguese
17.A-Z	Other, A-Z
21	Congresses
	Collected writings
25	Several authors
27	Individual authors
31	Encyclopedias, dictionaries, glossaries, etc.
40	Biography (Collective)
	For biography of classical Greek architects, see NA290.A+
	For biography of classical Roman architects, see NA340.A+
	For biography of special countries and special architects, see NA701+
	Directories
	Cf. TA12, Directories of engineering companies and engineers
	Cf. TH12+, Directories of building supply companies, builders, contractors
50	General
	United States
53	General
54.A-W	By state, A-W
55.A-Z	By city, A-Z
60.A-Z	Other countries, A-Z
65	Tours
	For tours of a special place, see NA701+
	Museums, see NA2400+
	Exhibitions, see NA2430+
	Architecture and the state
	Cf. NA4170+, Public buildings
	Cf. NA9050.5, Public architecture
100	General works

Architecture and the state -- Continued
104 Mutilation or defacement of architectural monuments
For works on mutilation, defacement, etc. of architecture found in particular places, see NA701+
Preservation and restoration of architectural monuments
Cf. N9100+, Protection of monuments and art works during wartime
Cf. NA9053.C6, City planning
Cf. TH3301+, Maintenance and repair of buildings
105 General works
United States
106 General works
107.A-W By state, A-W
108.A-Z By city, A-Z
109.A-Z Other regions or countries, A-Z
109.4.A-Z Special. By restorer, A-Z (Table N6)
110 Business community participation
111 Economic aspects
112 Study and teaching. Research
Examination and licensing of architects
120 General works
United States
123 General works
124.A-W By state, A-W
125.A-Z By city, A-Z
130.A-Z Other countries, A-Z
(135-150) Architects and the law
See class K
History
Including historical monuments treated from the architectural point of view
190 Historiography
200 General works
201 Folios
202 Pictorial works (with little or no text)
203 General special
203.3 Functionalism in architecture (General)
For functionalism as a special movement in the 20th century, see NA682.F8
203.5 Intercultural relations in architecture (General)
204 Handbooks of architectural styles
Cf. NA2810+, Orders of architecture
Primitive
Cf. GN413+, Ethnology
205 General works
(207) Primitive American architecture
See classes E-F

History -- Continued

208 Vernacular architecture

For works on the domestic vernacular architecture of a special place, see NA7201+

For works on the vernacular architecture of a special place, see NA701+

For works on the vernacular architecture of special types of buildings of a special place, see NA8200+

208.5 Grotesque in architecture

209 Lost architecture

For works on the lost architecture of a special place, see NA701+

For works on the lost domestic architecture of a special place, see NA7201+

Ancient architecture

210 General works

211 Folios

212 Middle East

Egypt

215 General works

216.A-Z Local, A-Z

Chaldea. Babylonia. Assyria

220 General works

221.A-Z Local, A-Z

Hittite Empire

223 General works

223.5.A-Z Local, A-Z

Persia

225 General works

226.A-Z Local, A-Z

Phoenicia. Cyprus. Carthaginia. Sardinia

230 General works

231.A-Z Local, A-Z

Judea. Syria

240 General works

243 Temple of Jerusalem. Solomon's Temple

245.A-Z Other special. By place, A-Z

Asia Minor

250 General works

251.A-Z Local, A-Z

For Greek cities (Ephesus, Halicarnassus, Pergamum, etc.), see NA285.A+

252.A-Z Other ancient, A-Z

252.D32 Dacia

Classical. Greek and Roman

260 General works

261 Folios

265 Pelasgic. "Cyclopean"

267 Minoan

Greek

270 General works

271 Folios

History
Ancient architecture
Classical. Greek and Roman
Greek -- Continued
Special classes of buildings and structures
Prefer classification by place NA279 NA285
274 Altars
275 Temples
277 Dwellings
Including houses, palaces, etc.
278.A-Z Others, A-Z
278.P6 Political meeting places
278.P78 Prytaneums
278.S85 Stoas
278.T5 Theaters
279.A-Z Special divisions, islands, etc., A-Z
e.g.
279.A8 Asia Minor
279.L5 Lesbos
279.M3 Magna Graecia
Special cities, towns, etc.
Including the Greek cities of Ionia, Magna Graecia, etc.
Athens
280 General works
281 Parthenon
283.A-Z Other special buildings, A-Z
283.A25 Acropolis
283.A27 Agora
283.E7 Erectheum
283.P76 Propylaea
283.T35 Temple of Athena Nike
285.A-Z Other, A-Z
e.g.
285.E6 Ephesus
285.H3 Halicarnassus
285.P3 Paestum
285.P4 Pergamum
290.A-Z Special architects, A-Z
e.g.
290.M5 Mnesicles
Ancient Italy
295 General works
300 Etruscan
301.A-Z Local, A-Z
Roman
Including the city of Rome
310 General works
311 Folios
312 Forums
Special classes of buildings and structures
Prefer classification by place (including individual buildings) NA327 NA335

History
Ancient architecture
Classical. Greek and Roman
Ancient Italy
Roman
Special classes of buildings and structures -- Continued
313 Ampitheaters. The Colosseum
(315) Arches, Memorial and triumphal
See NA9370.R6
317 Baths
320 Palaces
323 Temples
324 Villas
Cf. DG97, Roman antiquities
325.A-Z Others, A-Z
325.C7 Cryptoportici
325.G9 Gymnasiums
325.P64 Political meeting places
325.T5 Theaters
327.A-Z Special Italian cities, A-Z
e.g.
327.P6 Pompeii
Rome, see NA310+
335.A-Z Cities, divisions, islands outside of Italy, A-Z
e.g.
335.B2 Baalbec
335.L5 Libya
335.N5 Nîmes
335.P2 Palmyra
340.A-Z Special architects, A-Z
e.g.
340.V5 Vitruvius
Medieval architecture
Prefer classification by country
350 General works
351 Folios
Early Christian
360 General works
361 Folios
365 Carolingian architecture
Byzantine
370 General works
371 Folios
373 Modern designs in Byzantine style
Islamic architecture. Moorish architecture
Cf. NA4670, Mosques
380 General works
381 Folios
Moors in Spain
385 General works
386 Folios

History
Medieval architecture
Islamic architecture. Moorish architecture
Moors in Spain -- Continued
387 Alhambra
Other special countries, see NA701+
Buildings in Moorish style in non-Islamic countries
388.A2 General works
388.A3-Z Special, A-Z
388.W5 Wilhelma
Romanesque architecture
390 General works
391 Folios
Special countries, see NA701+
Norman architecture
423 General works
(425) Normandy
See NA1049
(427) Italy, Sicily
See NA1113, NA1119
(429) England
See NA963
Gothic architecture
For Gothic revival (18th and 19th centuries), see NA610
440 General works
441 Folios
(445) Great Britain, English Gothic
See NA963
447 Continental Gothic. General works
For special countries, see NA1003-NA1455
Gothic details
480 General works
Gothic arch and vault, keystones, see NA440+
483 Windows and window traceries
485 Moldings
487 Ornament
489 Other (not A-Z)
Military architecture
Cf. UG400+, Military engineering
490 General works
City walls and gates
493 General works
495 Gateways
Towers, see NA2930
497.A-Z Special countries, A-Z
499 Ottoman architecture outside of Turkey
For Turkey, see NA1361+

History -- Continued
Modern architecture
Class architectural movements identified with one country and largely one century under the country in NA701-NA1613
Prefer classification by country
500 General works
Renaissance. 16th century
510 General works
512.A-Z Special aspects or movements, A-Z
Special countries, see NA701+
590 Baroque. Rococo
595 Exoticism (General)
600 Neoclassicism (Greek and Roman revival)
603 Egyptian revival (General)
610 Gothic revival
(620) Tudor
See NA965
(625) Elizabethan
See NA965
18th century
627 General works
Gothic revival (18th and 19th centuries), see NA610
Greek and Roman revival, see NA600
630 Queen Anne (18th and 19th centuries)
Cf. NA707, United States (18th cent.)
Cf. NA710+, United States (19th cent.)
Cf. NA710, United States (19th cent.)
Cf. NA966+, Great Britain
640 Georgian
Cf. NA707, United States (18th cent.)
Cf. NA966+, Great Britain
American "Colonial", see NA707
642 19th and 20th centuries
19th century
645 General works
645.5.A-Z Special aspects or movements, A-Z
Divide like N6465
(650) Greek and Roman revival
See NA600
Egyptian revival, see NA710.5.E48
660 Swiss. Timber
670 Romanesque revival
For American Romanesque revival, see NA710.5.R65
20th century
673 Periodicals
680 General works
682.A-Z Special aspects or movements, A-Z
682.A78 Art deco architecture
682.B7 Brutalism
682.C65 Constructivism
682.D43 Deconstructivism

History
Modern architecture
19th and 20th centuries
20th century
Special aspects
or movements, A-Z -- Continued
682.E9 Expressionism
682.F8 Functionalism
682.I58 International style
682.O73 Organic architecture
682.P67 Postmodern architecture
682.S62 Socialist realism
682.T43 Team 10
701-1614 Architecture of special countries (Table N5 modified)
Including historical works discussing buildings of special materials located in special countries
In the application of Table 5 for "Special artists" read "Special architects, families and firms"
Establish special movements identified with one country and largely one century by adding .5 to the appropriate century number where possible and arranging movements alphabetically
Add country number in table to NA700
For special details and decorations, see NA2835+
For special details and decorations in special materials, see NA3680+
For technical works on design problems in special materials, including such problems when they pertain to special countries, see NA4100+
For ancient period prefer NA215-NA340
America
Latin America
20th century
702.5 General works
702.57.A-Z Special aspects or movements, A-Z
702.57.C64 Colonial revival
United States
707 Colonial period; 18th (and early 19th) century
19th century
710 General works
710.5.A-Z Special aspects or movements, A-Z
710.5.E25 Eclecticism
710.5.E48 Egyptian revival
710.5.G73 Greek revival
710.5.R65 Romanesque revival
710.5.V5 Victorian architecture
20th century
712 General works
712.5.A-Z Special aspects or movements, A-Z
Including regional movements
712.5.C48 Chicago Seven (Group of architects)
712.5.C55 Classicism (Late)
712.5.I57 International style

History
Architecture of special countries
America
United States
20th century
Special aspects
or movements, A-Z -- Continued
712.5.P67 Postmodern architecture
712.5.P73 Prairie school (Architecture)
Canada
19th century
744 General works
744.5.A-Z Special aspects or movements, A-Z
744.5.G67 Gothic revival
744.5.Q44 Queen Anne revival
South America
Brazil
19th century
854 General works
854.5.A-Z Special aspects or movements, A-Z
854.5.E26 Eclecticism
Chile
20th century
865 General works
865.5.A-Z Special aspects or movements, A-Z
865.5.I58 International style
Europe
Modern
19th century
957 General works
957.5.A-Z Special aspects or movements, A-Z
957.5.A78 Art nouveau architecture
957.5.E35 Egyptian revival
20th century
958 General works
958.5.A-Z Special aspects or movements, A-Z
958.5.E93 Expressionism
958.5.I58 International style
Special countries
Great Britain. England
Modern
17th-18th centuries
966 General works
966.5.A-Z Special aspects or movements, A-Z
966.5.G45 Georgian
966.5.G66 Gothic revival
966.5.N4 Neoclassicism
19th century
967 General works
967.5.A-Z Special aspects or movements, A-Z
967.5.G68 Gothic revival
967.5.V53 Victorian
20th century

History
Architecture of special countries
Europe
Special countries
Great Britain. England
Modern
20th century -- Continued
968 General works
968.5.A-Z Special aspects or movements, A-Z
968.5.E38 Edwardian
968.5.I58 International style
968.5.M68 Modern Architectural Research Group
Austria
Modern
20th century
1008 General works
1008.5.A-Z Special aspects or movements, A-Z
1008.5.C65 Coop Himmelblau (Group of architects)
Hungary
Modern
19th century
1019 General works
1019.5.A-Z Special aspects or movements, A-Z
1019.5.N45 Neoclassicism (Late)
Czechoslovakia. Czech Republic
Modern
17th-18th centuries
1029 General works
1029.5.A-Z Special aspects or movements, A-Z
1029.5.B35 Baroque
20th century
1031 General works
1031.5.A-Z Special aspects or movements, A-Z
1031.5.C83 Cubism
1031.5.F85 Functionalism
France
Modern
17th-18th centuries
1046 General works
1046.5.A-Z Special aspects or movements, A-Z
1046.5.N4 Neoclassicism
20th century
1048 General works
1048.5.A-Z Special aspects or movements, A-Z
1048.5.F85 Functionalism
1053.A-Z Special architects, A-Z
e.g.
1053.J4 Jeanneret-Gris, Charles Edouard, 1887-1965
Le Corbusier, 1887-1965, see NA1053.J4
Germany
Modern
17th-18th centuries
1066 General works

History
Architecture of special countries
Europe
Special countries
Germany
Modern
17th-18th centuries -- Continued
1066.5.A-Z Special aspects or movements, A-Z
1066.5.N46 Neoclassicism
19th century
1067 General works
1067.5.A-Z Special aspects or movements, A-Z
1067.5.N44 Neoclassicism (Late)
20th century
1068 General works
1068.5.A-Z Special aspects or movements, A-Z
1068.5.N37 National socialism
Italy
Modern
19th century
1117 General works
1117.5.A-Z Special aspects or movements, A-Z
1117.5.A7 Art nouveau
20th century
1118 General works
1118.5.A-Z Special aspects or movements, A-Z
1118.5.F7 Functionalism
1118.5.F87 Futurism
1118.5.G77 Gruppo romano architetti urbanisti
1118.5.S19 Gruppo S (Organization)
1118.5.S48 Gruppo 7 (Group of architects)
1118.5.S96 Superstudio (Group of architects)
1121.A-Z Other special cities, A-Z
e.g.
1121.V4 Venice
1123.A-Z Special architects, A-Z
e.g.
1123.B9 Buonarroti, Michel Angelo, 1475-1564
Michelangelo Buonarroti, 1475-1564, see NA1123.B9
Low countries
Holland (Netherlands)
Modern
19th century
1147 General works
1147.5.A-Z Special aspects or movements, A-Z
1147.5.A78 Art nouveau
20th century
1148 General works
1148.5.A-Z Special aspects or movements, A-Z
1148.5.A4 Amsterdamse school
1148.5.D42 De Stijl. Neoplasticism
1148.5.F86 Functionalism

History
Architecture of special countries
Europe
Special countries
Low countries
Holland (Netherlands)
Modern
20th century
Special aspects or movements, A-Z -- Continued
Stijl, De. Neoplasticism, see NA1148.5.D42
Belgium
Modern
19th century
1167 General works
1167.5.A-Z Special aspects or movements, A-Z
1167.5.A77 Art nouveau
1167.5.G67 Gothic revival
Russia
Modern
20th century
1188 General works
1188.5.A-Z Special aspects or movements, A-Z
1188.5.C64 Constructivism
Scandinavia
Modern
20th century
1208 General works
1208.5.A-Z Special aspects or movements, A-Z
1208.5.C55 Classicism
1208.5.F86 Functionalism
Denmark
Modern
19th century
1217 General works
1217.5.A-Z Special aspects or movements, A-Z
1217.5.N44 Neoclassicism (Late)
20th century
1218 General works
1218.5.A-Z Special aspects or movements, A-Z
1218.5.C53 Classicism (Late)
1218.5.P67 Postmodern architecture
Norway
Modern
20th century
1268 General works
1268.5.A-Z Special aspects or movements, A-Z
1268.5.P67 Postmodern architecture
Sweden
Modern
17th-18th centuries
1286 General works

History
Architecture of special countries
Europe
Special countries
Scandinavia
Sweden
Modern
17th-18th centuries -- Continued
1286.5.A-Z Special aspects or movements, A-Z
1286.5.C55 Classicism
20th century
1288 General works
1288.5.A-Z Special aspects or movements, A-Z
1288.5.F85 Functionalism
Switzerland
Modern
20th century
1348 General works
1348.5.A-Z Special aspects or movements, A-Z
1348.5.A72 ARCHICO (Association)
1348.5.C65 Constructivism
1361-1373.3 Turkey
Asia
Eastern Asia. China, Japan, etc.
Japan
20th century
1555 General works
1555.5.A-Z Special aspects or movements, A-Z
1555.5.P66 Postmodern architecture
1995 Architecture as a profession
1996 Business management for architects
1996.5 Data processing
The architect in legal relations
See class K
1997 Women architects
Study and teaching. Research
2000 General works
2005 General special
2101-2285 Special countries (Table N2)
Add country number in table to NA2100
Special schools
United States
2300.A-Z Special schools. By name, A-Z
Correspondence schools
2303 General works
2304.A-Z Special schools. By name, A-Z
2305.A-Z Other American. By country and school, A-Z
2310.A-Z Europe. By country and school, A-Z
2320.A-Z Other countries. By country and school, A-Z
Competitions
Including individual awards, prizes, etc.
2335 General and international
2340 United States

Competitions -- Continued
2345.A-Z Other American. By country, A-Z
Europe
2349 General works
2350.A-Z Special regions or countries, A-Z
2360.A-Z Other countries. By country, A-Z
Museums
2400.A-Z United States. By city and museum, A-Z
2405.A-Z Other American. By country and city, A-Z
2410.A-Z Europe. By country and city, A-Z
2420.A-Z Other countries. By country and city, A-Z
Exhibitions. By place
(2430) International
See NA2440-NA2460
Local
2440.A-Z United States. By city and gallery or other place of exhibition, A-Z
2445.A-Z Other American. By country and city, A-Z
Europe
2449 General works
2450.A-Z Special regions or countries, A-Z
2460.A-Z Other. By country and city, A-Z
General works
2500 Theory. Philosophy
Including aesthetics, architectonics, classification, semiotics
Cf. NA2760, Design
2510 Comprehensive works
2515 Early works to 1800
(2516) Quartos
2517 Folios
2520 1800-
(2521) Quartos
2522 Folios
2530 Outlines, syllabi, etc.
2540 General special
Including hints for architects, orientation, etc.
2540.5 Site planning
Architecture in relation to special subjects
Class here general works on the topics as well as the topics in a particular region, country, etc.
2541 Climate and architecture
2542.A-Z Special topics, A-Z
2542.A72 Arctic regions
2542.A73 Arid regions
2542.C75 Cold regions
2542.S6 Solar radiation
2542.T7 Tropics
2542.3 Energy conservation and architecture
Cf. TH6031, Environmental engineering systems
2542.35 Environmental aspects of architecture

Architecture in relation to special subjects -- Continued
2542.4 Human factors and architecture
Cf. NA6231.5, Psychological aspects of tall buildings
2542.7 Underground architecture
2542.8 Water and architecture
2543.A-Z Architecture in relation to other subjects, A-Z
Artist-architect collaboration, see N72.A75
Children, see NA2543.Y6
2543.H55 History
Leisure and architecture, see NA2543.R43
2543.M37 Mass media and architecture
2543.P4 Pedestrian traffic pattern inside buildings
Cf. NA9074, Pedestrian areas
Philosophy, see NA2500
2543.R43 Recreation and architecture
2543.S6 Society. Culture
2543.T43 Technology
2543.W65 Women
Cf. NA1997, Women architects
2543.Y6 Youth. Children
Architecture and the handicapped
2545.A1 General works
2545.A2-Z By special group, A-Z
2545.A3 Aged
Aged, Mentally handicapped, see NA2545.M4
Blind, see NA2545.V57
2545.C48 Children, Handicapped
Handicapped children, see NA2545.C48
2545.M4 Mentally handicapped
2545.P5 Physically handicapped
Physically handicapped students, see NA2545.S85
2545.S85 Students, Physically handicapped
2545.V57 Visually handicapped. Blind
2550 Works for general readers
Including Poetry of architecture, Seven lamps of architecture, etc.
2555 Juvenile works
Addresses, essays, lectures
2560 Collective
2563 Single
(2570) Business management for architects
See NA1996
Communication of information
2584 General works
2586 Information services
2588 Architecture and motion pictures
2590 Tables, pocketbooks, etc.
Cf. TH151, Building construction
2595 Miscellaneous maxims, etc.
Quotations, see PN6084.A75
2597 Anecdotes and curiosities of architecture and architects

2599 Facetiae, satire, etc.

Architectural criticism

2599.5 General works

Biography of architectural critics and historians

2599.7 Collective

2599.8.A-Z Individual, A-Z

2599.9 Book reviews

(2600-2635) Atlases, collections of plans, architectural sketchbooks, etc.

See NA205-NA2284, History of architecture, and NA4100-NA8480, Special classes of buildings

(2640-2645) Specifications

For engineering, see TA180, for general building specifications, see TH425, for special buildings, class with the building in classes NA, RA, TH, etc.

Architectural drawing

2695.A-Z Exhibitions. Collections. Museums. By country and collector or place of exhibition, A-Z

General works

2699 Early works through 1800

2700 1801-

2705 General special

2706.A-Z By region or country, A-Z

2707.A-Z Special artists, A-Z

e.g.

2707.B78 Buonarroti, Michel Angelo, 1475-1564

Michelangelo Buonarroti, 1475-1564, see NA2707.B78

Technique

Cf. NC730+, Drawing technique

2708 General works

2710 Perspective

Cf. NC748+, Graphic arts technique

Cf. T369, Mechanical drawing

2712 Measured drawing

2713 Working drawings

2714 Presentation drawings

2715 Shades and shadows

2718 Detailing

2725 Lettering

Cf. T371, Mechanical drawing

2726 Airbrushing

2726.3 Markers

2726.5 Watercolor

2728 Data processing

Class here works on data processing dealing with architecture including architectural drawing

Architectural design

2750 General works

Data processing, see NA2728

2760 Composition. Proportion

2765 Space

2770 Plan

Architectural design -- Continued
2775 Elevation
2780 Rendering in color, pen and ink, etc.
For special artists, see NA2707.A+
2790 Models and modeling
2793 Remodeling buildings for other use (General)
For remodeling of particular types of buildings, see NA4170+
For technical works on remodeling, see TH3401+
2794 Daylighting
2795 Color in architecture. Polychromy (General)
Including use of specific colors
For special centuries not limited to one country, see NA3330-NA3485
For special countries, see NA3501+
2796 Mirrors in architecture
2797 Photogrammetry in architecture
2800 Architectural acoustics
Orders of architecture
2810 Early work
2812 Folios
2815 Works since 1800
2817 Folios
Architectural details, motives, etc.
Class here works on special regions or countries
Cf. TH2025+, Building construction
2835 Periodicals
2840 General and miscellaneous
2841 Folios
Interiors
2850 General works
2851 Folios
2853 Entrances. Hallways
2856 Offices
For interior decoration, see NK2195.O4
Piers. Columns
2860 General works
2870 Capitals
2873 Bases
2875 Plinths. Socles
2880 Apses. Arches. Crypts. Vaults. Keystones
For Gothic arches and vaults, including keystones, see NA440+
2890 Domes
2900 Roofs
2910 Roof decoration (External)
2920 Gables. Pediments. Acroteria
2930 Towers. Spires
Including individual towers, such as the Eiffel Tower in Paris
Walls
2940 General works
2942 Niches

Architectural details, motives, etc. -- Continued
2950 Ceilings
2960 Moldings. Cornices. Corbels. Ancones
Cf. NA485, Gothic moldings
Cf. NK2120, Decoration
2965 Friezes
Cf. NK2120, Decoration
2970 Floors
Tiles
Cf. NA3750+, Mosaics
2980 General works
2985 Catalogs
Gateways and portes cochères, see NA8385
Doors and windows
Cf. NK2121, Decoration
3000 General works
3008 Awnings. Canopies. Marquees
3010 Doors and doorways
3020 Windows
Cf. NA483, Gothic windows
3030 Grilles. Fanlights
3040 Ornamental chimneys
Chimneypieces. Firebacks. Fireplaces. Mantels
3050 General works
3055 Catalogs
3060 Stairs. Balustrades
3070 Balconies. Galleries. Porches
Architectural metalwork (Decoration), see NA3940+
Architectural metalwork (Construction), see TH1651+
Architectural papier mâché, staff composition, see TH1550
Architectural decoration
Prefer classification by material
Cf. Class NK, Decoration and ornament
3310 Early works to 1800
3320 General works, 1801-
3321 Folios
Ancient
3330 General works
3331 Folios
3335 Egyptian
Classical
3340 General works
3341 Folios
3350 Greek
Roman
3360 General works
3370 Pompeian
Medieval
3390 General works
3391 Folios
3400 Early Christian
3410 Byzantine

Architectural decoration
Medieval -- Continued
3420 Romanesque
Gothic, see NA487
Modern
3450 General works
3460 Renaissance. 16th century
3461 Folios
3463 Baroque. Rococo
3465 Neoclassicism (Greek and Roman revival)
3467 18th century
3469 19th century
3470 Romanesque revival
3480 Gothic revival
3485 20th century
3501-3596.3 Special countries (Table N1)
Add country number in table to NA3500
Under each (1-number or decimal number countries):
.A1 *General works*
.A3A-.A3Z *Special regions, provinces, etc., A-Z*
.A5-.Z *Special cities, A-Z*
Under each (Cutter-number countries):
.x *General*
.x2A-.x2Z *Special cities, A-Z*
Painted decoration (Color use), see NA2795
Painted decoration (Architectural decoration), see ND1410+
Painted decoration (Decorative arts), see NK1+
Decoration in relief. Sculptured decoration
Cf. NB1137, Sculpture and architecture
For special countries, see NA3501+
3680 General works
3683.A-Z Special topics, A-Z
3683.A6 Animals
3683.C3 Caryatids
3683.G37 Gargoyles
3683.P5 Plants
3686 Catalogs
3690 Decorative plaster. Stucco
3695 Concrete
3696 Plastics
3700 Terra cotta
3703 Pressed brick
3705 Tiles (Floor and wall. Roof)
3710 Incrustation. Veneering
Paperhanging, see NK3375+, TH8441
Mosaic. Tesselated work. Terrazzo work
3750 General works
3752 Deterioration of mosaics
3752.5 Conservation and restoration of mosaics
3755.A-Z Museums. Collections. Exhibitions. By city and museum or collector, A-Z
Ancient

Architectural decoration
Mosaic. Tesselated work. Terrazzo work
Ancient -- Continued
3760 General works
3765 Greek
3770 Roman. Pompeian
Including individual mosaics and copies of individual mosaics
3780 Early Christian. Byzantine
Medieval
3788 General works
3790 Italian
3792.A-Z Other, A-Z
3792.N67 Norman
Modern
3810 General works
3820 Italian
3840 American and English
3850.A-Z Other, A-Z
3850.G3 German
3850.I5 Indic
3860.A-Z Special artists, A-Z
Stained glass, see NK5300+
3900 Woodwork
Cf. NK9600+, Decoration and ornament
Cf. TH1151+, Building construction
Metalwork
3940 General works
3950 Ironwork
Cf. NK8200+, Decoration and ornament
Cf. TH1651+, Building construction
3960.A-Z Other metals, A-Z
4010 Fixed furniture. Miscellaneous accessories
4050.A-Z Other, A-Z
4050.I5 Inscriptions
4050.N44 Neon lighting
Special classes of buildings
Classed by material
Class here technical works on design problems in special materials, including such problems when they pertain to special countries
For historical works discussing buildings of special materials located in special countries, see NA701+, General architecture; NA5201+, Religious architecture; NA7201+, Domestic architecture, etc.
Cf. NA7100+, Domestic architecture
Cf. TH1000+, Systems of building construction
4100 General works
4110 Wood
4115 Half-timbered
Masonry
4119 General works

Special classes of buildings
Classed by material
Masonry -- Continued
4120 Brick and tile
4125 Concrete
4130 Stone
4135 Iron and steel
4138 Aluminum
4140 Glass
4145.A-Z Other, A-Z
4145.A35 Adobe
Classed by form
4150 Basilicas
4160 Other special forms (not A-Z)
Classed by use
Including works on remodeling particular types of buildings for other use
Public buildings
4170 General works
4177 Multipurpose buildings
International
4180 General works
4183 League of Nations buildings
4184 United Nations buildings
4184.2 Unesco buildings
4185 Hague. Palace of Peace
4193 Pan American Union
4193.5 Soviet ėkonomicheskoĭ vzaimopomoshchi (Council for Mutual Economic Aid)
National, state, municipal, etc. Government buildings
Including documents of architectural departments
4201-4385 Special countries (Table N2)
Add country number in table to NA4200
Capitols. Parliament buildings
4410 General works
4411 United States
4412.A-W States, A-W
4413.A-Z Cities, A-Z
4415.A-Z Other countries, A-Z
Under each country:
.x General
.x2A-.x2Z Local, A-Z
Specifications
4416.A-Z United States. By city, A-Z
4417.A-Z Other countries. By country and city, A-Z
4420-4427 Government offices and bureaus. Prefectures, etc.
4420 General works
4421 United States
4422.A-W States, A-W
4423.A-Z United States government offices in special cities, A-Z

Special classes of buildings
Classed by use
Public buildings
National, state, municipal, etc. Government buildings
Government offices and bureaus. Prefectures, etc. -- Continued

4425.A-Z Other countries, A-Z
Apply table at NA4415.A-Z
Specifications
4426.A-Z United States. By city, A-Z
4427.A-Z Other countries. By country and city, A-Z
County buildings
Cf. NA4470+, Courthouses
4428 United States
4429.A-Z Other countries, A-Z
City halls. Townhalls
4430 General works
4431 United States
4432.A-W States, A-W
4433.A-Z Cities, A-Z
4435.A-Z Other countries, A-Z
Apply table at NA4415.A-Z
Great Britain
4435.G72A-Z Local, A-Z
4435.G72L6 London. Guildhall
Specifications
4436.A-Z United States. By city, A-Z
4437.A-Z Other countries. By country and city, A-Z
Official residences. Embassies
Cf. NA7710+, Palaces
4440 General works
4441 United States
4442.A-W States, A-W
4443.A-Z Cities, A-Z
e.g.
4443.W3 Washington (D.C.)
Including works on the White House and works on embassies
4445.A-Z Other countries, A-Z
Apply table at NA4415.A-Z
Specifications
4446.A-Z United States. By city, A-Z
4447.A-Z Other countries. By country and city, A-Z
Post offices
4450 General works
4451 United States
4452.A-W States, A-W
4453.A-Z Cities, A-Z
4455.A-Z Other countries, A-Z
Apply table at NA4415.A-Z
Specifications
4456.A-Z United States. By city, A-Z

Special classes of buildings
Classed by use
Public buildings
National, state, municipal, etc. Government buildings
Post offices
Specifications -- Continued
4457.A-Z Other countries. By country and city, A-Z
Customhouses
4460 General works
4461 United States
4462.A-W States, A-W
4463.A-Z Cities, A-Z
4465.A-Z Other countries, A-Z
Apply table at NA4415.A-Z
Specifications
4466.A-Z United States. By city, A-Z
4467.A-Z Other countries. By country and city, A-Z
Courthouses
4470 General works
4471 United States
4472.A-W States, A-W
4473.A-Z Cities, A-Z
4475.A-Z Other countries, A-Z
Apply table at NA4415.A-Z
Specifications
4476.A-Z United States. By city, A-Z
4477.A-Z Other countries. By country and city, A-Z
Prisons, see HV8805+
Armories, barracks, etc.
Cf. UC405.A+, Maintenance
4480 General works
4481 United States
4482.A-W States, A-W
4483.A-Z Cities, A-Z
4485.A-Z Other countries, A-Z
Apply table at NA4415.A-Z
Specifications
4486.A-Z United States. By city, A-Z
4487.A-Z Other countries. By country and city, A-Z
Police stations
4490 General works
4491 United States
4492.A-W States, A-W
4493.A-Z Cities, A-Z
4495.A-Z Other countries, A-Z
Apply table at NA4415.A-Z
Specifications
4496.A-Z United States. By city, A-Z
4497.A-Z Other countries. By country and city, A-Z
Fire stations
4500 General works
4501 United States

Special classes of buildings
Classed by use
Public buildings
National, state, municipal, etc. Government buildings
Fire stations
United States -- Continued
4502.A-W States, A-W
4503.A-Z Cities, A-Z
4505.A-Z Other countries, A-Z
Apply table at NA4415.A-Z
Specifications
4506.A-Z United States. By city, A-Z
4507.A-Z Other countries. By country and city, A-Z
4510.A-Z Other classes of buildings, A-Z
Almshouses, see NA6760+
Auditoriums, see NA6815
4510.C7 Community centers
4510.E7 Executive mansions
4510.F6 Forest department buildings
Hospitals, see RA967
4510.I6 Immigration stations
Libraries, see Z679+
4510.M5 Mints
Municipal auditoriums, see NA6815
4510.Q2 Quarantine stations
4510.R4 Refugees' camps, barracks, etc.
School buildings, see LB3201+
4510.V5 Visitors' centers
4510.W6 Weather bureau buildings
Religious buildings. Religious architecture
4590 Periodicals
4595 Congresses
4600 General works
4601 Folios
4605 Liturgy and architecture
Non-Christian
For special countries and special buildings, see NA5201+
4610 General works
Temples
Cf. NA215+, Egyptian temples
Cf. NA243, Temple of Jerusalem
Cf. NA275, Greek temples
Cf. NA323, Roman temples
4620 General works
4621 Folios
Rock temples. Cave temples
4640 General works
4641 Folios
4670 Mosques
4690 Synagogues
4710 Bahai temples

Special classes of buildings
Classed by use
Public buildings
Religious buildings.
Religious architecture -- Continued
Christian architecture
4790 Periodicals and societies
4795 Congresses
Dictionaries, see NA31
4800 General works
Including history, architectural symbolism, etc.
For symbolism of church art in general, see N8010+
4801 Folios
Plans and designs
4810 General works
4811 Folios
4813 Specifications
4815 Great churches of the world (General)
History
4817 Early Christian
Medieval
See NA5453
Renaissance
See NA5455
4823 17th and 18th centuries
4824 19th century
4825 20th century
4827 Interdenominational churches
Individual denominations
4828 Roman Catholic (General, Benedictine, Cistercian, etc.)
Cf. BX1970.3, Liturgical environment
4828.5 Protestant (General)
4829.A-Z Other, A-Z
4829.A6 Anglican
4829.B9 Byzantine
Cf. NA5082, Iconostases
4829.C3 Carolingian
4829.C5 Christian Science
4829.C64 Coptic
4829.F7 Friends
4829.L8 Lutheran
4829.M45 Mennonite
4829.M67 Morman
4829.S4 Seventh-Day Adventist
Special classes of buildings
For special countries and special buildings, see NA5201+
4830 Cathedrals
4840 Bishops' palaces
4850 Abbeys. Convents. Monasteries

Special classes of buildings
Classed by use
Public buildings
Religious buildings. Religious architecture
Christian architecture
Special classes of buildings -- Continued

4870 Chapels
4873 Martyria
4875 Shrines
Cf. NB1790+, Sculpture
4880 Parish houses
4890 Sunday school buildings
4900 Y.M.C.A. buildings
4910.A-Z Other buildings, A-Z
4950 Miscellaneous details
Including church doors
5000 Interior architectural decoration
Cf. NK2190+, Interior decoration of churches
Ecclesiastical furniture, etc.
For special countries, see NA5201+
5050 General works
5051 Folios
5060 Altars
5062 Baldachins
5065 Pulpits
5070 Baptismal fonts
5075 Choir stalls. Pews. Benches
5080 Screens. Rood screens. Reredos
5082 Iconostases
Cf. N8185.5+, Icons (Eastern Church)
5090 Candelabra. Chandeliers, etc.
5095.A-Z Other special, A-Z
5095.S2 Sacrament houses

Special classes of buildings
Classed by use
Public buildings
Religious buildings.
Religious architecture -- Continued
5201-6114 Religious architecture of special countries (Table N5 modified)
Class special buildings by city in which located. For buildings not located within a city, class in the number for cities, A-Z (or local, A-Z if there is no number for cities), but Cutter by name of building
For cities represented by a number, subarrange by Cuttering for name of building. For names beginning with some form of the word "Saint" (e.g. San, Santa, Sancta, etc.), Cutter "S" determining the number from the word following "Saint"
For cities represented by a Cutter number, expand the Cutter to provide for alphabetical arrangement of special buildings by name of building. For a building whose name begins with some form of the word "Saint," determine the Cutter number from the word following "Saint"
Add country number in table to NA5200
America
United States
5235.A-Z Cities, A-Z
e.g.
Boston churches
5235.B7 General works
5235.B75 Trinity Church
Europe
5453 Medieval
Special countries
Great Britain. England. Cathedrals, abbeys, etc.
5461 General works
England - Local
5470.A-Z London churches
5470.A1 General works
5470.S5 St. Paul's
5470.S6 St. Stephen's
5470.W5 Westminster Abbey
5471.A-Z Other English cities, A-Z
e.g.
5471.B3 Bath Abbey
5471.B47 Beverley Minster
5471.B8 Bristol Cathedral
5471.C2 Canterbury Cathedral
5471.C4 Carlisle Cathedral
5471.C5 Chester Cathedral

Special classes of buildings
Classed by use
Public buildings
Religious buildings. Religious architecture
Religious architecture of special countries
Europe
Special countries
Great Britain. England.
Cathedrals, abbeys, etc.
England - Local
Other English
cities, A-Z -- Continued

5471.C6 Chichester Cathedral
5471.C8 Christ Church Priory
5471.D9 Durham Cathedral
5471.E5 Ely Cathedral
5471.E9 Exeter Cathedral
5471.F9 Furness Abbey
5471.G5 Gloucester Cathedral
5471.H5 Hereford Cathedral
5471.L5 Lichfield Cathedral
5471.L7 Lincoln Cathedral
5471.M4 Manchester Cathedral
5471.N8 Norwich Cathedral
5471.O9 Oxford Cathedral
5471.P5 Peterborough Cathedral
5471.R7 Rochester Cathedral
5471.S2 Saint Albans Cathedral
5471.S5 Salisbury Cathedral
5471.T4 Tewkesbury Abbey
5471.W4 Wells Cathedral
Westminster Abbey, see NA5470.W5
5471.W6 Winchester Cathedral
5471.W8 Worchester Cathedral
5471.Y6 York Cathedral

Scottish cathedrals, abbeys, etc.
5481.A-Z Special cities, A-Z
e.g.
5481.G5 Glasgow

Welsh cathedrals, abbeys, etc.
5494.A-Z Special cities, A-Z
e.g.
5494.C9 Cwmhir
5494.L7 Llandaff
5494.S3 St. David's

France
Paris churches
5550.A1 General
5550.N7 Notre Dame
5550.S2 St. Ambroise
5550.S7 Ste. Chapelle

Germany

Special classes of buildings
Classed by use
Public buildings
Religious buildings. Religious architecture
Religious architecture of special countries
Europe
Special countries
Germany -- Continued
5586.A-Z Other cities, A-Z
e.g.
Cologne - Churches
5586.C68 General works
5586.C7 Cathedral. Dom
Italy
Rome - Churches
5620.A1 General works
5620.S3 S. Clemente
5620.S4 S. Giovanni in Laterano
5620.S6 S. Maria Maggiore (Basilica Liberiana)
5620.S8 S. Paolo fuori le Mura
5620.S9 S. Pietro (in Vaticano)
5621.A-Z Other cities, A-Z
e.g.
Florence - Churches
5621.F5 General works
5621.F6 S. Giovanni (Baptistery)
5621.F7 S. Maria del Fiore
5621.F75 S. Maria Novella
5621.F8 S. Miniato
Milan - Churches
5621.M5 General works
5621.M6 Duomo
5621.P4 Pavia. Certosa
Venice - Churches
5621.V4 General works
5621.V5 S. Marco
6115 Undertaking establishments
6117 Crematories, columbaria, etc.
Cemetery architecture
Including sepulchral monuments, tombs, mausoleums, etc.
Cf. NB1800+, Sculpture
6120 General works
6125 Design and plans
6127 Miscellaneous minor works
History
6130 General works
Ancient
Cf. NB143, Ancient bronzes
6132 General works
(6132.5) Egypt
See DT62.T6, DT63-DT63.5
6133 Assyria. Babylonia

Special classes of buildings
Classed by use
Public buildings
Cemetery architecture
History
Ancient -- Continued

6134 Persia. Media
6135 Judea. Syria
6136 Arabia
6137 Asia Minor
Halicarnassus, see NA285.H3
Classical
Cf. NB133.5.S46, Greek and Roman reliefs
6138 General works
6139 Greek
6140 Etruscan
6141 Roman. Pompeian
6142.A-Z Other ancient, A-Z
Medieval
For special countries and special monuments, see NA6149+
6143 General works
6145 Islamic. Moorish
6146 Romanesque
6147 Gothic
6148 Modern
Special countries
6149 America. North America
United States
6150 General works
6151.A-W By state, A-W
e.g.
6151.H3 Hawaii
6152.A-Z By city, A-Z
Canada
6153 General works
6154.A-Z Local, A-Z
6154.5 Latin America (General)
6155 Mexico
Central America
6156 General works
6157.A-Z By country, A-Z
West Indies
6158 General works
6159.A-Z Local, A-Z
South America
6160 General works
6161.A-Z By country, A-Z
Europe
6162 General works
6163 Great Britain
6164 Austria

Special classes of buildings
Classed by use
Public buildings
Cemetery architecture
History
Special countries
Europe -- Continued

6165 France
6166 Germany
6167 Italy
6168 Netherlands
6169 Belgium
6169.5 Portugal
6170 Russia
6172 Scandinavia
6174 Spain
6176 Switzerland
6177 Turkey
6178.A-Z Other, A-Z

Asia

6179 General works
6179.5 Afghanistan
6180 Turkey
6181 Iran
6182 Central Asia
Including Soviet Central Asia
6183 India
6183.2 Pakistan
6183.5 Ceylon

Indonesia. Malaysia

6184 General works
6185 Dutch East Indies
6186 Philippines

Eastern Asia

6187 General works
6188 China
6189 Japan
6189.5 Korea
6190 Northern Asia. Siberia

Africa

6191 General works
6192 Egypt
6194.A-Z Other countries, A-Z

Australia

6195 General works
6196.A-Z Local, A-Z
6197 New Zealand

Pacific islands

6198 General works
6199.A-Z Special, A-Z
e.g.
Hawaii, see NA6151.H3

Special classes of buildings
Classed by use
Public buildings -- Continued
Commercial buildings
Including commercial roadside buildings
Cf. TH4311+, Building construction
6210 General works
6212 United States
6214.A-Z Other countries, A-Z
Urban business centers
6215 General works
6216.A-Z By city and center, A-Z
6218 Shopping arcades. Shopping centers. Shopping malls
6218.5 Showrooms
Stores. Shops
6220 General works
6225 Shop fronts, etc.
6227.A-Z By business, A-Z
6227.B42 Beauty shops
6227.D45 Department stores
6227.J4 Jewelry stores
6227.S94 Supermarkets
Office buildings. Skyscrapers. Tall buildings
6230 General works
6231 Folios
6231.5 Psychological aspects of tall buildings
By region or country
United States
6232 General works
6233.A-Z Special buildings. By city and building, A-Z
e.g.
6233.N5E5 New York. Empire State Building
6233.N5S5 New York. Singer Building
6233.N5W66 New York. Woolworth Building
6234.A-Z Other regions or countries, A-Z
Under each country:
.x *General works*
.x2A-.x2Z *By city, A-Z*
Expand Cutter for city to provide for alphabetical arrangement of buildings
Banks
Cf. TH9734, Safes and vaults
6240 General works
United States
6241 General works
6243.A-Z Special buildings. By city and building, A-Z

Special classes of buildings
Classed by use
Public buildings
Commercial buildings
Banks -- Continued
6245.A-Z Other countries, A-Z
Under each country:
.x General works
.x2A-.x2Z By city, A-Z
Expand Cutter for city to provide for alphabetical arrangement of banks
Exchanges. Boards of trade
6250 General works
6253.A-Z Special buildings. By city and building, A-Z
Markets
Cf. NA9068, Marketplaces
6260 General works
6270 Cattle markets, stockyards, abattoirs
Cf. TS1970+, Packinghouse industries
6273 United States
6275.A-Z Other countries, A-Z
6280.A-Z Other, A-Z
Transportation and storage buildings
6290 General works
Airport buildings. Airport terminals
6300 General works
6301 United States
6302.A-W States, A-W
6303.A-Z Cities, A-Z
6305.A-Z Other countries, A-Z
Under each:
.x General works
.x2A-.x2Z Local, A-Z
6305.G7 Great Britain
6305.G72L6 London
Specifications
6306.A-Z United States. By city, A-Z
6307.A-Z Other countries. By country and city, A-Z
Railway stations, freight houses, etc.
Cf. TF300+, Railroad engineering and operation
6310 General works
6311 United States
6312.A-W States, A-W
6313.A-Z Cities, A-Z
6315.A-Z Other countries, A-Z
Apply table at NA6305.A-Z
6315.G7 Great Britain
6315.G72L6 London
Specifications
6316.A-Z United States. By city, A-Z
6317.A-Z Other countries. By country and city, A-Z
Bus terminals

Special classes of buildings
Classed by use
Public buildings
Transportation and storage buildings
Bus terminals -- Continued
6320 General works
6321 United States
6322.A-W States, A-W
6323.A-Z Cities, A-Z
6325.A-Z Other countries, A-Z
Apply table at NA6305.A-Z
Specifications
6326.A-Z United States. By city, A-Z
6327.A-Z Other countries. By country and city, A-Z
Dock buildings, ferryhouses, etc.
6330 General works
6332 United States
6333.A-Z Other regions or countries, A-Z
Warehouses
6340 General works
6342 United States
6343.A-Z Other regions or countries, A-Z
6350 Grain elevators
For grain elevator machinery, see TJ1415+
6360 Icehouses (Commercial)
For private icehouses, see NA8350
6370.A-Z Other, A-Z
6370.A87 Automobile service stations
Industrial architecture. Factories, mills, etc.
Cf. NA9053.I53, City planning
Cf. TH4511+, Building construction
6396 Congresses
6400 General works
6402 United States
6403.A-Z Other countries, A-Z
6405 Industrial parks
6410 Textile mills
Breweries. Distilleries. Wineries
6420 General works
6422 United States
6423.A-Z Other regions or countries, A-Z
6430 Foundries
6440 Machine shops
6450 Rolling mills
6460 Woodworking mills
6470 Carriage factories
Automobile industry facilities. Automobile factories
For automobile service stations, see NA6370.A87
6472 General works
6474.A-Z By factory, A-Z
6474.F53 Fiat-Lingotto

Special classes of buildings
Classed by use
Public buildings
Industrial architecture.
Factories, mills, etc.
Automobile industry facilities.
Automobile factories
By factory, A-Z -- Continued
6474.R45 Renault Centre (England)
6480 Papermills
6490 Flour mills
(6581) Mine buildings
See TH4561
6588 Service buildings for employees
6589.A-Z Other, A-Z
6589.N48 Newspaper buildings
6590-6597 Education departments
6590 General works
6591 United States
6592.A-W States, A-W
e.g.
6592.P4 Pennsylvania
6593.A-Z Cities, A-Z
6595.A-6495.Z Other countries, A-Z
Apply table at NA6305.A-Z
Specifications
6596.A-Z United States. By city, A-Z
6597.A-Z Other countries. By country and city, A-Z
Education buildings
Colleges and universities
For university and college physical facilities, see LB3223+
6600 General works
6602.A-Z Special types of buildings, A-Z
6602.A8 Auditoriums
6602.D6 Dormitories
6602.E6 Engineering schools
6602.M3 Mathematics
6602.M4 Medical
6602.P5 Physics laboratories
6602.S3 Science
6602.S7 Student unions
6602.T5 Theaters
United States
6603 General works
Special institutions
see classes LD, R, S, T, etc.
6605.A-Z Other regions and countries, A-Z
For special institutions, see classes LE-LG, R, S, T, etc.
(6608) Schools
See LB3205-LB3325

Special classes of buildings
Classed by use
Public buildings
Education buildings -- Continued
6610.A-Z Military academies. By city and school, A-Z
e.g.
6610.P2E3 Paris. École militaire
(6612) Libraries
See Z679
Museum architecture
6690 General works
6695 Art museums and galleries
For individual art museums or galleries, see N512-N3990
6700.A-Z Other individual museums. By city, A-Z
Exhibition buildings
6750.A1 General works
6750.A2A-Z By region or country, A-Z
6750.A3-Z Special. By city and building (or by name if non-urban), A-Z
e.g.
6750.N5C7 New York. Crystal Palace
6751 Research buildings. Laboratories
Cf. TH4652, Building construction
Halls of fame. Temples of fame
6753 General works
6755.A-Z Special by city (or by name if non-urban), A-Z
e.g.
6755.B3 Barmen, Ger. Ruhmeshalle
New York University. Hall of Fame, see E176.6
6755.W3 Walhalla (near Regensburg)
Charitable institutions. Asylums
Cf. Class HV, Social pathology
Cf. RC439, Asylums for the mentally ill
6760 General works
6761.A-Z Special. By city and building (or by name if non-urban), A-Z
(6763) Hospitals
See RA967
Group homes
6775 General works
By region or country
United States
6776 General works
6776.5.A-Z Local, A-Z
6777.A-Z Other regions or countries, A-Z
(6780) Prison architecture
See HV8805-HV8829
Buildings for recreation
6800 General works
6810 Casinos
Arts centers. Arts facilities
6812 General works

Special classes of buildings
Classed by use
Public buildings
Arts centers. Arts facilities -- Continued
6813.A-Z Special countries, A-Z
Under each country:
.x General
.x2A-.x2Z Special, by city (or by name if non-urban), A-Z
Great Britain
6813.G7 General works
6813.G8L6 London
6815 Auditoriums
Theaters. Opera houses. Music halls
General works
6820 Before 1800
6821 1801-
6826 Specifications
6828 Catalogs of equipment, supplies, etc.
United States
Including general material for cities, states, etc.
6830 General works
6835.A-Z By city and building, A-Z
e.g.
6835.E23G6 East Haddam, Conn. Goodspeed Opera House
6840.A-Z Other countries, A-Z
Under each country:
.x General works
.x2A-.x2Z By city, A-Z
Expand Cutter for city to provide for alphabetical arrangement of theaters
General material in a given city should precede material on individual theaters
6840.F7 France
6840.F72P36 Paris. Odeon
6840.F72P38 Paris. Opera House
Greek theaters, see NA278.T5
Roman theaters, see NA325.T5
Motion picture theaters
6845 General works
6846.A-Z By region or country, A-Z
Under each country:
.x General works
.x2A-.x2Z Special. By city, A-Z
6850 Panoramas
Amphitheaters. Stadia
6860 General works

Special classes of buildings
Classed by use
Public buildings
Amphitheaters. Stadia -- Continued
6862.A-Z By region or country, A-Z
Under each country:
.x General works
.x2A-.x2Z Special. By city (or by name if non-urban), A-Z
6870 Grandstands
Convention facilities, coliseums, lecture halls, etc.
6880 General works
6880.5.A-Z By region or country, A-Z
Apply table at NA6846.A-Z
6885 Radio, television stations, etc.
6890 Ice palaces
(6895) Bowling alleys
See GV907
(6900) Gymnasiums
See GV405, NA325.G9
(6910) Rinks
See GV849-GV852
6920 Boathouses
Cf. NA7970+, Boat clubs
(6925) Riding halls
See SF310
6930 Park buildings
Other public buildings
Restaurants, see NA7855+
7010 Baths and washhouses
(7020) Public comfort stations
See RA607
Domestic architecture. Houses. Dwellings
Cf. GT165+, Manners and customs
Cf. NA6775+, Group homes
Cf. NA9051+, Residential site planning
Cf. TH4805+, House construction
7100 Periodicals. Societies
7102 Congresses
7105 History (General)
General works
7109 Early works through 1800
7110 1801-
Planning
7115 General works
7115.3 Architects and housing developers
Climate and architecture
7116 General works
7117.A-Z Special topics, A-Z
Class here general works on the topics as well as works on the topics in a particular region, country, etc.

Special classes of buildings
Classed by use
Domestic architecture. Houses. Dwellings
Climate and architecture
Special topics, A-Z -- Continued
7117.A74 Arid regions
7117.C64 Cold regions
7117.S65 Solar radiation
7117.T74 Tropics
7117.3 Energy conservation and architecture
7117.5 Environmental aspects of architecture
7120 Popular works
7123 Historic houses (General)
7125 General special
Collections of plans and designs
7126 International
For other collections see country or type
American works
(7127) General
(7130) Folios
(7132) English works
(7133) French works
(7134) German works
(7135.A-Z) Other, A-Z
7140 Specifications (General)
7145 Prefabricated houses
Special materials
Prefer classification by country
7150 Brick
7155 Hollow tile
7160 Concrete. Stucco
7163 Pisé. Rammed earth
7165 Adobe
7170 Stone
7173 Wood
7175 Half-timbered houses
7180 Iron and steel
7195.A-Z Housing for special classes of persons, A-Z
Including works on special regions or countries
7195.A4 Aged
7195.A7 Architects
7195.A75 Artists
Physically handicapped, see NA2545.P5
7195.P7 Preschool children
7195.S5 Single people
7195.Y6 Youth

Special classes of buildings
Classed by use
Domestic architecture.
Houses. Dwellings -- Continued
7201-7477 Special countries (Table N3 modified)
Add country number in table to NA7200
For Colonial America, see NA707
For special architects, see NA737-NA1613
Under each (three number countries):
1 General works
2.A-2.Z Special divisions, regions, A-Z
3.A-3.Z Special cities, A-Z
Under each (one number or decimal number countries):
.A1 General works
.A2-.Z8 Special divisions, regions, A-Z
.Z9A-.Z9Z Special cities, A-Z
Under each (Cutter number countries):
.x General works
.x2A-.x2Z Special divisions, regions, A-Z
.x3A-.x3Z Special cities, A-Z
Europe
Great Britain. England
England
7331.A-Z English counties, A-Z
7332 London
7333.A-Z Other cities, A-Z
City houses. Mansions in cities
United States
7511 General works
7511.3.A-Z By region or state, A-Z
7511.4.A-Z By city, A-Z
Great Britain. England
7512 General works
7512.3.A-Z By region, country, county, etc., A-Z
7512.4.A-Z By city, A-Z
France
7513 General works
7513.3.A-Z By region or province, A-Z
7513.4.A-Z By city, A-Z
Germany
7514 General works
7514.3.A-Z By region or state, A-Z
7514.4.A-Z By city, A-Z
7515.A-Z Other countries, A-Z
Special forms of houses
Cf. NA7201+, By country
7520 Attached houses. Row houses
7521 Terrace houses
7523 Courtyard houses
7524 Hillside houses
7525 Double houses. Semi-detached houses
7530 Detached houses

Special classes of buildings
Classed by use
Domestic architecture. Houses. Dwellings
Special forms of houses -- Continued
7531 Earth sheltered houses
For method of construction, see TH4819.E27
7532 Geodesic dome houses
7540 Public works housing
Architectural works only
Cf. HD7285+, Housing (Economic history)
Dwellings for the working class
Cf. HD7285+, Housing (Economic history)
7550 General works
7551 United States
7552 Great Britain
7553 France
7554 Germany
7555.A-Z Other countries, A-Z
Workingmen's villages
7557 General works
7558.A-Z Special, by name, A-Z
Country homes. Small country houses
For farmhouses, see NA8208+
7560 General works
7561 United States
7562 Great Britain (English cottages, etc.)
7563 France
7564 Germany
7565 Italy
7566.A-Z Other countries, A-Z
Suburban homes. Bungalows
7570 General works
7571 United States
7572 Great Britain
7572.5.A-Z Other countries, A-Z
7573 Modern houses in "Colonial" style
Summerhouses. Vacation houses
Including seaside architecture
7574 General works
7575 United States
7576 Great Britain
7577 France
7578 Germany
7579.A-Z Other countries, A-Z
7580 Villas. Chalets
Ancient Roman villas, see NA324
United States
7586 General works
Including general material for cities, states, etc.
7587.A-Z Special villas. By city (or by name if non-urban), A-Z
Great Britain

Special classes of buildings
Classed by use
Domestic architecture. Houses. Dwellings
Villas. Chalets
Great Britain -- Continued
7588 General works
Including general material for cities, counties, etc.
7589.A-Z Special villas. By city (or by name if non-urban), A-Z
France
7590 General works
Including general material for cities, departments, etc.
7591.A-Z Special villas. By city (or by name if non-urban), A-Z
Germany
7592 General works
Including general material for cities, states, etc.
7593.A-Z Special villas. By city (or by name if non-urban), A-Z
Italy
7594 General works
Including general material for cities, provinces, etc.
7595.A-Z Special villas. By city (or by name if non-urban), A-Z
e.g.
7595.C29 Villa Carlotta, Italy
7595.R63 Rome. Villa Aldobrandini
7595.R65 Rome. Palazzo Baldassini
7596.A-Z Other countries, A-Z
Under each:
.x General works
.x2A-.x2Z Special villas. By city (or by name if non-urban), A-Z
Country houses, country seats, manor houses, etc.
7600 General works
United States
7610 General works
7613.A-W By state, A-W
7615.A-Z Special houses, A-Z
England
7620 General works
7621.A-Z By county, A-Z
7625.A-Z Special houses, A-Z
Other countries
See NA7241-NA7476
Castles. Châteaux. Palaces. Royal villas
General works
Austria. Hungary. Czechoslovak Republic

Special classes of buildings
Classed by use
Domestic architecture. Houses. Dwellings
Castles. Châteaux. Palaces. Royal villas
Austria. Hungary.
Czechoslovak Republic -- Continued
7720 General works
Including general material for cities, provinces, etc.
7721.A-Z Special. By city (or by name if non-urban), A-Z
Belgium
7725 General works
Including general material for cities, provinces, etc.
7726.A-Z Special. By city (or by name if non-urban), A-Z
Denmark
7730 General works
Including general material for cities, provinces, etc.
7731.A-Z Special. By city (or by name if non-urban), A-Z
France
7735 General works
Including general material for cities, provinces, etc.
7736.A-Z Special. By city (or by name if non-urban), A-Z
e.g.
7736.C45 Chambard, Château de
7736.P22 Paris. Château de Bagatelle
7736.P23 Paris. Château de Bercy
7736.P24 Paris. Hôtel de Soubise
Germany
7740 General works
Including general material for cities, provinces, etc.
7741.A-Z Special. By city (or by name if non-urban), A-Z
Great Britain
7745 General works
Including general material for cities, provinces, etc.
7746.A-Z Special. By city (or by name if non-urban), A-Z
Greece, Ancient, see NA277
Holland
7750 General works
Including general material for cities, provinces, etc.
7751.A-Z Special. By city (or by name if non-urban), A-Z

Special classes of buildings
Classed by use
Domestic architecture. Houses. Dwellings
Castles. Châteaux.
Palaces. Royal villas -- Continued
Italy
7755 General works
Including general material for cities, provinces, etc.
7756.A-Z Special. By city (or by name if non-urban), A-Z
Ancient Roman palaces, see NA320
Ancient Roman villas, see NA324
Japan
7757 General works
Including general material for cities, provinces, etc.
7758.A-Z Special. By city (or by name if non-urban), A-Z
Norway
7760 General works
Including general material for cities, provinces, etc.
7761.A-Z Special. By city (or by name if non-urban), A-Z
Poland
7763 General works
Including general material for cities, provinces, etc.
7764.A-Z Special. By city (or by name if non-urban), A-Z
Portugal
7765 General works
Including general material for cities, provinces, etc.
7766.A-Z Special. By city (or by name if non-urban), A-Z
Russia
7770 General works
Including general material for cities, provinces, etc.
7771.A-Z Special. By city (or by name if non-urban), A-Z
7775-7776 Spain
7775 General works
Including general material for cities, provinces, etc.
7776.A-Z Special. By city (or by name if non-urban), A-Z
Alhambra, see NA387
Sweden

Special classes of buildings
Classed by use
Domestic architecture. Houses. Dwellings
Castles. Châteaux. Palaces. Royal villas
Sweden -- Continued
7780 General works
Including general material for cities, provinces, etc.
7781.A-Z Special. By city (or by name if non-urban), A-Z
Switzerland
7785 General works
Including general material for cities, provinces, etc.
7786.A-Z Special. By city (or by name if non-urban), A-Z
Other countries, see NA701+
Hotels. Inns. Hotel lobbies
7800 General works
7810 For cities
7820 For resorts
7830 For country places
United States
7840 General works
7845.A-Z By city (or by name if non-urban), A-Z
7850.A-Z Other regions or countries, A-Z
Under each country:
.x General works
.x2A-.x2Z Special hotels or inns. By city (or name if non-urban), A-Z
Taverns. Pubs
7851 General works
United States
7852 General works
7852.5.A-Z By place, A-Z
7853.A-Z Other regions or countries, A-Z
Restaurants. Coffeehouses
Including chain restaurants, etc.
7855 General works
United States
7856 General works
7857.A-Z By place, A-Z
7858.A-Z Other regions or countries, A-Z
Under each country:
.x General works
.x2A-.x2Z Special restaurants or coffeehouses. By place, A-Z
Apartment houses. Flats. High-rise apartment buildings. Prefabricated apartment buildings
7860 General works
By region or country
United States
7861 General works

Special classes of buildings
Classed by use
Domestic architecture. Houses. Dwellings
Apartment houses. Flats. High-rise apartment buildings.
Prefabricated apartment buildings
By region or country
United States -- Continued
7862.A-Z By place, A-Z
7863.A-Z Other regions or countries, A-Z
Under each country:
.x General works
.x2A-.x2Z Special apartment houses. By place, A-Z
7880 Tenement houses
7882 Lofts
7884 Penthouses
Clubhouses
Cf. TH4800, Building construction
7910 General works
7911 United States
7912.A-W States, A-W
7913.A-Z Cities, A-Z
7915.A-Z Other countries, A-Z
Apply table at NA6305.A-Z
Specifications
7916.A-Z United States. By city, A-Z
7917.A-Z Other countries. By country and city, A-Z
City clubs
7920 General works
7921 United States
7922.A-W States, A-W
7923.A-Z Cities, A-Z
7925.A-Z Other countries, A-Z
Apply table at NA6305.A-Z
Specifications
7926.A-Z United States. By city, A-Z
7927.A-Z Other countries. By country and city, A-Z
Country clubs
7930 General
7931 United States
7932.A-W States, A-W
7933.A-Z Cities, A-Z
7935.A-Z Other countries, A-Z
Apply table at NA6305.A-Z
Specifications
7936.A-Z United States. By city, A-Z
7937.A-Z Other countries. By country and city, A-Z
Golf clubs
7940 General
7941 United States
7942.A-W States, A-W
7943.A-Z Cities, A-Z

Special classes of buildings
Classed by use
Clubhouses
Country clubs
Golf clubs -- Continued
7945.A-Z Other countries, A-Z
Apply table at NA6305.A-Z
Specifications
7946.A-Z United States. By city, A-Z
7947.A-Z Other countries. By country and city, A-Z
Cricket clubs
7950 General
7951 United States
7952.A-W States, A-W
7953.A-Z Cities, A-Z
7955.A-Z Other countries, A-Z
Apply table at NA6305.A-Z
Specifications
7956.A-Z United States. By city, A-Z
7957.A-Z Other countries. By country and city, A-Z
Athletic clubs
7960 General works
7961 United States
7962.A-W States, A-W
7963.A-Z Cities, A-Z
7965.A-Z Other countries, A-Z
Apply table at NA6305.A-Z
Specifications
7966.A-Z United States. By city, A-Z
7967.A-Z Other countries. By country and city, A-Z
Yacht clubs. Boat clubs
7970 General works
7971 United States
7972.A-W States, A-W
7973.A-Z Cities, A-Z
7975.A-Z Other countries, A-Z
Apply table at NA6305.A-Z
Specifications
7976.A-Z United States. By city, A-Z
7977.A-Z Other countries. By country and city, A-Z
Houses for societies
8000 General works
8001 United States
8002.A-W States, A-W
8003.A-Z Cities, A-Z
8005.A-Z Other countries, A-Z
Apply table at NA6305.A-Z
Secret societies
8010 General works
8011 United States
8012.A-W States, A-W
8013.A-Z Cities, A-Z

Special classes of buildings
Classed by use
Houses for societies
Secret societies -- Continued
8015.A-Z Other countries, A-Z
Apply table at NA6305.A-Z
College fraternities. Chapter houses
8020 General works
8021 United States
8022.A-W States, A-W
8023.A-Z Cities, A-Z
8025.A-Z Other countries, A-Z
Apply table at NA6305.A-Z
Guild houses. Confraternities' schools
8050 General works
8055 Austria
8060 Belgium
8065 Denmark
8070 France
8075 Germany
8080 Great Britain
For Guildhall, London, see NA4435.G72L6
8085 Holland
8090 Italy
8095 Norway
8100 Portugal
8105 Russia
8110 Spain
8115 Sweden
8120 Switzerland
8125.A-Z Other countries, A-Z
Farm architecture
Cf. S770+, Agriculture
Cf. TH4911+, Building
8200 General works
By region or country
8201 United States
8201.5 Europe
8202 Great Britain
8203 France
8204 Germany
8205 Italy
8206.A-Z Other regions or countries, A-Z
Farmhouses
8208 General works
By region or country
United States
8208.5 General works
8208.52.A-Z Local, A-Z
8210.A-Z Other regions or countries, A-Z
8220 Courtyards
Stables, see NA8340

Special classes of buildings
Classed by use
Farm architecture -- Continued
8230 Barns
Including housing for animals in general
8240 Granaries
8250 Dairies
8260.A-Z Other, A-Z
Minor buildings, outbuildings, gates, fences, etc.
8300 General works
8301 United States
8302 Great Britain
8303 France
8304 Germany
8305 Italy
8306.A-Z Other countries, A-Z
e.g.
8306.J2 Japan
8306.J22 Japanese teahouses: "Chasitsu"; "Sukiya"
8310 Lodges
8320 Servants' quarters
8330 Kitchens. Laundries
8340 Stables. Carriage houses
(8345) Fittings for stables, cowbarns, etc.
See SF92
8348 Garages
8350 Icehouses
Cf. NA6360, Commercial icehouses
8360 Conservatories. Garden rooms. Orangeries
8370 Dovecotes
(8372) Greenhouses
See SB416
8375 Terraces, patios, etc.
8380 Garden walls
8385 Gateways and portes cochères
Cf. NA493+, City gates
Gates and fences
8390 General works
8392 Ironwork
8450 Ornamental buildings for parks and gardens.
Pergolas. Bandstands
8455 Cave architecture
8460 Follies
8465 Rustic work
8470 Cabins, camps, etc.
8480 Portable buildings. Prefabricated buildings
Cf. HD9715.5, Economic aspects
Cf. NA7145, Prefabricated houses
Cf. TH1098, Building construction

Aesthetics of cities. City planning and beautifying
Class here works emphasizing architectural aspects
Cf. HT170+, Urban renewal. Urban development
For engineering works, see TD160+
For works dealing predominantly with the social, economic and political factors involved in city planning, see HT165.5+

NA

General works
9000 Periodicals. Societies. Collections
9010 Congresses
9010.5 Encyclopedias, dictionaries, glossaries, etc.
9012 Study and teaching. Research
9013 City planning as a profession
Exhibitions
9015.A-Z United States. By city and gallery or other place of exhibition, A-Z
9016.A-Z Other countries. By country and city, A-Z
9027 Early works (to 1870)
9030 1870-1944
9031 1945-
9035 Minor works
Addresses, essays, lectures
9040 Collections
9045 Single papers
9050 General special
Cf. HE353+, Traffic engineering
Cf. HF5843.5, Billboards, aesthetics, regulations, etc.
Special topics
Including works on special regions or countries
9050.5 Public architecture
Cf. NA4170+, Public buildings
Residential areas. Site planning
9051 General works
9051.4 Cluster housing
9051.5 Zero lot line housing
9052 Beautifications
Cf. SB472.7, Urban landscape architecture
9053.A-Z Others, A-Z
9053.B58 Blocks
9053.C3 Capitals (Cities)
9053.C48 Churches
9053.C57 Company town architecture
9053.C6 Conservation and restoration
Cf. CC135+, Archaeology
Dwellings, see NA9051+
9053.F8 Functionalism
9053.G7 Greenbelts
9053.H55 Historic districts
Including individual districts and their restoration
Housing, see NA9051+
9053.H76 Human factors

Aesthetics of cities. City planning and beautifying
Special topics
Others, A-Z -- Continued
9053.I53 Industrial buildings
Marketplaces, see NA9068
9053.M43 Megastructures
9053.N4 New towns. Garden cities
Including new city districts or sections
9053.O3 Office buildings
Pedestrian areas, see NA9074
Public spaces, see NA9053.S6
Public squares and promenades, see NA9070+
9053.R4 Recreation
Residential areas, see NA9051+
Restoration, see NA9053.C6
9053.S4 Skyscrapers
9053.S6 Space. Public spaces
9053.S7 Streets
Including individual streets and their restoration
9053.U7 Urban renewal
9053.W3 Walls
9053.W38 Waterfronts
Urban business centers, see NA6215+
(9060) Public parks and gardens
See SB481-SB485
9068 Marketplaces
Cf. NA6260+, Markets
Public squares and promenades
9070 General works
9072.A-Z Special squares. By city and square or promenade, A-Z
9074 Pedestrian areas
Cf. NA2543.P4, Pedestrian traffic pattern inside buildings
Cf. TE279.5+, Engineering
Biography
9080 Collective
For special countries, see NA9101+
9085.A-Z Individual, A-Z
Including collections of their designs
History
Cf. E59.C55, City planning in pre-Columbian America
9090 General works
9092 Ancient
Medieval
9093 General works
9093.9 Islamic
Modern
9094 General works
9094.3 Renaissance
9094.8 19th century

Aesthetics of cities. City planning and beautifying
History
Modern -- Continued
9095 20th century
9100 Collections of plans (not limited to a single country or city)
9101-9285 Special countries and cities (Table N2)
Add country number in table to NA9100
Ornamental structures (Monuments, arches, fountains, etc.)
General works
9319 Early works through 1800
9320 1801-
War memorials. National cemeteries
9325 General works
9330.A-Z Special countries, A-Z
Apply table at NA6305.A-Z
Monuments
Cf. NB1330+, Sculpture
Ancient
9335 General works
9340.A-Z Special cities or other local, A-Z
e.g.
9340.R4 Rome. Column of Marcus Aurelius
9343 Medieval
9345 Modern
Special countries
9347 United States
9348.A-Z Other countries, A-Z
e.g.
9348.H8 Hungary
Special cities or other local
9350.A-Z United States. By city, A-Z
e.g.
9350.W3W25 Washington Monument
9355.A-Z Other countries. By city, A-Z
For non-urban monuments, see NA9347+
9355.R7 Rome. Monument to Victor Emmanuel II
Memorial and triumphal arches
9360 General works
Ancient
9365 General works
9370.A-Z Special cities or other local, A-Z
e.g.
9370.R6-Z Rome. Arch of Constantine
9373 Medieval
Modern
9375 General works
Special countries
9377 United States
9378.A-Z Other countries, A-Z
9380.A-Z Special cities or other local, A-Z
e.g.

Aesthetics of cities. City planning and beautifying
Ornamental structures
(Monuments, arches, fountains, etc.)
Memorial and triumphal arches
Modern
Special cities
or other local, A-Z -- Continued
9380.N6 New York. Dewey arch
9380.P4 Paris. Arc de triomphe de l'Étoile
Obelisks (Egyptian), see DT62.O2
Fountains
Cf. NB1895, Wells
9400 General works
United States
9405 General works
9410.A-Z By city, A-Z
e.g.
9410.D6 Detroit. Scott Memorial Fountain
9413.A-Z Other countries, A-Z
e.g.
9413.F8 France
9415.A-Z Cities in other countries, A-Z
e.g.
9415.P2 Paris
9415.R7 Rome
9420 Catalogs
9425 Electric fountains
Wellheads
9426 General works
Special countries
9427 United States
9428.A-Z Other countries, A-Z

Sculpture
1 Periodicals and societies
Exhibitions (by place held)
Prefer classification by nationality, NB75 NB1113; by form, NB1293 NB1895; or by subject, NB1910 NB1950
16.A-Z United States. By city and museum or other place of exhibition, A-Z
17.A-Z Other countries. By country and city, A-Z
Special sculptors, see NB201+
Museums. Collections
Cf. NB87.A+, Special classical collections
20 Collective
23.A-Z Special countries, A-Z
Special museums
25.A-Z United States. By city and museum, A-Z
27.A-Z Other countries. By country and city, A-Z
30.A-Z Private collections. By collector, A-Z
Including exhibition catalogs and catalogs of auctions devoted to single private collections
Prefer classification by nationality or period
33 Catalogs of photographs of sculpture
35 Trade catalogs
36 Indexes to sculpture
Sculpture rental and lending colletions, see N378+
40 Congresses
Collected writings
43 Several authors
45.A-Z Individual authors, A-Z
50 Dictionaries. Encyclopedias
History
60 General works
61 Minor. Essays
61.3 Intercultural relations in sculpture (General)
61.5 Prehistoric sculpture
Primitive sculpture
Sculpture produced outside the traditions of the sculpture of Europe, the Mediterranean area, and Asia, i.e., the sculpture of the Negro people of sub-Saharan Africa and of the inhabitants of the islands of the Pacific Ocean, Australia, and some areas of the coast of Southeast Asia
For primitive sculpture of American Indians, See classes E-F
62 General works
64 General special
Special countries, see NB201+
Ancient sculpture
69 Early works to 1850
70 1850-
71.A-Z Special collections. By city and museum or private collector, A-Z
75 Egyptian
80 Assyro-Babylonian. Sumerian. Persian

History
Ancient sculpture -- Continued
85 Classical
86 Iconographies
87.A-Z Special collections. By city and museum or private collector, A-Z
Greek
90 General works
91.A-Z Special localities, A-Z (place of origin)
e.g.
91.A5 Aegina
91.A7 Athens
Special collections
92 Elgin marbles
Other, see NB87.A+
93 Color in Greek sculpture
94 General special
Special sculptors
98 Lysippus
100 Phidias
101 Polycletus
102 Praxiteles
103 Pythagoras of Rhegion
104 Scopas
105.A-Z Other, A-Z
108 Italian
110 Etruscan
115 Roman
116.A-Z Special Italian cities (other than Rome), A-Z
e.g.
116.P6 Pompeii
118.A-Z Remains in countries other than Italy, A-Z
e.g.
118.N5 Netherlands
120.A-Z Special sculptors, A-Z
130.A-Z Other ancient, A-Z
Limited to Mediterranean world and Middle East
130.C78 Cycladic
130.C8 Cypriote
130.J5 Jewish
130.L9 Lycian
130.P3 Palmyra
130.P46 Phrygian
130.S95 Sūsa (Libya)
Greek and Roman reliefs
133 General works
133.5.A-Z Special, A-Z
133.5.S46 Sepulchral monuments
Cf. NB143, Bronzes
133.5.T74 Triumphal arches
133.7.A-Z Special topics, A-Z
133.7.A65 Apollo (Greek deity)
133.7.A75 Assembly of gods

History
Ancient sculpture
Greek and Roman reliefs
Special topics, A-Z -- Continued

133.7.D56 Dionysus
133.7.H47 Hercules
133.7.L35 Landscape

Special materials of ancient sculpture other than stone
Bronzes

134 General works
135 Classical
140 Greek
141 Etruscan
Roman
142 General works
142.5.A-Z Special Italian cities (other than Rome), A-Z
142.7.A-Z In countries other than Italy, A-Z
143 Sepulchral monuments
145 Terra cottas
150 Statuettes. Figurines. Reliefs
153 Classical
155 Greek
157 Tanagra
158 Asia Minor
158.5.A-Z Other regions or countries, A-Z
158.7 Etruscan
158.9 Roman
159.A-Z Other special, A-Z
e.g.
159.E3 Egyptian

Glyptics (Carved gems, etc.), see NK5500+

Special subjects of ancient sculpture

160 Mythological
163.A-Z Special, A-Z
Aphrodite, see NB163.V5+
163.A7 Apollo (Greek deity)
163.A75 Artemis (Greek deity). Diana
Athena, see NB163.M5
163.C9 Cyrene
Diana, see NB163.A75
163.D5 Diomedes
163.D53 Dionysus (Greek deity)
163.D56 Dirce. Farnese bull
Farnese bull, see NB163.D56
163.F6 Fortuna (Roman deity). Tyche (Greek deity)
163.H4 Hercules. Heracles
163.J8 Jupiter (Roman deity). Zeus (Greek deity)
163.M3 Maia
163.M37 Mars (Roman deity)
163.M38 Marsyas (Greek deity)
163.M5 Minerva (Roman deity). Athena (Greek deity)
Nike, see NB163.V7

	History
	Ancient sculpture
	Special subjects of ancient sculpture
	Mythological
	Special, A-Z -- Continued
163.N5	Niobe
163.O7	Orestes
163.P6	Polyphemus
163.P8	Psyche (Greek deity)
163.S35	Satyrs
163.S4	Serapis (Egyptian deity)
	Tyche, see NB163.F6
	Venus (Roman deity). Aphrodite (Greek deity)
163.V5	General works
163.V6	Venus de Milo
163.V62A-Z	Other special types, A-Z
163.V62A55	Altovini
163.V62C67	Corinth
163.V62S3	Samos
163.V7	Victoria (Roman deity). Nike (Greek deity)
163.V8	Vulcan (Roman deity)
	Zeus, see NB163.J8
164	Personal
165.A-Z	Special, A-Z
165.A35	Agrippa, Marcus Vipsanius
165.A4	Alexander, the Great, 356-323 B.C.
165.A44	Amenhotep III, King of Egypt
165.A45	Amenkhotep, Priest
165.A5	Antinoüs, ca. 110-130
165.A55	Antonia Augusta, 36 B.C.-37 A.D.
165.A57	Antonine family
165.A9	Augustus, Emperor of Rome, 63 B.C.-14 A.D.
165.A95	Aurelius Antonius Marcus, Emperor of Rome, 121-180
165.C6	Commodus, Emperor of Rome, 161-192
165.G83	Gudea, of Lagash
165.H3	Hadrian, Emperor of Rome, 76-138
165.N4	Nefertiti, Queen of Egypt, 14th cent. B.C.
165.P3	Paullus, Lucius Aemilius, ca. 229-160 B.C.
165.P96	Pyrrhus, King of Epirus
165.S4	Sesostris III, King of Egypt
165.S45	Severus, Lucius Septimus, Emperor of Rome, 146-211
165.T47	Tetisheri, Queen of Egypt
165.T5	Thucydides
169	Other (not A-Z)
170	Medieval sculpture
171	Carolingian
172	Byzantine
175	Romanesque
180	Gothic

History -- Continued
185 Modern sculpture
Class special sculpture movements which are identified with one country and largely one century under country in NB201-NB1113
190 Renaissance
Italian, see NB615
193 17th and 18th centuries. Baroque. Rococo
197 19th and 20th centuries
19th century
197.3 General works
197.5.A-Z Special aspects or movements, A-Z
Subdivided like N6466 insofar as applicable
New sculpture (Art movement), see NB467.5.N48
20th century
198 General works
198.3.A-Z Private collections. By collector, A-Z
198.5.A-Z Special aspects or movements, A-Z
Subdivided like N6494 insofar as applicable
198.5.F6 Found objects
198.5.K5 Kinetic sculpture
198.5.S68 Sound sculpture
199 Jewish sculpture
201-1114 Special countries (Table N5 modified)
Establish special movements identified with one country and largely one century by adding .5 to the appropriate century number where possible and arranging movements alphabetically
Add country number in table to NB200
For sculpture in a particular material or on a special subject, see the material or subject
For ancient sculpture prefer NB69-NB169, when applicable
America
United States
20th century
212 General works
212.5.A-Z Special aspects or movements, A-Z
212.5.A27 Abstract expressionism
212.5.F68 Found objects sculpture
212.5.K54 Kinetic sculpture
212.5.S38 Sculpture Space (Studio)
Europe
Special countries
Great Britain. England
Modern
19th century
467 General works
467.5.A-Z Special aspects or movements, A-Z
467.5.N48 New sculpture
France
Modern
14th-16th centuries

History
Special countries
Europe
Special countries
France
Modern
14th-16th centuries -- Continued
545 General works
545.5.A-Z Special aspects, A-Z
545.5.M36 Mannerism. School of Fontainebleau
School of Fontainebleau, see NB545.5.M36
Germany
Modern
20th century
568 General works
568.5.A-Z Special aspects or movements, A-Z
568.5.F67 Formalhaut (Group)
568.5.K66 Gruppe Kontakt-Kunst (Hildescheim, Germany)
568.5.N37 National socialism
568.5.O34 Gruppe Odious
Italy
Modern
615 14th-16th centuries
1115 Sculptors - Collective biography
For individual sculptors, see NB98-NB105, NB120, and NB237-NB1114
Study and teaching
1120 General works
1125 United States
1130.A-Z Other countries, A-Z
Special schools
1132.A-Z United States. By name of school, A-Z
1133.A-Z Other countries. By country and name of school, A-Z
Competitions
Including individual awards, prizes, etc.
1134 General and international
1134.3 United States
1134.4.A-Z Other countries, A-Z
General works
1135 Theory. Aesthetics
1137 Relation to other arts. Sculpture and architecture
Cf. NA3680+, Architectural decoration
Treatises. Compends
1138 Early works through 1800
1140 1801-
Popular works
1142 General works
1142.5 Appreciation of sculpture
1143 Juvenile works
1145 Addresses, essays, lectures
1150 Atlases. Iconographies
For special sculptors, see NB98-NB105, NB237-NB1113

1160 Designs for sculpture
1170 Technique
1180 Modeling
Including clay, plaster, etc.
Cf. TT916, Handicraft
1185 Modeling in general casts
1190 Making of plaster casts
Cf. TT295, Plaster craft
1195 Instruments and apparatus
Special subjects, see NB1910+
1198 Mutilation or defacement of sculpture
For works on mutilation, defacement, etc. of sculpture in particular places, see NB201+
1199 Restoration of sculptures
1200.A-Z Special. By restorer, A-Z
Sculpture forgeries
1201 General works
1201.5.A-Z Special. By forger, or work of art, A-Z
Subarrange forgers by Table N6
1202 Sculpture materials
Sculpture in special materials
Class here works on special regions or countries
For special artists, see NB98-NB105, NB120, NB237-NB1113
1203 Soft sculpture
Cf. TT925, Handicraft
Stone
1208 General works
1209.A-Z By region or country, A-Z
1210.A-Z Special types, A-Z
1210.A4 Alabaster
1210.M3 Marble
1210.S55 Slate
1215 Cement. Concrete
1220 Metals
Cf. NK6400+, Metalwork
1230 Bronze
Cf. NK7900+, Bronzes
1240.A-Z Other metals, A-Z
1240.I75 Iron
1240.S7 Steel
1250 Wood. Driftwood
Cf. NK9700+, Wood carving
1255.A-Z Special. By country, A-Z
Ivory, see NK5800+
1265 Terra cotta
Cf. NK4267, Terra cotta ware
1270.A-Z Other materials, A-Z
Fabric, see NB1203
1270.G4 Glass
Cf. TT298, Glass craft
1270.G5 Glass fiber
Ice, see NK6030

Sculpture in special materials
Other materials, A-Z -- Continued
1270.N45 Neon
1270.P3 Paper
1270.P5 Plastic
1270.S3 Sand
Snow, see NK6030
1270.S6 Soap
1271 Found objects sculpture
Class here works of general interest
For works on found objects sculpture in particular places, see NB201+
For works on the special movement of the 20th century, see NB198.5.F6
1272 Mobiles. Kinetic sculpture
Class here works of general interest
Cf. TT899, Decorative crafts
For works on mobiles, kinetic sculpture, etc. in particular places, see NB201+
For works on the special movement of the 20th century, see NB198.5.K5
1275 Color in sculpture. Polychromy
Cf. NB93, Color in Greek sculpture
1277 Small sculpture
Including works on special regions or countries
1278 Sculpture gardens
Including works on sculpture gardens in special regions or countries
1280 Sculpture in relief (Bas-relief, high relief, etc.)
Including works on special regions or countries
Cf. NB133+, Greek and Roman reliefs
1282 Portals
1283.A-Z Special. By city or site, A-Z
1285 Doors
1287.A-Z Special. By city or site, A-Z
1287.F6 Florence. San Giovanni (Baptistry)
1288 Facades
1290 Monumental reliefs
1291.A-Z Special. By city (or name if non-urban), A-Z
1291.M3 Madarskiiat konnik
1291.P37 Pavia (Italy). Certosa di Pavia. Facciata
1291.S3 Schuylerville, N.Y. Saratoga Monument
Sculpture - Special forms
For works on statues, see general works on sculpture
For works of special sculptors, see NB98-NB1113
For special works of unknown sculptors, see NB69-NB199, NB201-NB1113

Sculpture - Special forms -- Continued
Portrait sculpture. Group portraits
For ancient portraits of an individual in the ancient world, see NB165.A+
For works on portraits of an individual man, see N7628.A+
For works on portraits of an individual woman, see N7639.A+
1293 General works
By period
1296 Ancient
1296.2 Egyptian
1296.3 Classical
1297 Medieval
1298 Renaissance and modern
1299 17th-18th centuries
1300 19th century
1301 20th century
By country
1303 United States
1305.A-Z Other countries, A-Z
1309 Busts
1310 Life masks. Death masks
For general works on masks, see GT1747+
For handicraft of making masks, see TT898
For masks of particular men, see N7628.A+
For masks of particular women, see N7639.A+
Equestrian statues
1312 General works
1313.A-Z By region or country, A-Z
Under each country:
.x General works
.x2A-.x2Z Special. By city (or by name if non-urban), A-Z
Sculptured monuments
Including rubbings
1330 General works
1340 Ancient
1350 Etruscan
1360 Greek and Roman
Cf. NB133.5.S46, Sepulchral reliefs
1370 Greek
1380 Roman
1390.A-Z Other. By country, A-Z
1420 Medieval
1450 Modern
1501-1685 Special countries (Table N2)
Add country number in table to NB1500
Public monuments, see NA9335+
Religious monuments
Cf. CC300+, Crosses
1750 General works

Sculpture - Special forms
  Religious monuments -- Continued
1753.A-Z Special. By place, A-Z
  e.g.
1753.G4 Geneva. Monument de la Réformation
  Shrines
1790 General works
1793.A-Z Special countries, A-Z
  Under each:
  .x General works
  .x2A-.x2Z Special. By city (or by name if non-urban), A-Z
  Sepulchral monuments
  Cf. NB133.5.S46, Greek and Roman reliefs
  Cf. NB143, Ancient bronzes
1800 General works
1805 Mausoleums
  Including individual mausoleums
1810 Sarcophagi
  Including individual sarcophagi
1820 Effigies
1830 Incised slabs
  Brasses. Incised bronzes
  Including rubbings
  Cf. TT912, Rubbing craft
1840 General works
  By country
1841 United States
1842 England
1843 France
1844 Germany
1845 Italy
1846.A-Z Other countries, A-Z
  Stone monuments, tablets, etc.
1850 General works
1851 Drawing and design
1853 Gothic styles
  By region or country
  United States
1855 General works
1856.A-Z Special places, A-Z
1857 Designs and catalogs
1859 Europe
1860 Great Britain. England
1862 Scotland
1863 Ireland
1865 France
1870 Germany
1875 Italy
1880.A-Z Other regions or countries, A-Z

Sculpture - Special forms -- Continued
Soldiers' and sailors' monuments
For historical works about soldiers' and sailors' monuments, see classes D-F
For technical works, see NA9325+
Vases, see NK4620+
1895 Wells
Special subjects
Class here general works on the topics as well as works on the topics in a particular region, country, etc.
Including technique, history, and collections
Religious subjects
1910 General works
1912.A-Z Special, A-Z
1912.A54 Angels
1912.A57 Anthony, of Padua, Saint
1912.A73 Arhats
1912.A92 Avalokiteśvara (Buddhist deity)
1912.B43 Bestiaries
1912.B83 Buddhist gods
1912.D42 Death
1912.D48 Devil
1912.D85 Durgā (Hindu deity)
1912.F34 Fall of man
1912.F64 Foliate head
1912.G35 Gaṇeśa (Hindu deity)
1912.G38 Gautama Buddha
1912.H33 Hachiman (Shinto deity)
1912.H55 Hindu gods and goddesses
1912.J34 Jaina gods
1912.J47 Jesus Christ
1912.J68 Joseph, Saint
1912.L34 Lajjā Gaurī (Hindu deity)
1912.M34 Maitreya (Buddhist deity)
1912.M37 Mary, Blessed Virgin, Saint
1912.P48 Peter, the Apostle, Saint
1912.S27 Saptamātṛkās (Hindu deities)
1912.S56 Siva (Hindu deity)
1912.S97 Sūrya (Hindu deity)
1912.T73 Tree of life
1912.V57 Vishnu (Hindu diety)
Mythology. Heroes. Legends
Cf. NB160, Ancient sculpture
1920 General works
1925.A-Z Special, A-Z
1925.R64 Roland (Legendary character)
Humans
Cf. NA3683.C3, Caryatids (Architecture)
Cf. NB164, Personal subjects in ancient sculpture
Cf. NB1293+, Portrait sculpture, busts, etc.
1930 General works

	Special subjects
	Humans -- Continued
1932	Special details of the human body (not A-Z)
	Including faces, heads, hands, feet, and other details
1935	Children
1936	Women
	Animals
1940	General works
1942.A-Z	Special, A-Z
1942.L55	Lions
1950	Plants
1952.A-Z	Other subjects or themes in sculpture, A-Z
1952.E76	Erotic sculpture
1952.O23	Occupations

Drawing. Design. Illustration
1 Periodicals and societies
5 Congresses
Encyclopedias, see N31
Dictionaries, see N33
Exhibitions (by place held)
Prefer classification by nationality or subject
15.A-Z United States. By city and museum or other place of exhibition, A-Z
17.A-Z Other countries. By country and city, A-Z
Museums and collections of drawings
20 Collective
23.A-Z Special countries, A-Z
Special museums
25.A-Z United States. By city and museum, A-Z
27.A-Z Other countries. By country and city, A-Z
Private collections
Including exhibition catalogs and catalogs of auctions devoted to single private collections
Prefer classification by subject, medium, period, or nationality
United States
30 Collective
31.A-Z Special. By collector, A-Z
33.A-Z Other regions or countries, A-Z
Under each country:
.x Collective
.x2A-.x2Z Special. By collector, A-Z
37 Catalogues raisonnés (General)
For special countries, see NC101+
Drawing rental and lending collections, see N378+
38 Sales catalogs
38.5 Auction catalogs
For private collections, see NC30+
Collected writings
40 Several authors
42.A-Z Individual authors, A-Z
45 Collective biography
For advertising designers, see NC999.2
For biography of illustrators, see NC961.6
For caricature artists, see NC1305
For general individual biography, see NC101+
For individual greeting card designers, see NC1868.A+
For individual poster artists, see NC1850.A+
History of drawing
Including books of reproductions of drawings
50 General works
52 Miscellaneous albums of drawings
53 General special
53.5 Intercultural relations in drawing (General)
54 Primitive
Cf. NK1177, Primitive ornament
55 Ancient

History of drawing
Ancient -- Continued
57 Greek
60 Roman
65.A-Z Other. By country, A-Z
65.E53 Egypt
70 Medieval
75.A-Z Special works, by name (artists unknown), A-Z
75.F55 Florentiner Skizzenbuch des internationalen Stils
75.J38 Jayadeva, 12th cent. Gītagovinda
75.L5 Liber depictus
75.R34 Reiner Musterbuch
75.W2 Warwick manuscript
75.W64 Wolfenbüttel Musterbuch
80 Modern
85 Renaissance. 16th century
86 17th century
18th century
87 General works
87.5.A-Z Drawings in special styles, A-Z
87.5.N46 Neoclassicism
89 19th and 20th centuries
19th century
90 General works
90.5.A-Z Drawings in special styles, A-Z
90.5.A7 Art nouveau
90.5.S96 Symbolism
95 20th century
95.5.A-Z Drawings in special styles, A-Z
95.5.A25 Abstract art
95.5.C83 Cubism
95.5.S9 Surrealism
101-377 Special countries (Table N3)
Prefer classification by subject except for special artists
Add country number in table to NC100
Under each (three number countries):
1 *General works*
2.A-2.Z *Local, A-Z*
3.A-3.Z *Special artists, A-Z*
Under each (one number or decimal number countries):
.A1 *General works*
.A2-.Z8 *Local, A-Z*
.Z9A-.Z9Z *Special artists, A-Z*
Under each (Cutter number countries):
.x *General works*
.x2A-.x2Z *Local, A-Z*
.x3A-.x3Z *Special artists, A-Z*
Europe
Great Britain. England
242.A-Z Special artists, A-Z
e.g.

History of drawing
Special countries
Europe
Great Britain. England
Special artists, A-Z -- Continued
242.T9 Turner, J. M. W. (Joseph Mallord William), 1775-1851
Italy
257.A-Z Special artists, A-Z
e.g.
257.B8 Buonarroti, Michel Angelo, 1475-1564
257.C56 Chirico, Giorgio de, 1888-
De Chirico, Giorgio, 1888- , see NC257.C56
Michelangelo Buonarroti, 1475-1564, see NC257.B8
Low countries
Netherlands
263.A-Z Special artists, A-Z
e.g.
263.G56 Gogh, Vincent van, 1853-1890
Van Gogh, Vincent, 1853-1890, see NC263.G56
Belgium
266.A-Z Special artists, A-Z
e. g.
266.D9 Dyck, Anthony van, Sir, 1599-1641
Van Dyck, Anthony, Sir, 1599-1641, see NC266.D9
Study and teaching
390 History
401-585 Special countries (Table N2)
Add country number in table to NC400
590 General works
593 General special
597 Outlines, syllabi, etc.
599 Examinations, questions, etc.
Instruction in elementary and secondary schools
610 Periodicals and societies
615 General works. Theory. Essays, etc.
620.A-Z Special systems of instruction, A-Z
Prefer classification by grade
Under each:
.x *Teachers' manuals*
.x2 *Textbooks*
Special grades
625 Kindergarten and primary
630 Elementary
635 Secondary
640 Correspondence school textbooks
650 Popular works for self-instruction
655 For children
Drawing rental and lending collections, see N378+
660 Studies and patterns for purposes of instruction
Cf. NC735, Studies for artists

Study and teaching -- Continued
670 Drawing books for children's amusements
For children's drawings, see N352+
Competitions
Including individual awards, prizes, etc.
673 General and international
674 United States
675.A-Z Other American. By region or country, A-Z
676.A-Z Europe. By region or country, A-Z
677.A-Z Other regions or countries. By region or country, A-Z
General works
703 Theory of design
Cf. NK1160+, Design in application to ornament
705 Early works to 1850
710 1851-
715 General special
720 Essays, lectures, etc.
725 Collectors' manuals
Technique
730 General works
735 Studies for artists
Cf. NC660, Studies and patterns for purposes of instruction
740 Composition
Balance. Rhythm. Symmetry. Porportion
745.A2 Early works to 1800
745.A3-Z 1801-
Perspective
748 History
749 Early works to 1800
750 1801-
(753) Studies of perspective in the works of special artists
See biography of the artist in appropriate classes
754 Line drawing
755 Light and shade
757 Reflections
758 Color drawing
Cf. NC870, Colored crayons
Cf. NC892, Colored pencils
760-825 Special subjects (Technique, history and collections)
Class here general works on the topics as well as works on the topics in a particular region, country, etc.
760 Art anatomy
Human figure
765 Figures. Proportions
Cf. N7570+, Human figure. Nude in art
770 Faces. Heads
Cf. N7573.3, Faces in art. Heads in art

Special subjects (Technique, history and collections)
Art anatomy
Human figure
Faces. Heads -- Continued
772 Collections of portrait drawings
Including self portraits
For works on portraits of an individual man, see N7628.A+
For works on portraits of an individual woman, see N7639.A+
773 Sketching of portraits
Cf. HV8073.4, Police composite drawings
Cf. NC860, Crayon portraits
774 Hands, feet and other details
775 Drapery on the human figure
776 Other drapery studies
778 Pinup art
Animal and wildlife anatomy and drawing
780 General works
780.5 Extinct animals. Dinosaurs. Prehistoric animals. Fossil animals
780.7 Endangered species
781 Fishes. Sharks. Whales. Marine fauna
782 Birds
783 Insects
783.8.A-Z Other animals, A-Z
783.8.C63 Cats. Kittens
783.8.D47 Desert animals
783.8.F67 Forest animals
783.8.G73 Grassland animals
783.8.H65 Horses
Kittens, see NC783.8.C63
783.8.P48 Pets
783.8.R45 Reptiles
783.8.Z64 Zoo animals
785 Action in art
787 Animal locomotion
Cf. QP301+, Movement (Physiology)
790 Landscapes
795 Sketching
799 Sketching machines
800 Landscape studies
805 Trees. Plants. Flowers
Cf. NK1560+, Design and ornament
810 Trees
815 Plants and flowers
817 Marine drawing
825.A-Z Other subjects, A-Z
825.A4 Airplanes
825.A47 Algeria
825.A53 Androids
825.A63 Armenia
825.A65 Arms and armor

Special subjects (Technique, history and collections)
Other subjects, A-Z -- Continued

825.A8 Automobiles
825.B6 Boats
825.B7 Bridges
825.B8 Buildings
825.C37 Cartoon characters
825.C49 Christmas
825.C5 Churches
825.C53 Circle
825.C56 Circus
825.C6 Costumes
825.D72 Dragons
825.E38 Egypt
825.E55 Emotions
825.E76 Erotic drawing
825.G3 Gardens
825.G64 Golf
825.G73 Greece
825.H32 Halloween
825.H4 Heraldic emblems
825.H55 Hindu gods and goddesses
825.H65 Holiday decorations
825.H85 Hunting
825.I42 Indian arts and crafts
825.I45 Interior decoration
825.I5 Interiors
825.M3 Machines (Nontechnical drawings)
Cf. TJ227+, Technical machine drawings
825.M6 Monsters
825.M64 Motor vehicles
825.M8 Musicians. Musical instruments
825.M9 Mythology
825.N34 Nature
825.N86 Numbers
825.O3 Occupations
825.O88 Outdoor life
(825.P5) Picture books
see NC965.85
825.R6 Rockets
825.S34 Science fiction
825.S5 Ships
825.S58 Space vehicles
825.S62 Sports
825.S74 Still life
825.T47 Terezín (Czech Republic: Concentration camp)
825.T7 Trains
825.T76 Trucks
825.T87 Turkey
825.U48 Underground movements
825.U5 Uniforms
825.V45 Vehicles
825.W47 West (U.S.)

Special subjects (Technique, history and collections)
  Other subjects, A-Z -- Continued
825.W67 Words
Graphic art materials (Technique, history and collections)
  For individual artists, see NC101+
845 General works
847 Paper
850 Charcoal. Charcoal and crayon
855 Crayon
860 Crayon portraits
865 Blackboard drawing. Chalk talks
  Cf. T361, Technical blackboard drawing
870 Colored crayons. Wax crayons
875 Stump drawing
Markers
877.8 General works
878 Dry markers
878.6 Felt markers
880 Pastel
885 Pastels (Reproductions)
Pencil
890 General works
892 Colored pencils
895 Pencil drawings (Reproductions)
Silverpoint
900 General works
902 Silverpoint drawings (Reproductions)
905 Pen and ink
  Cf. ND2460, India ink and sepia brush work
Silhouettes
910 General works
  Including silhouette cuttings
910.2.A-Z By region or country, A-Z
910.5.A-Z Special artists, A-Z
915.A-Z Other, A-Z
915.A35 Airbrush art
915.D6 Doodles. Doodling
915.R8 Rubbings. Frottage. Brass rubbing
  Cf. NK3632+, Non-Roman calligraphy
  Cf. TT912, Rubbing craft
915.S4 Scratchboard drawing
915.S7 Spatter-ink art
930 Conservation and restoration of drawings
  Cf. NE380, Conservation and restoration of prints
950 Drawing for reproduction
Courtroom art
953 General works
953.5.A-Z By region or country, A-Z
953.8.A-Z Special artists, A-Z

Drawing for reproduction -- Continued
960 Illustration
Cf. N8020+, Bible illustration
Cf. NE890+, Artists' illustrated books
Cf. Z276, Book decoration and ornamentation
Cf. Z1023, Illustrated books
Museums. Collections. Exhibitions
961.A-Z United States. By city and museum or other place of exhibition, A-Z
961.5.A-Z Other countries. By country and city, A-Z
961.55.A-Z Private collections. By collector, A-Z
961.6 Collective biography
For individual biography in special countries, see NC975+
961.63 Directories
961.7.A-Z Special subjects, A-Z
961.7.A54 Animals
961.7.D46 Detective and mysteries
961.7.F34 Fables
961.7.F66 Fountains
Mystery stories, see NC961.7.D46
961.7.P67 Portraits
961.7.S34 Science fiction
963.A-Z Special styles, A-Z
963.A77 Art nouveau
963.S87 Surrealism
Illustration of children's books
For works by artists of special countries, see NC975+
965 General works
965.7.A-Z Special subjects, A-Z
965.7.A54 Animals
965.7.T73 Transportation
965.8.A-Z Special characters, persons, or classes of persons, A-Z
965.8.C45 Children
965.8.P56 Pinocchio (Fictitious character)
965.85 Picture books
965.9 Coloring books
Textbook illustration
966 General works
966.5.A-Z By region or country, A-Z
966.8.A-Z Special artists, A-Z
Periodical illustration
For works by artists of special countries, see NC975+
968 General works
968.5.A-Z Special subjects, A-Z
968.5.C45 Christmas
968.5.H6 Horror tales
968.5.S33 Science fiction
968.5.W35 War
970 Newspaper illustration

Drawing for reproduction -- Continued
Map cover illustration
972 General works
972.2.A-Z By region or country, A-Z
972.4.A-Z Special artists, A-Z
Book cover design
Cf. Z266+, Bookbinding
Cf. Z276, Book decoration and ornamentation
973 General works
973.5.A-Z By region or country, A-Z
973.8.A-Z Special artists, A-Z
Magazine covers
For works by artists of special countries, see NC975+
974 General works
974.2.A-Z Special subjects, A-Z
974.2.P54 Pinup art
974.3.A-Z Magazine covers in special styles, A-Z
974.3.A78 Art nouveau
974.4.A-Z Special magazines. By title of magazine, A-Z
Illustration in special countries
United States
975 General works
975.5.A-Z Special illustrators, A-Z
Canada
975.6 General works
975.7.A-Z Special illustrators, A-Z
975.8 Latin America (General)
975.9 South America (General)
976.A-Z Individual Latin American countries, A-Z
Under each:
.x General works
.x2A-.x2Z Special illustrators, A-Z
977 Europe (General)
Great Britain
978 General works
978.5.A-Z Special illustrators, A-Z
Austrian, German, and Swiss (Collectively), see NC980.8
Austria
979 General works
979.5.A-Z Special illustrators, A-Z
France
980 General works
980.5.A-Z Special illustrators, A-Z
980.8 German, Austrian, and Swiss (Collectively)
Germany
Including the former West Germany
981 General works
981.5.A-Z Special illustrators, A-Z
Former East Germany
981.6 General works
981.62.A-Z Special illustrators, A-Z

Illustration in special countries
Europe (General) -- Continued
Italy
982 General works
982.5.A-Z Special illustrators, A-Z
Low countries
Netherlands
983 General works
983.5.A-Z Special illustrators, A-Z
Belgium
984 General works
984.5.A-Z Special illustrators, A-Z
Russia in Europe
985 General works
985.5.A-Z Special illustrators, A-Z
Scandinavia
986 General works
986.5.A-Z Special illustrators, A-Z
Spain
987 General works
987.5.A-Z Special illustrators, A-Z
Swiss, Austrian, and German (Collectively), see NC980.8
Switzerland
988 General works
988.5.A-Z Special illustrators, A-Z
989.A-Z Other European, A-Z
Bulgaria
989.B8 General works
989.B82A-Z Special illustrators, A-Z
Czech Republic
989.C9 General works
989.C92A-Z Special illustrators, A-Z
Hungary
989.H8 General works
989.H82A-Z Special illustrators, A-Z
Poland
989.P6 General works
989.P62A-Z Special illustrators, A-Z
Portugal
989.P7 General works
989.P72A-Z Special illustrators, A-Z
990 Asia
China
990.5 General works
990.6.A-Z Special illustrators, A-Z
Japan
991 General works
991.5.A-Z Special illustrators, A-Z
992.A-Z Other Asian, A-Z
Armenia
992.A74 General works
992.A742A-Z Special illustrators, A-Z

Illustration in special countries
Asia
Other Asian, A-Z -- Continued
Kirghizistan
992.K5 General works
992.K52A-Z Special illustrators, A-Z
Uzbekistan
992.U95 General works
992.U952A-Z Special illustrators, A-Z
Africa
993.A1 General works
993.A2-Z By country, A2-Z
Apply table at NC976.A-Z
Australia
994 General works
994.5.A-Z Special illustrators, A-Z
New Zealand
995 General works
995.5.A-Z Special illustrators, A-Z
995.8.A-Z Other countries, A-Z
Apply table at NC976.A-Z
(996) Indexes to illustrations (General)
See N7525
Commercial art. Advertising art
Cf. HF5841, Signs in advertising
Cf. HF5851, Advertising cards
Cf. HF6133, Cuts in advertising
Cf. T351+, Mechanical drawing, industrial drawing
Cf. TS171+, Industrial design
997.A1 Periodicals and societies. Yearbooks
997.A2 Congresses
997.A3A-Z Collections. By collector or institution, A-Z
997.A4A-Z Exhibitions. By place, A-Z
997.A5 General works
History
998 General works
By period
998.2 Early to 1900
998.4 1900-
998.45.A-Z Special styles or movements, A-Z
998.45.A7 Art deco
998.45.D33 Dada
998.45.F87 Futurism
By region or country
United States
998.5.A1 General works
998.5.A2-Z By region or state, A-Z
Under each state:
.x *General works*
.x2A-.x2Z *By city, A-Z*

Commercial art. Advertising art
History
By region or country -- Continued
998.6.A-Z Other regions or countries, A-Z
Under each country:
.x General works
.x2A-.x2Z By city, A-Z
999 Directories
999.2 Collective biography
Individual advertising designers, families, and firms
999.4.A-Z United States. By designer, etc., A-Z
999.6.A-Z Other countries. By country and designer, etc., A-Z
1000 Study and teaching. Techniques
Prefer NC850 NC915 for graphic art materials and techniques, where applicable
1001 Commercial art as a profession
Including advertising art, graphic design, illustration
1001.5 Awards, prizes, etc.
1001.6 Economics of commercial art
1002.A-Z Special types of advertising art, A-Z
Class here general works on the topics as well as works on the topics in a particular region, country, etc.
Including individual collections
1002.A4 Almanacs
1002.B49 Beverage paraphernalia
1002.B7 Broadsides
Cf. NC1800+, Posters
1002.C3 Calendars
1002.C4 Cards
Cf. GV1235+, Playing cards
Cf. HF5851, Advertising cards
Cf. NC1860+, Pictorial cards of greeting
Cf. NE965+, Tradesmen's cards and billheads
1002.C46 Children's paraphernalia
1002.C5 Cigar bands
1002.C68 Cosmetics
1002.F35 Fans
1002.L3 Labels
1002.L47 Letterheads
1002.L63 Logography
(1002.M3) Match covers, matchbox labels
See NC1889-NC1890
1002.M4 Menus
Posters, see NC1800+
1002.P7 Programs. Playbills
1002.W72 Wrappers
1003 Trademark design
Cf. NE965+, Advertising cards and billheads
Cf. T325, Trademarks

(1005-1260) Books of reproductions of drawings
See NC50-NC376, for history of drawing, or NC760-NC825, for special subjects
(1265) Children's drawings
See N352
Printed ephemera. Imagerie populaire
Classify here only works too broad to be classified under NE430-794, Wood and metal engraving; NE1030-1196, Wood engraving; NE1634-1815, Metal engraving; or NE1850-1879, Color prints
Cf. HE6182+, Stamps
Cf. HF5841, Signs in advertising
Cf. HF5851, Advertising cards
Cf. HF6133, Cuts in advertising
Cf. NC998.2, Advertising art (Early)
Cf. Z1029.5, Special classes of books
1280 General works
Chapbooks, see PN970+
American chapbooks, see PS472+
French chapbooks, see PQ803+
English chapbooks, see PR972+
Illustrated chapbooks
See Class NE, wood engraving, etc.
Broadsides, calendars, cards, etc, see NC1002.A+
Invitations, announcements, calling cards, etc, see NC1880
1282.A-Z By subject, A-Z
1282.T43 Teddy bears
1282.T73 Travel
1284.A-Z By country, A-Z
Caricature. Pictorial humor and satire
Cf. NC1878.W58, Picture postcards
For comic books, strips, etc., see PN6700+
1300 Periodicals and societies. Yearbooks
1302 Congresses
1305 Collective biography
For individual biography, including biography of cartoonists whose work may be in Classes D-F, see NC1400+
Exhibitions (by place held)
Prefer classification by nationality or subject
1310.A-Z United States. By city and museum or other place of exhibition, A-Z
1312.A-Z Other countries. By country and city, A-Z
Museums and collections
1313 Collective
1314.A-Z Special countries, A-Z
Special museums
1315.A-Z United States. By city and museum, A-Z
1316.A-Z Other countries. By country and city, A-Z
1318.A-Z Private collections. By collector, A-Z
1320 General works (technique, etc.)
History

Caricature. Pictorial humor and satire
History -- Continued
1325 General works
1330 Ancient
1335 Medieval
1340 Modern
1345 18th century
1350 19th century
1355 20th century
Special countries
1400 America
1410 North America
United States
1420 General works
1423 Before 19th century
1425 19th century
1426 20th century
1426.3.A-Z Special works. By name, A-Z
1427.A-Z Collections and exhibitions of works produced in the United States. By city and museum or other place of exhibition, A-Z
For special artists, see NC1429.A+
1428.A-Z Collections from special newspapers or periodicals. By name of publication, A-Z
1429.A-Z Special artists, A-Z
e.g.
1429.P35 Partch, Virgil Franklin, 1916-
Vip, 1916- , see NC1429.P35
Canada
1440 General works
1443 Before 19th century
1445 19th century
1446 20th century
1446.3.A-Z Special works. By name, A-Z
1447.A-Z Collections and exhibitions of works produced in Canada. By city and museum or other place of exhibition, A-Z
For special artists, see NC1449.A+
1448.A-Z Collections from special newspapers or periodicals. By name of publication, A-Z
1449.A-Z Special artists, A-Z
1450 Latin America
1455.A-Z Special countries, A-Z
1460.A-Z Special artists, A-Z
e.g.
1460.A68 Arbach
1460.F24 Falcón
Henfil, see NC1460.S6
1460.L3 Lavado, J. S.
1460.M46 Mendez
Quino, see NC1460.L3
1460.S6 Sousa, Henrique de
1461 West Indies

Caricature. Pictorial humor and satire
History
Special countries
West Indies -- Continued
1462.A-Z Special countries, A-Z
1463.A-Z Special artists, A-Z
1465 Europe
Great Britain
1470 General works
1473 Before 19th century
1475 19th century
1476 20th century
1476.3.A-Z Special works. By name, A-Z
1477.A-Z Collections and exhibitions of works produced in Great Britain. By city and museum or other place of exhibition, A-Z
For special artists, see NC1479.A+
1478.A-Z Collections from special newspapers or periodicals. By name of publication, A-Z
1479.A-Z Special artists, A-Z
Ireland
1479.3 General works
1479.5.A-Z Special artists, A-Z
Austria
1480 General works
1483 Before 19th century
1485 19th century
1486 20th century
1486.3.A-Z Special works. By name, A-Z
1487.A-Z Collections and exhibitions of works produced in Austria. By city and museum or other place of exhibition, A-Z
For special artists, see NC1489.A+
1488.A-Z Collections from special newspapers or periodicals. By name of publication, A-Z
1489.A-Z Special artists, A-Z
France
1490 General works
1493 Before 19th century
1495 19th century
1496 20th century
1496.3.A-Z Special works. By name, A-Z
1497.A-Z Collections and exhibitions of works produced in France. By city and museum or other place of exhibition, A-Z
For special artists, see NC1499.A+
1498.A-Z Collections from special newspapers or periodicals. By name of publication, A-Z
1499.A-Z Special artists, A-Z
e.g.
Chaval, 1915-1968, see NC1499.L28
1499.L28 Le Louarn, Yvan Francis, 1915-1968
Germany

Caricature. Pictorial humor and satire
History
Special countries
Europe
Germany -- Continued
1500 General works
1503 Before 19th century
1505 19th century
1506 20th century
1506.3.A-Z Special works. By name, A-Z
1507.A-Z Collections and exhibitions of works produced in Germany. By city and museum or other place of exhibition, A-Z
For special artists, see NC1509.A+
1508.A-Z Collections from special newspapers or periodicals. By name of publication, A-Z
1509.A-Z Special artists, A-Z
e.g.
1509.B8 Busch, Wilhelm
Greece
1510 General works
1513 Before 19th century
1515 19th century
1516 20th century
1516.3.A-Z Special works. By name, A-Z
1517.A-Z Collections and exhibitions of works produced in Greece. By city and museum or other place of exhibition, A-Z
For special artists, see NC1519.A+
1518.A-Z Collections from special newspapers or periodicals. By name of publication, A-Z
1519.A-Z Special artists, A-Z
Italy
1520 General works
1523 Before 19th century
1525 19th century
1526 20th century
1526.3.A-Z Special works. By name, A-Z
1527.A-Z Collections and exhibitions of works produced in Italy. By city and museum or other place of exhibition, A-Z
For special artists, see NC1529.A+
1528.A-Z Collections from special newspapers or periodicals. By name of publication, A-Z
1529.A-Z Special artists, A-Z
Low countries
1530 General works
1533 Before 19th century
1535 19th century
1536 20th century
1536.3.A-Z Special works. By name, A-Z

	Caricature. Pictorial humor and satire
	History
	Special countries
	Europe
	Low countries -- Continued
1537.A-Z	Collections and exhibitions of works produced in the Low countries. By city and museum or other place of exhibition, A-Z For special artists, see NC1539.A+
1538.A-Z	Collections from special newspapers or periodicals. By name of publication, A-Z
1539.A-Z	Special artists, A-Z
	Holland (Netherlands)
1540	General works
1543	Before 19th century
1545	19th century
1546	20th century
1546.3.A-Z	Special works. By name, A-Z
1547.A-Z	Collections and exhibitions of works produced in the Netherlands. By city and museum or other place of exhibition, A-Z For special artists, see NC1549.A+
1548.A-Z	Collections from special newspapers or periodicals. By name of publication, A-Z
1549.A-Z	Special artists, A-Z
	Belgium. Flanders. Wallonia
1550	General works
1553	Before 19th century
1555	19th century
1556	20th century
1556.3.A-Z	Special works. By name, A-Z
1557.A-Z	Collections and exhibitions of works produced in Belgium. By city and museum or other place of exhibition, A-Z For special artists, see NC1559.A+
1558.A-Z	Collections from special newspapers or periodicals. By name of publication, A-Z
1559.A-Z	Special artists, A-Z
	Russia
1570	General works
1573	Before 19th century
1575	19th century
1576	20th century
1576.3.A-Z	Special works. By name, A-Z
1577.A-Z	Collections and exhibitions of works produced in Russia. By city and museum or other place of exhibition, A-Z For special artists, see NC1579.A+
1578.A-Z	Collections from special newspapers or periodicals. By name of publication, A-Z
1579.A-Z	Special artists, A-Z
	Scandinavia
1580	General works

Caricature. Pictorial humor and satire
History
Special countries
Europe
Scandinavia -- Continued
1583 Before 19th century
1585 19th century
1586 20th century
1586.3.A-Z Special works. By name, A-Z
1587.A-Z Collections and exhibitions of works produced in Scandinavia. By city and museum or other place of exhibition, A-Z
For special artists, see NC1589.A+
1588.A-Z Collections from special newspapers or periodicals. By name of publication, A-Z
1589.A-Z Special artists, A-Z
Denmark
1590 General works
1593 Before 19th century
1595 19th century
1596 20th century
1596.3.A-Z Special works. By name, A-Z
1597.A-Z Collections and exhibitions of works produced in Denmark. By city and museum or other place of exhibition, A-Z
For special artists, see NC1599.A+
1598.A-Z Collections from special newspapers or periodicals. By name of publication, A-Z
1599.A-Z Special artists, A-Z
Iceland
1600 General works
1603 Before 19th century
1605 19th century
1606 20th century
1606.3.A-Z Special works. By name, A-Z
1607.A-Z Collections and exhibitions of works produced in Iceland. By city and museum or other place of exhibition, A-Z
For special artists, see NC1609.A+
1608.A-Z Collections from special newspapers or periodicals. By name of publication, A-Z
1609.A-Z Special artists, A-Z
Norway
1610 General works
1613 Before 19th century
1615 19th century
1616 20th century
1616.3.A-Z Special works. By name, A-Z
1617.A-Z Collections and exhibitions of works produced in Norway. By city and museum or other place of exhibition, A-Z
For special artists, see NC1619.A+

Caricature. Pictorial humor and satire
History
Special countries
Europe
Scandinavia
Norway -- Continued
1618.A-Z Collections from special newspapers or periodicals. By name of publication, A-Z
1619.A-Z Special artists, A-Z
Sweden
1620 General works
1623 Before 19th century
1625 19th century
1626 20th century
1626.3.A-Z Special works. By name, A-Z
1627.A-Z Collections and exhibitions of works produced in Sweden. By city and museum or other place of exhibition, A-Z
For special artists, see NC1629.A+
1628.A-Z Collections from special newspapers or periodicals. By name of publication, A-Z
1629.A-Z Special artists, A-Z
Spain and Portugal. Spain
1630 General works
1633 Before 19th century
1635 19th century
1636 20th century
1636.3.A-Z Special works. By name, A-Z
1637.A-Z Collections and exhibitions of works produced in both Spain and Portugal or in Spain alone. By city and museum or other place of exhibition, A-Z
For special artists, see NC1639.A+
1638.A-Z Collections from special newspapers or periodicals. By name of publication, A-Z
1639.A-Z Special artists, A-Z
Portugal
1640 General works
1643 Before 19th century
1645 19th century
1646 20th century
1646.3.A-Z Special works. By name, A-Z
1647.A-Z Collections and exhibitions of works produced in Portugal. By city and museum or other place of exhibition, A-Z
For special artists, see NC1649.A+
1648.A-Z Collections from special newspapers or periodicals. By name of publication, A-Z
1649.A-Z Special artists, A-Z
Switzerland
1650 General works
1653 Before 19th century
1655 19th century

Caricature. Pictorial humor and satire
History
Special countries
Europe
Switzerland -- Continued
1656 20th century
1656.3.A-Z Special works. By name, A-Z
1657.A-Z Collections and exhibitions of works produced in Switzerland. By city and museum or other place of exhibition, A-Z
For special artists, see NC1659.A+
1658.A-Z Collections from special newspapers or periodicals. By name of publication, A-Z
1659.A-Z Special artists, A-Z
1660.A-Z Other European countries, A-Z
1660.B8 Bulgaria
1660.C9 Czech Republic
1660.F5 Finland
1660.H8 Hungary
1660.P6 Poland
1660.R6 Romania
1660.T9 Turkey
1660.Y8 Former Yugoslavia
1670.A-Z Special artists of other countries, A-Z
1680 Asia
China
1690 General works
1693 Before 19th century
1695 19th century
1696 20th century
1696.3.A-Z Special works. By name, A-Z
1697.A-Z Collections and exhibitions of works produced in China. By city and museum or other place of exhibition, A-Z
For special artists, see NC1699.A+
1698.A-Z Collections from special newspapers or periodicals. By name of publication, A-Z
1699.A-Z Special artists, A-Z
Japan
1700 General works
1703 Before 19th century
1705 19th century
1706 20th century
1706.3.A-Z Special works. By name, A-Z
1707.A-Z Collections and exhibitions of works produced in Japan. By city and museum or other place of exhibition, A-Z
For special artists, see NC1709.A+
1708.A-Z Collections from special newspapers or periodicals. By name of publication, A-Z
1709.A-Z Special artists, A-Z
India
1710 General works

Caricature. Pictorial humor and satire
History
Special countries
Asia
India -- Continued
1713 Before 19th century
1715 19th century
1716 20th century
1716.3.A-Z Special works. By name, A-Z
1717.A-Z Collections and exhibitions of works produced in India. By city and museum or other place of exhibition, A-Z
For special artists, see NC1719.A+
1718.A-Z Collections from special newspapers or periodicals. By name of publication, A-Z
1719.A-Z Special artists, A-Z
1720.A-Z Other Asian countries, A-Z
1729.A-Z Special artists of other Asian countries, A-Z
1730 Africa
1740.A-Z Special countries, A-Z
1749.A-Z Special artists, A-Z
Australia
1750 General works
1753 Before 19th century
1755 19th century
1756 20th century
1756.3.A-Z Special works. By name, A-Z
1757.A-Z Collections and exhibitions of works produced in Australia. By city and museum or other place of exhibition, A-Z
For special artists, see NC1759.A+
1758.A-Z Collections from special newspapers or periodicals. By name of publication, A-Z
1759.A-Z Special artists, A-Z
New Zealand
1760 General works
1761.A-Z Special artists, A-Z
1762.A-Z Other, A-Z
Under each:
.x *General works*
.x2A-.x2Z *Special artists, A-Z*
Guam
1762.G8 General works
1762.G82.A-82.Z Special artists, A-Z
1763.A-Z Special subjects, A-Z
For historical events and personages, see classes D-F
For works for special regions or countries, see NC1400+
1763.A3 Actors
1763.A4 Aeronautics
1763.A45 AIDS (Disease)
1763.A55 Alien labor
1763.A6 Aquatic sports

Caricature. Pictorial humor and satire
Special subjects, A-Z -- Continued

1763.A66 Art
1763.A7 Astronautics
1763.A8 Automobiles
Cf. NC1763.W6, Women automobile drivers
1763.B6 Booksellers and bookselling
1763.B8 Business
1763.C35 Cats
1763.C45 Children
1763.C47 City and town life
1763.C5 Clergy
1763.C6 Communism
1763.C65 Contract bridge
1763.D2 Dancing. Dancers
1763.D3 Dentistry
1763.D7 Dreams
1763.D85 Dwellings
1763.E25 Economic assistance
1763.E5 Entertaining
1763.F48 Fire extinction. Fire prevention
Fire prevention, see NC1763.F48
1763.F5 Fishing
1763.G6 Golf
1763.H34 Health resorts
1763.H38 Heart
1763.H4 Heating
1763.H5 Historic preservation
1763.I5 Inventions
1763.J4 Jews
1763.L3 Law. Lawyers
1763.L4 Left- and right-handedness
1763.M3 Marriage
1763.M32 Masks
1763.M4 Medicine. Physicians
1763.M5 Military service
1763.M56 Moon
1763.M6 Motion pictures
1763.O95 Ozone
1763.P3 Parent and child
1763.P45 Photography
(1763.P5) Physicians
See NC1763.M4
1763.P56 Pinocchio (Fictitious character)
1763.P65 Plumbing

Caricature. Pictorial humor and satire
Special subjects, A-Z -- Continued
1763.P66 Politics
Class here general works on political cartoons, including general collections of political cartoons
For collections of political cartoons pertaining to individual countries or events, see classes D-F
For the history of political cartooning in individual countries, see NC1400+
1763.P67 Pollution
1763.P68 Postage stamps
1763.P7 Pregnancy
1763.P75 Professions
1763.P77 Prohibition
1763.P78 Psychoanalysis
1763.P8 Publicity
1763.R3 Railroads
1763.S4 Science
1763.S5 Sex
1763.S53 Sick
1763.S7 Sports
1763.T4 Teaching machines
1763.T48 Theater audiences
1763.T6 Tobacco-pipes
Town life, see NC1763.C47
1763.T7 Tramps
1763.V3 Vacations
1763.W3 War
Water sports, see NC1763.A6
1763.W6 Women. Women automobile drivers
Comic books, strips, etc.
Class here works on how to draw comics
For comics as a literary form, see PN6700+
1764 General works
1764.5.A-Z Special regions or countries, A-Z
Apply table at NC1762.A-Z
Motion picture cartoons
Cf. PN1997.5, Cartoon plays, scenarios, etc.
1765 General works
1766.A-Z By country, A-Z
Under each country:
.x *General*
.x2A-.x2 *Special artists, A-Z*
.x3A-.x3Z *Special works. By title, A-Z*
1766.U53R34 Raggedy Ann and Andy
Posters
1800 Periodicals and societies. Yearbooks
Exhibitions
1805.A-Z United States. By city and museum or other place of exhibition, A-Z
1806.A-Z Other countries. By country and city, A-Z

Posters -- Continued
History
Modern
1806.45 General works
1806.7 19th century
1806.8 20th century
1807.A-Z Special countries, A-Z
For special subjects, see NC1849.A+
1810 General works (Technique, etc.)
1815 General special
Including censorship
1817 Juvenile works
Museums and collections
1820 Collective
1823.A-Z Special countries, A-Z
Special museums
1825.A-Z United States. By city and museum, A-Z
1827.A-Z Other countries. By country and city, A-Z
Private collections
Including exhibition catalogs and catalogs of auctions devoted to single private collections
United States
1830 Collective
1831.A-Z Special, by collector, A-Z
1833.A-Z Other regions or countries, A-Z
Apply table at NC33.A-Z
1840 Trade catalogs
1845.A-Z Posters in special styles, A-Z
1845.A68 Art deco
1845.A7 Art nouveau
1849.A-Z Special topics, A-Z
Class here general works on the topics as well as works on the topics in a particular region, country, etc.
1849.A29 Advertising
1849.A35 Airlines
1849.A44 Alcoholic beverages
1849.A46 Alps
1849.A53 Animals
1849.A76 Art exhibitions
1849.A95 Automobiles
1849.B35 Banks and banking
1849.B43 Beer
1849.B52 Bicycles
1849.B57 Birth control
1849.B84 Bullfights
Cigarettes, see NC1849.T63
Cigars, see NC1849.T63
1849.C57 Circus
1849.C63 Coca-Cola Company
1849.D35 Dance
1849.E84 Etiquette
1849.F38 Fashion

Posters
Special topics, A-Z -- Continued
Film posters, see PN1995.9.P5
Individual artists of film posters, see NC1850.A+
1849.H43 Health resorts, watering places, etc.
1849.H66 Hotels
1849.H68 Household appliances
1849.H94 Hygiene
1849.H95 Hygiene products
1849.M43 Medicine
Olympic games, see GV721.75
Outer space, see NC1849.S63
1849.P42 Peace
Political posters
See the topic in classes D-F and J
1849.P82 Publishers and publishing
1849.R34 Railroads
1849.R42 Real estate business
1849.S42 Sea
1849.S47 Shoes
1849.S63 Space
1849.S66 Sports
1849.T45 Tennis
Theatrical posters, see PN2098+
1849.T63 Tobacco trade. Cigars. Cigarettes
1849.T68 Tourist trade
1849.T7 Transportation
Watering places, see NC1849.H43
1849.W65 Women
1850.A-Z Posters by special artists
Vignettes
1855 General works
By region or country
1856 United States
1857.A-Z Other regions or countries, A-Z
1858.A-Z Trade catalogs. By compiler, A-Z
Pictorial cards of greeting
Cf. PN171.G74, Authorship
1860 General (technique, etc.)
1861.A-Z Exhibitions. Collections. Museums. By country and collector or place of exhibition, A-Z
1864.A-Z Publishers' catalogs. By firm, A-Z
1864.H3 Hallmark Cards, Inc.
1866.A-Z Special occasions, A-Z
1866.A6 Anniversary
1866.C5 Christmas
1866.N3 New Year
1866.V3 Valentine
1867.A-Z Special styles, A-Z
1867.B53 Biedermeier
1867.T45 Three-dimensional
1868.A-Z Special designers, A-Z
Picture postcards

NC

Picture postcards -- Continued
1870 Periodicals
Exhibitions
1871.A-Z United States. By city and museum or other place of exhibition, A-Z
1871.5.A-Z Other countries. By country and city, A-Z
1872 General works
1875.A-Z Collections. By country and collector, A-Z
Publishers
1875.5 General works
1876.A-Z By country, A-Z
1877.A-Z Individual firms, A-Z
Including catalogs
1878.A-Z Special subjects, A-Z
For picture postcards depicting special places, persons, or events, see the place, person, or event
1878.A37 Afro-Americans
1878.A97 Automobiles
1878.B53 Bicycles
Boats, see NC1878.S4
1878.C36 Cats
1878.C55 Children's postcards
1878.D6 Dolls
1878.E7 Erotica. Pinup art
1878.F37 Fashion
Humor, see NC1878.W58
1878.L68 Love
1878.M68 Motion picture actors and actresses
Opera houses, see NC1878.T48
1878.P3 Patriotism
1878.P45 Photography
Pinup art, see NC1878.E7
1878.P6 Politics
1878.P74 Propaganda
1878.R34 Railroads
1878.R68 Royal portraits
1878.S4 Sea. Ships. Boats
Ships, see NC1878.S4
1878.S78 Street-railroads
1878.T48 Theaters. Opera houses
1878.T73 Travel
1878.W58 Wit and humor
1878.W64 Women
1878.5.A-Z Picture postcards in special styles, A-Z
1878.5.A75 Art nouveau
1878.7.A-Z Special countries, A-Z
1879.A-Z Special artists, A-Z

1880 Invitations, social announcements, calling cards
Use especially for non-illustrated cards and papers
Cf. HF5851, Advertising cards
Cf. NE965+, Tradesmen's cards
Cf. NE2710, Engraved letters and monograms
Cf. NK3630, Specimens of decorative lettering

Book jackets. Phonorecord jackets
1882 General works
1882.5.A-Z Exhibitions. Collections. Museums. By country and collector or place of exhibition, A-Z
1882.7.A-Z Special subjects, A-Z
1882.7.J39 Jazz album covers
1882.7.R62 Rock music record jackets
1882.7.S35 Science fiction
1883.A-Z Special countries, A-Z
1883.3.A-Z Special artists, A-Z

Cigar, cigarette, and tobacco labels
1883.5 General works
1883.6.A-Z Special countries, A-Z

Matchcovers. Matchbox labels
1889 General works
1890.A-Z Special countries, A-Z

Seals (Christmas, etc.)
Cf. HE6184.S42, Seals and labels (Philately)
1895 General works
1896.A-Z Special regions or countries, A-Z

1900 Copying, enlarging, and reduction of drawings
Cf. TR900+, Photography
1920 Pantograph
1940 Transfer processes

Painting
Periodicals, see N1+
Societies, see N10+
Congresses, see N21
Exhibitions, see N4390+
Museums and collections, see N400+, N5198+
Collected writings
25 Several authors
27 Individual authors
30 Encyclopedias
31 Dictionaries
Biography
For special countries, see ND201+
Collective
34 Early works to 1800
35 1801-
36 Popular works
38 Women painters
Individual artists, see ND201+
40 Catalogues raisonnés (General)
For special countries or artists, see ND201+
45 Other general catalogs of paintings. Indexes to paintings
For catalogs of lantern slides of paintings, see N4040.A+
For catalogs of reproductions of paintings, see N4035.A+
For indexes to portraits, see N7620
45.5 Appraisal of paintings
Prices of paintings. Sales catalogs
Class with subject, medium, period, or nationality, if possible
46 Early works to 1800
47 1801-
(48) Auction catalogs, dealers' catalogs since 1801
See N5220-5299, and N8640-N8650
History
49 Early works to 1800
50 General works
53 General special
For comparisons of ancient and modern painting, special influences and relationships between different cultures, see N7428.5
53.5 Outlines, syllabi
55 Chronological lists
60 Ancient and medieval
Ancient
70 General works
73 General special
75 Egyptian
100 Classical
110 Greek
115.A-Z Special painters, A-Z

History
Ancient
Classical -- Continued
118 Ancient Italy (General)
For Etruscan painting, see ND130.E8
120 Roman
125 Pompeian
127.A-Z Special painters, A-Z
130.A-Z Other ancient, A-Z
130.E8 Etruscan
135 Early Christian
Cf. N7840, Art of the catacombs
137 Medieval and modern painting
138 Folios
Medieval
140 General works
141 General special
141.5 Carolingian
142 Byzantine
143 Romanesque
144 Gothic
146 Islamic painting
Cf. ND2955, Illumination of books
150 Old masters
Prefer classification by century or nationality
Modern
160 General works
By century
Under each century a "General" number is provided, followed by a number for "Special aspects or movements." The latter is used for historical movements, etc., which are considered international
Special painting movements which are identified with one country and largely one century are classified where possible under country in ND201-ND1114
For individual painters, see ND201+
Renaissance. 15th-16th centuries
170 General works
Special countries, see ND201+
172.A-Z Special aspects or movements, A-Z
Divide like N6375
172.M3 Mannerist painting
177 17th and 18th centuries
17th century
180 General works
Special countries, see ND201+
182.A-Z Special aspects or movements, A-Z
Divide like N6415
18th century
186 General works
Special countries, see ND201+

History
Modern
By century
17th and 18th centuries
18th century -- Continued
188.A-Z Special aspects or movements, A-Z
Divide like N6425
189 19th and 20th centuries
19th century
190 General works
Special countries, see ND201+
192.A-Z Special aspects or movements, A-Z
Divide like N6465
192.I4 Impressionist painting
192.R6 Romantic painting
20th century
195 General works
Special countries, see ND201+
196.A-Z Special aspects or movements, A-Z
Divide like N6494
196.A2 Abstract painting
196.A25 Abstract expressionism
196.E9 Expressionist painting
197 Buddhist painting
(198) Islamic painting
See ND146
199 Jewish painting
Cf. N7414.75+, Jewish art
201-1114 Special countries (Table N5 modified)
Class here painting movements which are identified with one country and largely one century.
Assign numbers for special painting movements by adding .5 to the appropriate century number where possible under a country and using the movement as represented in the corresponding country and century in N6501-N7413
Add country number in table to ND200
Europe
Special countries
Great Britain. England
Modern
19th century
Including the Regency, Victorian, Edwardian periods
467 General works
467.5.A-Z Special aspects or movements, A-Z
467.5.P7 Preraphaelites. Preraphaelitism
France
Modern
19th century
547 General works
547.5.A-Z Special aspects or movements, A-Z
547.5.I4 Impressionism

History
Special countries
Europe
Special countries
France -- Continued
553.A-Z Special artists, A-Z
e.g.
553.G3 Gelée, Claude, called Claude Lorraine, 1600-1682
Lorraine, Claude, 1600-1682, see ND553.G3
Germany
Modern
17th-18th centuries
566 General works
566.5.A-Z Special aspects or movements, A-Z
566.5.B3 Baroque
20th century
568 General works
568.5.A-Z Special aspects or movements, A-Z
568.5.E9 Expressionism
Italy
623.A-Z Special artists, A-Z
e.g.
Angelico, Fra, 1387-1455, see ND623.F5
623.B23 Barbieri, Giovanni, Francesco, 1591-1666
623.B567 Bon, Angelo del, 1898-1952
623.B9 Buonarroti, Michel Angelo, 1475-1564
623.C2 Canal, Antonio, 1697-1768
Canaletto, 1697-1768, see ND623.C2
623.C56 Chirico, Giorgio de, 1888-
De Chirico, Giorgio, 1888- , see ND623.C56
Del Bon, Angelo, 1898-1952, see ND623.B567
623.F5 Fiesole, Giovanni da, called Fra Angelico, 1387-1455
Fra Angelico, 1387-1455, see ND623.F5
623.F78 Francesca, Piero della, 1416?-1492
623.G6 Giotto, 1266?-1337
Guercino, 1591-1666, see ND623.B23
Michelangelo Buonarroti, 1475-1564, see ND623.B9
Piero, della Francesca, 1416?-1492, see ND623.F78
623.R7 Rosa, Salvatore, 1615-1673
Titian, 1477-1576, see ND623.T7
623.T7 Tiziano, Vecelli, 1477-1576
Low countries
Belgium
673.A-Z Special artists, A-Z
e.g.
673.D9 Dyck, Anthony van, Sir, 1559-1641
Van Dyck, Anthony, Sir, 1599-1641, see ND673.D9
Russia

History
Special countries
Europe
Special countries
Russia -- Continued
699.A-Z Special artists, A-Z
e.g.
699.S48 Shevchenko, Taras, 1814-1861
699.V5 Vereshchagin, V.
Spain
813.A-Z Special artists, A-Z
e.g.
El Greco, 1541?-1614, see ND813.T4
Greco, 1541?-1614, see ND813.T4
813.T4 Theotocopuli, Dominico, called El Greco, 1541?-1614
Study and teaching
1115 General works
1120 General special
Special countries and schools, see N81+
Competitions, see N393+
General works
1130 Early works to 1800
1133 Comprehensive works
1135 1800-
1140 General special
Popular works
1142 General works
1143 Appreciation of painting
1145 Famous pictures described and interpreted
1146 Juvenile works
Picture study for elementary schools, see N366+
Picture rental and lending collections, see N378+
1150 Essays, lectures, etc.
1155 Anecdotes of painters and painting
1156 Facetiae, satire, caricatures, etc.
1158.A-Z Painting in relation to other subjects, A-Z
Class here general works on the topics as well as works on the topics in a particular region, country, etc.
1158.M66 Motion pictures
1158.P74 Psychoanalysis
1158.S45 Semiotics
1159 Small paintings
Including works on special regions or countries
(1160-1240) Books of reproductions
See ND49-ND1113, ND1290-ND1460
Catalogs of reproductions of paintings, including Unesco catalogs, see N4035.A+

(1242-1257) Art treasures of special countries
Class books on miscellaneous collections belonging to more than one museum or gallery in a country with the country in N510-N3990.
Class treasures of one museum under the number for the museum in N510-N3990
Class collections of native art of a country in N6501-N7413, or ND201-ND1113
(1259-1286) Technique. Styles. Materials and methods
See ND1470-ND1620
Special subjects of painting
Including technique, history and collections
For subjects for watercolor painting, see ND2190+
1288 Choice of subject. Titles. Themes and motives
Cf. ND45, Indexes to paintings
Human figure painting
1290 General works
1290.5 Nudes
1290.7 Female nudes
1290.8 Male nudes
Special countries
1292 United States
1293.A-Z Other countries, A-Z
Portraits. Group portraits. Self-portraits
For works on portraits of an individual man, see N7628.A+
For works on portraits of an individual woman, see N7639.A+
1300 General works
Exhibitions. Museums
Prefer special country, ND1311-ND1327, or special artist ND1329
1301.A-Z United States. By city and gallery or other place of exhibition, A-Z
1301.5.A-Z Other countries. By country and city, A-Z
1301.6.A-Z Private collections. By collector, A-Z
1302 Technical manuals
History
1303 General works
1304 General special
Including conversation pieces
1305 Ancient
1307 Medieval
1308 15th-16th centuries
Modern (since 15th century)
1309 General works
1309.2 16th century
1309.3 17th century
1309.4 18th century
1309.5 19th century
1309.6 20th century
Special countries
United States

Special subjects of painting
Portraits. Group portraits. Self-portraits
History
Special countries
United States -- Continued

1311	General works
	By period
1311.1	17th-18th centuries
1311.2	19th century
1311.3	20th century
	By region, state, etc.
1311.5	New England
1311.6	South
1311.65	Central States
1311.7	West
1311.75	Pacific States
1311.8.A-W	By state, A-W
1311.9.A-Z	By city, A-Z
1312.A-Z	Other American, A-Z
	Under each country:
	.x General works
	.x2 16th century
	.x3 17th century
	.x4 18th century
	.x5 19th century
	.x6 20th century
	Mexico
1312.M4	General works
1312.M42	16th century
1312.M43	17th century
1312.M44	18th century
1312.M45	19th century
1312.M46	20th century
	Europe
1313	General works
1313.2	16th century
1313.3	17th century
1313.4	18th century
1313.5	19th century
1313.6	20th century
	Great Britain
1314	General works
1314.2	16th century
1314.3	17th century
1314.4	18th century
1314.5	19th century
1314.6	20th century
	Austria
1315	General works
1315.2	16th century
1315.3	17th century
1315.4	18th century
1315.5	19th century

Special subjects of painting
Portraits. Group portraits. Self-portraits
History
Special countries
Europe
Austria -- Continued

1315.6 20th century

France

1316 General works
1316.2 16th century
1316.3 17th century
1316.4 18th century
1316.5 19th century
1316.6 20th century

Germany

1317 General works
1317.2 16th century
1317.3 17th century
1317.4 18th century
1317.5 19th century
1317.6 20th century
1317.7 Germany (East)

Italy

1318 General works
1318.2 16th century
1318.3 17th century
1318.4 18th century
1318.5 19th century
1318.6 20th century

Netherlands. Belgium

1319 General works
1319.2 16th century
1319.3 17th century
1319.4 18th century
1319.5 19th century
1319.6 20th century

Russia

1320 General works
1320.2 16th century
1320.3 17th century
1320.4 18th century
1320.5 19th century
1320.6 20th century

Scandinavia

1321 General works
1321.2 16th century
1321.3 17th century
1321.4 18th century
1321.5 19th century
1321.6 20th century

Spain and Portugal

1322 General works
1322.2 16th century

Special subjects of painting
Portraits. Group portraits. Self-portraits
History
Special countries
Europe
Spain and Portugal -- Continued
1322.3 17th century
1322.4 18th century
1322.5 19th century
1322.6 20th century
Switzerland
1323 General works
1323.2 16th century
1323.3 17th century
1323.4 18th century
1323.5 19th century
1323.6 20th century
1324.A-Z Other European, A-Z
Apply table at ND1312.A-Z
Orient
1325 General works
1325.2 16th century
1325.3 17th century
1325.4 18th century
1325.5 19th century
1325.6 20th century
China and Japan
1326 General works
1326.2 16th century
1326.3 17th century
1326.4 18th century
1326.5 19th century
1326.6 20th century
1326.8.A-Z Other Oriental countries, A-Z
Apply table at ND1312.A-Z
1327.A-Z Other countries, A-Z
Apply table at ND1312.A-Z
Biography of portrait painters
1328 Collective
1329.A-Z Individual, A-Z
Including collections of their work
e.g.
1329.D93 Dyck, Anthony van, Sir, 1559-1641
Van Dyck, Anthony, Sir, 1559-1641, see ND1329.D93
1329.3.A-Z Special subjects, A-Z
Class here general works on the topics as well as works on the topics in a particular region, country, etc.
1329.3.A38 Actors
1329.3.A74 Aristocracy
1329.3.C45 Children
1329.3.M45 Men
1329.3.P74 Priests

Special subjects of painting
Portraits. Group portraits. Self-portraits
Special subjects, A-Z -- Continued
1329.3.W6 Women
Portrait miniatures. Miniature painting
Cf. ND2900+, Illuminating of manuscripts and books
General works
1329.8 Early works through 1800
1329.9 1801-
1330 Technique
Exhibitions. Museums
1333.A-Z United States. By city and museum or other place of exhibition, A-Z
1335.A-Z Other countries. By country and city, A-Z
1335.6.A-Z Private collections. By collector, A-Z
1336 Biography (Collective)
History
1337.A2 General works
1337.A3-Z Special regions or countries, A-Z
Under each country:
.x General works
.x2A-.x2Z Special artists, A-Z
Landscape painting
1340 General works
1341 Sketching
1342 Technical manuals
History
1343 General works
1345 Ancient
1347 Medieval
1348 15th-16th centuries
Modern (since 15th century)
1349 General works
1349.2 16th century
1349.3 17th century
1349.4 18th century
1349.5 19th century
1349.6 20th century
Special countries
United States
1351 General works
1351.2 16th century
1351.3 17th century
1351.4 18th century
1351.5 19th century
1351.6 20th century
1352.A-Z Other American, A-Z
Apply table at ND1312.A-Z
Europe
1353 General works
1353.2 16th century
1353.3 17th century

ND

Special subjects of painting
Landscape painting
History
Special countries
Europe -- Continued
1353.4 18th century
1353.5 19th century
1353.6 20th century
Great Britain
1354 General works
1354.2 16th century
1354.3 17th century
1354.4 18th century
1354.5 19th century
1354.6 20th century
Austria
1355 General works
1355.2 16th century
1355.3 17th century
1355.4 18th century
1355.5 19th century
1355.6 20th century
France
1356 General works
1356.2 16th century
1356.3 17th century
1356.4 18th century
1356.5 19th century
1356.6 20th century
Germany
1357 General works
1357.2 16th century
1357.3 17th century
1357.4 18th century
1357.5 19th century
1357.6 20th century
Italy
1358 General works
1358.2 16th century
1358.3 17th century
1358.4 18th century
1358.5 19th century
1358.6 20th century
Netherlands. Belgium
1359 General works
1359.2 16th century
1359.3 17th century
1359.4 18th century
1359.5 19th century
1359.6 20th century
Russia
For Russia in Asia, see ND1365.5
1360 General works

Special subjects of painting
Landscape painting
History
Special countries
Europe
Russia -- Continued
1360.2 16th century
1360.3 17th century
1360.4 18th century
1360.5 19th century
1360.6 20th century
Scandinavia
1361 General works
1361.2 16th century
1361.3 17th century
1361.4 18th century
1361.5 19th century
1361.6 20th century
Spain and Portugal
1362 General works
1362.2 16th century
1362.3 17th century
1362.4 18th century
1362.5 19th century
1362.6 20th century
Switzerland
1363 General works
1363.2 16th century
1363.3 17th century
1363.4 18th century
1363.5 19th century
1363.6 20th century
1364.A-Z Other European, A-Z
Apply table at ND1312.A-Z
Asia. The Orient
1365 General works
1365.5 Russia in Asia
China, Japan, Korea
1366 General works
China
1366.7 General works
1366.715 Pre-16th century
1366.72 16th century
1366.73 17th century
1366.74 18th century
1366.75 19th century
1366.76 20th century
Japan
1366.8 General works
1366.815 Pre-16th century
1366.82 16th century
1366.83 17th century
1366.84 18th century

Special subjects of painting
Landscape painting
History
Special countries
Asia. The Orient
China, Japan, Korea
Japan -- Continued
1366.85 19th century
1366.86 20th century
Korea
1366.9 General works
1366.915 Pre-16th century
1366.92 16th century
1366.93 17th century
1366.94 18th century
1366.95 19th century
1366.96 20th century
1367.A-Z Other countries (including Asian), A-Z
Apply table at ND1312.A-Z
Marine painting
1370 General works
Special countries
United States
1372 General works
1372.2 16th century
1372.3 17th century
1372.4 18th century
1372.5 19th century
1372.6 20th century
1373.A-Z Other countries, A-Z
Apply table at ND1312.A-Z
Biography of marine painters
1374 Collective
1375.A-Z Individual, A-Z
Including collections of their work
Animals. Birds
1380 General works
Special countries
United States
1382 General works
1382.2 16th century
1382.3 17th century
1382.4 18th century
1382.5 19th century
1382.6 20th century
1383.A-Z Other countries, A-Z
Apply table at ND1312.A-Z
Sports. Hunting, fishing, etc.
1385 General works
Special countries
United States
1387 General works
1387.2 16th century

Special subjects of painting
Sports. Hunting, fishing, etc.
Special countries
United States -- Continued
1387.3 17th century
1387.4 18th century
1387.5 19th century
1387.6 20th century
1388.A-Z Other countries, A-Z
Apply table at ND1312.A-Z
Still life
1390 General works
Special countries
United States
1392 General works
1392.2 16th century
1392.3 17th century
1392.4 18th century
1392.5 19th century
1392.6 20th century
1393.A-Z Other countries, A-Z
Apply table at ND1312.A-Z
Plants. Trees. Flowers. Fruit
1400 General works
Special countries
United States
1402 General works
1402.2 16th century
1402.3 17th century
1402.4 18th century
1402.5 19th century
1402.6 20th century
1403.A-Z Other countries, A-Z
Apply table at ND1312.A-Z
Other subjects
Architectural
1410 General works
Special countries
United States
1411 General works
1411.2 16th century
1411.3 17th century
1411.4 18th century
1411.5 19th century
1411.6 20th century
1412.A-Z Other countries, A-Z
Apply table at ND1312.A-Z
Mythological. Symbolical
1420 General works
Special countries
United States
1421 General works
1421.2 16th century

Special subjects of painting
Other subjects
Mythological. Symbolical
Special countries
United States -- Continued
1421.3 17th century
1421.4 18th century
1421.5 19th century
1421.6 20th century
1422.A-Z Other countries, A-Z
Apply table at ND1312.A-Z
Religious
For icons of the Eastern Church, see N8185.5+
1430 General works
Special countries
United States
1431 General works
1431.2 16th century
1431.3 17th century
1431.4 18th century
1431.5 19th century
1431.6 20th century
1432.A-Z Other countries, A-Z
Apply table at ND1312.A-Z
Historical
1440 General works
Special countries
United States
1441 General works
1441.2 16th century
1441.3 17th century
1441.4 18th century
1441.5 19th century
1441.6 20th century
1442.A-Z Other countries, A-Z
Apply table at ND1312.A-Z
Genre
1450 General works
Special countries
United States
1451 General works
1451.2 16th century
1451.3 17th century
1451.4 18th century
1451.5 19th century
1451.6 20th century
1452.A-Z Other countries, A-Z
Apply table at ND1312.A-Z
Calligraphy as painting
1454 Periodicals. Societies. Congresses
1454.5.A-Z Exhibitions. Collections. Museums. By country and collector or place of exhibition, A-Z
1455 General works

	Special subjects of painting
	Other subjects
	Calligraphy as painting -- Continued
1456	General special
1457.A-Z	Special, A-Z
	Arabic
1457.A7	Periodicals. Societies. Congresses
1457.A72A-Z	Exhibitions. Collections. Museums. By city, A-Z
1457.A725A-Z	Private collections. By collector, A-Z
1457.A73	General works
1457.A74	History
1457.A75	Collective biography
1457.A76A-Z	Special artists, A-Z
1457.A77A-Z	Special works, by name (artists unknown), A-Z
	Buddhist
1457.B83	Periodicals. Societies. Congresses
1457.B832A-Z	Exhibitions. Collections. Museums. By city, A-Z
1457.B8325A-Z	Private collections. By collector, A-Z
1457.B833	General works
1457.B834	History
1457.B835	Collective biography
1457.B836A-Z	Special artists, A-Z
1457.B837A-Z	Special works, by name (artists unknown), A-Z
	Chinese
1457.C5	Periodicals. Societies. Congresses
1457.C52A-Z	Exhibitions. Collections. Museums. By city, A-Z
1457.C525A-Z	Private collections. By collector, A-Z
1457.C53	General works
1457.C54	History
1457.C55	Collective biography
1457.C56A-Z	Special artists, A-Z
1457.C57A-Z	Special works, by name (artists unknown), A-Z
	Islamic
1457.I8	Periodicals. Societies. Congresses
1457.I82A-Z	Exhibitions. Collections. Museums. By city, A-Z
1457.I825A-Z	Private collections. By collector, A-Z
1457.I83	General works
1457.I84	History
1457.I85	Collective biography
1457.I86A-Z	Special artists, A-Z
1457.I87A-Z	Special works, by name (artists unknown), A-Z
	Japanese
1457.J3	Periodicals. Societies. Congresses
1457.J32A-Z	Exhibitions. Collections. Museums. By city, A-Z
1457.J325A-Z	Private collections. By collector, A-Z
1457.J33	General works
1457.J34	History
1457.J35	Collective biography

Special subjects of painting
Other subjects
Calligraphy as painting
Special, A-Z
Japanese -- Continued

1457.J36A-Z Special artists, A-Z
1457.J37A-Z Special works, by name (artists unknown), A-Z

Korean

1457.K6 Periodicals. Societies. Congresses
1457.K62A-Z Exhibitions. Collections. Museums. By city, A-Z
1457.K625A-Z Private collections. By collector, A-Z
1457.K63 General works
1457.K64 History
1457.K65 Collective biography
1457.K66A-Z Special artists, A-Z
1457.K67A-Z Special works, by name (artists unknown), A-Z

Zen

1457.Z4 Periodicals. Societies. Congresses
1457.Z42A-Z Exhibitions. Collections. Museums. By city, A-Z
1457.Z425A-Z Private collections. By collector, A-Z
1457.Z43 General works
1457.Z44 History
1457.Z45 Collective biography
1457.Z46A-Z Special artists, A-Z
1457.Z47A-Z Special works, by name (artists unknown), A-Z

1460.A-Z Miscellaneous, A-Z

Class here general works on the topics as well as works on the topics in a particular region, country, etc.

1460.A34 Adirondack Mountains (New York)
1460.A37 Aeronautics
1460.A65 Aragon (Spain)
1460.A7 Artists' studios
1460.A88 Australia
1460.B35 Bali Island (Indonesia)
1460.B36 Bathing beaches
1460.B37 Battles
1460.B44 Belle-Ile-en-Mer (France)
1460.B47 Bernese Alps (Switzerland)
1460.B67 Bordeaux (France)
1460.B7 Brazil
1460.B76 Brittany
1460.B85 Bullfights
1460.C32 Calcutta (India)
1460.C34 California
1460.C35 Campagna di Roma (Italy)
1460.C43 Ch'ang-ch'ing hsien (China)
1460.C48 Children

Cf. ND1329.3.C45, Portraits

1460.C55 Circus
1460.C63 Classical architecture

Special subjects of painting
Other subjects
Miscellaneous, A-Z -- Continued

1460.C65 Concarneau (France)
1460.C66 Constance, Lake of
1460.C67 Cotentin (France)
1460.C68 Country life
1460.C74 Crespina (Italy)
1460.D34 Dancers. Dancing
1460.D65 Domestics
1460.D68 Douarnenez (France)
1460.D82 Dubrovnik (Croatia)
1460.D87 Düsseldorf (Germany)
1460.E35 Egypt
1460.E43 Elbe River (Czech Republic and Germany)
1460.E53 Engadine (Switzerland)
1460.E75 Erotic painting
1460.E95 Exoticism
1460.F34 Family
1460.F35 Fantasy
1460.F36 Farm life
1460.F55 Finistère (France)
1460.F56 Florence (Italy)
1460.G37 Gardens
1460.G44 Geneva, Lake
1460.G46 Gennevilliers (France)
1460.G73 Grand Canal (China)
1460.H34 Hague (Netherlands)
1460.H38 Hauts-de-Seine (France)
1460.H65 Home
1460.H66 Hopeh Province (China)
1460.I73 Iran
1460.I83 Italy
1460.K37 Karelia (Russia)
1460.K55 Kirin Province (China)
1460.L33 Labor. Laboring classes. Working class
1460.L38 Laval (Québec)
1460.L43 Lebanon
1460.L45 Leisure class
1460.L48 L'Estaque (France)
1460.L68 Love
1460.M43 Medicine
1460.M45 Mediterranean Region
1460.M48 Mexico
1460.M64 Moon. Moonlight
Moonlight, see ND1460.M64
1460.M66 Moscow (Russia)
1460.M87 Musical instruments
1460.N38 Nature
1460.N48 New York (N.Y.)
1460.N67 Normandy (France)
1460.N87 Nursing
1460.P35 Painting (as a theme)

Special subjects of painting
Other subjects
Miscellaneous, A-Z -- Continued
1460.P38 Paris (France)
1460.P39 Pas-de-Calais (France)
1460.P47 Personal space
1460.P65 Port Louis (Mauritius)
1460.P67 Porto (Portugal)
1460.P83 Puerto Rico
1460.Q43 Québec (Québec)
1460.R3 Railroads
1460.R32 Rainbow
1460.R83 Rugs, Oriental
1460.S23 Sainte-Victoire Mountain (France)
1460.S24 San Francisco (Calif.)
1460.S28 Sauzon (France)
1460.S45 Sidon (Lebanon)
1460.S55 Skies
1460.S62 Snow
1460.S63 Social problems
Soldiers, see ND1460.W37
1460.T54 Time
1460.T95 Tyrol (Austria)
1460.U54 United States
1460.V32 Val d'Oise (France)
1460.V34 Valais (Switzerland)
1460.V37 Vases, Greek
1460.V39 Vaud (Switzwerland)
1460.V45 Venice (Italy)
1460.V47 Versailles (France)
1460.W37 War
Including soldiers as artists, except where the subject matter is entirely unrelated to military subjects
For collections of paintings about a specific war, see the war in classes D-F. For works by a particular artist, see the artist under medium and nationality
1460.W54 Wine
1460.W55 Winter
1460.W65 Women
Cf. ND1290.7, Female nudes
Cf. ND1329.3.W6, Portraits
1460.W95 Wyoming
Painting technique and styles
Technique
Cf. ND1500+, Materials and methods
1470 Periodicals

Painting technique and styles
Technique -- Continued

1471 General works

Including histories of painting techniques or comparisons of various painting media, from the viewpoint of the historian rather than the artist

For technical manuals for the artist, see ND1500+

1473 Technical manuals for amateur painters

Cf. ND1620, Amateurs' manuals for painting on china, etc.

1475 Composition

Styles

Class here general discussions of stylistic elements in painting, especially those too general to go under one century or one country

For special styles related to historical movements in art, prefer "special aspects or movements" numbers under History of painting, ND172-ND196, or under special countries

1480 General works

1481 General special

1482.A-Z Special styles, A-Z

1482.A16 Abstraction

Cf. ND196.A2, History of abstract painting

1482.C5 Classicism

Prefer ND100 ND127 or ND188.N4 where applicable

1482.E9 Expressionism

Cf. ND196.E9, History of expressionist painting

1482.I6 Impressionism

Cf. ND192.I4, History of impressionist painting

Cf. ND547.5.I4, French impressionism

1482.M3 Mannerism

Cf. ND172.M3, History of Mannerist painting

1482.P7 Primitive painting. Naive painting

Cf. N7432.5.P7, Primitivism

1482.R4 Realist painting. Naturalism

1482.R6 Romantic painting

Cf. ND192.R6, History of romantic painting

1484 Light

Including shade and shadows, daylight, etc.

Color

General works

1486 Early works to 1800

1488 1800-

1489 General special

1490 Popular works

1492 Technical works

e.g. plates of color standards

1493.A-Z Special color systems, A-Z

e.g.

Painting technique and styles
Color
Special color systems, A-Z -- Continued
1493.M8 Munsell
1493.O8 Ostwald
1495.A-Z Special aspects of color, A-Z
1495.P8 Psychology of color in art
1495.S9 Symbolism
Painting materials and methods
1500 General. Technical manuals for artists
For works on special themes in special painting media, see the theme
Cf. ND1370+, Seascape in polymer painting
Cf. ND1471, General studies of painting technique (Comparisons of styles, etc.)
Cf. ND1473, Technical manuals for amateurs
1505 General special
1510 Pigments
1530 Varnishes
1535 Synthetic pigments and media
e.g. Acrylic polymers, other plastic paints
Including works on synthetic paints with aqueous bases
1536 Rollers
1538 Brushes
1539 Painting knives and other implements
Including works on palette knife painting
1550.A-Z Trade catalogs. By firm, A-Z
Special surfaces for painting
Cf. ND2470, Fresco painting
Cf. TT385, Tole painting
1560 General works
Fabrics (Canvas, linen)
1570 General works
1572 Silk, satin, and other fabrics (Kensington, Lustra, etc.)
1573 Transparency painting of fabrics
1575 Wood
Cf. NK2703, Decorative furniture painting
1580 Stone
1585 Paper
Cf. ND2370, Fore-edge painting
1587 Vellum
Glass
For glass painting in general, see NK5300+
1595 Lantern slides (Hand painted)
Cf. TR505, Photography
For catalogs of color slides of works of art, see N4040.A+
1605 Metal
1615 Ivory
1618 Plastics

Painting materials and methods
Special surfaces for painting -- Continued
1620 Amateurs' manuals for painting on china, satin, glass, etc.
For china painting, china and glass painting, see NK4605+
For glass painting, see NK5304
1625 Silk, satin, and other fabrics (Kensington, Lustra, etc.)
Examination and conservation of paintings
1630 General works
1632 Mutilation or defacement of paintings
For thefts of works of art, see N8795+
For works on mutilation, defacement, etc. of paintings in particular places, see ND201+
1635 Technical examination: Expertising, x-ray, micrography, etc.
1637 Attribution and reattribution
1638 Deterioration of paintings
Preservation and care of paintings
1640 General works
1643.A-Z Special collections, A-Z
Restoration
For works on the conservation and restoration of art found in particular places, see ND201+
1650 General works
1651.A-Z Exhibitions. Collections. Museums. By country and place of exhibition, A-Z
1653.A-Z Special. By restorer, A-Z
1655 Copying and reproducing of paintings
Do not use for books of reproductions of paintings
Cf. N4035.A+, Trade catalogs and catalogs of reproductions
1656.A-Z Special. By painter or work of art copied, A-Z
Subarrange painters by Table N6
1660 Painting forgeries
1662.A-Z Special. By forger, or work of art, A-Z
Subarrange forgers by Table N6
Watercolor painting
1700 Periodicals
Societies
1711 United States
1712.A-Z Other American countries, A-Z
1713 Great Britain
1714 France
1715 Germany. Austria
1716 Italy
1717 Netherlands. Belgium
1718 Scandinavia
1719 Spain and Portugal
1720 Switzerland
1721.A-Z Other countries, A-Z
Museums. Collections

Watercolor painting
Museums. Collections -- Continued
1725.A-Z United States. By city and museum or collector, A-Z
1727.A-Z Other countries. By country and city, or country and collector, A-Z
1731-1735 Exhibitions (by place held)
Prefer classification by societies, ND1171 ND1721; by nationality ND1801 ND2094; or by subject ND290 ND2365
1731.A-Z United States. By city and museum or other place of exhibition, A-Z
1733.A-Z Great Britain. By city and museum or other place of exhibition, A-Z
1735.A-Z Other countries. By country and city, A-Z
Collected writings
1740 Several authors
1742 Individual authors
1750 Biography (Collective)
Prefer classification by special countries
History
1760 General works
1770 Ancient
1780 Medieval
1790 Modern
1795 17th-18th centuries
1797 19th century
1798 20th century
1801-2094.5 Special countries (Table N4)
Add country number in table to ND1800
Under each country (4-number countries):
1 General works
2.A-2.Z Special divisions, A-Z
3.A-3.Z Special cities, A-Z
4.A-4.Z Special artists, A-Z
Under each (3-number countries):
1 General works
2.A-2.Z Local, A-Z
3.A-3.Z Special artists, A-Z
Under each (2-number countries):
1.A1 General works
1.A2-1.Z Local, A-Z
2.A-2.Z Special artists, A-Z
Under each (1-number countries):
.A1 General works
.A2-.Z7 Local, A-Z
.Z8A-.Z8Z Special artists, A-Z
Under each (Cutter-number countries):
.x General
.x2A-.x2Z Local, A-Z
.x3A-.x3Z Special artists, A-Z
2095.A-Z Special works, by name (artist unknown), A-Z (regardless of country)
Study and teaching

Watercolor painting
Study and teaching -- Continued
2110 General works
2113 Outlines, syllabi, etc.
2115.A-Z Special topics, A-Z
General works
2125 Early works to 1800
2130 1800-
(2133-2145) Technical treatises
See ND2420-ND2440
2150 Addresses, essays, lectures
(2160) Reproductions of watercolors (General)
See ND1760-ND2094, and ND2190-ND2365
Special countries and special artists, see ND1801+
Special subjects of watercolor painting (Technique, history and collections)
Human figure
2190 General works
2191 United States
2192.A-Z Other countries, A-Z
Portraits
2200 General works
2201 United States
2202.A-Z Other countries, A-Z
Nature
2237 General works
By region or country
2238 United States
2239.A-Z Other regions or countries, A-Z
Landscapes
2240 General works
2241 Sketching
By region or country
2242 United States
2243.A-Z Other regions or countries, A-Z
Trees. Plants
2244 General works
By region or country
2245 United States
2246.A-Z Other regions or countries, A-Z
Marines
2270 General works
2271 United States
2272.A-Z Other countries, A-Z
Animals. Birds
2280 General works
2281 United States
2282.A-Z Other countries, A-Z
Still life
2290 General works
2291 United States
2292.A-Z Other countries, A-Z
Flowers. Fruit

Watercolor painting
Special subjects of watercolor painting (Technique, history and collections)
Still life
Flowers. Fruit -- Continued
2300 General works
2301 United States
2302.A-Z Other countries, A-Z
Architectural subjects
Cf. NA2726.5, Architectural drawing
2310 General works
2311 United States
2312.A-Z Other countries, A-Z
Genre
2350 General works
2351 United States
2352.A-Z Other countries, A-Z
Religious subjects
2360 General works
2361 United States
2362.A-Z Other countries, A-Z
2365 Other (not A-Z)
2370 Fore-edge painting
(2380-2395) Materials for watercolor painting
See ND2420-ND2495
2397 Outline design cards
2399 Painting books for children
Cf. ND2440, Technique of watercolor painting (Juvenile)
Cf. ND2490, Finger painting
Children's watercolors, see N352+
Techniques of watercolor painting. Materials and special media
For special countries and artists, see ND1801+
2420 General works
2422 General special
2425.A-Z Trade catalogs. By firm, A-Z
Transparent watercolor
2430 General works. Technical manuals
2435 Special elements of technique
2440 Minor technical. Juvenile
Cf. ND2399, Painting books for children
Cf. ND2490, Finger painting
Other methods and media
For special countries and artists, see ND1801+
2460 India-ink and sepia brush work. Neutral tints
2462 Sumi painting. Haiga
2463 Nanga
2465 Tempera. Gouache. Casein. Distemper
2468 Egg tempera
2470 Fresco
For history of murals painted in fresco technique, see ND2550+

Watercolor painting
Techniques of watercolor painting. Materials and special media
Other methods and media
Tempera. Gouache. Casein. Distemper -- Continued
2480 Encaustic
2490 Finger painting
2492 Stencil painting
Cf. NE2240+, Stencil prints
Cf. NK8650+, Stencil work (Decorative)
2495 Other (not A-Z)
Synthetic pigments and media, see ND1535
Mural painting
Including fresco and other techniques
Cf. ND2470, Fresco
Cf. NK2119, Ceilings, walls, floors (Interior decoration)
2550 General works
2550.5 Attribution and reattribution
2551 Deterioration of murals
2552 Restoration of murals
2555 Ancient and medieval
2560 Ancient
2565 Etruscan
2570 Greek. Hellenistic
2575 Roman. Pompeian. Herculanean
2578 Medieval
2578.3 Sogdian
2579 Carolingian
2580 Romanesque
2583 Byzantine
2590 Modern
2601-2877 Special countries (Table N3 modified)
Add country number in table to ND2600
Under each (three number countries):
1 *General works*
2.A-2.Z *Special divisions, regions, A-Z*
3.A-3.Z *Special cities, A-Z*
Under each (one number or decimal number countries):
.A1 *General works*
.A2-.Z8 *Special divisions, regions, A-Z*
.Z9A-.Z9Z *Special cities, A-Z*
Under each (Cutter number countries):
.x *General works*
.x2A-.x2Z *Special divisions, regions, A-Z*
.x3A-.x3Z *Special cities, A-Z*
Europe
Great Britain. England
2731.A-Z English counties, A-Z
2732.A-Z London. By building, A-Z
2733.A-Z Other local, A-Z
e.g.

Mural painting
Special countries
Europe
Great Britain. England
Other local, A-Z -- Continued
2733.S8 Stratford-on-Avon
Special artists
See ND237-ND1113
Panoramas, etc.
Here are entered works on painted panoramas
For panoramas descriptive of special places or events, see classes D-F
For works in a variety of media and formats, see N7436.5+
2880 General works
2880.5.A-Z By region or country, A-Z
2881.A-Z By special artists, A-Z
Dioramas
Including miniature and juvenile
2882 General works
2882.5.A-Z Special artists, A-Z
2883 Cosmoramas
Scene painting. Painted theater curtains
Including paintings as designs for stage settings
2885 General works
2887.A-Z Special countries, A-Z
2888.A-Z Special artists, A-Z
Illuminating of manuscripts and books
2889 Dictionaries
2890 Biographical dictionaries
2893 Exhibitions
2894.A-Z Collections in special countries, A-Z
e.g.
2894.S7 Spain
Collections in special libraries and museums
2895.A-Z United States. By city and institution, A-Z
2896.A-Z Other American. By country and city, A-Z
2897.A-Z Great Britain. By city and institution, A-Z
2898.A-Z Other European countries. By country and city, A-Z
2899.A-Z Other countries. By country and city, A-Z
2899.5 Sales catalogs
History
2900 General works
2910 Ancient
2920 Medieval
2930 Early Christian. Byzantine
2935 Hebrew
2940 Anglo-Saxon. Celtic. Irish
2950 Carolingian
2955 Islamic
2960 Romanesque
2980 Gothic
2990 Renaissance

Illuminating of manuscripts and books
  History -- Continued
    Asian, see ND3237
3001-3294.5 Special countries (Table N4)
      Add country number in table to ND3000
      Apply table at ND1801-2094.5
3237 Asia. The Orient
  General works
    Including technique
3305 Early works to 1800
3310 Treatises since 1800
3320 General special
3325 Addresses, essays, lectures
3327.A-Z Special techniques, A-Z
3327.G54 Gilding
3327.G74 Grisaille
  Special elements and subjects
3333 Astrology
3334 Borders
3335 Initials. Ornaments
3336 Occupations
3337 Human figure. Portraits
3338 Religious subjects
3339 Animals. Birds
3340 Plants. Flowers. Trees
3341 Landscapes
3342 Interiors. Still life
3343 Architecture
3343.5 Musical instruments. Musicians
  Histories and reproductions of special illuminated works
3345 Societies (for the reproduction of illuminated manuscripts)
3350 Series. Collections
    Special works
      In providing for special works by name, Cutter for the first significant element in the uniform title, unless otherwise indicated
      Bibles
3355 General works
3355.5.A-Z Special Bibles. By name, A-Z
3355.5.A37 Aetatibus mundi imagines
3355.5.A45 Codex Amiatinus
3355.5.B52 Bibliothèque nationale (France). Manuscript. Syr. 341
3355.5.B62 Bodleian Library. Manuscript. Laud misc. 752
3355.5.C63 Codex Vindobonensis 2554
3355.5.F53 Figurae bibliorum
3355.5.L35 Lambeth Bible
3355.5.M67 Moutier-Grandval Bible
3355.5.N38 Národní muzeum v Praze. Manuscript. XIIB13
3355.5.N43 Necksei-Lipócz Bible
3355.5.P56 Biblia Płocka

Illuminating of manuscripts and books
Histories and reproductions of special illuminated works
Special works
Bibles
Special Bibles. By name, A-Z -- Continued

3355.5.S35 San Paolo Bible
3355.5.T67 Topkapı i Sarayı i Müzesi. Kütüphane. Manuscript. 52
3355.5.W55 Winchester Bible

Old Testaments

3356 General works
3356.5.A-Z Special Bibles. By name, A-Z
3356.5.A35 Admonter Bible
3356.5.B47 Berlin. Preussische Staatsbibliothek. Mss. (Theol. lat. fol. 485)
3356.5.C66 Copenhagen. Universitet. Bibliothek. Mss. (Arnamag. 227 fol.)
3356.5.N36 Naples Bible (Vienna. Nationalbibliothek. Mss. (1191))
3356.5.W46 Wenzelsbibel
3357.A-Z Psalters, A-Z
e.g.
3357.A1 Collected
3357.5.E4 Egbert psalter (Codex Gertrudianus)
3358.A-Z Other special parts of the Old Testament, A-Z
e.g.
3358.5.P5 Pentateuch
3358.5.S8 Song of Solomon

New Testaments

3359.A2 General works
3359.A3-Z Evangelaries, A-Z
3359.C56 Codex aureus Epternacensis
3359.C57 Codex purpureus Rossanensis
3359.C78 Cologne Gospels
3359.D87 Book of Durrow
3359.E62 Erfurter codex aureus
3359.G46 Gladzori Avetaran
3359.G84 Gundohinus Gospels
3359.H44 Evangeliar Heinrichs des Löwen
3359.K35 Kaiser Heinrich III's Evangelistar
3359.K36 Kaiser Otto III's Evangelary, Aachen
3359.K4 Book of Kells
3359.L5 Lindisfarne Gospels
3359.M42 Miroslavljevo jevanđelje
3359.N48 New York Cruciform Lectionary
3359.Q43 Quedlinburg Gospels
3359.T47 Tetraevangheliarul Sucevița 23
3359.T48 Tetraevangheliarul Sucevița 24
3359.U82 Uta-Evangelistar
3361.A-Z Special parts, A-Z
3361.E57 Epistles of Paul
Revelation (Apocalypse)

Illuminating of manuscripts and books
Histories and reproductions of special illuminated works
Special works
Bibles
New Testaments
Special parts, A-Z
Revelation (Apocalypse) -- Continued
3361.R5 General works
3361.R52.A-Z Individual. By name, A-Z, and date
3361.R52.B43 Beatus, Saint, Presbyter of Liebana, d. 798. In Apocalipsin
3361.R52.B63 Bodleian Library. Manuscript. Douce 180
3361.R52.D95 Dyson Perrins Apocalypse
3361.R52.L53 Université de Liège. Bibliothèque. Manuscript. Willaert no. 6
3362.5 Benedictionals
Books of hours
3363.A1 General works
3363.A2-Z Special, A-Z
e.g.
3363.B5 Hours of the Duc de Berry
3365 Breviaries
e.g.
3365.G7 Grimani breviary
Sacramentaries
3370 General works
3370.5.A-Z Special, A-Z
3370.5.S7 St. Gall, Switzerland. Stiftsbibliothek. MSS. (341)
Missals
3374.8 General works
3375.A-Z Special, A-Z
3375.B52 Biblioteca apostolica vaticana. Manuscript. Cod. Cap. 63B
3375.M47 Messale di Barbara
3375.N68 Novacella (Abbey of Augustinian canons). Biblioteca. Manuscript. C20
3375.S55 Slujebnicul mitropolitului Ştefan al Ungrovlahiei
Other service books. Prayer books (other than above)
3380 General works
3380.4.A-Z Special, A-Z
3380.4.A58 Antifonario della cattedrale di Volterra
3380.4.C67 Corvinus graduale
3380.4.H33 Haggadah
3380.4.K72 Kraków. Katedra. Kapituła Metropolitalna. Archiwum. MSS. (KP42-44) (The Gradual of Jan Olbracht)
3380.4.L43 Lectionarium Sigebergense
3380.4.L52 Liber viventium Fabariensis
3380.4.R65 Rothchild canticles

	Illuminating of manuscripts and books
	Histories and reproductions of special illuminated works
	Special works
	Other service books. Prayer books (other than above)
	Special, A-Z -- Continued
3380.4.R66	Rothchild maḥzor
3385.A-Z	Other religious works, A-Z
3385.B53	Biblioteca apostolica vaticana. Manuscript. Barb. Lat. 592
3385.B54	Bibliotheca Bodmeriana. Manuscript. Cod. Bodmer 127
3385.H5	Herrad von Landsberg, abbess of Hohenburg, d. 1195. Hortus deliciarum
3385.J63	Joannes, of Damascus, Saint. Sacra parallela
3385.M27	Madrid. Biblioteca Nacional. MSS (Vit. 14-1)
3385.M3	Magyar Anjou legendárium
3385.N53	Nicholas, of Lyra, ca. 1270-1349. Postillae perpetuae
3385.O67	Országos Széchényi Könyvtár. Manuscript. Cod. Lat. 396
3385.P37	Paris. Bibliothèque nationale. MSS. (Fr. 2090-2092). Vie de St. Denis
3385.P65	Pov͡iest′ o vid͡ienii Koz′my igumena
3385.S54	ŏ Šišatovački apostl
3385.S65	Speculum humanae salvationis
	Vie de St. Denis, see ND3385.P37
3385.V58	Vita Sancti Augustini imaginibus adornata
3385.W87	Württembergisçhe Landesbibliothek. Manuscript. Cod. hist. 4 415
3390	Cartularies
3395.A-Z	Classical authors, A-Z
3399.A-Z	Other secular works, A-Z
3399.A2	Abu al-Faẓl ibn Mubārak, 1551-1602. Akbarnāmah
	Alfonso X, el Sabio, King of Castile and Leon, 1221-1284
3399.A5	Lapidario del rey D. Alfonso X
3399.A52	Libro de ajedrez, dados y tablas
3399.A72	Arif Çelebi, d. 1561. Sulaymānnāmah
3399.A9	ʹAyyūqī. Varqah va Gulshāh
3399.B18	Babar, Emperor of Hindustan, 1483-1530. Bābar-nāmah
3399.B25	Baisonqur-Handschrift
3399.B33	Bartholomaeus, Anglicus, 13th cent. De proprietatibus rerum
3399.B48	Biblioteka Jagiellońska. Manuscript. 35/64 Acc.
3399.B62	Boccaccio, Giovanni, 1313-1375. De mulieribus claris
3399.B64	Bodleian Library. Manuscript. Bodley 283
3399.C44	Codex Arcerianus A.

Illuminating of manuscripts and books
Histories and
reproductions of special illuminated works
Special works
Other secular works, A-Z -- Continued

3399.C48 Codex Wenceslai
3399.C49 Codice Casanatense 1889
Dāstān-i Amīr Hamzah (Persian romance), see ND3399.Q5
3399.D43 Decembrio, Pier Candido, 1399-1477. De omnium animalium natura
3399.F5 Firdawsī. Shāhnāmah.
3399.F62 Floire and Blancheflor
3399.F68 Fouquet, Jean, ca. 1420-ca. 1480. Grandes chroniques de France
3399.G45 Georgius Zothorus Zaparus Fendulus. 12th cent. Liber astrologiae
3399.G63 Gottfried, von Strassburg, 13th cent. Tristan
3399.G67 Grandes chroniques de France
3399.G68 Gratian, 12th cent. Decretum
3399.H26 Harīrī, 1054-1122. Maqāmāt
3399.H4 Heidelberger Liederhandschrift, Grosse (Manessische Handschrift)
3399.H47 Histoire ancienne jusqu'à César
Hrabanus Maurus, Abp., 784?-856
3399.H79 De rerum naturis
3399.H8 De universo
3399.H9 Hünernâme
3399.I15 Ibn Buṭlān, d. ca. 1068. Theatrum sanitatis
3399.J38 Jayadeva, 12th cent. Gītagovinda
3399.J4 Jenský kodex
3399.J6 Joannes Scylitzes, fl. 1081. Historiarum compendium
3399.K32 Kalīlah wa-Dimnah
3399.K37 Kapituła Sandomierska. Archiwum. MSS. 114
3399.K45 Kherenhüller-Chronik
3399.K65 Konrad, von Ammenhausen, 14th cent. Schachzabelbuch
3399.L413 Leiden Aratea
3399.L43 Leitura nova
3399.L44 Lenzi, Domenico. Libro del biadaiolo
3399.L55 Liu, Shang, 8th cent. Hu chia shih pa p'ai
3399.L58 Livre des fais d'Alexandre le Grande
3399.M244 Mandeville, John, Sir. Itinerarium. (British Library. Manuscript. Additional 24189)
Manessische Handschrift, see ND3399.H4
3399.M55 Mi'rāj nāmah
3399.M6 Mouseion Hierōn Eikonōn
3399.N5 Niẓāmī Ganjavī, 1140 or 41-1202 or 3. Khamsah
3399.N66 Notitia dignitatum
3399.P35 Paris, Matthew, 1200-1259. Chronica majora

Illuminating of manuscripts and books
Histories and reproductions of special illuminated works
Special works
Other secular works, A-Z -- Continued

3399.P65 Pisa. Università. Biblioteca. MSS. (Codice 536)
3399.P87 Puranas. Bhāgavatapurāṇa
3399.Q5 Qiṣṣat al-Amīr Hamzah (Arabic romance). Dāstān-i Amīr Hamzah (Persian romance)
3399.R33 Rashīd al-Dīn Tabīb, 1247?-1318. Jāmi 'al-tavārīkh
3399.R4 René I, d'Anjou, King of Naples and Jerusalem, 1409-1480. Livre du cuer d'amours espris
3399.S37 Schwazer Bergbuch
3399.S42 Scot, Michael, ca. 1175-ca. 1234. Liber introductorius
3399.S47 Sercambi, Giovanni, 1347-1424. Le Chroniche di Giovanni Sercambi, Lucchese
3399.S5 Sforza manuscript
3399.S75 St. Veiter Bruchstück
3399.T85 Tulasīdāsa, 1532-1623. Rāmacaritamānasa
3399.T9 Ṭūṭī 'nāmah
3399.V33 Vālmīki. Rāmāyaṇa
3399.V44 Vergilius Romanus (Cod. vat. 3867)
3399.V46 Vergilius Vaticanus
3399.W37 Weingartner Liederhandschrift
3399.W4 Weltchronik. Toggenburg Weltchronik

Modern illuminated books
Including imitations of medieval works

3410.A-Z Works by special artists, A-Z
3416 Collaborations and compilations

Print media
In general classify works on reproductions of paintings, drawings, etc. ("prints" in a popular but incorrect usage of the word) under the medium of the original, e.g. NC, ND, etc. Consult the scope notes at the head of NE400 and NE1850 for additional information
Printmaking and engraving
1 Periodicals and societies
3 Congresses
10 Yearbooks
20 Encyclopedias
25 Dictionaries
30 Directories
Exhibitions (by place held)
Prefer classification by nationality or subject
(40) International
See NE42-NE45
42.A-Z United States. By city and gallery or other place of exhibition, A-Z
45.A-Z Other countries. By country and city, A-Z
Museums. Collections
Public (Art galleries, Print departments, etc.)
53.A-Z United States. By city and museum or collector, A-Z
55.A-Z Other countries. By country and city, A-Z
Private
Including exhibition catalogs and catalogs of auctions devoted to single private collections
Prefer classification by subject, medium, period, or nationality
57.A-Z United States. By collector, A-Z
59.A-Z Other countries. By country and collector, A-Z
Biography of print collectors
59.5 Collective
59.7.A-Z Individual, A-Z
60 Organization and administration of museums, galleries and collections
Print rental and lending collections, see N378+
61 Printmaking as a profession
62 Economic aspects of printmaking
Sales catalogs
63 Before 1801
65 Auction catalogs, 1801-
For auction catalogs of private collections, see NE57+
70 Dealers' catalogs, 1801-
75 Publishers' catalogs, 1801-
For catalogs on a specific subject, medium, period, or nationality, see the subject, medium, period, or nationality

Printmaking and engraving -- Continued
(80) Catalogs of special engravers
See NE501-NE794
For etchers, wood engravers, etc., see special subject
85 Prices of prints
Cf. NE880+, Collectors' manuals
Biography
(88) Collective
See NE800
Individual
See NE468, or special countries under special categories
90 Catalogues raisonnés. Peintre-graveurs
For history of printmaking, see NE400+
Engraved portraits. Self-portraits
218 General works
Exhibitions (by place held)
Prefer classification by nationality or subject
219.A-Z United States. By city and gallery or other place of exhibition, A-Z
219.2.A-Z Other countries. By country and city, A-Z
Catalogs of engraved portraits
220 General
Public collections
230.A-Z United States. By city and museum or collector, A-Z
232.A-Z Other countries. By country and city, A-Z
Private collections
240.A-Z United States. By collector, A-Z
242.A-Z Other countries. By country and collector, A-Z
250.A-Z Sales catalogs. By dealer or auction house, A-Z
Special countries
United States
260 General
262 17th-18th centuries
263 19th century
264 20th century
Europe
264.5 General
Great Britain
265 General
266.A-Z By county, A-Z
270 France
275 Germany
280 Italy
285 Netherlands
290 Russia
295 Scandinavia
300 Spain and Portugal
310.A-Z Other countries, A-Z

Printmaking and engraving
Engraved portraits. Self-portraits
Catalogs of engraved portraits -- Continued
(320) Special persons
See N7628, or N7639
For special saints, see N8080
(330) Portrait prints by special artists
See NE501-NE794
(370) Engravings after special artists
Classify with artist under medium of original
380 Conservation and restoration of prints
Cf. NC930, Conservation and restoration of drawings
Cf. Z110.C7, Conservation and restoration of manuscripts
Collected works
390 Several authors
395.A-Z Individual authors, A-Z
History of printmaking
Including collections of prints in book form and works on wood and metal engraving treated jointly
Here are included engravings (and facsimiles) noteworthy for their age, method of execution, or artistic excellence, but not works in which the process of reproduction is secondary in interest to the works of art thus represented
Certain subjects are to be classed independently of the method of reproduction. For example, see N7720 for Dance of Death; see NE218+ for portraits NE501-NE794
For engravings of drawings, outline sketches, caricatures, etc., by famous artists (one or several), see NC
Cf. NE1030+, History of wood engraving
Cf. NE1980+, History of etching
For Catalogues raisonnés, see NE90
400 General
402 Intercultural relations in prints (General)
Ancient
405 General works
410 Oriental
Cf. NE1310+, Japanese prints
415.A-Z Classical Orient, A-Z
420.A-Z Others, A-Z
e.g.
420.R6 Rome
Modern
430 General works
14th-17th centuries
440 General works
441 Collections in book form
441.5.A-Z Special aspects or movements, A-Z
441.5.R44 Renaissance

NE

Printmaking and engraving
History of printmaking
Modern
14th-17th centuries -- Continued
16th century
444 General works
444.5.A-Z Special aspects or movements, A-Z
444.5.M35 Mannerism
445 Einblattdruck series
450.A-Z Other series, A-Z
468.A-Z Anonymous engravers; unnamed masters, A-Z
468.A5 Master of the Amsterdam Cabinet
468.B3 Master of the Banderoles (Master of 1464)
468.E2 Master E. S. of 1466
468.G3 Master of the Gardens of Love
468.P6 Master of the Playing-cards
468.W2 Master W. of the Gable
Other special engravers, see NE501+
17th-19th centuries
470 General works
471 Collections in book form
475 17th century
476 Collections in book form
480 18th century
481 Collections in book form
485 19th century
486 Collections in book form
487.A-Z Special aspects or movements, A-Z
Divide like N6465
20th century
490 General works
491 Collections in book form
492.A-Z Special aspects or movements, A-Z
Divide like N6494

Printmaking and engraving
History of printmaking -- Continued
501-794.5 Special countries (Table N4 modified)
Including works on printmaking in general, on metal engraving alone, or on wood and metal engraving
Add country number in table to NE500
Cf. NE1310+, Japanese prints
Cf. NE2001+, Etching (Special countries)
Cf. NE2237+, Serigraphy (Special countries)
Cf. NE2301+, Lithography (Special countries)
For wood engraving alone, see NE1101+
For Cutter number and 1-number countries use only indicated number in table; for 2-number countries use first number only
Under 3-number countries:
1 General works
1.2 17th-18th centuries
1.3 19th century
1.4 20th century
1.6.A-1.6.Z Special aspects or movements, A-Z
2.A-2.Z Local, A-Z
3.A-3.Z Special artists, A-Z
Under 4-number countries:
1 General works
1.2 17th-18th centuries
1.3 19th century
1.4 20th century
1.6.A-1.6.Z Special aspects or movements, A-Z
2.A-2.Z Special divisions, A-Z
3.A-3.Z Special cities, A-Z
4.A-4.Z Special artists, A-Z
United States
508.3.A-Z Special aspects or movements, A-Z
508.3.A27 Abstract printmaking
508.3.P45 Photo-realism
508.3.P67 Pop art
508.3.S63 Social realism
Mexico
544.6.A-Z Special aspects or movements, A-Z
544.6.T34 Taller de Gráfica Popular (Mexico City, Mexico)
Europe
Germany
651.6.A-Z Special aspects or movements, A-Z
651.6.F44 Fels (Artists' group)
Low countries
Belgium
671.6.A-Z Special aspects or movements, A-Z
671.6.B5 De Bloedschuit (Engravers' Group)
674.A-Z Special artists, A-Z
e. g.
674.D95 Dyck, Anthony van Sir, 1559-1641

Printmaking and engraving
History of printmaking
Special countries
Europe
Low countries
Belgium
Special artists, A-Z -- Continued
Van Dyck, Anthony, Sir, 1559-1641, see NE674.D95
Scandinavia
Denmark
683.6.A-Z Special aspects or movements, A-Z
683.6.A74 Arme og ben (Group) (Denmark)
Sweden
695.6.A-Z Special aspects or movements, A-Z
695.6.N6 Nio-gruppen. IX-gruppen
Asia. The Orient
Eastern Asia
771-773 Japan
Biography
For special countries, see NE501+
800 Collective
(803-817) By century
See NE501-NE794.5
(805) Unnamed pre 18th century masters
See NE468
Special artists, see NE501+
820 Engravers' marks, monograms, etc.
General works. Treatises
Before 1851
Technical
830 General
835 Minor
840 Popular
1851-
Technical
850 General
855 Minor
860 Popular
863 General special
e.g. suppressed plates
865 Addresses, essays, lectures
Collectors' manuals
880 Before 1851
885 1851-

Printmaking and engraving
General works. Treatises -- Continued
Artists' illustrated books
Class here works about books richly illustrated with original prints by well known artists and published in limited editions. Class here also collections of such books or illustrations from them by several artists.
For artists' illustrated books in a single print medium, see the medium
For artists' illustrated books by specific artists, see the artist in the specific medium
890 General works
892.A-Z By region or country, A-Z
Miniature prints
893 General works
893.5.A-Z Museums. Collections. Exhibitions. By city and museum or collector, A-Z
Large prints
897 General works
898.A-Z By region or country, A-Z
(900-950) Collections of prints in book form
See NE400-NE794, and NE953-NE962
Special subjects
Class here general collections (wood and metal engraving) and wood engravings
For special subjects in other print media, see the specific media
Cf. NE1400+, Metal engraving
951 Choice of subject. Titles. Themes and motives
Flower and fruit prints
953 General works
Special countries. By country of origin
953.2 United States
953.3.A-Z Other countries, A-Z
Landscapes. Views
954 General works
Special countries. By country of origin
954.2 United States
954.3.A-Z Other countries, A-Z
Military prints
955 General works
Special countries. By country of origin
955.2 United States
955.3.A-Z Other countries, A-Z
Naval and marine prints
957 General works
Special countries. By country of origin
957.2 United States
957.3.A-Z Other countries, A-Z
Religious prints
958 General works

NE

Printmaking and engraving
Special subjects
Religious prints -- Continued
Special countries. By country of origin
958.2 United States
958.3.A-Z Other countries, A-Z
Sporting prints
960 General works
Special countries. By country of origin
960.2 United States
960.3.A-Z Other countries, A-Z
962.A-Z Other subjects, A-Z
Class here general works on the topics as well as works on the topics in a particular region, country, etc.
962.A43 Adam and Eve
962.A46 Alchemy
962.A48 Allegories
962.A49 America
962.A5 Animals
962.A52 Animals, Mythical
962.A72 Architecture
962.B28 Ballet
962.B3 Balloons
962.B74 Bridges
962.B84 Bullfights
962.C3 Carriages and carts
962.C34 Cats
962.C35 Caves
962.C47 Children
962.C48 Circus
962.C5 Cities and towns
962.C67 Costume
962.C7 Cricket
962.D3 Dancing
962.D4 Deadly sins
962.D42 Death
Demonology, see NE962.D48
962.D48 Devil. Demonology
962.D7 Drinking
962.E6 The erotic
962.F37 Fashion
962.F45 Festivals
962.F65 Folklore
962.G3 Gardens
962.G67 Granada
962.G7 Grotesque
962.H3 Hair
962.H35 Hand
962.H44 Heilungkiang Province (China)
962.H6 Horsemanship
962.H83 Hudson River Valley (N.Y. and N.J.)
962.I53 Industry

Printmaking and engraving
Special subjects
Other subjects, A-Z -- Continued
962.M35 Manners and customs
962.M4 Medicine
962.M43 Melancholy
962.M44 Men
Mythical animals, see NE962.A52
962.N54 Night
962.N67 North America
962.O25 Occupations. Professions
962.P4 Peddling
962.P56 Plants
962.P64 Politics
Professions, see NE962.O25
962.R85 Ruins
Seals (Numismatics), see CD5001+
962.S47 Sexism
962.S7 Street music and musicians
962.S8 Suffering
962.T73 Transportation
962.V45 Venice (Italy)
962.W37 War
962.W48 West (U.S.)
962.W5 Whaling
962.W56 Witchcraft
962.W65 Women
Portraits, see NE218+
Bookplates, see Z993+
Tradesmen's cards and billheads
Class here works of primarily pictorial or typographic interest
Cf. HF5851, Advertising cards
Cf. NC1002.C4, Cards
For trademark design, see NC1003
965 General works
Special countries
965.2 United States
965.3.A-Z Other countries, A-Z
Study and teaching
970 General works
973 General special
Competitions
Including individual awards, prizes, etc.
975 General and international
975.3 United States
975.4.A-Z Other countries, A-Z
976 Printmaking materials
Instruments and apparatus
977 General works
978 Catalogs

Wood engraving. Woodcuts. Xylography. Block printing
Cf. GV1235+, Playing cards
Cf. Z240+, Incunabula and block books
1000 Periodicals and societies
Exhibitions
1010.A-Z United States. By city and gallery or other place of exhibition, A-Z
1012.A-Z Other countries. By country and city, A-Z
Collections
Public
1020.A-Z United States. By city and museum or collector, A-Z
1022.A-Z Other countries. By country and city, A-Z
Private
1025.A-Z United States. By collector, A-Z
1027.A-Z Other countries. By country and collector, A-Z
History. Collections of wood engravings (in book form)
1030 General works
1032 Miscellaneous collections of woodcuts in book form
Ancient
1035 General works
1037.A-Z Special works, A-Z
1037.K35 Kanjur
Medieval
14th century
1045 General works
1047 Collections in book form
Modern
1048 General works
1049 Collections in book form
15th-17th centuries
For special countries and artists, see NE1101+
1050 General works
Collections in book form
1052 General
1055 Series
Special artists, see NE1101+
Special works
1070 Bibles
1075.A-Z Others, A-Z
Cf. Z241+, Block books
1075.C64 Colonna, Francesco, d. 1527. Hypnerotomachia Poliphili
1075.C73 Cranach, Hans, d. 1537. Passional Christi und Antichristi
1075.O83 Ovide moralisé
18th-20th centuries
For special countries and artists, see NE1101+
1080 General works
1082 Collections in book form
18th century
1085 General works

Wood engraving. Woodcuts. Xylography. Block printing
History. Collections of wood engravings (in book form)
Modern
18th-20th centuries
18th century
General works -- Continued
1087 Collections in book form
1088.A-Z Special works, A-Z
1088.J8 Justine, by Marquis de Sade
19th century
1090 General works
1092 Collections in book form
1093.A-Z Special works, A-Z
20th century
1095 General works
1096 Collections in book form
1097.A-Z Special works, A-Z
1101-1196.3 Special countries (Table N1 modified)
Librarians may prefer to keep all special artists in NE together under NE501 NE794 regardless of medium
Add country number in table to NE1100
For Japanese wood engravings, see NE1310+
Under each country (except United States or countries assigned decimal numbers or Cutter numbers):
.2 *17th-18th century*
.25 *19th century*
.3 *20th century*
.35.A-.35.Z *Special aspects or movements, A-Z*
.35.F38 *Fauvism*
.4.A-.4.Z *Local, A-Z*
.5.A-.5.Z *Special artists, A-Z*
Special subjects, see NE951+
Wood engravers (Lives and works)
1200 Collective
(1205-1217) Special artists
See NE1101-NE1196
Treatises. Manuals
Before 1851
1220 Technical
1223 Popular
1851-
1225 Technical
1227 Popular
1233 Addresses, essays, lectures
(1235-1295) Collections of woodcuts and wood engravings in book form
See NE1030-NE1196
For block books, see Z240-Z241
Colored wood engravings and woodcuts
1300 General works

Wood engraving. Woodcuts. Xylography. Block printing
Colored wood engravings and woodcuts -- Continued
By period
1300.2 Early to 1900
1300.4 20th century
Special countries and artists
United States
1300.5 General works
1300.6.A-Z Special artists, A-Z
1300.8.A-Z Other regions or countries, A-Z
For Japan, see NE1310+
Under each country:
.x *General works*
.x2A-.x2Z *Special artists, A-Z*
Japanese colored wood engravings. Ukiyoe prints
Including color prints, hangas, etc.
For reproductions of colored prints of a special period, see the period
1310 General works
Exhibitions (by place held)
1314.A-Z United States. By city and museum or other place of exhibition, A-Z
1315.A-Z Other countries. By country and city, A-Z
Museums. Collections
1317.A-Z United States. By city and museum or collector, A-Z
1318.A-Z Other countries. By country and city or collector, A-Z
History
Early through 1900
1321 General works
1321.4 Collections in book form
1321.5 Folios
1321.7 Kamakura-Momoyama period (1185-1600)
Edo period (1600-1868)
1321.8 General works
1321.85.A-Z Special aspects or movements, A-Z
1321.85.K38 Katsukawa school
1321.85.S87 Surimono
1321.85.U82 Utagawa school of Ukiyoe
1322 Meiji period (1868-1912)
20th century
1323 General works
1323.4 Collections in book form
1323.5 Folios
1325.A-Z Special artists, A-Z
1326 Artists' marks
1326.5.A-Z Special subjects, A-Z
Smoking paraphernalia, see NE1326.5.T62
1326.5.S85 Sugoroku boards
1326.5.S87 Sumo
1326.5.T62 Tobacco. Smoking paraphernalia

Wood engraving. Woodcuts.
Xylography. Block printing -- Continued
Linoleum block prints
Cf. NK9504, Textile decoration
1330 General works
1331 Linoleum prints in color
Special countries
1332 United States
1334.A-Z Other countries, A-Z
1336.A-Z Special artists, A-Z
Libraries may prefer to keep all special artists in Class NE together under NE501 NE794 regardless of print medium
Fish prints. Gyotaku
1340 General works
1341.A-Z By region or country, A-Z
Under each country:
.x General works
.x2A-.x2Z Local, A-Z
.x3 Collective biography
.x4A-.x4Z Special artists, A-Z
Potato prints
1344 General works
1345.A-Z By region or country, A-Z
Apply table at NE1341.A-Z
Other materials used in relief printing
1350 General works
1352.A-Z Special materials, A-Z
1352.C3 Cardboard
1352.L8 Lucite
Cf. NE1849.L8, Intaglio
Metal engraving. Copper, steel, etc.
Including works on combined intaglio processes
Cf. NE1750+, Copper engraving
For non-metallic materials used in intaglio printmaking, see NE1849.A+
1400 Periodicals and societies
Exhibitions
1410.A-Z United States. By city and gallery or other place of exhibition, A-Z
1412.A-Z Other countries. By country and city, A-Z
Collections
Public
1415.A-Z United States. By city and museum or collector, A-Z
1417.A-Z Other countries. By country and city, A-Z
Private
1420.A-Z United States. By collector, A-Z
1422.A-Z Other countries. By country and collector, A-Z
(1430-1495) History
See NE1634-NE1749

NE

Metal engraving. Copper, steel, etc. -- Continued
(1600-1617) Metal engravers
For collective biography, see NE800
For special artists, see NE501-NE794, NE468
Treatises on intaglio processes
1620 Before 1851
1851-
1625 Technical
1630 Popular
Collectors' manuals, see NE880+
History. Collections in book form
For special countries and artists, see NE501+
For unnamed master engravers, see NE468.A+
1634 General works
1635 Miscellaneous books of engravings
1637 Ancient
1637.5 Medieval
1638 14th century
Modern
15th-17th centuries
1639 General history
1640 Collected engravings in book form
1641 Folios
1655 15th century
1656 Collected engravings in book form
1665 16th century
1666 Collected engravings in book form
17th century
1670 General history
1671 Collected engravings in book form
Special subjects
1675 Religious
1680 Mythological and symbolical
1683 Emblems
1685 Historical
1690.A-Z Other, A-Z
18th-20th centuries
See also Mezzotints, aquatints, etc.
1695 General history
1700 Collected engravings in book form
1701 Folios
18th century
Including works on prints produced before the period of steel engraving began, ca. 1820
1710 General history
1711 Collected engravings in book form
Special subjects
1712 Religious subjects
Cf. NE1070, Bibles (Woodcuts)
1713 Figures
Including Shakespeare's heroines
For portraits, see NE218+
1714 Landscapes. Marines. Views

Metal engraving. Copper, steel, etc.
History. Collections in book form
Modern
15th-17th centuries
18th century
Special subjects -- Continued

1715 Mythological subjects
1716 Symbolical subjects. Symbolism. Fables, etc.
1717 Historical subjects
1718 Still life. Animals, birds, etc.
1719.A-Z Other, A-Z

19th century (General)
Period of steel engraving, 1820-1875

1720.5 General history
1721 Collected engravings in book form

Special subjects

1722 Religious subjects
1723 Figures
For portraits, see NE218+
1724 Landscapes. Marines. Views
1725 Mythological subjects
1726 Symbolical subjects. Symbolism. Fables, etc.
1727 Historical subjects
1728 Still life. Animals, birds, etc.
1729.A-Z Other subjects, A-Z

Period of photographic processes, 1875-

1730 General history
1731 Collected engravings in book form

Special subjects

1732 Religious subjects
1733 Figures
For portraits, see NE218+
1734 Landscapes. Marines. Views
1735 Mythological subjects
1736 Symbolical subjects. Symbolism. Fables, etc.
1737 Historical subjects
1738 Still life. Animals, birds, etc.
1739.A-Z Other subjects, A-Z

20th century

1740 General history
1741 Collected engravings in book form

Special subjects

1742 Religious subjects
1743 Figures
For portraits, see NE218+
1744 Landscapes. Marines. Views
1745 Mythological subjects
1746 Symbolical subjects. Symbolism. Fables, etc.
1747 Historical subjects

Metal engraving. Copper, steel, etc.
History. Collections in book form
Modern
18th-20th centuries
20th century
Special subjects -- Continued
1748 Still life. Animals, birds, etc.
1749.A-Z Other subjects, A-Z
Special countries and artists, see NE501+
Unnamed master engravers, see NE468.A+
Copper engraving
Including etching
1750 General works
History (by period), see NE1634+
Treatises. Manuals
1760 Before 1851
1851-
1770 Technical
1775 Popular
Special countries and artists, see NE501+
(1785) Line engraving
See NE1400-NE1775
1795 Stipple engraving
(1805) Steel engraving
See NE1400-NE1775
Mezzotint engraving
1815 General works
1816.A-Z Special countries, A-Z
1816.5.A-Z Special artists, A-Z
(1820-1840) Aquatint
See NE2230
Dry point, see NE2220+
(1843-1846) Seriography (Silk screen printing)
See NE2236-NE2239.7
1849.A-Z Other materials used in engraving and intaglio techniques, A-Z
1849.G5 Glass
Prefer this number for discussion of glass used in making prints
Cf. NE2690, Engraving on glass
1849.L8 Lucite
Cf. NE1352.L8, Relief printing
1849.Z5 Zinc

Metal engraving. Copper, steel, etc. -- Continued
Color prints (General or produced by metal engraving alone)
Including works on hand colored prints, on original color engraving and etching, and on color reproduction processes before the period of photographic processes (i.e., before ca. 1875) which are of interest for their technique in producing fine prints. See also the scope note above NE400
Cf. NE1300+, Color woodcuts
For works on color reproductions, photo-mechanically reproduced after original paintings or drawings, see N4035.A+
1850 General works
By period
1855 18th century
1857 19th century
1858 20th century
Special countries and artists, see NE501+
1860.A-Z Special publishers, printers, etc., A-Z
For publishers of color reproductions, see N4035.A+
1865.A-Z Special media, A-Z
Aquatint, see NE1865.E8
1865.E6 Engraving (Metal and wood) - General
1865.E8 Etching and aquatint
Japanese prints in miscellaneous media, see NE771+
Japanese wood engravings, see NE1310+
(1865.L5) Linoleum cuts
See NE1331
Lithography, see NE2500+
1865.M4 Mezzotint
Photoengraving, see TR970
Serigraphy, see NE2236+
Stencil, see NE2240+
(1865.W6) Wood engraving and woodcuts
See NE1300-NE1300.8
1870 General collections in book form
Special countries and artists, see NE501+
Special subjects
1872 Religious subjects
1873 Figures
For portraits, see NE218+
1874 Landscapes. Marines. Views
1875 Mythological subjects
1876 Symbolical subjects. Symbolism. Fables, etc.
1877 Historical subjects
1878 Still life. Animals, birds, etc.
1879.A-Z Other, A-Z
Etching and aquatint
1940 Periodicals and societies
Museums. Collections

Etching and aquatint
Museums. Collections -- Continued
Public
1945.A-Z United States. By city and museum or collector, A-Z
1946.A-Z Other countries. By country and city, A-Z
Private
1947.A-Z United States. By collector, A-Z
1948.A-Z Other countries. By country and collector, A-Z
Exhibitions (by place held)
Prefer classification by nationality or subject
(1950) International
See NE1952-NE1955
1952.A-Z United States. By city and gallery or other place of exhibition, A-Z
1955.A-Z Other countries. By country and city, A-Z
1960.A-Z Dealers' catalogs. By firm, A-Z
Collected writings
1970 Several authors
1975 Individual authors
History. Collections of etchings in book form
Prefer classification by special country or artist, NE2001 NE2096
1980 General history
1981 General collections
1982 Folios
15th-17th centuries
1984 General works
1985 Folios
18th-20th centuries
1987 General works
1988 Folios
18th century
1990 General works
1992 Folios
19th century
1994 General works
1995 Folios
20th century
1997 General works
1998 Folios

Etching and aquatint
History. Collections
of etchings in book form -- Continued
2001-2096.3 Special countries (Table N1 modified)
Librarians may prefer to keep all special artists in Class NE together under NE501 NE794 regardless of print medium
Add country number in table to NE2000
For special movements by country, see NE501-NE794
Under each country (except United States or countries assigned decimal numbers or Cutter numbers):
.2 17th-18th centuries
.25 19th century
.3 20th century
.4.A-.4.Z Local, A-Z
.5.A-.5.Z Special artists, A-Z
Europe
Low countries
Belgium
2055.5.A-Z Special artists, A-Z
e. g.
2055.5.D92 Dyck, Anthony van, Sir, 1559-1641
Van Dyck, Anthony, Sir, 1559-1641, see NE2055.5.D92
Biography
2110 Collective
For special countries, see NE2001+
(2115) Individual artists
See NE2001-NE2096
Color etching, see NE1865.E8
General works
2120 Early (to 1850)
Since 1850
2130 Technical
2135 Popular
2140 Addresses, essays, lectures
Special subjects
2141 Religious subjects
Human figures
2142 General works
Portraits, see NE218+
2143 Landscapes
2144 Marines
2145 Animals. Birds
Still life
2146 General works
2147 Flowers. Fruit
2148 Architectural subjects
2149.A-Z Other, A-Z
2149.W37 War
(2150-2210) Collections in book form
See NE1980-NE2096

NE

Etching and aquatint -- Continued
Dry point
2220 General works
2225.A-Z Work of special artists, A-Z
Libraries may prefer to keep all special artists in Class NE together under NE501 NE794 regardless of print medium
Aquatint
2230 General works
Special countries and artists, see NE2001+
Special subjects, see NE2141+
Color aquatint, see NE1865.E8
Collagraph
2232 General works
2232.5.A-Z Work of special artists, A-Z
Libraries may prefer to keep all special artists in Class NE together under NE501 NE794 regardless of print medium
Serigraphy (Silk screen printing)
Including color serigraphy
Cf. TT273, Arts and crafts
2236 General works
Special countries and artists
United States
2237 General works
2237.5.A-Z Special artists, A-Z
Libraries may prefer to keep all special artists in Class NE together under NE501 NE794 regardless of print medium
Corita, 1918- , see NE2237.5.K4
2237.5.K4 Kent, Corita, 1918-
2238.A-Z Other countries, A-Z
2238.5.A-Z Special artists, A-Z (regardless of country)
Libraries may prefer to keep all special artists in Class NE together under NE501 NE794 regardless of print medium
Special subjects
Human figures
2239 General works
Portraits, see NE218+
2239.1 Landscapes. Marines
2239.2 Animals. Birds
Still life
2239.3 General works
2239.4 Flowers. Fruits
2239.5 Architectural subjects
2239.6 Religious subjects
2239.7.A-Z Other, A-Z
Other stencil techniques used in printmaking
Including color stencil prints
Cf. ND2492, Watercolor stencil painting
Cf. NK8650+, Stencil work
2240 General works

Serigraphy (Silk screen printing)
Other stencil techniques
used in printmaking -- Continued
2240.5.A-Z By region or country, A-Z
2240.6.A-Z Special artists, A-Z
Libraries may prefer to keep all special artists in Class NE together under NE501 NE794 regardless of print medium
Monotype (Printmaking)
2242 General works
History
2242.5 General works
2243 17th-19th centuries
2244 20th century
2245.A-Z By region or country, A-Z
2246.A-Z Special artists, A-Z (regardless of country)
Libraries may prefer to keep all special artists in Class NE together under NE501 NE794 regardless of print medium
Lithography
2250 Periodicals and societies
Museums. Collections
Public
2260.A-Z United States. By city and museum or collector, A-Z
2262.A-Z Other countries. By country and city, A-Z
Private
2264.A-Z United States. By collector, A-Z
2266.A-Z Other countries. By country and collector, A-Z
Exhibitions (by place held)
Prefer classification by nationality or subject
(2270) International
See NE2272-NE2275
2272.A-Z United States. By city and gallery or other place of exhibition, A-Z
2275.A-Z Other countries. By country and city, A-Z
2280.A-Z Dealers' catalogs. By firm, A-Z
2283 Directories
Collected writings
2285 Several authors
2290 Individual authors
History. Collections in book form
2295 General works
2296 Folios
2297 19th century
2298 20th century
2301-2396.3 Special countries (Table N1 modified)
Add country number in table to NE2300
For special movements, by country, see NE501-NE794
Apply table at NE2001-2096.3
Biography
2410 Collective

NE

Lithography
Biography -- Continued
(2415) Special lithographers
See NE2301-NE2396
General works
2420 Early (to 1850)
Since 1850
2425 Technical
2430 Popular
2435 Addresses, essays, lectures
(2450) Collections in book form
See NE2295-NE2398
Special subjects
2452 Religious subjects
2453 Figures
2454 Landscapes. Views
2455 Mythological subjects
2456 Symbolical subjects
2457 Historical subjects
(2458) Portraits
See NE220-NE310
2459.A-Z Other, A-Z
2480 Study and teaching
Instruments and apparatus
2490 General works
2495 Catalogs
Chromolithography
History. Collections in book form
2500 General works
2502 19th century
By region or country
2505 United States
2506.A-Z Other regions or countries, A-Z
2507.A-Z Special artists, families, firms, A-Z
2515 Technique
Special subjects
2522 Religious subjects
2523 Figures
Portraits, see NE218+
2524 Landscapes. Marines. Views
2525 Mythological subjects
2526 Symbolical subjects. Symbolism. Fables, etc.
2527 Historical subjects
2528 Still life. Animals, birds, etc.
2529.A-Z Other, A-Z
Substitutes for lithographic stone
2540 General works
2550 Zinc
2560 Aluminum
Offset lithography
2562 General works
By region or country
2562.5 United States

Offset lithography
By region or country -- Continued
2562.7.A-Z Other regions or countries, A-Z
2562.9.A-Z Special artists, families, firms, A-Z
2570 Other mechanical processes (not A-Z)
Photoengraving, see TR925+
(2590) Special publishers, firms, etc., A-Z
See NE1860
(2600-2680) Collections of prints
See NE2820-NE2825
Lumiprints. Clichés verres
Including other techniques in which the artist draws or paints the "negative" on glass or plastic, and uses photosensitive paper to print it
2685 General works
2685.5.A-Z By region or country, A-Z
2685.8.A-Z Special artists, families, firms, A-Z
2690 Engravings on glass
Cf. NE1849.G5, Glass used in intaglio printmaking
Cf. NE2685+, Lumiprints; Clichés verres
Cf. NK5100+, Glass and stained glass
Cf. TT298, Glass craft
Ornamental engraving on metal for printing
Cf. NK6520+, Chasing, engraving, etc.
2700 General works
2710 Letters, monograms, etc.
2715 Stationery engraving
2720 Machine engraving
Cf. HG350, Bank note engraving
2740 Miscellaneous minor engraving (not A-Z)
Including engraving on shelf fungi, etc.
Niello engraving, see NK6525
Playing cards, see GV1235+
Ex libris, see Z993+
Printing of engravings (Especially commercial applications)
Cf. Z257, Printing of pictures, illustrations, etc.
2800 Periodicals and societies
2802 History
Biography. Plate printers
2803.A1 General
2803.A3-Z Special printers, A-Z
General works
2805 Early (to 1850)
2810 Since 1850
2815 Miscellaneous minor works. Machinery and supplies
Trade publications
2820 To 1880
2825 Since 1880
Special media
2830 Wood engravings
2840 Copper engravings

Printing of engravings
(Especially commercial applications)
Special media -- Continued
2850 Steel engravings
2860 Lithographs
2870 Zincographs
2880.A-Z Other mechanical processes, A-Z
2890 Photomechanical processes
Including rotogravure printing
Cf. TR925+, Photography
Copy art. Copying machine art
3000 General works
3001.A-Z Special regions or countries, A-Z
3002.A-Z Special artists, A-Z

Decorative arts. Applied arts. Decoration and ornament
Including antiques in general
Periodicals
1 American and English
2 French
3 German
4 Italian
5 Spanish and Portuguese
6 Dutch
7 Russian
8.A-Z Other, A-Z
9 Yearbooks
Societies
11 American
12 English
13 French
14 German
15 Italian
16 Spanish and Portuguese
17 Dutch
18 Russian
19.A-Z Other, A-Z
21 Congresses
Collected writings
25 Several authors
27 Individual authors
28 Encyclopedias
30 Dictionaries
Cf. NK1165, Design dictionaries
Study and teaching
50 Periodicals and societies
60 General works
65 General special
70 Art crafts for children

Study and teaching -- Continued
101-377 Special countries (Table N3)
Add country number in table to NK100
Under each:
TABLE NK101/1:
Table for 3 number countries
1 *General works*
2.A-Z *Special divisions, regions, A-Z*
3.A-Z *Special cities, A-Z*
TABLE NK101/2:
Table for 1 number or decimal number countries
.A1 *General works*
.A2A-.Z8Z *Special divisions, regions, A-Z*
.Z9A-Z *Special cities, A-Z*
TABLE NK101/3:
Table for Cutter number countries
.x *General works*
.x2A-Z *Special divisions, regions, A-Z*
.x3A-Z *Special cities, A-Z*
Special schools
410.A-Z United States. By city and school, A-Z
420.A-Z Other American. By country and school, A-Z
430.A-Z Europe. By country and school, A-Z
440.A-Z Other countries. By country and school, A-Z
Museums, galleries, etc.
Cf. NK613+, Ancient museums
Cf. NK633.A+, Egyptian museums
Biography of museum personnel
446 Collective
446.2.A-Z Individual, A-Z
450 General works
460.A-Z United States. By city and museum, A-Z
470.A-Z Other American. By country and city, A-Z
Europe
475 Collective
480.A-Z By city, A-Z
e.g.
480.B5 Berlin. Kunstgewerbemuseum
480.D8 Dresden. Grünes Gewölbe
490.A-Z Other. By city, A-Z
(492) Miniature objects (Collections)
See NK8470-NK8475
(493) Toys
See NK9509-NK9509.8
(494.A-Z) Special miniatures, A-Z
See NK8475
Exhibitions. By place held
Prefer classification by subject or nationality
(510) International
See NK512-NK520
512.A-Z United States. By city and museum or other place of exhibition, A-Z

Exhibitions. By place held -- Continued
520.A-Z Other countries. By country and city, A-Z
Private collections
United States
530 Collective
535.A-Z Special. By collector, A-Z
540.A-Z Other American. By country, A-Z
Under each:
.x Collective
.x2A-.x2Z Special collections. By collector, A-Z
550.A-Z European. By country, A-Z
Apply table at NK540.A-Z
560.A-Z Other countries, A-Z
Apply table at NK540.A-Z
570 Auction catalogs
For collections of known owners, see NK530+
History
600 General works
602 Intercultural relations in the decorative arts (General)
605 Primitive
Folk and decorative art of ethnic groups not limited to one country
607 General works
608.A-Z Special, A-Z
608.A78 Arumanian
608.F54 Finno-Ugrian
608.H55 Hmong (Asian people)
608.J48 Jewish
For Jewish religious applied art, see NK1672
608.L37 Lapp
608.M65 Mongolian
Ancient
610 General
Exhibitions. Museums
613.A-Z United States. By city and museum or other place of exhibition, A-Z
614.A-Z Other countries. By country and city, A-Z
615.A-Z Private collections. By collector, A-Z
620 Oriental
Egyptian
630 General works
633.A-Z Exhibitions. Museums. By country and city, A-Z
635.A-Z Collections. By country, A-Z
640 Assyro-Babylonian
650 Persian
660 Phoenician
Classical
665 General works
670 Greek
675 Etruscan
680 Roman

NK

History
  Ancient -- Continued
685.A-Z Other ancient, A-Z
  e.g.
685.C8 Crete
  Medieval
700 General works
703 Frankish
705 Irish (Early)
710 Anglo-Saxon
715 Early Christian. Byzantine
  Arabic. Islamic
720 General works
725 Moors in Spain
730 Romanesque
740 Gothic
  Modern
750 General works
760 Renaissance. 15th-16th centuries
770 17th-18th centuries
775 19th century
775.5.A-Z Special styles, A-Z
775.5.A7 Art nouveau
775.5.E25 Eclecticism
789 20th century
789.5.A-Z Special styles, A-Z
789.5.A7 Art deco

History -- Continued

801-1094.5 Special countries (Table N4)

Add country number in table to NK800

For Jewish applied art, see NK608.J48

For Jewish religious applied art, see NK1672

Under each country:

TABLE NK801/1:

Table for 4-number countries

1 *General works*

2.A-Z *Special divisions, A-Z*

3.A-Z *Special cities, A-Z*

4.A-Z *Special artists, A-Z*

TABLE NK801/2:

Table for 3-number countries

1 *General works*

2.A-Z *Local, A-Z*

3.A-Z *Special artists, A-Z*

TABLE NK801/3:

Table for 2-number countries

1.A1 *General works*

1.A2-Z *Local, A-Z*

2.A2-Z *Special artists, A-Z*

TABLE NK801/4:

Table for 1-number countries

.A1 *General works*

.A2-.Z7 *Local, A-Z*

.Z8A-Z *Special artists, A-Z*

TABLE NK801/5:

Table for Cutter-number countries

.x *General*

.x2A-Z *Local, A-Z*

.x3A-Z *Special artists, A-Z*

United States

806 Colonial period; 18th (and early 19th) century

General works

1100 Early works to 1800

1105 1800-

1110 General special

Including outlines and syllabi

(1115-1120) Collected designs

See NK1530-NK1535

1125 Collectors' manuals (Miscellaneous art objects and antiques)

Cf. AM200+, Collectors and collecting (General)

1125.A1-A5 Periodicals

1125.A6-Z General works

1127 Directories

Including directories of antique appraisers, authors, auctioneers, dealers, publishers, etc.

1127.5 Preservation of art objects and antiques. Cleaning. Restoration

1128 Reproduction of art objects and antiques

1130 Technique

General works -- Continued
1132 Addresses, essays, lectures
Dealers' catalogs
Cf. NK1149.A+, Special arts and crafts shops, etc.
1133.A-Z General. By dealer, A-Z
1133.2.A-Z Special auction sales. By dealer, A-Z
For catalogs of auctions of single private collections, see NK530+
Biography of antique dealers
1133.25 Collective
1133.26.A-Z Individual, A-Z
1133.28 Antiques business
1133.3 Mail-order business
Arts and crafts movement
Class here only works on the movement in England and the United States fostered in the last quarter of the 19th century by William Morris, et al.
For works on other local arts and crafts organizations, see NK801+
1135 Periodicals
1136 Societies
1137 Exhibition of societies
History
1140 General works
1141 United States
1142 Great Britain
Other countries, see NK801+
1145 General works
Addresses, essays, lectures
1147 Collections
1148 Single papers
1149.A-Z Special shops, A-Z
1149.5 Women in the arts and crafts movement
(1151-1158) Industrial design
See TS171-TS171.6
Decoration and ornament. Design
1160 Periodicals and societies
1164 Congresses
1165 Dictionaries
1166 Collective biography
For special countries and designers, see NK1401+
1167 Directories
1170 Study and teaching
For textbooks, etc., see NK1510
1172 Vocational guidance
1173 Business management for designers
1174 Women designers
History
1175 General works
1177 Primitive ornament. Evolution of decorative art
Cf. GN418.4, Anthropology
Cf. NC54, Primitive drawing

Decoration and ornament. Design
History -- Continued
Ancient
1180 General works
1183 General special
1185 Oriental
1190 Egyptian
1195 Assyro-Babylonian
1205 Persian
1215 Phoenician
Classical
1225 General works
1230 Greek
1235 Etruscan
Roman
1240 General
1245 Pompeian
1250.A-Z Other ancient, A-Z
Medieval
1260 General works
1263 General special
1264 Irish. Celtic
1264.3 Germanic
1264.5 Norse
Early Christian, see NK1652.1
Byzantine, see NK1652.25
Arabic. Islamic. Moorish
Cf. N6260+, Moorish art
Cf. NK1575, Arabesques
1270 General works
1275 Moors in Spain
1285 Romanesque
1295 Gothic
Modern
1320 General works
15th-16th centuries. Renaissance
1330 General works
(1332-1339) Special countries
See NK1401-NK1496
17th-18th centuries
1340 General works
1345 Baroque
1350 Louis XIV
1352 William and Mary
1355 Rococo. Louis XV. Régence
1360 Louis XVI
1365 Directoire
19th century
1370 General works
1372 Empire (1st)
1374 Biedermeier
1376 Empire (2d)
1378 Victorian

Decoration and ornament. Design
History
Modern
19th century -- Continued
1380 Art nouveau
1382.A-Z Other special, A-Z
Arts and crafts movement, see NK1135+
1382.L6 Louis Philippe
1382.N46 Neoclassicism
20th century
1390 General works
1394 International style
Including Mies van der Rohe, Neutra, Le Corbusier
1396.A-Z Other special, A-Z
1396.A45 Alchimia (Group)
1396.A76 Art deco
1396.M46 Memphis (Group)
1396.P66 Postmodernism
1396.S63 Société des artistes décorateurs (France)
1396.S65 Sottsass associati (Milan, Italy)
1401-1496.3 Special countries (Table N1)
Add country number in table to NK1400
Under each (1-number or decimal-number countries):
.A1 General works
.A3A-.A3Z Special regions, provinces, etc., A-Z
.A5-.Z7 Special cities, A-Z
.Z8 Collective biography
.Z9A-.Z9Z Special artists, A-Z
Under each (Cutter-number countries):
.x General works
.x2A-.x2Z Local, A-Z
.x3 Collective biography
.x4A-.x4Z Special artists, A-Z
(1498.A-Z) Decoration and ornament in the work of special artists, A-Z
See the artist
1505 Theory of ornament and design
1510 General works
1520 General special
Including miniature decorative design
1525 Addresses, essays, lectures
Collections of designs
1530 General
1531 Film catalogs
1533 Minor
1535.A-Z Special artists, A-Z
Special elements or subjects in decoration and ornament or design
1548 Color
1550 Human figure
1553 Nature in ornament
1555 Animals. Birds

Decoration and ornament. Design
Special elements or subjects in decoration and ornament or design -- Continued
Plants. Trees. Flowers
1560 General works
1565 Conventionalized forms
1566.A-Z Special forms, A-Z
1566.R67 Rosemaling
Cf. TT385, Handicrafts
1570 Linear. Geometric. Latticework
For alphabets, calligraphy, initials, see NK3600+
1575 Arabesques. Paisley design
1580 Scrolls
1585 Allegorical figures, emblems, etc.
1590.A-Z Other, A-Z
1590.A53 Angels
1590.B66 Books and reading
1590.B73 Brassieres
1590.E76 Erotic art
1590.H64 Holidays
Reading, see NK1590.B66
1590.S56 Shoes
1590.W37 Water waves
1590.Z63 Zodiac
Religious art (Decorative and applied)
Including ceremonial art
Cf. NK2190+, Interior decoration
Cf. NK4850, Ecclesiastical vestments
Cf. NK7215, Ecclesiastical plate
Cf. NK9310, Ecclesiastical embroidery
1648 General
Christian
1650 General works
1652 History
1652.1 Early Christian
1652.2 Medieval
1652.25 Byzantine
1652.3 Renaissance. 16th century
1652.4 17th-18th centuries
1652.5 19th century
1652.6 20th century
1653.A-Z Special countries, A-Z
e.g.
1653.S7 Spain
1655.A-Z Special cities, A-Z
e.g.
1655.B34 Barcelona
1656.A-Z Special denominations, A-Z
e.g.
1656.M4 Methodist
1657 Trade catalogs, etc.
Museums. Collections

NK

Religious art (Decorative and applied)
Christian
Museums. Collections -- Continued
1658.A-Z United States. By institution, A-Z
1658.5.A-Z Other countries. By country and city, A-Z
Exhibitions (by place held)
1660.A-Z United States. By city and museum or other place of exhibition, A-Z
1660.5.A-Z Other countries. By country and city, A-Z
Non-Christian
1670 General works
Special religions
1672 Jewish
1674 Islamic
1676 Buddhist
1677 Hindu
1678.A-Z Other, A-Z
1678.T36 Taoist
Interior decoration. House decoration
Including decorative painting
Cf. TX309, Home economics
1700 Periodicals and societies
1702 Congresses
1704 Dictionaries
1705 Directories
History and styles
1710 General works
Ancient
1720 General works
1730 Oriental
1740 Egyptian
Greek and Roman
1750 General works
1760 Greek
1770 Roman. Pompeian
1780.A-Z Other, A-Z
Medieval
1800 General works
1810 Early Christian. Byzantine
1820 Arabic. Islamic. Moorish
1830 Romanesque
1840 Gothic
Modern
1860 General works
1870 15th-16th centuries. Renaissance
17th-18th centuries
1880 General works
1890 Louis XIII
1900 Louis XIV
1910 Baroque
1920 Rococo. Louis XV. Regency
1930 Louis XVI
1940 Directoire

Interior decoration. House decoration
History and styles
Modern -- Continued
19th century
1960 General works
1962 Empire (1st)
1964 Biedermeier
1966 Empire (2d)
1968 Victorian
1970 Art nouveau
1972.A-Z Other special, A-Z
20th century
1980 General works
1984 International style
Including Mies van der Rohe, Neutra, Le Corbusier
1986.A-Z Other special, A-Z
1986.A78 Art deco
1986.O73 Organic design
1986.R8 Rustic style
Special countries
2000 America
North America
2001 General works
United States
2002 General works
2003 Colonial period to 1830
2003.5 19th century. Victorian period
2004 20th century
2004.2 Collective biography
2004.3 Special designers, A-Z
Including collections of their designs
2005-2096.3 Other countries (Table N1)
Add country number in table to NK2000
Apply table at NK1401-1496.3
General works
2105 Early works to 1850
2110 1850-
2113 General special
Including psychological aspects
Perspective, see NC748+
2113.5 Rendering
2115 Popular works. Minor manuals, etc.
2115.3.A-Z For special classes of persons, A-Z
2115.3.A76 Artisans
2115.3.A78 Artists
Bachelors, see NK2115.3.S55
2115.3.I57 Interior decorators
2115.3.S55 Single men. Bachelors
2115.5.A-Z Special elements in interior decoration, A-Z
2115.5.A25 Accessories
2115.5.A42 Americana
2115.5.A5 Antiques

Interior decoration. House decoration
Special elements in
interior decoration, A-Z -- Continued
2115.5.A83 Audio-visual equipment
2115.5.C44 Ceramics
2115.5.C45 Christmas decorations
2115.5.C58 Collectibles
2115.5.C6 Color
Including individual colors
2115.5.D73 Drapery
2115.5.E84 Ethnic art
2115.5.F3 Fabrics
Cf. TT387+, Soft home furnishings
2115.5.F55 Floor coverings
2115.5.F68 Found objects
2115.5.F77 Furniture
House plants, see SB419.25
2115.5.I55 Industrial equipment
Kilims, see NK2115.5.R77
2115.5.L5 Lighting. Lighting fixtures
Cf. TH7700+, Lighting in buildings
2115.5.P47 Photographs
2115.5.P48 Pictures
Plants, see SB419.25
2115.5.P5 Plastics
2115.5.Q54 Quilts
2115.5.R77 Rugs. Kilims
2115.5.T54 Tiles
2115.5.V53 Victoriana
2115.5.W3 Wall coverings
Cf. NK3375+, Wallpapers
2115.5.W57 Wire
2115.5.W66 Wood
2115.8 Collective biography
For biography of special countries, see NK2005+
For biography of special designers or decorators, see NK2004.3
2116 Interior decoration as a profession
2116.2 Economic aspects of the profession
Study and teaching
2116.4 General
By country
2116.5 United States
2116.6.A-Z Other countries, A-Z
2117.A-Z Special rooms, A-Z
2117.A8 Attics
2117.B3 Basements
2117.B33 Bathrooms
2117.B4 Bedrooms
2117.C4 Children's rooms
2117.D5 Dining rooms
2117.D7 Drawing rooms
2117.E5 Entrance halls

Interior decoration. House decoration
Special rooms, A-Z -- Continued
Family rooms, see NK2117.R4
Game rooms, see NK2117.R4
2117.G37 Garden rooms
Hobby rooms, see NK2117.R4
2117.K5 Kitchens
2117.L46 Libraries, Home
2117.L5 Living rooms
2117.M54 Miniature rooms
2117.N87 Nurseries
2117.R4 Recreation rooms
2117.S8 Storage rooms
Special parts of rooms
2119 Ceilings. Walls. Floors
Cf. NK2115.5.W3, Wall coverings
Cf. NK3375+, Wallpapers
2120 Friezes, moldings, etc.
Cf. NA2960, Architecture - Moldings, etc.
Cf. NA2965, Architecture - Friezes
2121 Doors and windows
2125 Addresses, essays, lectures
Collections of designs
2130 Various sources
(2135.A-Z) By special artists, A-Z
See NK2004.3, and NK2005-NK2096
Trade publications
2137 General
2138 Auction sales. By name of owner, if known
Decorative painting (Commercial and industrial)
Cf. ND2550+, Mural painting
Cf. TH8001+, Decoration and decorative furnishings
2140 Periodicals
History
For special buildings, see NA1+
2150 General works
2155 Ancient
2165 Medieval
2170 Modern
2175 General works
2180.A-Z Design by special artists. By artist, A-Z
Church decoration
Cf. NA5000, Architectural decoration
Cf. NK1648+, Religious art
2190 General works

Interior decoration. House decoration
Church decoration -- Continued
2192.A-Z By region or country, A-Z
Under each country:
.x General works
.x2A-.x2Z Local, A-Z
.x25A-.x25Z By church, A-Z
.x3 Collective biography
.x4A-.x4Z Special artists, A-Z
2195.A-Z Decoration of other special buildings, A-Z
For classification of special types of rooms, see NK2117.A+
2195.A6 Apartment houses. Apartments
2195.B34 Bakeries
2195.B36 Banks
Bars, see NK2195.R4
Cabarets, see NK2195.N55
Coffeehouses, see NK2195.R4
2195.H43 Health facilities
2195.H6 Hotels. Motels
2195.L63 Log cabins
2195.M6 Model houses
2195.N55 Nightclubs. Cabarets
2195.O4 Offices
Including all kinds of offices, such as architectural offices, dental offices, etc.
For interior architecture, see NA2856
2195.P8 Public buildings
Resort houses, see NK2195.V34
2195.R4 Restaurants. Bars. Coffeehouses. Taverns
2195.R87 Rural homes. British cottages. Farmhouses
Schools, see LB3257
2195.S56 Showrooms
2195.S89 Stores
Including specific types of stores, such as bookstores
Summerhouses, see NK2195.V34
Taverns, see NK2195.R4
2195.V34 Vacation homes. Resort houses. Summerhouses
Furniture
Cf. NA5050+, Ecclesiastical furniture
2200 Periodicals
2205 Dictionaries
2206 Directories
Exhibitions (by place held)
2210.A-Z United States. By city and museum or other place of exhibition, A-Z
2211.A-Z Other countries. By country and city, A-Z
Museums
2215.A-Z United States. By city and museum, A-Z
2216.A-Z Other countries. By country and city, A-Z
2220.A-Z Private collections. By collection or collector, A-Z
2229 Early works to 1850

Furniture -- Continued
2230 1850-
2231 General special
2235 Styles
Prefer classification by period or country
2240 Collectors' manuals. "Old furniture," etc.
2250 Addresses, essays, etc.
2260 Collection of designs from several sources
Prefer classification by period or country
2265 Dealers' catalogs, etc.
Study and teaching
2267 General works
2268.A-Z Schools, by city, A-Z
History
2270 General works
Ancient
2280 General works
2285 Oriental
2290 Egyptian
2295 Assyro-Babylonian
2305 Greek
2310 Etruscan
2315 Roman. Pompeian
2320.A-Z Other, A-Z
Medieval
2335 General works
2340 Romanesque
2345 Gothic
Modern
2350 General works
2355 Renaissance. 15-16th centuries
17th-18th centuries
2360 General works
2365 Baroque
2370 Louis XIV
2375 Rococo. Louis XV. Regency
2380 Louis XVI
2382 Directoire
19th century
2385 General works
2386 Empire (1st)
2387 Biedermeier
2388 Empire (2d)
2390 Victorian
2392 Art nouveau
2394.A-2294.Z Other special, A-Z
20th century
2395 General works
2397 International style
Including Mies van der Rohe, Neutra, Le Corbusier
2399.A-Z Other special, A-Z
2399.S87 Surrealist

NK

Furniture
History -- Continued
2401-2694.5 Special countries (Table N4)
Add country number in table to NK2400
Under each (4-number countries):
1 General works
2 Old furniture to 1830
3 1831-
4.A-4.Z Special designers, A-Z. Including individuals, families, and firms
Under each (3-number countries):
1 General works
2.A-2.Z Local, A-Z
3.A-3.Z Special designers, A-Z
Under each (2-number countries):
1.A1 General works
1.A2-1.Z Local, A-Z
2.A-2.Z Special designers
Under each (1-number countries):
.A1 General works
.A2-.Z7 Local, A-Z
.Z8A-.Z8Z Special designers, A-Z
Under each (Cutter-number countries):
.x General works
.x2A-.x2Z Local, A-Z
.x3A-.x3Z Special designers, A-Z
United States
2406 Colonial period; 18th (and early 19th) century
Europe
Great Britain. England
2542.A-Z Individual designers, A-Z
e.g.
2542.C5 Chippendale
2542.H5 Hepplewhite
2542.S4 Shearer, Thomas, fl. 1788
2542.S5 Sheraton
France
2548 Louis XIV-Louis XVI
2702 Architect-designed furniture
For special countries, see NK2401+
2703 Decorative furniture painting. Painted furniture
Cf. TT305, Painting of furniture as a craft
For special countries, see NK2401+
2705 Gilt furniture
For special countries, see NK2401+
2709 Incrustation and stonework applied to furniture
For special regions or countries, see NK2401+
2710 Marquetry and inlaid woods applied to furniture
For special regions or countries, see NK2401+
2712 Built-in furniture
2712.5 Unit furniture
2712.6 Bamboo furniture
2712.63 Bentwood furniture

Furniture -- Continued
2712.7 Wicker furniture
Special articles of furniture
Prefer classification by material
2713 Beds
2715 Chairs. Miniature chairs
2720 Clockcases
2725 Coffers. Chests
2727 Cupboards, sideboards, etc.
2736 Sofas
2740 Tables. Desks. Shelves. Bookshelves
2750 Miniature furniture. Children's furniture
Cf. NK4891.3+, Doll furniture
Rugs. Carpets
Cf. NK2115.5.R77, Interior decoration
2775 Periodicals
Exhibitions. By place held
2780.A-Z United States. By city and museum or other place of exhibition, A-Z
2781.A-Z Other countries. By country and city, A-Z
Museums
2785.A-Z United States. By city and museum, A-Z
2786.A-Z Other countries. By country and city, A-Z
2790.A-Z Private collections. By collection, A-Z
2795 General works. Collectors' manuals
Oriental rugs, see NK2808+
2799 Dealers' catalogs, etc.
History
2800 General works
2803 Ancient
2805 Medieval
2807 Modern
Oriental
Including kilims
2808 General works
2808.5 Conservation and restoration
2809.A-Z Special, A-Z
2809.B34 Baluchi
2809.C3 Caucasian
2809.I8 Islamic
Including prayer rugs
2809.K87 Kurdish
2809.P4 Persian. Iranian
2809.Y8 Yuruk
2809.5 Oriental rugs as an investment
2810 Trade publications
2811 North America
2812 United States

Rugs. Carpets -- Continued

2813-2896.3 Other countries (Table N1 modified)
Add country number in table to NK2800
For Iran, see NK2809.P4
For Oriental countries (General), see NK2808+
Under each (1-number or decimal-number countries):
.A1 General works
.A3A-.A3Z Special regions, provinces, etc., A-Z
.A5-.Z Special cities, A-Z
Under each (Cutter-number countries):
.x General
.x2A-.x2Z Special cities, A-Z

2897 Collective biography

2898.A-Z Special artists, A-Z

2910 Screens

Tapestries. Wall hangings
Cf. TS1780, Machine-made tapestry
Cf. TT849, Hand-loom weaving

2975 Periodicals and societies

Exhibitions. By place held

2980.A-Z United States. By city and museum or other place of exhibition, A-Z

2981.A-Z Other countries. By country and city, A-Z

Museums

2985.A-Z United States. By city and museum, A-Z

2986.A-Z Other countries. By country and city, A-Z

2990.A-Z Private collections. By collection, A-Z

2995 General works

2995.5 Technique

2997 Conservation and restoration
For works on the conservation and restoration of tapestries found in particular places, see NK3011+
For works on the conservation and restoration of tapestries found in particular places, see NK3013+

2999 Dealers' catalogs

History

3000 General works

3003 Ancient

3005 Medieval

3007 Modern

3007.4 Baroque

3007.85 20th century

Special countries

3011 North America

3012 United States

Tapestries. Wall hangings
History
Special countries -- Continued
3013-3096.3 Other countries (Table N1 modified)
Add country number in table to NK3000
Under each (1-number or decimal-number countries):
.A1 General works
.A3A-.A3Z Special artists, A-Z
.A4A-.A4Z Special aspects or movements, A-Z
.A5-.Z Other special, A-Z
Under each (Cutter-number countries):
.x General works
.x2A-.x2Z Special artists, A-Z
.x25A-.x25Z Special aspects or movements, A-Z
.x3A-.x3Z Other special, A-Z
Europe
3049 France
3049.A3A-Z Special artists, A-Z
e.g.
3049.A3L8 Lurçat, Jean, 1892-1966
3049.A5-Z Other special, A-Z
3049.B3 Bayeux tapestry
3049.G7 Gobelin tapestry
Upholstery. Drapery
3175 Periodicals
Exhibitions. By place held
3180.A-Z United States. By city and museum or other place of exhibition, A-Z
3181.A-Z Other countries. By country and city, A-Z
Museums
3185.A-Z United States. By city and museum, A-Z
3186.A-Z Other countries. By country and city, A-Z
3195 General works
3197 Collected designs
3199 Dealers' catalogs
History
3200 General works
3203 Ancient
3205 Medieval
Modern
3207 General works
Special countries
3211 North America
3212 United States
3213-3296.3 Other countries (Table N1)
Add country number in table to NK3200
Apply table at NK2813-2896.3
Wallpapers
3375 Periodicals
Exhibitions
3380.A-Z United States. By city and museum or other place of exhibitions, A-Z

Wallpapers
Exhibitions -- Continued
3381.A-Z Other countries. By country and city, A-Z
Museums
3385.A-Z United States. By city and museum, A-Z
3386.A-Z Other countries. By country and city, A-Z
3395 General works
3399 Dealers' catalogs
History
3400 General works
Special countries
3412 United States
3413-3496.3 Other countries (Table N1)
Add country number in table to NK3400
Apply table at NK2813-2896.3
3505 Lincrusta-Walton
Woodwork, see NK9600+
Other arts and art industries
Subjects are arranged in an alphabetical sequence; however since a large number of subjects are broad in scope and supplied with subtopics, it is suggested that the general index to the schedule be used in locating any subject
Wherever practicable, objects of glass, metal, wood, etc. are classed under the material, e.g. For ancient ceramic lamps, see NK4680
Alphabets. Calligraphy. Initials
Class here material where consideration is primarily aesthetic
Cf. NA2725, Architectural drawing (Lettering)
Cf. ND3335, Illumination
Cf. NE2710, Engraving
Cf. T371, Mechanical drawing (Lettering)
Cf. TT360, Sign painting, showcards, etc.
Cf. Z43+, Penmanship
Cf. Z250+, Type and typefounding
For general works on writing, see Z44
3600 General works
Roman
3603 General works
Including Gothic forms derived from the Roman
3605 Ancient
3610 Medieval
3615 14th-18th centuries
3620 19th-20th centuries
3625.A-Z Special styles of lettering, A-Z
3625.A7 Art deco
3625.A73 Art nouveau
3625.I85 Italics
3625.R66 Roman capitals
3625.V53 Victorian
3630 Specimens of decorative lettering
3630.3.A-Z Special applications of lettering, A-Z

Other arts and art industries
Alphabets. Calligraphy. Initials
Roman
Special applications of lettering, A-Z -- Continued

3630.3.S46 Sepulchral monuments
3630.3.S54 Signs and signboards
Stonework (General), see NK8705
3630.3.S77 Street names
3630.4.A-Z Special topics, A-Z
3630.4.B67 Borders
3630.4.W67 Words
3630.6.A-Z By region or country, A-Z
3631.A-Z Special artists, A-Z

Non-Roman
Including rubbings
For calligraphy as painting, see ND1454+

3632 General works
Special alphabets, characters, scripts, etc. (Table N13)
3633 Arabic (Table N13)
3634 Chinese (Table N13)
3635 Cyrillic (Table N13)
3636 Hebrew (Table N13)
3636.5 Islamic (Table N13)
3637 Japanese (Table N13)
3639.A-Z Other, by language, A-Z
3639.P4 Persian (Table N14)
3639.T45 Thai (Table N14)
3639.T53 Tibetan (Table N14)
3639.U73 Urdu (Table N14)
3640 Monograms, marks, etc.

Automata
For music boxes, see ML1066

3649 General works
3649.2.A-Z Special artists, A-Z

Bamboo
For bamboo baskets, see NK3649.5+
For bamboo furniture, see NK2712.6

3649.3 General works
3649.35.A-Z By region or country, A-Z
Under each country:
.x General works
.x2A-.x2Z Local, A-Z
.x3 Collective biography
.x4A-.x4Z Special artists, A-Z

Basketwork
Cf. TS910, Industrial basketmaking
Cf. TT879.B3, Handcrafts

3649.5 General works
3649.55.A-Z By region or country, A-Z
Apply table at NK3649.35.A-Z

Other arts and art industries -- Continued
Beadwork. Ojime
Cf. NK5440.B34, Glass beads
3650 General works
3650.5.A-Z By region or country, A-Z
Apply table at NK3649.35.A-Z
3651 Bear collectibles
3651.5 Beer collectibles
Cf. NK5440.B6, Beer bottles
Cf. NK8459.B36, Beer cans. Beer trays
Cf. NK8551.25.B43, Beer neon signs
3653 Bells. Handbells. Tap bells
For bells in a particular material, see the material
Cf. CC200+, History of bells
Cf. TS583+, Manufacture of bells
3654 Betel chewing paraphernalia
Cf. NK8459.B47, Betel cutters
3655 Birdcages
3660 Book ornamentation
Cf. NC973+, Cover design
Cf. ND2889+, Illumination
Cf. NK3600+, Alphabets and initials
Cf. Z266+, Binding
Cf. Z276, Book arts (General)
Cf. Z1023, Illustrated books
3665 Boxes. Caskets
Cf. ML1066, Music boxes
Cf. NK4696.5, Cigar boxes
Cf. NK6080, Inro
Cf. NK6213, Lunchboxes
Cf. NK9550, Trunks
Brush stands
3667 General works
3667.2.A-Z By region or country, A-Z
Apply table at NK3649.35.A-Z
Buttons. Insignia
For buttons made of special materials, see the material
3668.5 General works
Special types
3669 Campaign insignia
3670 Clothing and dress
3685 Candlesticks
Prefer classification by material
3690 Candy containers. Candy dispensers
Prefer classification by material
Canes, see NK8645
3695 Cat collectibles
3697 Cathédrale de Strasbourg collectibles
Ceramics
Cf. TP785+, Chemical technology
Cf. TT919+, Pottery craft
3700 Periodicals and societies

Other arts and art industries
Ceramics -- Continued
3703 Congresses
Exhibitions. By place held
(3710) International
See NK3712-NK3720
3712.A-Z United States. By city and museum or other place of exhibition, A-Z
3720.A-Z Other countries. By country and city, A-Z
Museums. Collections
Public
3728 Collective
3730.A-Z United States. By city and museum, A-Z
3735.A-Z Other countries. By country and city, A-Z
Private
3740.A-Z United States. By collector, A-Z
3745.A-Z Other countries. By country and collector, A-Z
Dealers' catalogs, etc, see NK4255
3760 Collected writings
3770 Dictionaries. Encyclopedias
History
3780 General works
3785 General special
3787 Outlines, syllabi, etc.
3795 Primitive
For aspects other than aesthetic, see GN433
Ancient
3800 General works
3803 General special
3805 Oriental
3810 Egyptian
3820 Assyro-Babylonian
3825 Persian
3830 Phoenician. Punic
Classical
3835 General works
3840 Greek
Cf. NK4645+, Vases
3843 Mycenaean and pre-Mycenaean
3845 Etruscan
3850 Roman (Arretine, terra sigillata, etc.)
3855.A-Z Other ancient, A-Z
Medieval
3870 General works
3880 Islamic
3885 Merovingian
Modern
3900 General works
19th century
3920 General works
3920.3.A-Z Special styles, A-Z
3920.3.A77 Art nouveau
3930 20th century

Other arts and art industries
Ceramics
History
Modern
20th century -- Continued
3930.3.A-Z Special styles, A-Z
3930.3.A77 Art deco
4001-4185 Special countries (Table N2 modified)
Add country number in table to NK4000
For individual potters, see NK4210.A+
United States
4025.A-W States, A-W
4025.P4 Pennsylvania German ware
Ethnic groups
4028.3.A-Z Special, A-Z
For American Indian pottery, see E98.P8
Asia. The Orient
Eastern Asia
China
4165 General works
By period
Prefer classification by place
4165.2 Pre T'ang
4165.22 Early through Chou dynasty (To 221 B.C.)
4165.23 Ch'in-Han dynasties (221 B.C.-220 A.D.)
4165.24 Three kingdoms-Sui dynasty (220-618)
4165.3 T'ang-Five dynasties (618-960)
4165.4 Sung-Yuan dynasties (960-1368)
4165.5 Ming-Manchu (Ch'ing) dynasties (1368-1912)
4165.6 19th century
4165.7 20th century
4166.A-Z Local, A-Z
Japan
4167 General works
By period
Prefer classification by place
Early to 1868
4167.2 General works
To 1600
4167.215 General works
4167.22 Early through Tempyo period (To 794 A.D.)
4167.3 Fujiwara (Heian) period (794-1185)
4167.4 Kamakura - Momoyama periods (1185-1600)
4167.5 Tokugawa (Edo) period (1600-1868)
4167.55 19th century
4167.6 Meiji period (1868-1912)
4167.7 20th century
4167.73 Taishō period (1912-1926)

Other arts and art industries
Ceramics
History
Special countries
Asia. The Orient
Eastern Asia
Japan
By period
20th century -- Continued
4167.78.A-Z Special aspects or movements, A-Z
4167.78.S63 Sodeisha
4168.A-Z Local, A-Z
4200 Collective biography
4210.A-Z Individual potters, families, and firms, A-Z
e.g.
4210.B63 Böttger, Johann Friedrich
4210.P3 Palissy, Bernard, 1510?-1590
4210.W4 Wedgwood, Josiah, 1730-1795
4215 Potters' marks
General works. Treatises
4220 To 1800
4225 1800-
4230 Collectors' manuals (How to identify old china, etc.)
Cf. NK4215, Potters' marks
4233 Preservation. Cleaning. Restoration
4235 General special
4240 Juvenile works
4245 Addresses, essays, lectures
4250 Collections of designs
4255 Trade publications
Earthenware
For ancient earthenware vases, see NK4645-NK4654
For ancient earthenware, see NK3800+
For special countries, see NK4001+
4260 General works
Unglazed
4265 General works
4265.5 Biscuit ware
4267 Terra cotta
Cf. NK4325, Robbia ware
4270 Glazed and enameled ware
Glazed ware (Lead glaze)
4275 General works
4277 Blue and white transfer ware. Willowware
4278 Creamware
4280 Graffito decorated
4283 Redware
4285 Slip decorated
For Pennsylvania German ware, see NK4025.P4
Leadless glazes
4287 General works
4289 Raqqa ware

NK

Other arts and art industries
Ceramics
Earthenware -- Continued
Enameled ware
Including tin and other opaque enamels; faience
For enamel glaze on metal base, see NK6510+

4290 General works
Delft ware
4295 Dutch and general
4295.5.A-Z Other regions or countries, A-Z
e.g.
4295.5.G7 Great Britain
Faience
For tiles, see NK4670+
4305 French and general
4305.5.A-Z Other regions or countries, A-Z
For individual factories, see NK4210.A+
4310 Hispano-Moresque
Majolica
4315 Italian and general
4320.A-Z Other regions or countries, A-Z
e.g.
4320.M5 Mexico
4325 Robbia ware
4335 Wedgwood
For biography of Josiah Wedgwood, 1730-1795, see NK4210.W4
4340.A-Z Other special, A-Z
4340.B4 Berlin faience
4340.B6 Black basaltes
4340.B7 Brunswick faience
4340.C3 Canakkale
4340.C44 Çeladon ware
4340.D3 Davenport
4340.D4 Dedham
4340.F68 Franciscan ware
4340.F7 Frankfurt am Main
4340.G38 Gaudy ware
4340.G7 Grueby
4340.H3 Habaner ware
4340.I9 İznik
4340.J7 Jugtown
4340.K73 Kütahya
4340.K75 Kutani
4340.M28 Marseille
4340.M3 Martinware
4340.N47 Newcomb pottery
4340.O7 Oribe
4340.P6 Portneuf
4340.P73 Pratt ware
4340.R3 Raku
4340.R6 Rockingham
4340.R7 Rookwood

Other arts and art industries
Ceramics
Earthenware
Enameled ware
Other special, A-Z -- Continued
4340.R75 Rosemeade pottery
4340.R78 Royal Copley
4340.R79 Royal Haeger pottery
4340.S5 Shino
Spatterware, see NK4340.S65
4340.S65 Sponged ware. Spatterware
4340.S9 Swansea
4340.T3 Talavera
4340.T67 Torquay
4340.U54 University of North Dakota pottery
4340.W4 Wemyss ware
4340.Y44 Yellow ware
4340.Y84 Yüeh
Stoneware (Grès de Flandres, Steinzeug, Steingut)
4360 General works
By region or country
4364 United States
4365.A-Z Other regions or countries, A-Z
4367.A-Z Special wares, A-Z
4367.B67 Böttger ware
For biography of Johann Freidrich Böttger, 1682-1719, and for works on Böttger ware together with Böttger porcelain (early Meissen porcelain), see NK4210.B63
4367.C7 Creussen pottery
4367.D7 Doulton
4367.I35 I-hsing ware
4367.I7 Ironstone china
Porcelain
4370 General works
4373 General special
Including 18th century porcelain
Special varieties
For China trade porcelain and its varieties, see NK4565.5
4374 Armorial
4375 Soft porcelain
For special varieties and countries, see NK4380-NK4584
4380 Dresden (Meissen)
4390 Sèvres
4395 Worchester
4399.A-Z Other special, A-Z
4399.A4 American Belleek
4399.A7 Arita
4399.B4 Berlin
4399.B58 Blue and white ware

NK

Other arts and art industries
Ceramics
Porcelain
Special varieties
Other special, A-Z -- Continued

4399.B7 Bow
4399.B75 Bristol
4399.C27 Capodimonte
4399.C3 Caughley
4399.C47 Ch'ai ware
4399.C5 Chelsea
4399.C55 Coalport
4399.C6 Copenhagen
4399.D4 Derby
4399.F8 Frankenthal
4399.F87 Fürstenberg
4399.G45 Geisha girl porcelain
4399.H3 Hague
4399.H4 Haviland china
4399.H57 Hirado
4399.H8 Hutchenreuther
4399.I4 Imari
4399.K3 Kakiemon
4399.K87 Kutani
4399.L5 Limoges
4399.L53 Liverpool
4399.L6 Longton Hall
4399.L7 Lowestoft
4399.L9 Lusterware
4399.M43 Medici
4399.N25 Nabeshima
4399.N3 Nantgarw
4399.N4 New Hall
4399.N9 Nyon
4399.P3 Parian
4399.P33 Paris
4399.P55 Plymouth
4399.R6 Rockingham
4399.R7 Rozenburg
4399.S9 Swansea
4399.T45 Thuringian ware
4399.T55 Ting ware
4399.T6 Tournai
4399.T68 Tōzan
4399.V5 Vienna
4399.V55 Vincennes
4401-4585 Special countries (Table N2 modified)
Add country number in table to NK4400
Asia. The Orient
Eastern Asia
China
4565 General works

Other arts and art industries
Ceramics
Porcelain
Special countries
Asia. The Orient
Eastern Asia
China -- Continued
By period
Prefer classification by place

4565.2 Pre T'ang
4565.22 Early through Chou dynasty (To 221 B.C.)
4565.23 Ch'in-Han dynasties (221 B.C.-220 A.D.)
4565.24 Three kingdoms-Sui dynasty (220-618)
4565.3 T'ang-Five dynasties (618-960)
4565.4 Sung-Yuan dynasties (960-1368)
4565.5 Ming-Manchu (Ch'ing) dynasties (1368-1912)
4565.6 19th century
4565.7 20th century
4566.A-4166.Z Local, A-Z
Japan
4567 General works
By period
Prefer classification by place
Early to 1868
4567.2 General works
To 1600
4567.215 General works
4567.22 Early through Tempyo period (To 794 A.D.)
4567.3 Fujiwara (Heian) period (794-1185)
4567.4 Kamakura-Momoyama periods (1185-1600)
4567.5 Tokugawa (Edo) period (1600-1868)
4567.55 19th century
4567.6 Meiji period
4567.7 20th century
4567.73 Taishō period (1912-1926)
4568.A-Z Local, A-Z
4600 Decoration of pottery
China painting
4605 General works
4605.5.A-Z Special regions or countries, A-Z
Under each country:
.x General works
.x2A-.x2Z Local, A-Z
.x3A-.x3Z Special artists, A-Z
4607 Transfer printing
Cf. NK4277, Blue and white transfer ware (Earthenware)

NK

Other arts and art industries
Ceramics -- Continued
(4610) Firing (for amateurs)
See TT920
Special objects
Vases
4620 General works
Exhibitions
4621.A-Z United States. By city and museum or other place of exhibition, A-Z
4622.A-Z Other countries. By country and city, A-Z
Museums, collections, etc.
Public
4623.A-Z United States. By city and museum, A-Z
4623.5.A-Z Other countries. By country and city, A-Z
Private
4624.A-Z United States. By collector, A-Z
4624.5.A-Z Other countries. By country and collector, A-Z
Stone vases
4625.A1 General works
4625.A2-Z Special, A-Z
4625.W3 Warwick vase
Special periods
Prefer classification by country
4640 Ancient
4642 Medieval
4643 Modern
Greek vases and their decorations
For museums and collections, see NK4623+
4645 General works
Including Etruscan and other local
For Etruscan vases alone, see NK4654+
4646 Mycenean and pre-Mycenean
4647 Geometric
4648 Black-figured
4649 Red-figured
4649.5 White-ground. Slipware
4650.A-Z Other special varieties, A-Z
4650.A6 Amphora
4650.A84 Askos
4650.B83 Bucchero
4650.D8 Drinking cups (Cylix, etc.)
4650.H9 Hydria
4650.L47 Lebes gamikos
4650.L5 Lecythi
4650.M44 Megarian bowls
4650.O48 Olpes
4650.P55 Phialae
4650.P75 Psykters
4650.R5 Rhyta
4650.S8 Stamnos

Other arts and art industries
Ceramics
Special objects
Vases
Greek vases and their decorations -- Continued

(4652) Special vase-painters
See ND115

4653.A-Z Special vases, A-Z
e.g.

4653.P7 Portland vase

Roman vases. Arretine vases. Etruscan vases
For special Etruscan vase painters, see ND130.E8
For special Roman vase painters, see ND127.A+

4654 General works

4654.5.A-Z Special varieties, A-Z

4654.5.B83 Bucchero

4654.5.P38 Paterae

4655 Chinese and Japanese vases

4655.6.A-Z Special works, by name (artists unknown), A-Z

4657.A-Z Others, by country, A-Z

4659 Portraits in pottery

4660 Statuettes. Ornamental figures
For ancient statuettes and ornamental figures, see NB150

Tiles. Earthenware stoves

4670 General works

4670.5.A-Z Exhibitions. Collections. Museums. By country and collector or place of exhibition, A-Z

4670.7.A-Z Special regions or countries, A-Z
Under each country:
.x General
.x2A-.x2Z Local, A-Z
.x3A-.x3Z Special artists, A-Z

4675 Trade publications (Art tiles)

4678 Ampullae

4680 Lamps (Ancient)

4690 Braziers

4695.A-Z Other objects, A-Z

4695.A6 Apothecary jars

4695.B44 Bells. Handbells

4695.C5 Chamber pots

4695.C518 Character jugs

4695.C52 Character steins

4695.C6 Coffeepots

4695.C66 Cookie jars

4695.C73 Cream pots

4695.C8 Cups

Dolls, see NK4894.4.C55

4695.E4 Eggcups

4695.F54 Figural planters

4695.F6 Food warmers

Other arts and art industries
Ceramics
Special objects
Other objects, A-Z -- Continued
Handbells, see NK4695.B44
4695.H43 Head vase planters
4695.L5 Lids
4695.M8 Mustache cups
4695.M83 Mustard pots
4695.P45 Pillows
4695.P5 Pitchers
4695.P55 Plates
4695.P6 Pouring vessels. Decanters
4695.R44 Relief-decorated jugs
4695.S23 Salt and pepper shakers
4695.S26 Santos
4695.S5 Shaving mugs
4695.S65 Solitaires
4695.S73 Steins
4695.S76 Storage jars
4695.T33 Tableware
4695.T43 Teapots
4695.T53 Tobacco jars and boxes
4695.T55 Tobacco-pipes
4695.T6 Toby jugs
4695.T64 Toothbrush holders
4695.T87 Tureens
4695.W34 Wall pockets
4695.W45 Whiskey jugs
4695.5 Cheese dishes
4696 Chessmen. Chess sets
Cf. TT896.55, Handicraft
4696.2.A-Z By region or country, A-Z
4696.25.A-Z Special artists, A-Z
4696.35 Chips. Gambling chips
4696.4 Christmas collectibles
4696.5 Cigar boxes
4698 Coin banks
4698.5 Containers
Prefer classification by material
Costume and its accessories
Cf. GT500+, Manners and customs
Cf. TT490+, Clothing manufacture
For ecclesiastical vestments, see NK4850
For military uniforms, see UC480+
4700 Periodicals and societies
4700.5 Congresses
4700.6 Dictionaries
4700.7 Directories

Other arts and art industries
Costume and its accessories -- Continued
Exhibitions (By place held)
Class here works on general exhibitions
For exhibitions on special periods not limited to a particular country, see NK4707-NK4710.3
For exhibitions on special countries, see NK4711-NK4796

4701.A-Z United States. By city and museum or other place of exhibition, A-Z
4701.5.A-Z Other countries. By country and city, A-Z
Museums
4701.8 Collective
4702.A-Z United States. By city and museum, A-Z
4702.5.A-Z Other countries. By country and city, A-Z
Special periods
See NK4707-NK4710.3
4703.A-Z Private collections. By collection, A-Z
4704 General. Collectors' manuals
4704.3 Deterioration
4704.5 Conservation and restoration
4705 Collected designs
4705.5 Auction catalogs
History
4706 General works
4706.4.A-Z Ethnic groups not limited to one country, A-Z
4706.4.B35 Baluchi
4706.4.C44 Celts
4706.4.H56 Hmong (Asian people)
4706.4.J48 Jews
4706.4.T45 Thracians
4706.4.T83 Tuaregs
4707 Ancient
4707.15 Egyptian
4707.2 Etruscan
4707.3 Classical
4707.4 Early Christian
4708 Medieval
4708.7 Buddhist
4708.8 Byzantine
4708.9 Islamic
4708.92 Romanesque
4708.923 Gothic
4709 Modern
4709.2.A-Z Special styles, A-Z
4709.2.G76 Grotesque
4709.3 Renaissance
4709.6 Baroque
4709.65 18th century
4709.7 Rococo
4709.8 19th century
4709.85.A-Z Special styles, A-Z
4709.85.A7 Art nouveau

	Other arts and art industries
	Costume and its accessories
	History
	Modern
	19th century
	Special styles, A-Z -- Continued
4709.85.B53	Biedermeier
4709.85.E24	Eclecticism
4709.85.I84	Islamic
4709.85.V53	Victorian
4710	20th century
4710.3.A-Z	Special styles, A-Z
4710.3.A78	Art deco
4711	North America
4712	United States
4712.5	Latin America
4713-4796.3	Other countries (Table N1)
	Add country number in table to NK4700
	Apply table at NK2813-2896.3
4797	Collective biography
4798.A-Z	Special artists, A-Z
	Including families and firms
4799	Dealers' catalogs
4850	Ecclesiastical vestments
	Wearable art
4860	General works
4860.5.A-Z	By region or country, A-Z
	Apply table at NK3649.35.A-Z
	Special articles
4870	Fans
4890.A-Z	Other articles, A-Z
4890.B4	Belts. Belt buckles
4890.B62	Bola ties
4890.B67	Braid
4890.B8	Buttonhooks
4890.C36	Cashmere shawls
4890.C47	Charms
4890.C63	Combs, Ornamental
4890.C65	Compacts
4890.C67	Costume jewelry
4890.E86	Ethnic jewelry (General)
	Glass jewelry, see NK5440.J48
4890.H34	Handbags. Plastic handbags
4890.H4	Head-gear
4890.J4	Jeans
4890.M37	Masks
	Ornamental combs, see NK4890.C63
	Plastic handbags, see NK4890.H34
4890.P55	Plastic jewelry
4890.P67	Porcelain jewelry
4890.R48	Rhinestone jewelry
4890.S45	Shirts
	Including Aloha shirts, T-shirts, etc.

Other arts and art industries
Costume and its accessories
Special articles
Other articles, A-Z -- Continued
4890.S5 Shoe buckles
4890.3 Darning eggs
For darning eggs in a particular material, see the material
4890.5 Decoys
For decoys in a particular material, see the material
4891 Distaffs
Dolls and dollhouses
Including doll furniture, paper dolls, action figures, etc.
Cf. GV1218.5+, Games and amusements
Cf. NK2117.M54, Miniature rooms
Cf. TS2301.T7, Toy manufacture
Cf. TT175+, Dolls (Handicrafts)
4891.3 Congresses
4891.35 Directories
4891.5 Competitions
Including individual awards, prizes, etc.
4892.A-Z Exhibitions. Museums. By country and city, A-Z
4892.5.A-Z Private collections. By collector, A-Z
4893 General works. Collectors' manuals
4893.3 Trademarks
History
4894.A2 General works
4894.A3-Z By region or country, A-Z
4894.15 Collective biography
4894.2.A-Z Special artists, A-Z
4894.3.A-Z Special types of dolls, A-Z
4894.3.B33 Baby dolls
4894.3.B37 Barbie dolls
4894.3.B53 Black dolls
4894.3.B58 Bleuette dolls
4894.3.B68 Boy dolls
4894.3.C44 Celebrity dolls
4894.3.C67 Costume dolls
4894.3.F37 Fashion dolls
4894.3.F73 Francie dolls
G.I. Joe figures, see NK8475.M5
4894.3.G55 Ginny dolls
4894.3.M43 Mechanical dolls
4894.3.N47 Nesting dolls
4894.3.P37 Patsy dolls
4894.3.P85 Pullstring dolls
4894.3.R34 Raggedy Ann and Andy dolls
4894.3.S25 Santa dolls
4894.3.S56 Shirley Temple dolls
4894.3.T35 Tammy dolls
4894.3.T76 Troll dolls

Other arts and art industries
Dolls and dollhouses -- Continued
4894.4.A-Z Dolls in special materials, A-Z
4894.4.B57 Bisque dolls
4894.4.C44 Celluloid dolls
4894.4.C55 China dolls
4894.4.C57 Cloth dolls. Rag dolls
4894.4.C65 Composition dolls
4894.4.H37 Hard plastic dolls
Rag dolls, see NK4894.4.C57
4894.4.W37 Wax dolls
4894.5 Door knockers
4894.6 Doorstops
Drinking vessels
Prefer classification by material
Cf. NK4650.D8, Ancient Greek vessels
4895 General works
4895.5.A-Z Special types, A-Z
4895.5.M8 Mugs
4898 Duck calls. Turkey calls
Prefer classification by material
4898.5 Duck collectibles
4900 Easter eggs
Cf. TT896.7, Handicraft of egg decoration
Enamel
Cf. TS700+, Metal finishing
Cf. TT382.6, Handicraft
For enameled earthenware, see NK4290+
For enameled glass, see NK5439.E5
For enameled metalwork, see NK6510+
4997 Periodicals. Societies
4998 Congresses. Yearbooks
4999.A-Z Museums. Collections. Exhibitions. By city and museum or collector, A-Z
5000 General works
5001 General special
History
5003 General works
5003.2.A-Z Ethnic groups not limited to one country, A-Z
5003.2.C44 Celts
5003.3 Medieval
Modern
5003.45 General works
5003.8 20th century
5004.A-Z By country, A-Z
5008.A-Z Special artists, A-Z
Cloisonné
5010 General works
5013 Byzantine
5014 Renaissance
5015 Chinese and Japanese
5015.4.A-Z By region or country, A-Z
5015.5.A-Z Special artists, A-Z

Other arts and art industries
Enamel -- Continued
Champlevé
5016 General works
5016.5 Medieval
5017.5 Romanesque
5019.A-Z By region or country, A-Z
Apply table at NK4670.7.A-Z
Painted enamel
5020 General works
5021 Medieval
5022 Renaissance
5024.A-Z By region or country, A-Z
Apply table at NK4670.7.A-Z
Fairground art
Including merry-go-round art, carnival and sideshow banners, etc.
Cf. TT898.2, Handicraft of carousel horses
5030 General works
By region or country
5033 United States
5035.A-Z Other regions or countries, A-Z
Floral arrangements, see SB449+
Gambling chips, see NK4696.35
5080 Gesso
Cf. NB1180, Modeling in plaster
Cf. NB1190, Making plaster casts
Cf. NK5735, Plaster reproductions of gems
Glass
Cf. TT298, Glass craft
5100 Periodicals and societies
5100.5 Congresses
5100.6 Dictionaries
5100.7 Directories
Exhibitions (By place held)
Class here works on general exhibitions
For exhibitions on special periods not limited to a particular country, see NK5107-NK5110.3
For exhibitions on special countries, see NK5111-NK5196
5101.A-Z United States. By city and museum or other place of exhibition, A-Z
5101.5.A-Z Other countries. By country and city, A-Z
Museums
5101.8 Collective
5102.A-Z United States. By city and museum, A-Z
5102.5.A-Z Other countries. By country and city, A-Z
Special periods
See NK5307-NK5310.3
5103.A-Z Private collections. By collection, A-Z
5104 General. Collectors' manuals
5104.5 Conservation and restoration
5105 Collected designs

Other arts and art industries
Glass -- Continued
5105.5 Auction catalogs
History
5106 General works
5106.4.A-Z Ethnic groups not limited to one country, A-Z
5107 Ancient
5107.15 Egyptian
5107.2 Etruscan
5107.3 Classical
5107.4 Early Christian
5108 Medieval
5108.7 Buddhist
5108.8 Byzantine
5108.9 Islamic
5108.92 Romanesque
5108.923 Gothic
5109 Modern
5109.2.A-Z Special styles, A-Z
5109.2.G76 Grotesque
5109.3 Renaissance
5109.6 Baroque
5109.65 18th century
5109.7 Rococo
5109.8 19th century
5109.85.A-Z Special styles, A-Z
5109.85.A7 Art nouveau
5109.85.B53 Biedermeier
5109.85.E24 Eclecticism
5109.85.V53 Victorian
5110 20th century
5110.3.A-Z Special styles, A-Z
5110.3.A78 Art deco
5111 North America
5112 United States
5112.5 Latin America
5113-5196.3 Other countries (Table N1)
Add country number in table to NK5100
Apply table at NK2813-2896.3
5197 Collective biography
5198.A-Z Special artists, A-Z
5199 Dealers' catalogs
Crystal glass. Cut glass. Engraved glass. Pressed glass
5200 Periodicals. Societies
5200.5.A-Z Exhibitions. Collections. Museums. By country and collector or place of exhibition, A-Z
5201 General works
5202 History
By region or country
5203 United States
5204.A-Z Other regions or countries, A-Z
5205.A-Z Special artists, families, firms, A-Z

Other arts and art industries
Glass -- Continued
Colored glass. Pâte de verre
5206 General works
5207.A-Z By region or country, A-Z
Stained glass. Glass painting
Cf. TH8271+, Decoration of buildings
Cf. TP863+, Manufacture
Cf. TT298, Handicrafts
5300 Periodicals and societies
5300.5 Congresses
5300.6 Dictionaries
5300.7 Directories
Exhibitions (By place held)
Class here works on general exhibitions
For exhibitions on special periods not limited to a particular country, see NK5307-NK5310.3
For exhibitions on special countries, see NK5311-NK5396
5301.A-Z United States. By city and museum or other place of exhibition, A-Z
5301.5.A-Z Other countries. By country and city, A-Z
Museums
5301.8 Collective
5302.A-Z United States. By city and museum, A-Z
5302.5.A-Z Other countries. By country and city, A-Z
Special periods
See NK5107-NK5110.3
5303.A-Z Private collections. By collection, A-Z
5304 General. Collectors' manuals
5304.5 Conservation and restoration
5305 Collected designs
5305.5 Auction catalogs
History
5306 General works
5306.4.A-Z Ethnic groups not limited to one country, A-Z
5307 Ancient
5307.15 Egyptian
5307.2 Etruscan
5307.3 Classical
5307.4 Early Christian
5308 Medieval
5308.7 Buddhist
5308.8 Byzantine
5308.9 Islamic
5308.92 Romanesque
5308.923 Gothic
5309 Modern
5309.2.A-Z Special styles, A-Z
5309.2.G76 Grotesque
5309.3 Renaissance
5309.6 Baroque

Other arts and art industries
Glass
Stained glass. Glass painting
History
Modern -- Continued
5309.65 18th century
5309.7 Rococo
5309.8 19th century
5309.85.A-Z Special styles, A-Z
5309.85.A7 Art nouveau
5309.85.B53 Biedermeier
5309.85.E24 Eclecticism
5309.85.V53 Victorian
5310 20th century
5310.3.A-Z Special styles, A-Z
5310.3.A78 Art deco
5311 North America
5312 United States
5312.5 Latin America
5313-5396.3 Other countries (Table N1)
Add country number in table to NK5300
Apply table at NK2813-2896.3
5397 Collective biography
5398.A-Z Special artists, A-Z
5399 Dealers' catalogs
5410 Glass painting for amateurs
5420 Leaded glass
5430 Mosaic glass
Glass underpainting. Hinterglasmalerei
For icons of the Eastern Church, see N8185.5+
5431 Periodicals. Societies
5431.5.A-Z Exhibitions. Collections. Museums. By country and collector or place of exhibition, A-Z
5432 General works
5433 History
By region or country
5434 United States
5435.A-Z Other regions or countries, A-Z
5436.A-Z Special artists, families, firms, A-Z
5438 Portraits on glassware
5439.A-Z Other special types of glass, A-Z
5439.A77 Art glass
5439.B54 Black glass
5439.C33 Cameo glass
5439.C35 Carnival glass
5439.C73 Crackle glass
5439.C85 Custard glass
5439.D44 Depression glass
5439.E5 Enameled glass
5439.G64 Goofus glass
5439.L34 Lacy glass
5439.M37 Mary Gregory glass
5439.M54 Milk glass

Other arts and art industries
Glass
Other special types of glass, A-Z -- Continued
5439.O6 Opal glass
5439.P36 Pattern glass
5439.P95 Pyrex
5439.R82 Ruby glass
5439.V37 Vaseline glass
5440.A-Z Special articles of glass, A-Z
5440.A55 Animals. Covered animal dishes
5440.B34 Beads
5440.B37 Bells
5440.B6 Bottles
5440.B86 Buttons
5440.C26 Candlesticks
5440.C3 Candy containers
5440.C48 Chandeliers
5440.C57 Christmas ornaments
Covered animal dishes, see NK5440.A55
5440.C75 Cruets
5440.C8 Cup plates
5440.D4 Decanters
5440.D75 Drinking glasses
Including Hedwig glasses
5440.D85 Dwarf ale glasses
5440.E4 Electric insulators
5440.E83 Epergnes
5440.F3 Fairy lamps
5440.F38 Figurines
5440.F4 Fishing floats
5440.F66 Footed salvers
5440.F7 Fruit jars
5440.G6 Goblets
5440.J48 Jewelry
5440.K44 Kerosene lamps
5440.K54 Knives
5440.L3 Lampshades
5440.P3 Paperweights. Snowdomes
5440.S3 Salt shakers
5440.S49 Shoes
5440.S53 Shot glasses
Snowdomes, see NK5440.P3
5440.S8 Sulphides
5440.T68 Toothpick holders
Glyptic arts
Carving or engraving of gems and hard stones, shells, coral, ivory, boxwood, ebony, etc.
5500 General works
Gems (Engraved stones)
Exhibitions. By place held
5505.A-Z United States. By city and museum or other place of exhibition, A-Z
5506.A-Z Other countries. By country and city, A-Z

NK

Other arts and art industries
Glyptic arts
Gems (Engraved stones) -- Continued
Museums
5510.A-Z United States. By city and museum, A-Z
5511.A-Z Other countries. By country and city, A-Z
5515.A-Z Private collections. By collector, A-Z
5517 Catalogues raisonnés
5520 Dealers' catalogs
General works
5523 Early works to 1800
5525 1800-
5528 General special
5530 Collectors' manuals
5540 Addresses, essays, lectures
5545 Collections of designs
History
5550 General works
Ancient
5555 General works
5557 Oriental
Egyptian
5559 General works
5561 Scarabs
5563 Assyro-Babylonian
Classical. Greek and Roman
5565 General works
5566 General special
e.g. starred gems
5580.A-Z Other ancient, A-Z
5585 Medieval
5595 Modern
5601-5696.3 Special countries (Table N1)
Add country number in table to NK5600
Apply table at NK2813-2896.3
5698.A-Z Special artists, A-Z
Special varieties
Cameos
5720 General works
5720.5 By region or country, A-Z
5722 Special pieces (not A-Z)
e.g. Gonzaga cameo
5730 Intaglios
5733.A-Z Special subjects, A-Z
5733.J9 Jupiter (Roman deity)
5735 Plaster reproductions of gems
Jade carving. Jade art objects
5750 General works

Other arts and art industries
Glyptic arts
Jade carving. Jade art objects -- Continued
5750.2.A-Z Special regions or countries, A-Z
Under each country:
.x General works
.x2A-.x2Z Local, A-Z
.x3 Collective biography
.x4A-.x4Z Individual artists, A-Z
5755 Jet
Ivory carving. Ivories
Exhibitions. By place held
5800.A-Z United States. By city and museum or other place of exhibition, A-Z
5801.A-Z Other countries. By country and city, A-Z
Museums
5810.A-Z United States. By city and museum, A-Z
5811.A-Z Other countries. By country and city, A-Z
5815.A-Z Private collections. By collector, A-Z
5820 Dealers' catalogs
5825 General works
5835 General special
5840 Addresses, essays, etc.
History
5850 General works
5860 Ancient
Medieval
5870 General works
5872 Byzantine
5875 Gothic
Modern
5890 General works
5895 15th-16th centuries
5896 17th-18th centuries
5897 19th-20th centuries
5901-5996.3 Special countries (Table N1)
Add country number in table to NK5900
Apply table at NK2813-2896.3
5998.A-Z Special artists, A-Z
6000 Amber carving. Amber art objects
Bamboo carving, see NK3649.3+
6010 Coral carving. Coral art objects
Horn and bone carving
Cf. TS1050, Manufacture
Cf. TT288, Bone and horn craft
6020 General works
6020.5.A-Z By region or country, A-Z
Apply table at NK3649.35.A-Z
6022 Scrimshaw
6030 Ice carving. Snow sculpture

NK

Other arts and art industries
Glyptic arts -- Continued
Inkstands. Inksticks. Inkstones. Inkwells
Cf. TP946+, Ink manufacture
Cf. Z45, Writing. Calligraphy. Penmanship
Cf. Z112, Paleography
6035 General works
6035.2.A-Z By region or country, A-Z
Apply table at NK3649.35.A-Z
6045 Meerschaum. Meerschaum tobacco-pipes
Netsuke carving. Netsukes. Chinese belt toggles
6050 General works
6052.A-Z Special artists, A-Z
6058 Soapstone carving. Soapstone art objects
6060 Tortoiseshell carving. Tortoiseshell art objects
6075 Gourds. Gourd craft
Cf. TT873.5, Handicraft
6076 Hairwork
6076.5 Halloween collectibles
6077 Holiday decorations
Cf. NK4696.4, Christmas decorations
Cf. NK4900, Easter eggs
Cf. NK6076.5, Halloween collectibles
6077.3 Horse collectibles
6077.5 Hunting collectibles
6078 Incense burners and containers
6080 Inro
Insignia, see NK3668.5+
6100 Ju-i (Scepters)
6140 Kitchen collectibles
Cf. TX656+, Equipment, appliances, utensils, etc.
6150 Knife rests
For knife rests in a particular material, see the material
6196 Lamps
Prefer classification by material
Cf. NK4680, Ceramic lamps (Ancient)
Cf. NK8475.L3, Miniature lamps
Leatherwork
Cf. Z266+, Bookbinding
6200 General works
6202.A-Z By region or country, A-Z
Apply table at NK3649.35.A-Z
6210 Leather bottles, blackjacks, etc.
6213 Lunchboxes
6215 Marbles (Game)
6220 Match holders
For match holders in a particular material, see the material
6300 Measuring tapes. Tape measures
Metalwork
6400 Periodicals and societies

Other arts and art industries
Metalwork -- Continued
6400.5 Congresses
6400.6 Dictionaries
6400.7 Directories
Exhibitions (By place held)
Class here works on general exhibitions
For exhibitions on special periods not limited to a particular country, see NK6407-NK6410.3
For exhibitions on special countries, see NK6411-NK6496
6401.A-Z United States. By city and museum or other place of exhibition, A-Z
6401.5.A-Z Other countries. By country and city, A-Z
Museums
6401.8 Collective
6402.A-Z United States. By city and museum, A-Z
6402.5.A-Z Other countries. By country and city, A-Z
Special periods
See NK6407 NK6410.3
6403.A-Z Private collections. By collection, A-Z
6404 General. Collectors' manuals
6404.5 Conservation and restoration
6405 Collected designs
6405.5 Auction catalogs
History
6406 General works
6406.4.A-Z Ethnic groups not limited to one country, A-Z
6407 Ancient
6407.15 Egyptian
6407.2 Etruscan
6407.3 Classical
Cf. DG137, Roman antiquities
6407.4 Early Christian
6408 Medieval
6408.7 Buddhist
6408.8 Byzantine
6408.9 Islamic
6408.92 Romanesque
6408.923 Gothic
6409 Modern
6409.2.A-Z Special styles, A-Z
6409.2.G76 Grotesque
6409.3 Renaissance
6409.6 Baroque
6409.65 18th century
6409.7 Rococo
6409.8 19th century
6409.85.A-Z Special styles, A-Z
6409.85.A7 Art nouveau
6409.85.B53 Biedermeier
6409.85.E24 Eclecticism
6409.85.V53 Victorian

Other arts and art industries
Metalwork
History
Modern -- Continued
6410 20th century
6410.3.A-Z Special styles, A-Z
6410.3.A78 Art deco
6411 North America
6412 United States
6412.5 Latin America
6413-6496.3 Other countries (Table N1)
Add country number in table to NK6400
Apply table at NK2813-2896.3
6497 Collective biography
6498.A-Z Special artists, A-Z
Including families and firms
6499 Dealers' catalogs
Enameling, coloring, etc.
6510 General works
6511.A-Z Special topics, A-Z
6511.G72 Graniteware
6511.S53 Signs and signboards
6512.A-Z Special artists, A-Z
Chasing, engraving, etc.
6520 General works
6521.A-Z Special topics, A-Z
6522.A-Z Special artists, A-Z
6525 Inlay work
Including damascening, niello, bidri ware, etc.
6530 Hammered work and its imitations
Including repoussé and chasing combined
6535 Modeling of metal
Arms and armor
Prefer Class U, except for collections of art museums
Cf. GN497.5+, Anthropology
Cf. U799+, Military science
6600 Periodicals and societies
6600.5 Congresses
6600.6 Dictionaries
6600.7 Directories
Exhibitions (By place held)
Class here works on general art exhibitions
For exhibitions on special periods not limited to a particular country, see NK6607-NK6610.3
For exhibitions on special countries, see NK6611-NK6696
6601.A-Z United States. By city and museum or other place of exhibition, A-Z
6601.5.A-Z Other countries. By country and city, A-Z
Museums
6601.8 Collective

Other arts and art industries
Metalwork
Arms and armor
Museums -- Continued

6602.A-Z United States. By city and museum, A-Z
6602.5.A-Z Other countries. By country and city, A-Z
e.g.
6602.5.B4B8 Belgium. Brussels
Special periods
See NK6607-NK6610.3
6603.A-Z Private collections. By collection, A-Z
6604 General. Collectors' manuals
6604.5 Conservation and restoration
6605 Collected designs
6605.5 Auction catalogs
History
6606 General works
6606.4.A-Z Ethnic groups not limited to one country, A-Z
6607 Ancient
6607.15 Egyptian
6607.2 Etruscan
6607.3 Classical
6607.4 Early Christian
6608 Medieval
6608.7 Buddhist
6608.8 Byzantine
6608.9 Islamic
6608.92 Romanesque
6608.923 Gothic
6609 Modern
6609.2.A-Z Special styles, A-Z
6609.2.G76 Grotesque
6609.3 Renaissance
6609.6 Baroque
6609.65 18th century
6609.7 Rococo
6609.8 19th century
6609.85.A-Z Special styles, A-Z
6609.85.A7 Art nouveau
6609.85.B53 Biedermeier
6609.85.E24 Eclecticism
6609.85.V53 Victorian
6610 20th century
6610.3.A-Z Special styles, A-Z
6610.3.A78 Art deco
6611 North America
6612 United States
6612.5 Latin America
6613-6696.3 Other countries (Table N1)
Add country number in table to NK6600
Apply table at NK2813-2896.3
6697 Collective biography

Other arts and art industries
Metalwork
Arms and armor -- Continued
6698.A-Z Special artists, A-Z
Including families and firms
6699 Dealers' catalogs
Swords. Sword guards. Sword mountings
For Tsubas, see NK6784
6700 Periodicals and societies
6700.5 Congresses
6700.6 Dictionaries
6700.7 Directories
Exhibitions (By place held)
Class here works on general exhibitions related to the decorative arts and swords
For exhibitions on special periods not limited to a particular country, see NK6707-NK6710.3
For exhibitions on special countries, see NK6711-NK6796
6701.A-Z United States. By city and museum or other place of exhibition, A-Z
6701.5.A-Z Other countries. By country and city, A-Z
Museums
6701.8 Collective
6702.A-Z United States. By city and museum, A-Z
6702.5.A-Z Other countries. By country and city, A-Z
Special periods
See NK6707-NK6710.3
6703.A-Z Private collections. By collection, A-Z
6704 General. Collectors' manuals
6704.5 Conservation and restoration
6705 Collected designs
6705.5 Auction catalogs
History
6706 General works
6706.4.A-Z Ethnic groups not limited to one country, A-Z
6707 Ancient
6707.15 Egyptian
6707.2 Etruscan
6707.3 Classical
6707.4 Early Christian
6708 Medieval
6708.7 Buddhist
6708.8 Byzantine
6708.9 Islamic
6708.92 Romanesque
6708.923 Gothic
6709 Modern
6709.2.A-Z Special styles, A-Z
6709.2.G76 Grotesque
6709.3 Renaissance
6709.6 Baroque

Other arts and art industries
Metalwork
Arms and armor
Swords. Sword guards. Sword mounting
History
Modern -- Continued
6709.65 18th century
6709.7 Rococo
6709.8 19th century
6709.85.A-Z Special styles, A-Z
6709.85.A7 Art nouveau
6709.85.B53 Biedermeier
6709.85.E24 Eclecticism
6709.85.V53 Victorian
6710 20th century
6710.3.A-Z Special styles, A-Z
6710.3.A78 Art deco
6711 North America
6712 United States
6712.5 Latin America
6713-6796.3 Other countries (Table N1)
Add country number in table to NK6700
Apply table at NK2813-2896.3
6772 Asia. The Orient
6782 Eastern Asia
6784 Japan
6797 Collective biography
6798.A-Z Special artists, A-Z
Including families and firms
6799 Dealers' catalogs
6805 Daggers
6808 Shields
Firearms. Guns and pistols
6900 Periodicals and societies
6900.5 Congresses
6900.6 Dictionaries
6900.7 Directories
Exhibitions (By place held)
Class here works on general exhibitions of firearms and the decorative arts
For exhibitions on special periods not limited to a particular country, see NK6907-NK6910.3
For exhibitions on special countries, see NK6911-NK6996
6901.A-Z United States. By city and museum or other place of exhibition, A-Z
6901.5.A-Z Other countries. By country and city, A-Z
Museums
6901.8 Collective
6902.A-Z United States. By city and museum, A-Z
6902.5.A-Z Other countries. By country and city, A-Z

Other arts and art industries
Metalwork
Arms and armor
Firearms. Guns and pistols
Museums -- Continued
Special periods
See NK6907-NK6910.3
6903.A-Z Private collections. By collection, A-Z
6904 General. Collectors' manuals
6904.5 Conservation and restoration
6905 Collected designs
6905.5 Auction catalogs
History
6906 General works
6906.4.A-Z Ethnic groups not limited to one country, A-Z
6907 Ancient
6908 Medieval
6909 Modern
6909.2.A-Z Special styles, A-Z
6909.2.G76 Grotesque
6909.3 Renaissance
6909.6 Baroque
6909.65 18th century
6909.7 Rococo
6909.8 19th century
6909.85.A-Z Special styles, A-Z
6909.85.A7 Art nouveau
6909.85.B53 Biedermeier
6909.85.E24 Eclecticism
6909.85.V53 Victorian
6910 20th century
6910.3.A-Z Special styles, A-Z
6910.3.A78 Art deco
6911 North America
6912 United States
6912.5 Latin America
6913-6996.3 Other countries (Table N1)
Add country number in table to NK6900
Apply table at NK2813-2896.3
6997 Collective biography
6998.A-Z Special artists, A-Z
Including families and firms
6999 Dealers' catalogs
(7000-7099) Coins and medals
See Class CJ, Numismatics
Gold and silver. Plate. Jewelry
For church plate, see NK7215
7100 Periodicals and societies
7100.5 Congresses
7100.6 Dictionaries
7100.7 Directories

Other arts and art industries
Metalwork
Gold and silver. Plate. Jewelry -- Continued
Exhibitions (By place held)
Class here works on general exhibitions.
For exhibitions on special periods not limited to a particular country, see NK7107-NK7110.3
For exhibitions on special countries, see NK7111-NK7196

7101.A-Z United States. By city and museum or other place of exhibition, A-Z
7101.5.A-Z Other countries. By country and city, A-Z
Museums
7101.8 Collective
7102.A-Z United States. By city and museum, A-Z
7102.5.A-Z Other countries. By country and city, A-Z
Special periods
See NK7807-NK7810.3
7103.A-Z Private collections, A-Z
7104 General. Collectors' manuals
7104.5 Conservation and restoration
7105 Collected designs
7105.5 Auction catalogs
History
7106 General works
7106.4.A-Z Ethnic groups not limited to one country, A-Z
7106.4.C44 Celts
7106.4.T45 Thracians
7107 Ancient
7107.15 Egyptian
7107.2 Etruscan
7107.3 Classical
7107.4 Early Christian
7108 Medieval
7108.7 Buddhist
7108.8 Byzantine
7108.9 Islamic
7108.92 Romanesque
7108.923 Gothic
7109 Modern
7109.2.A-Z Special styles, A-Z
7109.2.G76 Grotesque
7109.3 Renaissance
7109.6 Baroque
7109.65 18th century
7109.7 Rococo
7109.8 19th century
7109.85.A-Z Special styles, A-Z
7109.85.A7 Art nouveau
7109.85.B53 Biedermeier
7109.85.E24 Eclecticism
7109.85.V53 Victorian

Other arts and art industries
Metalwork
Gold and silver. Plate. Jewelry
History
Modern -- Continued
7110 20th century
7110.3.A-Z Special styles, A-Z
7110.3.A78 Art deco
7111 North America
7112 United States
7112.5 Latin America
7113-7196.3 Other countries (Table N1)
Add country number in table to NK7100
Apply table at NK2813-2896.3
7197 Collective biography
7198.A-Z Special artists, A-Z
Including families and firms
7199 Dealers' catalogs
7210 Hallmarks and other marks
7215 Ecclesiastical plate (Chalices, patens, etc.)
7218 Miscellaneous plate
Including gold and silver trophies of Charles V
Gold plate, vases, etc.
Prefer NK7112 NK7196
7220 General works
7225 Special (not A-Z)
e.g. Golden patera of Rennes
Silverwork, vases, etc.
Prefer NK7112 NK7196
7230 General works
7233 Special pieces (not A-Z)
Including Disk of Theodosius
Silver flatware
7234 General works
7234.5 Servers
7235 Spoons
7236.A-Z Other special topics, A-Z
7236.M65 Monteiths
7236.M88 Mustard pots
7236.N44 Nefs
7236.T55 Thimbles
Silver-plated ware
Cf. TS675, Electroplated ware (Catalogs)
7240 General works
By region or country
7240.5 United States
7241.A-Z Other regions or countries, A-Z
7241.5.A-Z Special artists, families, firms, A-Z
7242.A-Z Special topics, A-Z
7242.F55 Flatware
7242.N3 Napkin rings
7250 Sheffield plate

Other arts and art industries
Metalwork
Gold and silver. Plate. Jewelry -- Continued
Jewelry
Cf. GT2250+, History of costume
Cf. TS740+, Jewelry manufacture
Cf. TT212, Jewelry craft
For costume jewelry, see NK4890.C67
For ethnic jewelry (General), see NK4890.E86
7300 Periodicals and societies
7300.5 Congresses
7300.6 Dictionaries
7300.7 Directories
Exhibitions (By place held)
Class here works on general exhibitions.
For exhibitions on special periods not limited to a particular country, see NK7307-NK7310.3
For exhibitions on special countries, see NK7311-NK7396
7301.A-Z United States. By city and museum or other place of exhibition, A-Z
7301.5.A-Z Other countries. By country and city, A-Z
Museums
7301.8 Collective
7302.A-Z United States. By city and museum, A-Z
7302.5.A-Z Other countries. By country and city, A-Z
Special periods
See NK7307-NK7310.3
7303.A-Z Private collections. By collection, A-Z
7304 General. Collectors' manuals
7304.5 Conservation and restoration
7305 Collected designs
7305.5 Auction catalogs
History
7306 General works
7306.4.A-Z Ethnic groups not limited to one country, A-Z
7307 Ancient
7307.15 Egyptian
7307.2 Etruscan
7307.3 Classical
7307.4 Early Christian
7308 Medieval
7308.7 Buddhist
7308.8 Byzantine
7308.9 Islamic
7308.92 Romanesque
7308.923 Gothic
7309 Modern
7309.2.A-Z Special styles, A-Z
7309.2.G76 Grotesque
7309.3 Renaissance
7309.6 Baroque

Other arts and art industries
Metalwork
Gold and silver. Plate. Jewelry
Jewelry
History
Modern -- Continued
7309.65 18th century
7309.7 Rococo
7309.8 19th century
7309.85.A-Z Special styles, A-Z
7309.85.A7 Art nouveau
7309.85.B53 Biedermeier
7309.85.E24 Eclecticism
7309.85.V53 Victorian
7310 20th century
7310.3.A-Z Special styles, A-Z
7310.3.A78 Art deco
7311 North America
7312 United States
7312.5 Latin America
7313-7396.3 Other countries (Table N1)
Add country number in table to NK7300
Apply table at NK2813-2896.3
7397 Collective biography
7398.A-Z Special artists, A-Z
Including families and firms
7399 Dealers' catalogs
Crown jewels, insignia, regalia
Prefer NK7407 to NK7401 NK7403 for ancient
Cf. CR4480+, Heraldry
7400 Periodicals
Exhibitions. By place held
7401.A-Z United States. By city and museum or other place of exhibition, A-Z
7401.5.A-Z Other countries. By country and city, A-Z
Museums
7402.A-Z United States. By city and museum, A-Z
7402.5.A-Z Other countries. By country and city, A-Z
7403.A-Z Collections. By collection, A-Z
7404 General works
7405 Collected designs
History
7406 General works
By period
7407 Ancient
7408 Medieval
7409 Modern
By country
7411 North America
7412 United States
7415.A-Z Other countries, A-Z
e.g.
7415.A8 Austria

Other arts and art industries
Metalwork
Gold and silver. Plate. Jewelry
Jewelry
Crown jewels, insignia, regalia
History -- Continued
7417.A-Z Special artists, A-Z
7419 Trade catalogs, etc.
7422 Chains
7422.4 Bridal crowns
7425 Maces (Ceremonial)
Rings
7440 Periodicals
Exhibitions. By place held
7441.A-Z United States. By city and museum or other place of exhibition, A-Z
7441.5.A-Z Other countries. By country and city, A-Z
Museums
7442.A-Z United States. By city and museum, A-Z
7442.5.A-Z Other countries. By country and city, A-Z
7443.A-Z Collections. By collection, A-Z
7444 General works
7445 Collected designs
History
7446 General works
By period
7447 Ancient
7448 Medieval
7449 Modern
By country
7451 North America
7452 United States
7455.A-Z Other countries, A-Z
7457.A-Z Special artists, A-Z
7459 Trade catalogs, etc.
Watches and clocks
Including pocket watches and wrist watches
For clockcases, see NK2720
7480 Periodicals
Exhibitions. By place held
7481.A-Z United States. By city and museum or other place of exhibition, A-Z
7481.5.A-Z Other countries. By country and city, A-Z
Museums
7482.A-Z United States. By city and museum, A-Z
7482.5.A-Z Other countries. By country and city, A-Z
7483.A-Z Collections. By collection, A-Z
7484 General works
7485 Collected designs
History
7486 General works
By period
7487 Ancient

Other arts and art industries
Metalwork
Gold and silver. Plate. Jewelry
Jewelry
Watches and clocks
History
By period -- Continued
7488 Medieval
7489 Modern
By country
7491 North America
7492 United States
7495.A-Z Other countries, A-Z
7497.A-Z Special artists, A-Z
7499 Trade catalogs, etc.
7500.A-Z Special kinds of clocks and watches, A-Z
7500.A38 Advertising clocks
7500.B35 Banjo clocks
7500.C65 Comic strip character clocks and watches
7500.L34 Lantern clocks
7500.L65 Longcase clocks
7500.S53 Shelf clocks
7502 Balance cocks
7502.5 Watch fobs
7503 Watch keys
7504 Watch holders
Precious stones
Cf. NK5505+, Glyptic arts
7650 General works
Diamonds
7658 Collections
7660 General works
7663 Special (not A-Z)
e.g. Koh-i-noor (Diamond)
7680 Pearls
7690.A-Z Others, A-Z
7695 Other (not A-Z)
7700 Aluminum work
Brasses
Including works on brass, bronze, and copper
7800 Periodicals and societies
7800.5 Congresses
7800.6 Dictionaries
7800.7 Directories
Exhibitions (By place held)
Class here works on general exhibitions.
For exhibitions on special periods not limited to a particular country, see NK7807-NK7810.3
For exhibitions on special countries, see NK7811-NK7896
7801.A-Z United States. By city and museum or other place of exhibition, A-Z

Other arts and art industries
Metalwork
Brasses
Exhibitions (By place held) -- Continued
7801.5.A-Z Other countries. By country and city, A-Z
Museums
7801.8 Collective
7802.A-Z United States. By city and museum, A-Z
7802.5.A-Z Other countries. By country and city, A-Z
Special periods
See NK7807-NK7810.3
7803.A-Z Private collections. By collection, A-Z
7804 General. Collectors' manuals
7804.5 Conservation and restoration
7805 Collected designs
7805.5 Auction catalogs
History
7806 General works
7806.4.A-Z Ethnic groups not limited to one country, A-Z
7807 Ancient
7807.15 Egyptian
7807.2 Etruscan
7807.3 Classical
7807.4 Early Christian
7808 Medieval
7808.7 Buddhist
7808.8 Byzantine
7808.9 Islamic
7808.92 Romanesque
7808.923 Gothic
7809 Modern
7809.2.A-Z Special styles, A-Z
7809.2.G76 Grotesque
7809.3 Renaissance
7809.6 Baroque
7809.65 18th century
7809.7 Rococo
7809.8 19th century
7809.85.A-Z Special styles, A-Z
7809.85.A7 Art nouveau
7809.85.B53 Biedermeier
7809.85.E24 Eclecticism
7809.85.V53 Victorian
7810 20th century
7810.3.A-Z Special styles, A-Z
7810.3.A78 Art deco
7811 North America
7812 United States
7812.5 Latin America
7813-7896.3 Other countries (Table N1)
Add country number in table to NK7800
Apply table at NK2813-2896.3
7897 Collective biography

Other arts and art industries
Metalwork
Brasses -- Continued
7898.A-Z Special artists, A-Z
Including families and firms
7899 Dealers' catalogs
Bronzes. Gilt bronzes
7900 Periodicals and societies
7900.5 Congresses
7900.6 Dictionaries
7900.7 Directories
Exhibitions (By place held)
Class here works on general exhibitions.
For exhibitions on special periods not limited to a particular country, see NK7907-NK7910.3
For exhibitions on special countries, see NK7911-NK7996
7901.A-Z United States. By city and museum or other place of exhibition, A-Z
7901.5.A-Z Other countries. By country and city, A-Z
Museums
7901.8 Collective
7902.A-Z United States. By city and museum, A-Z
7902.5.A-Z Other countries. By country and city, A-Z
Special periods
See NK7907-NK7910.3
7903.A-Z Private collections. By collection, A-Z
7904 General. Collectors' manuals
7904.5 Conservation and restoration
7905 Collected designs
7905.5 Auction catalogs
History
7906 General works
7906.4.A-Z Ethnic groups not limited to one country, A-Z
7907 Ancient
7907.15 Egyptian
7907.2 Etruscan
7907.3 Classical
7907.4 Early Christian
7908 Medieval
7908.7 Buddhist
7908.8 Byzantine
7908.9 Islamic
7908.92 Romanesque
7908.923 Gothic
7909 Modern
7909.2.A-Z Special styles, A-Z
7909.2.G76 Grotesque
7909.3 Renaissance
7909.6 Baroque
7909.65 18th century
7909.7 Rococo

Other arts and art industries
Metalwork
Bronzes. Gilt bronzes
History
Modern -- Continued
7909.8 19th century
7909.85.A-Z Special styles, A-Z
7909.85.A7 Art nouveau
7909.85.B53 Biedermeier
7909.85.E24 Eclecticism
7909.85.V53 Victorian
7910 20th century
7910.3.A-Z Special styles, A-Z
7910.3.A78 Art deco
7911 North America
7912 United States
7912.5 Latin America
7913-7996.3 Other countries (Table N1 modified)
Add country number in table to NK7900
Under each (1-number or decimal number countries) (except China):
.A1 General works
.A3A-.A3Z Special regions, provinces, etc., A-Z
.A5-.Z Special cities, A-Z
Under each (Cutter-number countries):
.x General
.x2A-.x2Z Special cities, A-Z
Asia. The Orient
7982 Eastern Asia
7983 China
7983.A1 General works
7983.A3A-Z Special regions, provinces, etc., A-Z
7983.A5A-Z Special cities, A-Z
By period
Prefer classification by place
7983.2 Pre T'ang
7983.22 Early through Chou dynasty (To 221 B.C.)
7983.23 Ch'in-Han dynasties (221 B.C.-220 A.D.)
7983.24 Three kingdoms-Sui dynasty (220-618)
7983.3 T'ang-Five dynasties (618-960)
7983.4 Sung-Yuan dynasties (960-1368)
7983.5 Ming-Manchu (Ch'ing) dynasties (1368-1912)
7983.6 19th century
7983.7 20th century
7997 Collective biography
7998.A-Z Special artists, A-Z
Including families and firms
7999 Dealers' catalogs
8000 Special pieces (not A-Z)
e. g. Wade cup
Chrome-plated metalwork
8030 General works
By region or country

Other arts and art industries
Metalwork
Chrome-plated metalwork
By region or country -- Continued
8032 United States
8033.A-Z Other regions or countries, A-Z
8035.A-Z Special artists, A-Z
Copperwork
8100 Periodicals and societies
8100.5 Congresses
8100.6 Dictionaries
8100.7 Directories
Exhibitions (By place held)
Class here works on general exhibitions.
For exhibitions on special periods not limited to a particular country, see NK8107-NK8110.3
For exhibitions on special countries, see NK8111-NK8196
8101.A-Z United States. By city and museum or other place of exhibition, A-Z
8101.5.A-Z Other countries. By country and city, A-Z
Museums
8101.8 Collective
8102.A-Z United States. By city and museum, A-Z
8102.5.A-Z Other countries. By country and city, A-Z
Special periods
See NK8107-NK8110.3
8103.A-Z Private collections. By collection, A-Z
8104 General. Collectors' manuals
8104.5 Conservation and restoration
8105 Collected designs
8105.5 Auction catalogs
History
8106 General works
8106.4.A-Z Ethnic groups not limited to one country, A-Z
8107 Ancient
8107.15 Egyptian
8107.2 Etruscan
8107.3 Classical
8107.4 Early Christian
8108 Medieval
8108.7 Buddhist
8108.8 Byzantine
8108.9 Islamic
8108.92 Romanesque
8108.923 Gothic
8109 Modern
8109.2.A-Z Special styles, A-Z
8109.2.G76 Grotesque
8109.3 Renaissance
8109.6 Baroque
8109.65 18th century

Other arts and art industries
Metalwork
Copperwork
History
Modern -- Continued
8109.7 Rococo
8109.8 19th century
8109.85.A-Z Special styles, A-Z
8109.85.A7 Art nouveau
8109.85.B53 Biedermeier
8109.85.E24 Eclecticism
8109.85.V53 Victorian
8110 20th century
8110.3.A-Z Special styles, A-Z
8110.3.A78 Art deco
8111 North America
8112 United States
8112.5 Latin America
8113-8196.3 Other countries (Table N1)
Add country number in table to NK8100
Apply table at NK2813-2896.3
8197 Collective biography
8198.A-Z Special artists, A-Z
Including families and firms
8199 Dealers' catalogs
Ironwork. Cast iron work
8200 Periodicals and societies
8200.5 Congresses
8200.6 Dictionaries
8200.7 Directories
Exhibitions (By place held)
Class here works on general exhibitions.
For exhibitions on special periods not limited to a particular country, see NK8207-NK8210.3
For exhibitions on special countries, see NK8211-NK8296
8201.A-Z United States. By city and museum or other place of exhibition, A-Z
8201.5.A-Z Other countries. By country and city, A-Z
Museums
8201.8 Collective
8202.A-Z United States. By city and museum, A-Z
8202.5.A-Z Other countries. By country and city, A-Z
Special periods
See NK8207-NK8210.3
8203.A-Z Private collections. By collection, A-Z
8204 General. Collectors' manuals
8204.5 Conservation and restoration
8205 Collected designs
8205.5 Auction catalogs
History
8206 General works

Other arts and art industries
Metalwork
Ironwork. Cast iron work
History -- Continued

8206.4.A-Z	Ethnic groups not limited to one country, A-Z
8207	Ancient
8207.15	Egyptian
8207.2	Etruscan
8207.3	Classical
8207.4	Early Christian
8208	Medieval
8208.7	Buddhist
8208.8	Byzantine
8208.9	Islamic
8208.92	Romanesque
8208.923	Gothic
8209	Modern
8209.2.A-Z	Special styles, A-Z
8209.2.G76	Grotesque
8209.3	Renaissance
8209.6	Baroque
8209.65	18th century
8209.7	Rococo
8209.8	19th century
8209.85.A-Z	Special styles, A-Z
8209.85.A7	Art nouveau
8209.85.B53	Biedermeier
8209.85.E24	Eclecticism
8209.85.V53	Victorian
8210	20th century
8210.3.A-Z	Special styles, A-Z
8210.3.A78	Art deco
8211	North America
8212	United States
8212.5	Latin America
8213-8296.3	Other countries (Table N1) Add country number in table to NK8200 Apply table at NK2813-2896.3
8297	Collective biography
8298.A-Z	Special artists, A-Z Including families and firms
8299	Dealers' catalogs
8350	Leadwork
8380	Nickel silver
8400-8420	Pewter. Britannia metal Cf. TT266.3, Handicrafts
8400	Periodicals
	Exhibitions. By place held
8401.A-Z	United States. By city and museum or other place of exhibition, A-Z
8401.5.A-Z	Other countries. By country and city, A-Z
	Museums
8402.A-Z	United States. By city and museum, A-Z

Other arts and art industries
Metalwork
Pewter. Britannia metal
Museums -- Continued
8402.5.A-Z Other countries. By country and city, A-Z
8403.A-Z Collections. By collection, A-Z
8404 General works
8405 Collected designs
History
8406 General works
By period
8407 Ancient
8408 Medieval
8409 Modern
By country
8411 North America
8412 United States
8415.A-Z Other countries, A-Z
8417.A-Z Special artists, A-Z
8419 Trade catalogs, etc.
8420 Pewter marks
8425 Tinwork
Cf. TT266+, Handicraft
Miscellaneous articles of metal
8428 Crosses
Cf. CC300+, Archaeology
8430 Cutlery
8438 Lanterns. Light fixtures
Mirrors
Cf. TT898.3, Handicraft
8440 General works
8440.2.A-Z By region or country, A-Z
Apply table at NK3649.35.A-Z
8450 Spoons (General)
Cf. NK7235, Silver spoons
Toys
8454 General works
8454.2.A-Z By region or country, A-Z
Apply table at NK3649.35.A-Z
8459.A-Z Other, A-Z
8459.A38 Advertising tins
8459.B36 Beer cans. Beer trays
8459.B4 Belts
8459.B47 Betel cutters
Cf. NK3654, Betel chewing paraphernalia
8459.C67 Corkscrews
8459.D64 Doorknobs
Cf. TH2279, Building design and construction
8459.F57 Firebacks
8459.K4 Kettles
Including ancient Greek tripods
8459.M36 Matchboxes

Other arts and art industries
Metalwork
Miscellaneous articles of metal
Other, A-Z -- Continued
8459.M6 Mortars
8459.O64 Openers (Implements)
8459.S3 Samovars
8459.W3 Waffle irons
8459.W55 Windmill weights
Miniature objects
8470 General works
8473.A-Z By region or country, A-Z
8473.5.A-Z Special artists, A-Z
8475.A-Z Special, A-Z
Including works on special regions or countries
8475.B6 Bottles
Including beer and liquor bottles
Cf. NK8475.P47, Perfume bottles
8475.B8 Buildings
8475.C3 Cases
Dolls and dollhouses, see NK4891.3+
8475.F53 Fiberwork
Furniture, see NK2750
8475.G55 Glassware
8475.L3 Lamps
8475.M5 Military (Model soldiers, etc.)
Including G.I. Joe figures
Cf. GV1218.T55, Children's games
Cf. U311, Military sciences
8475.M66 Mosaics
8475.P47 Perfume bottles
8475.P65 Porcelain. Pottery
Pottery, see NK8475.P65
8475.R48 Retail stores
Rooms, see NK2117.M54
8475.S45 Sewing machines
8475.S55 Silverwork
8475.T33 Tableware
Toys, see NK9509+
8475.W66 Wood-carving
Molds
8490 For foods
e. g., Bread molds, cooky molds, etc.
8491 Other molds (not A-Z)
8500 Mosaic ornaments and jewelry
Cf. NK8475.M66, Miniature mosaics
8550 Musical instruments (Art collections)
8551 Needlework boxes
Cf. NK9100+, Needlework
Neon signs
8551.2 General works
8551.25.A-Z Special, A-Z
8551.25.B43 Beer signs

Other arts and art industries -- Continued
8551.3 Nutcrackers
For nutcrackers in a particular material, see the material
8552 Ocean liner collectibles
Olympic games collectibles, see GV721.75
Paper and paper articles. Decorated paper. Decoupage
Cf. N6494.P34, Paper art
Cf. NB1270.P3, Paper sculpture
Cf. NK4891.3+, Paper dolls
Cf. NK8475.M5, Paper soldiers
Cf. TT870+, Decorative paperwork
Cf. TT892, Paper flowers
8552.5.A-Z Exhibitions. Collections. Museums. By country and collector or place of exhibition, A-Z
8553 General works
8553.2.A-Z By region or country, A-Z
8553.5.A-Z Special artists, A-Z
8554 Watermarks
Cf. Z237, Watermarks in printing
Papier mâché
Cf. TT871, Papier mâché craft
8555 General works
8555.5.A-Z Special regions and countries, A-Z
Apply table at NK3649.35.A-Z
8560 Pattern printing (Handicraft)
8580 Permodello modeling
8590 Piqué-work
8592 Pitchers
Prefer classification by material
8593 Plaques
Plastic materials
Including collectibles
8595 General works
8595.2.A-Z Special articles of plastic, A-Z
8595.2.C45 Character toys
Hard plastic dolls, see NK4894.4.H37
Plastic handbags, see NK4890.H34
Plastic jewelry, see NK4890.P55
8596 Plates
Prefer classification by material
8598 Powder flasks
Pyrography
Cf. TT199.8, Handicraft
8600 Periodicals
8605 General works

Other arts and art industries
Pyrography -- Continued
8605.5.A-Z Special regions or countries, A-Z
Under each country:
.x General works
.x2.A-.x2.Z Local, A-Z
.x3 Collective biography
.x4.A-.x4.Z Special artists, A-Z
8608 Rabbit collectibles
8610 Rattles
8640 Salt dishes. Salt shakers. Salt and pepper shakers
Prefer classification by material
8643 Shellcraft
8643.3 Shopping bags
For bags in a particular material, see the material
8643.45 Signs and signboards
For signs and signboards in a particular material, see the material
8644 Spoons
For spoons in a particular material, see the material, e.g., NK7235, Silver spoons; NK8450, Metal spoons; etc.
8645 Staffs (Sticks, canes, etc.)
Prefer classification by material
8647 Steins
Prefer classification by material
Stencil work (Decorative)
Cf. ND2492, Stencil painting
Cf. NE2236+, Serigraphy
Cf. TT270+, Arts and crafts
8650 Periodicals
Exhibitions. By place held
8651.A-Z United States. By city and museum or other place of exhibition, A-Z
8651.5.A-Z Other countries. By country and city, A-Z
Museums
8652.A-Z United States. By city and museum, A-Z
8652.5.A-Z Other countries. By country and city, A-Z
8653.A-Z Collections. By collection, A-Z
8654 General works
8655 Collected designs
History
8656 General works
By period
8657 Ancient
8658 Medieval
8659 Modern
By country
8661 North America
8662 United States
8665.A-Z Other countries, A-Z
8667.A-Z Special artists, A-Z
8669 Trade catalogs, etc.

Other arts and art industries -- Continued
Sticks, see NK8645
Stonework. Marble work
Cf. NB1+, Sculpture
8700 General works
8700.5.A-Z Special regions and countries, A-Z
Apply table at NK3649.35.A-Z
8705 Lettering
8713 Stone lanterns
Cf. SB473.5, Garden ornaments and furniture
8714 Straw work
8715 Suiseki. Ornamental rocks
Tableware
For tableware in a particular material, see the material
Cf. NK8475.T33, Miniature tableware
8725 General works
8725.5.A-Z Special artists, A-Z
Tape measures, see NK6300
8730 Teapots
Prefer classification by material
Teddy bears
8740 General works
8740.2.A-Z Special kinds of bears, A-Z
8740.2.W54 Winnie the Pooh
8740.5.A-Z Special artists, A-Z
8745 Tennis collectibles
Textile arts and art needlework
Cf. TT699+, Handicrafts
8800 Periodicals and societies
8800.5 Congresses
8800.6 Dictionaries
8800.7 Directories
Exhibitions (By place held)
Class here works on general exhibitions. For exhibitions on special periods not limited to a particular country, see NK8807-NK8810.3, for exhibitions on special countries, see NK8811-NK8896
8801.A-Z United States. By city and museum or other place of exhibition, A-Z
8801.5.A-Z Other countries. By country and city, A-Z
Museums
8801.8 Collective
8802.A-Z United States. By city and museum, A-Z
8802.5.A-Z Other countries. By country and city, A-Z
Special periods
For special periods, see NK8807-NK8810.3
8803.A-Z Private collections. By collection, A-Z
8804 General. Collectors' manuals
8804.5 Conservation and restoration
8805 Collected designs
8805.5 Auction catalogs

NK

	Other arts and art industries
	Textile arts and art needlework -- Continued
	History
8806	General works
8806.4.A-Z	Ethnic groups not limited to one country, A-Z
8807	Ancient
8807.15	Egyptian
8807.2	Etruscan
8807.3	Classical
8807.4	Early Christian
8808	Medieval
8808.7	Buddhist
8808.8	Byzantine
8808.9	Islamic
8808.92	Romanesque
8808.923	Gothic
8809	Modern
8809.2.A-Z	Special styles, A-Z
8809.2.G76	Grotesque
8809.3	Renaissance
8809.6	Baroque
8809.65	18th century
8809.7	Rococo
8809.8	19th century
8809.85.A-Z	Special styles, A-Z
8809.85.A7	Art nouveau
8809.85.B53	Biedermeier
8809.85.E24	Eclecticism
8809.85.V53	Victorian
8810	20th century
8810.3.A-Z	Special styles, A-Z
8810.3.A78	Art deco
8811	North America
8812	United States
8812.5	Latin America
8813-8896.3	Other countries (Table N1) Add country number in table to NK8800 Apply table at NK2813-2896.3
8872	Asia. The Orient
8877	Southeastern Asia
8880	Indonesia. Dutch East Indies
8897	Collective biography
8898.A-Z	Special artists, A-Z Including families and firms
8899	Dealers' catalogs
8899.5.A-Z	By material, A-Z
8899.5.W65	Wool
	Woven fabrics Cf. NK2775+, Rugs and carpets Cf. NK2975+, Tapestries Cf. NK3175+, Upholstery, drapery Cf. NK4700+, Costume
8900	Periodicals and societies

Other arts and art industries
Textile arts and art needlework
Woven fabrics -- Continued

8900.5 Congresses
8900.6 Dictionaries
8900.7 Directories
Exhibitions (By place held)
Class here works on general exhibitions. For exhibitions on special periods not limited to a particular country, see NK8907-NK8910.3, for exhibitions on special countries, see NK8911-NK8996
8901.A-Z United States. By city and museum or other place of exhibition, A-Z
8901.5.A-Z Other countries. By country and city, A-Z
Museums
8901.8 Collective
8902.A-Z United States. By city and museum, A-Z
8902.5.A-Z Other countries. By country and city, A-Z
Special periods
For special periods, see NK8907-NK8910.3
8903.A-Z Private collections. By collection, A-Z
8904 General. Collectors' manuals
8904.5 Conservation and restoration
8905 Collected designs
8905.5 Auction catalogs
History
8906 General works
8906.4.A-Z Ethnic groups not limited to one country, A-Z
8906.4.B35 Baluchi
8907 Ancient
8907.15 Egyptian
8907.2 Etruscan
8907.3 Classical
8907.4 Early Christian
8908 Medieval
8908.7 Buddhist
8908.8 Byzantine
8908.9 Islamic
8908.92 Romanesque
8908.923 Gothic
8909 Modern
8909.2.A-Z Special styles, A-Z
8909.2.G76 Grotesque
8909.3 Renaissance
8909.6 Baroque
8909.65 18th century
8909.7 Rococo
8909.8 19th century
8909.85.A-Z Special styles, A-Z
8909.85.A7 Art nouveau
8909.85.B53 Biedermeier
8909.85.E24 Eclecticism

Other arts and art industries
Textile arts and art needlework
Woven fabrics
History
Modern
19th century
Special styles, A-Z -- Continued
8909.85.V53 Victorian
8910 20th century
8910.3.A-Z Special styles, A-Z
8910.3.A78 Art deco
8911 North America
8912 United States
8912.5 Latin America
8913-8996.3 Other countries (Table N1)
Add country number in table to NK8900
Apply table at NK2813-2896.3
8997 Collective biography
8998.A-Z Special artists, A-Z
Including families and firms
8999 Dealers' catalogs
9002 Silk pictures
9010 Calamanco
Needlework
Including samplers, quilts, etc.
Cf. NK8551, Needlework boxes
9100 Periodicals and societies
9100.5 Congresses
9100.6 Dictionaries
9100.7 Directories
Exhibitions (By place held)
Class here works on general exhibitions. For exhibitions on special periods not limited to a particular country, see NK9107-NK9110.3, for exhibitions on special countries, see NK9111-NK9196
9101.A-Z United States. By city and museum or other place of exhibition, A-Z
9101.5.A-Z Other countries. By country and city, A-Z
Museums
9101.8 Collective
9102.A-Z United States. By city and museum, A-Z
9102.5.A-Z Other countries. By country and city, A-Z
Special periods
For special periods, see NK9107-NK9110.3
9103.A-Z Private collections. By collection, A-Z
9104 General. Collectors' manuals
9104.5 Conservation and restoration
9105 Collected designs
9105.5 Auction catalogs
History
9106 General works
9106.4.A-Z Ethnic groups not limited to one country, A-Z

Other arts and art industries
Textile arts and art needlework
Needlework
History
Ethnic groups not limited to one country, A-Z -- Continued
9106.4.H56 Hmong (Asian people)
9107 Ancient
9107.15 Egyptian
9107.2 Etruscan
9107.3 Classical
9107.4 Early Christian
9108 Medieval
9108.7 Buddhist
9108.8 Byzantine
9108.9 Islamic
9108.92 Romanesque
9108.923 Gothic
9109 Modern
9109.2.A-Z Special styles, A-Z
9109.2.G76 Grotesque
9109.3 Renaissance
9109.6 Baroque
9109.65 18th century
9109.7 Rococo
9109.8 19th century
9109.85.A-Z Special styles, A-Z
9109.85.A7 Art nouveau
9109.85.B53 Biedermeier
9109.85.E24 Eclecticism
9109.85.V53 Victorian
9110 20th century
9110.3.A-Z Special styles, A-Z
9110.3.A78 Art deco
9111 North America
9112 United States
9112.5 Latin America
9113-9196.3 Other countries (Table N1)
Add country number in table to NK9100
Apply table at NK2813-2896.3
9197 Collective biography
9198.A-Z Special artists, A-Z
Including families and firms
9199 Dealers' catalogs
Embroidery
Including ethnic embroidery
9200 Periodicals and societies
9200.5 Congresses
9200.6 Dictionaries
9200.7 Directories

Other arts and art industries
Textile arts and art needlework
Needlework
Embroidery -- Continued
Exhibitions (By place held)
Class here works on general exhibitions. For exhibitions on special periods not limited to a particular country, see NK9207-NK9210.3, for exhibitions on special countries, see NK9211-NK9296

9201.A-Z United States. By city and museum or other place of exhibition, A-Z
9201.5.A-Z Other countries. By country and city, A-Z
Museums
9201.8 Collective
9202.A-Z United States. By city and museum, A-Z
9202.5.A-Z Other countries. By country and city, A-Z
Special periods
For special periods, see NK9207-NK9210.3
9203.A-Z Private collections. By collection, A-Z
9204 General. Collectors' manuals
9204.5 Conservation and restoration
9205 Collected designs
9205.5 Auction catalogs
History
9206 General works
9206.4.A-Z Ethnic groups not limited to one country, A-Z
9207 Ancient
9207.15 Egyptian
9207.2 Etruscan
9207.3 Classical
9207.4 Early Christian
9208 Medieval
9208.7 Buddhist
9208.8 Byzantine
9208.9 Islamic
9208.92 Romanesque
9208.923 Gothic
9209 Modern
9209.2.A-Z Special styles, A-Z
9209.2.G76 Grotesque
9209.3 Renaissance
9209.6 Baroque
9209.65 18th century
9209.7 Rococo
9209.8 19th century
9209.85.A-Z Special styles, A-Z
9209.85.A7 Art nouveau
9209.85.B53 Biedermeier
9209.85.E24 Eclecticism
9209.85.V53 Victorian
9210 20th century
9210.3.A-Z Special styles, A-Z

Other arts and art industries
Textile arts and art needlework
Needlework
Embroidery
History
Modern
20th century
Special styles, A-Z -- Continued

9210.3.A78 Art deco
9211 North America
9212 United States
9212.5 Latin America
9213-9296.3 Other countries (Table N1)
Add country number in table to NK9200
Apply table at NK2813-2896.3
9297 Collective biography
9298.A-Z Special artists, A-Z
Including families and firms
9299 Dealers' catalogs
9310 Ecclesiastical embroidery
9315 Fabric pictures

Lace
9400 Periodicals and societies
9400.5 Congresses
9400.6 Dictionaries
9400.7 Directories
Exhibitions (By place held)
Class here works on general exhibitions. For exhibitions on special periods not limited to a particular country, see NK9407-NK9410.3, for exhibitions on special countries, see NK9411-NK9496
9401.A-Z United States. By city and museum or other place of exhibition, A-Z
9401.5.A-Z Other countries. By country and city, A-Z
Museums
9401.8 Collective
9402.A-Z United States. By city and museum, A-Z
9402.5.A-Z Other countries. By country and city, A-Z
Special periods
For special periods, see NK9407-NK9410.3
9403.A-Z Private collections. By collection, A-Z
9404 General. Collectors' manuals
9404.5 Conservation and restoration
9405 Collected designs
9405.5 Auction catalogs
History
9406 General works
9406.4.A-Z Ethnic groups not limited to one country, A-Z
9407 Ancient
9407.15 Egyptian
9407.2 Etruscan
9407.3 Classical

Other arts and art industries
Textile arts and art needlework
Needlework
Lace
History
Ancient -- Continued

9407.4	Early Christian
9408	Medieval
9408.7	Buddhist
9408.8	Byzantine
9408.9	Islamic
9408.92	Romanesque
9408.923	Gothic
9409	Modern
9409.2.A-Z	Special styles, A-Z
9409.2.G76	Grotesque
9409.3	Renaissance
9409.6	Baroque
9409.65	18th century
9409.7	Rococo
9409.8	19th century
9409.85.A-Z	Special styles, A-Z
9409.85.A7	Art nouveau
9409.85.B53	Biedermeier
9409.85.E24	Eclecticism
9409.85.V53	Victorian
9410	20th century
9410.3.A-Z	Special styles, A-Z
9410.3.A78	Art deco
9411	North America
9412	United States
9412.5	Latin America
9413-9496.3	Other countries (Table N1) Add country number in table to NK9400 Apply table at NK2813-2896.3
9497	Collective biography
9498.A-Z	Special artists, A-Z Including families and firms
9499	Dealers' catalogs
	Textile decoration Cf. TP897+, Dyeing, textile printing Cf. TT851+, Textile crafts For stencil work, see NK8650+
9500	General works
9502	Collective biography
9502.5.A-Z	Special artists, A-Z
	Batik Cf. NK8880, Dutch East Indian textiles
9503	General works
9503.2.A-Z	Special regions or countries, A-Z Apply table at NK3649.35.A-Z
9504	Block printing
9504.7	Resist-dyed textiles

Other arts and art industries
Textile arts and art needlework
Textile decoration -- Continued
Textile painting
9505 General works
9505.2.A-Z Special regions or countries, A-Z
Apply table at NK3649.35.A-Z
9505.5 Tie-dyeing
9505.7 Thimbles
Cf. NK7236.T55, Silver thimbles
9505.75 Thread winders
9507 Tobacco jars, boxes, etc.
Prefer classification by material
9508 Toothpick holders
For toothpick holders in a particular material, see the material
Toys
Prefer classification by material
Cf. GN799.T7, Prehistoric toys
Cf. GV1218.5+, Games and amusements
Cf. LB1029.T6, Educational toys
Cf. NK8470+, Miniature objects
Cf. TS2301.T7, Toy manufacture
Cf. TT174+, Handicrafts
9509 General works
9509.15 Directories
Exhibitions
9509.2.A-Z United States. By city and museum or other place of exhibition, A-Z
9509.3.A-Z Other countries. By country and city, A-Z
Museums. Collections
9509.4.A-Z United States. By city and museum, A-Z
9509.5.A-Z Other countries. By country and city, A-Z
9509.6.A-Z Private collections. By collector, A-Z
9509.65.A-Z Special regions or countries, A-Z
Apply table at NK3649.35.A-Z
9509.7 Boys' toys
9509.8 Girls' toys
9509.95.A-Z Special types of toys, A-Z
9509.95.C43 Character toys
9509.95.C57 Circus toys
Dolls and dollhouses, see NK4891.3+
9509.95.H67 Horses
9509.95.S63 Soft animal toys
Teddy bears, see NK8740+
9509.95.T68 Tops
9509.95.W85 Whistles
9510 Transfer pictures (Decalcomania)
Cf. NK4607, Transfer printing on pottery
9530 Trays
Cf. NK8459.B36, Beer trays
9540 Trivets
9550 Trunks

Other arts and art industries -- Continued
Turkey calls, see NK4898
9560 Visiting card cases
Prefer classification by material
Wax modeling. Wax portraits. Ceroplastic
Cf. GV1836, Waxworks
Cf. TT866, Wax craft
9580 General works
9581 Religious articles
9581.5.A-Z By region or country, A-Z
9582.A-Z Special artists, A-Z
9585 Weather vanes
Woodwork
Cf. NA2970, Floors
Cf. NA3900, Architectural decoration (Woodwork)
Cf. NA5050+, Ecclesiastical furniture
9600 Periodicals and societies
9600.5 Congresses
9600.6 Dictionaries
9600.7 Directories
Exhibitions (By place held)
Class here works on general exhibitions. For exhibitions on special periods not limited to a particular country, see NK9607-NK9610.3, for exhibitions on special countries, see NK9611-NK9696
9601.A-Z United States. By city and museum or other place of exhibition, A-Z
9601.5.A-Z Other countries. By country and city, A-Z
Museums
9601.8 Collective
9602.A-Z United States. By city and museum, A-Z
9602.5.A-Z Other countries. By country and city, A-Z
Special periods
See NK9607 NK9610.3
9603.A-Z Private collections. By collection, A-Z
9604 General. Collectors' manuals
9604.5 Conservation and restoration
9605 Collected designs
9605.5 Auction catalogs
History
9606 General works
9606.4.A-Z Ethnic groups not limited to one country, A-Z
9607 Ancient
9607.15 Egyptian
9607.2 Etruscan
9607.3 Classical
9607.4 Early Christian
9608 Medieval
9608.7 Buddhist
9608.8 Byzantine
9608.9 Islamic
9608.92 Romanesque

Other arts and art industries
Woodwork
History
Medieval -- Continued
9608.923 Gothic
9609 Modern
9609.2.A-Z Special styles, A-Z
9609.2.G76 Grotesque
9609.3 Renaissance
9609.6 Baroque
9609.65 18th century
9609.7 Rococo
9609.8 19th century
9609.85.A-Z Special styles, A-Z
9609.85.A7 Art nouveau
9609.85.B53 Biedermeier
9609.85.E24 Eclecticism
9609.85.V53 Victorian
9610 20th century
9610.3.A-Z Special styles, A-Z
9610.3.A78 Art deco
9611 North America
9612 United States
9612.5 Latin America
9613-9696.3 Other countries (Table N1)
Add country number in table to NK9600
Apply table at NK2813-2896.3
9697 Collective biography
9698.A-Z Special artists, A-Z
9699 Dealers' catalogs
Wood carving
For wood carving of American Indians, see classes E-F
Cf. NB1250, Sculpture in wood
9700 Periodicals and societies
9700.5 Congresses
9700.6 Dictionaries
9700.7 Directories
Exhibitions (By place held)
Class here works on general exhibitions. For exhibitions on special periods not limited to a particular country, see NK9707-NK9710.3, for exhibitions on special countries, see NK9711-NK9796
9701.A-Z United States. By city and museum or other place of exhibition, A-Z
9701.5.A-Z Other countries. By country and city, A-Z
Museums
9701.8 Collective
9702.A-Z United States. By city and museum, A-Z
9702.5.A-Z Other countries. By country and city, A-Z
Special periods
See NK9707 NK9710.3

NK

Other arts and art industries
Woodwork
Wood carving -- Continued
9703.A-Z Private collections. By collection, A-Z
9704 General. Collectors' manuals
9704.5 Conservation and restoration
9705 Collected designs
9705.5 Auction catalogs
History
9706 General works
9706.4.A-Z Ethnic groups not limited to one country, A-Z
9707 Ancient
9707.15 Egyptian
9707.2 Etruscan
9707.3 Classical
9707.4 Early Christian
9708 Medieval
9708.7 Buddhist
9708.8 Byzantine
9708.9 Islamic
9708.92 Romanesque
9708.923 Gothic
9709 Modern
9709.2.A-Z Special styles, A-Z
9709.2.G76 Grotesque
9709.3 Renaissance
9709.6 Baroque
9709.65 18th century
9709.7 Rococo
9709.8 19th century
9709.85.A-Z Special styles, A-Z
9709.85.A7 Art nouveau
9709.85.B53 Biedermeier
9709.85.E24 Eclecticism
9709.85.V53 Victorian
9710 20th century
9710.3.A-Z Special styles, A-Z
9710.3.A78 Art deco
9711 North America
9712 United States
9712.5 Latin America
9713-9796.3 Other countries (Table N1)
Add country number in table to NK9700
Apply table at NK2813-2896.3
9797 Collective biography
9798.A-Z Special artists, A-Z
9799 Dealers' catalogs
Lacquer
9900 General works
9900.5.A-Z Exhibitions. Collections. Museums. By country and collector or place of exhibition, A-Z
9900.7.A-Z Special regions or countries, A-Z
Apply table at NK4670.7.A-Z

Other arts and art industries
Woodwork -- Continued
Marquetry. Inlaying
Cf. NK2710, Inlaid furniture, etc.

9920 General works
9924.A-Z By region or country, A-Z
9925.A-Z Special artists, A-Z
9930 Fretwork
9950 Other (not A-Z)
9955.A-Z Miscellaneous articles of wood, A-Z
9955.B43 Beehives
9955.B6 Boxes
Canes, see NK9955.S72
9955.D8 Dummy board figures
9955.G35 Gameboards
9955.M5 Mirror cases
9955.S72 Staffs (Sticks, canes, etc.)
Sticks, see NK9955.S72
9955.T69 Toys
Cf. TT174.5.W6, Handicraft
(9990.A-Z) Miscellaneous articles, A-Z
See (in alphabetical position) NK3600-NK9955, e.g. Automata, see NK3649, Boxes, see NK3665, Candlesticks, see NK3685, Chessmen, see NK4696

Arts in general
Including works dealing with two or more of the fine arts media, i.e. literature, performing arts (dance, motion pictures, music, opera, theater) or the visual arts
Works on any one of these subjects are classified with the subject in classes GV, M, N, P, TR
Periodicals
1.A1 Polyglot
1.A12-Z American and English
2 French
3 German
4 Italian
5 Dutch and Flemish
6 Russian. Slavic
6.5 Scandinavian
7 Spanish and Portuguese
8.A-Z Other (including Oriental), A-Z
9 Yearbooks
Societies. Councils
20 General
International
21 General
21.2.A-Z Special, A-Z
United States
22 General
24.A-W By state, A-W
26.A-Z By city or other local organization, A-Z
28.A-Z Other regions or countries, A-Z
Under each country:
.x General works
.x2A-.x2Z Special societies or councils. By name, A-Z
50 Congresses
Cf. NX420+, Exhibitions, festivals of the arts
Collected writings
Including addresses, essays, lectures
60 Several authors
65 Individual authors
67 Anecdotes, facetiae, curiosities of the arts and artists
70 Encyclopedias
80 Dictionaries of terms
Biography
Class here biography of those creative in several arts
For biography of special countries, see NX501+
90 Collective
93.A-Z Individual, A-Z
Directories
100 General
110 United States
120.A-Z Other countries, A-Z
(150-159) Theory and philosophy
See Class BH, Aesthetics

160 Creation in the arts
The arts as a profession. Artists
Including management, grants, etc.
163 General works
164.A-Z Special classes of artists, A-Z
164.B55 Blacks. Afro-Americans
164.C47 Children
Negroes, see NX164.B55
164.P7 Prisoners
164.W65 Women
Special countries, see NX501+
165 Psychology of the arts and the artist
Interrelationships among the arts in general
Cf. ML3849, Music and other arts
Cf. PN53, Literature and other arts
Cf. PN1069, Poetry and other arts
Cf. PN1637, Drama and other visual arts
Cf. PN1995.3, Motion pictures and literature
170 General works
175 General special
180.A-Z The arts in relation to other subjects, A-Z
Class here general works on the topics as well as works on the topics in a particular region, country, etc.
Cf. N72.A+, The visual arts in relation to other subjects
180.A35 Aged and the arts
180.A36 AIDS (Disease)
180.A74 Armed Forces and the arts
180.A77 Artists and community
180.C44 Censorship
180.C45 Children and the arts
Christianity and the arts, see BR115.A8
Communism and the arts, see HX521
180.C93 Cybernetics and the arts
180.D78 Drugs and the arts
180.E8 Ethics
180.F3 Fascism
180.F4 Feminism and the arts
180.F74 Freedom and the arts
180.F76 Freemasonry and the arts
180.H34 Handicapped
180.H6 Homosexuality and the arts
180.M3 Mass media and the arts
180.M33 Mathematics
Medicine and the arts, see R702.5
180.M68 Motherhood
180.P48 Phonorecords and the arts
180.P64 Politics
180.P7 Psychoanalysis and the arts
180.R37 Recreation and the arts
180.R4 Religion and the arts
180.R45 Revolutions

The arts in relation to other subjects, A-Z -- Continued
180.S3 Science and the arts
180.S46 Semiotics and the arts
Socialism and the arts, see HX521
180.S57 Socialist realism in the arts
180.S6 Society. Culture
Sound recordings and the arts, see NX180.P48
The state and the arts, see NX720+
180.T4 Technology and the arts
180.T44 Television and the arts
180.T67 Tourist trade
180.T7 Trade unions and the arts
180.Y68 Youth and the arts
Communication of information
190 General works
192 Information services
200 Styles in the arts
For studies of specific styles in the arts prefer classificaiton in NX540-NX596, History of the arts
205 Attribution
210 Taste
Cf. BH301.K5, Theory and philosophy of kitsch
Cf. NX600.K5, Kitsch in the arts
212 Performance in the arts
Cf. NX600.P47, Performance art
Cf. PN1560+, Performing arts
220 Arts audiences
230 Citizen participation
260 Computer applications. Data processing
Study and teaching. Research
280 General works
282 General special
Art teacher training, recruiting, etc.
284 General works
By region or country
United States
284.3 General works
284.4.A-Z By region or state, A-Z
284.5.A-Z Other regions or countries, A-Z
Audiovisual materials
Including films on the arts, filmstrips, sound recordings, etc.
285 General works
286 Select lists
287.A-Z Dealers' catalogs. By dealer, A-Z
History
290 General works
292 Before 1900
294 Since 1900

Study and teaching. Research
History -- Continued
301-396.3 Special countries (Table N1)
Add country number in table to NX300
Under each (1-number or decimal number countries):
.A1 General works
.A3A-.A3Z Special regions, provinces, etc., A-Z
.A5-.Z Special cities, A-Z
Under each (Cutter-number countries):
.x General
.x2A-.x2Z Special cities, A-Z
396.5 Artists as teachers
Scholarships. Fellowships. Internships
396.6 Directories
397 General works
By country
398 United States
399.A-Z Other countries, A-Z
Schools of fine and applied arts
400 General
Special schools
405.A-Z United States. By city and school, A-Z
407.A-Z Other American. By country and school, A-Z
409.A-Z Europe. By country and school, A-Z
410.A-Z Other countries. By country and school, A-Z
Competitions
Including individual awards, prizes, etc.
411 General and international
412 United States
413.A-Z Other American. By country, A-Z
414.A-Z Europe. By country, A-Z
415.A-Z Other countries. By country, A-Z
Exhibitions. Festivals of the arts
420 General works
Special countries
United States
425 General works
427.A-Z Local, A-Z
430.A-Z Other countries, A-Z
Under each:
.x General works
.x2A-.x2Z Local, A-Z
History of the arts
440 General works
445 General special
447 Outlines. Syllabi
447.5 Chronological lists
By period
448 Ancient
448.5 Classical
449 Medieval
Modern
449.5 General works

History of the arts
By period
Modern -- Continued
450 16th-17th centuries
16th century. Renaissance
450.5 General works
450.6.A-Z Special aspects or movements, A-Z
450.6.M3 Mannerism
17th century
451 General works
451.5.A-Z Special aspects or movements, A-Z
451.5.B3 Baroque
451.5.C55 Classicism
451.5.N3 Naturalism
18th century
452 General works
452.5.A-Z Special aspects or movements, A-Z
452.5.N4 Neoclassicism (General, and Early)
452.5.R6 Rococo
452.5.R64 Romanticism (Early)
19th century
454 General works
454.5.A-Z Special aspects or movements, A-Z
454.5.A25 Abstract art
454.5.A7 Art nouveau. Jugendstil
454.5.B5 Biedermeier
454.5.E25 Eclecticism
454.5.E35 Edwardian art
454.5.E48 Egyptian Revival (Art)
454.5.G68 Gothic revival
454.5.I4 Impressionism
454.5.K5 Kitsch
454.5.M63 Modernism
454.5.N4 Neoclassicism (Late)
454.5.N44 Neo-impressionism
454.5.P6 Post-impressionism
454.5.P7 Pre-Raphaelites
454.5.P74 Primitivism
454.5.R4 Realism
454.5.R45 Renaissance revival
454.5.R6 Romantic movement
454.5.S9 Symbolism
454.5.V5 Victorian art
20th century
456 General works
456.5.A-Z Special aspects or movements, A-Z
456.5.A2 Abstract art
456.5.A25 Abstract expressionism
456.5.A35 Air art
456.5.A66 Appropriation
456.5.A7 Art deco
456.5.A8 Assemblage
456.5.B63 Body art

History of the arts
By period
Modern
20th century
Special aspects
or movements, A-Z -- Continued

456.5.C45	Cercle et carré (Group)
456.5.C47	Chenal (Group)
456.5.C5	CoBrA
456.5.C6	Collage. Papiers collés
456.5.C63	Conceptual art
456.5.C635	Concrete art
456.5.C64	Constructivism
456.5.C8	Cubism
456.5.D3	Dadaism
456.5.E27	Earthworks (Art)
456.5.E43	Electricity. Electronics
456.5.E6	Environment (Art)
456.5.E87	Experiments in Art and Technology
456.5.E9	Expressionism
456.5.F28	Fascism
456.5.F3	Fauvism
456.5.F47	Fiberwork
456.5.F5	Figurative art
456.5.F55	Fluxus (Group of artists)
456.5.F6	Found objects
456.5.F7	Functionalism
456.5.F8	Futurism
456.5.G72	Groupe de recherche d'art visuel. GRAV
456.5.I55	Impressionism (Late)
456.5.I56	Installations (Art)
456.5.I58	Internationale situationniste
456.5.K5	Kinetic art
456.5.K54	Kitsch
456.5.L3	Lasers
456.5.L4	Lettrism. Letter-pictures
456.5.M3	Magic realism
456.5.M35	Mail art
456.5.M5	Minimal art
456.5.M64	Modernism
456.5.M8	Multiple art
456.5.N3	Narrative art
456.5.N34	Naturalism
456.5.O6	Op art. Optical art. Perceptual art
456.5.P34	Paper art
456.5.P42	Photo-realism. New realism
456.5.P6	Pop art. Neodadaism. Neo-realism
456.5.P66	Postmodernism
456.5.P7	Primitivism. Groupe Henri Rousseau
456.5.P74	Projection art
456.5.P79	Psychedelic art
456.5.R3	Ratilly (Artists' colony)
456.5.R4	Realism

History of the arts
By period
Modern
20th century
Special aspects
or movements, A-Z -- Continued
456.5.R44 Relief art
456.5.R65 Romanticism
456.5.S24 Salon des réalités nouvelles
456.5.S47 Serial art
456.5.S65 Socialist realism
456.5.S7 Spatialism
456.5.S8 Surrealism
456.5.T94 Typewriter art
456.5.V53 Video art
456.5.W5 Wiener Secession
456.5.Z42 Zebra (Group of artists)
457 1900-1950
458 1950-
501-596.3 Special countries (Table N1)
Add country number in table to NX500
For the arts of the American Indians, see classes E-F
For biography of individuals not identified with any country, see NX93.A+
Under each (1-number or decimal-number countries):
.A1 General works
.A3A-.A3Z Special regions, provinces, etc., A-Z
.A5-.Z7 Special cities, A-Z
.Z8 Collective biography
.Z9A-.Z9Z Special artists, A-Z
Under each (Cutter-number countries):
.x General works
.x2A-.x2Z Local, A-Z
.x3 Collective biography
.x4A-.x4Z Special artists, A-Z
Europe
Italy
552.Z9A-Z Special artists, A-Z
e.g.
Chirico, Giorgio de, 1888, see NX552.Z9D43
552.Z9D43 De Chirico, Giorgio, 1888-
600.A-Z Special movements, A-Z
Class here material not limited to one country
For classification by country, see NX501+
600.A27 Abstract
600.A6 Art deco
600.A7 Art nouveau
600.B37 Baroque
600.C5 Classicism
600.C57 Collage
600.C6 Conceptual art
600.C64 Concrete art
600.C8 Cubism

History of the arts
Special movements, A-Z -- Continued
600.D3 Dadaism
600.D42 De Stijl. Neoplasticism
600.E9 Expressionism
600.F8 Futurism
600.I8 Impressionism
600.K5 Kitsch
Cf. BH301.K5, Theory and philosophy of kitsch
600.L4 Lettrism
600.M33 Magic realism
Neoplasticism, see NX600.D42
600.P47 Performance art
600.P66 Pop art
600.R4 Realism
600.R46 Revival
600.R6 Romanticism
Stijl, De. Neoplasticism, see NX600.D42
600.S9 Surrealism
600.S95 Symbolism
600.W53 Wiener Secession
General works
619 Early works through 1800
620 1801-
Influences and relationships between cultures
627 General works
628 Influences of Oriental arts on Western arts, and vice versa
629 Arts of minority groups (General)
For groups in particular places, see NX501+
632 Primitive arts
Class here works on arts produced outside the traditions of the arts of Europe, the Mediterranean area and Asia, that is primarily arts produced in the traditions of the indigenous peoples of sub-Saharan Africa, the islands of the Pacific Ocean, Australia and parts of the Malay Archipelago
Does not include "primitive" or "naive" artists who, while seemingly untutored, work in the traditions of European folk arts
Cf. N5310.7+, Primitive art
633 Juvenile works
634 Economics of the arts
Cf. N8600, Economics of art
635 Reproduction of works of art
636 Forgery of works of art
Criticism in the arts
Cf. N7475+, Visual arts
640 General works
Biography of arts critics
640.2 Collective
640.5.A-Z Individual, A-Z

Criticism in the arts -- Continued
643 Appreciation of the arts
645 Book reviews
650.A-Z Special subjects or topics, A-Z
Class here general works on the topics as well as works on the topics in a particular region, country, etc.
650.A28 Absinthe
650.A3 Aeronautics
650.A33 AIDS (Disease)
650.A43 Asceticism
650.A44 Allegories
Cf. N7710+, Allegories in the visual arts
650.A55 Animals
650.A6 Apocalyptic art
650.A73 Asceticism
650.B4 Beaches
650.B64 Bohemianism
650.B84 Bullfights. Bullfighters
650.C26 Cannibalism
650.C29 Castles
650.C3 Cats
650.C6 Christianity in the arts
650.C63 Christmas
650.C66 Cities and towns in the arts
650.C67 Cockaigne. Fool's paradise. Schlaraffenland
650.C676 Colors
650.C678 Comic, The
650.C68 Concentration camps
650.C69 Country life
650.C73 Cranes (Birds)
650.D34 Dance of death
Cf. N7720.A1A+, Dance of death in the visual arts
650.D35 Dancing
For dancing in motion pictures, television, etc., see GV1779
650.D4 Death
Demonology, see NX652.D48
650.D45 Desire
650.D63 Dogs
650.D66 Donkeys
650.D72 Dragons
650.D74 Dreams
650.E7 Erotica. Pornography
Cf. HQ471, Pornography and society
650.E85 Exoticism
650.F35 Falcons
650.F36 Fantastic, The (Aesthetics). Fantasy
650.F45 Feminine beauty (Aesthetics)
For visual arts, see N7629+
650.F55 Flight
650.F57 Flowers

Special subjects or topics, A-Z -- Continued

	Fool's paradise, see NX650.C67
650.G64	Golf
650.G7	Grotesque
650.H42	Hell
650.H44	Heroes
650.H5	History in the arts
650.H6	Homosexuality in the arts
650.H67	Horror
650.H72	Human abnormalities
650.H74	Human figure
650.H76	Human life cycle
650.H8	Humanism
650.H85	Hunting
650.I34	Idealism in the arts
650.I74	Irony
650.L32	Labor. Laboring classes. Working class
650.L33	Labyrinths
650.L34	Landscape
650.L54	Life
650.L68	Love
650.M26	Machinery
650.M3	Masks
650.M45	Memory
650.M48	Metamorphosis
650.M53	Middle Ages
650.M534	Milazzo (Italy), Battle of, 1860
650.M536	Mirrors
650.M55	Monsters
650.M57	Months
650.M6	Moon
650.M68	Mouth of hell
650.M9	Mythology
650.N35	Narcissism
650.N37	Narration
650.N376	National characteristics
650.N38	Nature
650.N52	Nibelungen
650.N54	Nightmares
650.N65	Nostalgia
650.N83	Nude
650.P35	Paradise
650.P37	Parody
650.P38	Pastoral art
650.P4	Peace
650.P5	Pitchers
650.P53	Plants
650.P6	Politics in the arts
650.P64	Privacy
650.P65	Proportion
650.P7	Psychoanalysis in the arts
650.R33	Rabbits
650.R36	Rape

	Special subjects or topics, A-Z -- Continued
650.R4	Religion in the arts
650.R45	Repetition
650.R63	Roosters
650.R65	Roses
650.R83	Rugs, Oriental
650.S28	Scatology
	Schlaraffenland, see NX650.C67
650.S3	Science fiction in the arts
650.S4	Sea
650.S43	Seasons
	Signs and symbols, see NX650.W75
650.S58	Skyscrapers
650.S68	Sound
650.S8	Space in the arts
650.S85	Stone
650.T45	Temperance (Virtue) in the arts
650.T47	Ten virgins (Parable)
650.T5	Time in the arts
650.T73	Travel
650.T74	Trees
650.U5	Underground movements
650.U53	Unicorns
650.V47	Vietnamese Conflict, 1961-1975
650.V5	Violence in the arts
650.W3	War in the arts
650.W48	Whales
650.W56	Wild boar
650.W75	Writing. Signs and symbols
	Characters, persons, classes of persons, and ethnic groups
651.8	General works
652.A-Z	By name of character, person, class of persons, or ethnic group, A-Z
652.A37	Afro-Americans
652.A53	Amazons
652.A55	Angels
652.A6	Apollo (Greek deity)
652.A7	Arthur, King
652.B54	Billy, the Kid
652.C34	Caesar, Julius
652.C48	Children
652.C49	Chimney sweeps
652.C494	Cinderella (Legendary character)
652.C5	Clowns
652.D25	Daphne
652.D3	David, King of Israel
	Demonology, see NX652.D48
652.D48	Devil. Demonology
652.D56	Dionysus (Greek deity)
652.D64	Don Juan
652.D86	Duplessis, Marie, 1824-1847
652.D88	Dwarfs

Characters, persons,
classes of persons, and ethnic groups
By name of character,
person, class of persons,
or ethnic group, A-Z -- Continued

652.E56 Entertainers
652.E8 Eulenspiegel
652.F36 Father and child
652.F38 Faust, d. ca. 1540
652.F45 Femmes fatales
652.F5 Fishermen
652.F65 Fools and jesters
652.F69 Francesca, da Rimini, d. ca. 1285
652.F7 Francis, of Assisi, Saint, 1182-1226
652.G3 Galatea
652.G33 Galilei, Galileo, 1564-1642
652.G35 Ganymede
652.G38 Gay artists. Lesbian artists
652.G55 Girls
652.G63 Gods, Greek
652.H35 Handicapped
652.H4 Hercules
652.I53 Indians of North America
Iseult (Legendary character), see NX652.T75
652.J36 Jan III Sobieski, King of Poland, 1629-1696
Jesters, see NX652.F65
652.J62 Joan, of Arc, Saint, 1412-1431
652.J64 Jonah (Biblical character)
652.K45 Kennedy, John F. (John Fitzgerald), 1917-1963
652.K65 Kore
Lesbian artists, see NX652.G38
652.M25 Mary, Blessed Virgin, Saint
652.M27 Mary Magdalene, Saint
652.M3 Mazepa, Ivan Stepanovych, Hetman of the Cossacks, 1644-1709
652.M42 Mercury (Roman deity)
652.M64 Mothers
652.N44 Niels Ebbesen, d. 1340
652.N5 Nine Worthies
652.N87 Nurses
652.O3 Odysseus
652.O7 Orpheus
652.O78 O'Shea, Kathleen, Countess
652.O8 Osiris
652.P4 Penelope
652.P43 Perseus
652.P47 Philosophers
652.P55 Pied Piper of Hamelin
652.P83 Punchinello (Fictitious character)
652.P87 Pygmalion
652.P9 Pyramus and Thisbe
652.S24 Salome
652.S42 Sebastian, Saint

Characters, persons,
classes of persons, and ethnic groups
By name of character,
person, class of persons,
or ethnic group, A-Z -- Continued

652.T37 Tasso, Torquato, 1544-1595
652.T39 Tell, Wilhelm
652.T4 Teresa, Saint
652.T75 Tristan (Legendary character)
Ulysses, see NX652.O3
652.W38 Wayland the Smith
652.W6 Women
653.A-Z Special geographic areas and places as subjects, A-Z
Class here general works on the topics as well as works on the topics in a particular region, country, etc.
e.g.
653.I83 Italy
653.M5 Minas Gerais (Brazil)
653.P38 Parnassus Mountain (Greece)
653.T7 Troy
653.W47 West (U.S.)
653.Y67 Yosemite Valley (Calif.)
Religious arts
654 General works
Christian arts
655 Periodicals and societies
656 Collections. Congresses
Exhibitions
(657) International
See NX658-NX659
658.A-Z United States. By city and gallery or other place of exhibition, A-Z
659.A-Z Other countries. By country and city, A-Z
660 General works
661 General special
History
662 General works
663.A-Z By country, A-Z
Non-Christian arts
670 General works
673 General special
Special religious arts
Buddhist (Table N11)
676 General works
Special subjects, characters, etc.
676.2 Gautama Buddha
676.3.A-Z Other, A-Z
676.3.Z45 Zen
680 Hindu (Table N11)
680.3.A-Z Special subjects or topics, A-Z
680.3.C48 Chakra
680.3.K37 Kārttikeya (Hindu diety)

Religious arts
Non-Christian arts
Special religious arts
Hindu
Special subjects or topics, A-Z -- Continued
680.3.K75 Krishna (Hindu deity)
680.3.L34 Lakshmi (Hindu deity)
680.3.R35 Rāma (Hindu deity)
684 Jewish (Table N11)
688 Islamic (Table N11)
692.A-Z Other religious arts, A-Z
692.B35 Bahai (Table N12)
692.S5 Shinto (Table N12)
694.A-Z Special topics, A-Z
Patronage of the arts
700 General works
Biography of arts patrons
701 Collective
701.2.A-Z Individual, A-Z
705 General special
e.g. Cooperation between private foundations and local or federal government
705.5.A-Z Special regions or countries, A-Z
Under each country:
.x General
.x2A-.x2Z Local, A-z
Non-governmental patronage
Including private individuals, corporate patrons, and private foundations
710 General works
Special
711.A-Z By country, A-Z
712.A-Z By patron, A-Z
Governmental patronage
720 General works
Special countries
United States
730 General works
735 Federal
740 State (General)
742.A-Z By state, A-W
Under each:
.x General
.x2A-.x2Z By county, city, etc., A-Z
745 Local (General)
750.A-Z Other countries, A-Z
Administration of the arts. Administrators. Arts boards
Including arts administration training
760 General works
Special countries
United States
765 General works

NX

Administration of the arts.
  Administrators. Arts boards
 Special countries
  United States -- Continued
767.A-Z   Local, A-Z
768.A-Z   Special administrators, A-Z
770.A-Z   Other countries, A-Z
     Under each country:
   .x   *General*
   .x2A-.x2Z   *Local, A-Z*
   .x3A-.x3Z   *Special administrators, A-Z*
775 Voluntarism in the arts
776 United States
776.5.A-Z   Local, A-Z
777.A-Z Other countries, A-Z
    Under each country:
  .x   *General works*
  .x2A-.x2Z   *Local, A-Z*
Arts centers. Arts facilities
  Including general publications of arts centers and facilities
  For architecture of arts centers and arts facilities, see NA6812+
798 General works
 Special countries
  United States
800   General works
805.A-Z   Local, A-Z
820.A-Z   Other countries, A-Z
     Apply table at NX777.A-Z

01	America
01.5	Latin America
02	North America
	United States
03	General works
03.5	Colonial period; 18th (and early 19th) century
03.7	19th century
04	20th century
04.5	Northeastern States
04.7	Atlantic States
05	New England
05.5	Middle Atlantic States
06	South
07	Central
08	West
08.5	Northwestern States
08.6	Southwestern States
09	Pacific States
10.A-W	States, A-W
	e.g.
	Each state may be subarranged:
	.x *General works*
	.x2A-.x2Z *Local (other than cities), A-Z*
10.H3	Hawaii
	Virginia
10.V8	General works
10.V82F3	Fairfax County
11.A-Z	Cities, A-Z
12.A-Z	Special artists, A-Z
	Including families and firms
	Ethnic groups
12.2	General works
12.3.A-Z	Special, A-Z
12.3.A35	Afro-Americans. Negroes. Blacks
12.3.A4	American Indians
	For traditional arts and crafts, see Classes E-F
12.3.A83	Asian Americans
	Blacks, see 12.3.A35
12.3.H57	Hispanic Americans
12.3.I85	Italian Americans
12.3.L3	Latin Americans
12.3.L35	Latvian Americans
12.3.M4	Mexican Americans
(12.3.N4)	Negroes
	See N1 12.3.A35
	Spanish Americans, see 12.3.H57
12.3.S82	Swedish Americans
13-13.3	Canada
	Ethnic groups
13.2	General works
13.3.A-Z	Special, A-Z
13.3.G47	Germans
	Latin America, see 01.5

Tables

14	Mexico
	Central America
15	General works
16	Belize. British Honduras
17	Costa Rica
18	Guatemala
19	Honduras
20	Nicaragua
21	Panama
22	El Salvador
	West Indies
23	General works
24	Bahamas
25	Cuba
26	Haiti
27	Jamaica
28	Puerto Rico
29.A-Z	Other, A-Z
	South America
30	General works
31	Argentina
32	Bolivia
33	Brazil
34	Chile
35	Colombia
36	Ecuador
37	Guyana (British Guiana)
37.2	Surinam (Dutch Guiana)
37.4	French Guiana
38	Paraguay
39	Peru
40	Uruguay
41	Venezuela
	Europe
42	General works
	Class here general works and also works on Northern Europe, Eastern Europe, Southern Europe, etc. with no area Cutter subarrangement
	Great Britain. England
43	General works
44.A-Z	England. Local, A-Z
	Scotland
45.A1	General works
45.A3A-Z	Special regions, counties, etc., A-Z
45.A5-Z	Special cities, A-Z
	Ireland
46.A1	General works
46.A3A-Z	Special regions, counties, etc., A-Z
46.A5-Z	Special cities, A-Z
	Wales
47.A1	General works
47.A3A-Z	Special regions, counties, etc., A-Z
47.A5-Z	Special cities, A-Z

	Europe
	Great Britain. England -- Continued
47.6.A-Z	Special artists, A-Z
	Including special individuals, families, or firms of England, Scotland, Ireland, or Wales
	Austrian, German, and Swiss, see 49.6
48	Austria
49	France
49.6	German, Austrian, and Swiss (Collectively)
	German, Flemish, and Dutch, see 52.6
50	Germany
	Including the former West Germany
	For Alsace-Lorraine, see 49
50.6	Former East Germany
51	Greece
52	Italy
52.6	Dutch, Flemish, and German (Collectively)
	Low countries
53	General works
54	Holland (Netherlands)
55	Belgium
55.6	Luxembourg
56	Russia in Europe. Russia (Federation)
	Class Siberia as a local here
	For Caucasian republics, see 75.7.A12-Z
	Scandinavia
57	General works
58	Denmark
59	Iceland
60	Norway
61	Sweden
62	Spain
	Class here also works on both Spain and Portugal
63	Portugal
	Swiss, Austrian, and German, see 49.6
64	Switzerland
65	Turkey
	Balkan States
66	General works
67	Bulgaria
(68)	Montenegro
	See N1 71.Y8
69	Romania
(70)	Serbia
	See N1 71.Y8
71.A-Z	Other regions or countries, A-Z
71.A4	Albania
	Baltic Sea Region, see 71.B34
71.B34	Baltic States. Baltic Sea Region
71.B44	Belarus
71.C76	Croatia
71.C9	Czech Republic
71.E88	Estonia

Tables

	Europe
	Other regions or countries, A-Z -- Continued
71.F5	Finland
71.H8	Hungary
71.L38	Latvia
71.L57	Lithuania
71.M32	Macedonia (Region)
71.M35	Malta
71.M64	Moldova
71.P6	Poland
71.S54	Slovakia
71.S56	Slovenia
71.U47	Ukraine
71.Y8	Yugoslavia
71.5	Mediterranean Region
	Asia. The Orient
72	General works
	Southwestern Asia. Middle East
73	General works
73.6.A-Z	By region or country, A-Z
73.6.A68	Arabian Peninsula
73.6.A7	Armenia (Historical region)
	For Armenia (Republic), see 75.7.A7
73.6.B33	Bahrain
73.6.C9	Cyprus
73.6.I7	Iraq
73.6.J6	Jordan
73.6.K8	Kuwait
73.6.L4	Lebanon
73.6.O45	Oman
73.6.Q36	Qatar
73.6.S2	Saudi Arabia
73.6.S9	Syria
73.6.U54	United Arab Emirates
73.6.Y4	Yemen
73.6.Y42	Yemen (People's Democratic Republic)
73.7	Israel. Palestine
74	Iran. Persia
	Central Asia
75	General works
	Class here also works on Russia in Asia as a whole
	For Siberia, see 56
75.6	Afghanistan
	Russia in Asia
	General works, see 75
75.7.A2-Z	By republic, A-Z
75.7.A7	Armenia (Republic)
	For historical Armenia, see 73.6.A7
75.7.A9	Azerbaijan
75.7.D3	Daghestan
75.7.G4	Georgia (Republic)
75.7.K3	Kazakhstan

	Asia. The Orient
	Central Asia
	Russia in Asia
	By republic, A-Z -- Continued
75.7.K5	Kirghizistan
75.7.T3	Tajikistan
75.7.T8	Turkmenistan
75.7.T85	Tuva
75.7.U9	Uzbekistan
	Southern Asia
75.8	General works
76	India
76.6	Sri Lanka. Ceylon
76.7	Pakistan
76.8.A-Z	Other countries, A-Z
	Southeastern Asia
77	General works
77.6	Burma
	French Indochina
78	General works
78.6.A-Z	By country, A-Z
78.6.C3	Cambodia (Khmer)
78.6.L3	Laos
78.6.V5	Vietnam. South Vietnam
78.6.V55	Vietnam (Democratic Republic, 1946-)
78.7	Thailand. Siam
79	Malaysia. Malaya
	Sabah, Singapore and Sarawak and Malaya are treated as locals of Malaysia here
80	Indonesia. Dutch East Indies
	Java, Sumatra, Kalimantan and West Irian are treated as locals of Indonesia here
81	Philippines
	Eastern Asia
82	General works
83	China
	Taiwan and Hong Kong are treated as locals of China in this table
84	Japan
84.6	Korea
84.7	Korea (Democratic People's Republic)
86.A-Z	Other countries, A-Z
	Africa
87	General works
	North Africa
87.6	General works
87.65	Algeria
87.7	Libya
87.75	Morocco
87.8	Sudan
87.85	Tunisia
88	Egypt
88.3	Coptic

Africa
North Africa -- Continued
88.6.A-Z Other North Africa, A-Z
88.6.I3 Ifni
88.6.S6 Spanish Sahara. Western Sahara
88.7 Ethiopia
88.75 Sub-Saharan Africa
Eastern Africa
88.8 General works
88.9.A-Z By country, A-Z
88.9.B8 Burundi
88.9.C6 Comoro Islands
88.9.F7 French Somaliland
88.9.K4 Kenya
88.9.M3 Madagascar
88.9.M6 Mozambique
88.9.R8 Rwanda
88.9.S6 Somali Republic
88.9.T3 Tanzania
88.9.Z3 Zanzibar
Western Africa
89 General works
89.3 French-speaking West Africa
89.6.A-Z By country, A-Z
89.6.A5 Angola
Benin, see 89.6.D3
89.6.B87 Burkina Faso. Upper Volta
89.6.C3 Cameroon
89.6.C4 Central African Republic
89.6.C5 Chad
89.6.C6 Congo (Democratic Republic). Belgian Congo. Zaire
89.6.C7 Congo (Brazzaville)
89.6.D3 Dahomey. Benin
89.6.G25 Gabon
89.6.G3 Gambia
89.6.G5 Ghana
89.6.G8 Guinea
89.6.I8 Ivory Coast. Côte d'Ivoire
89.6.L5 Liberia
89.6.M3 Mali
89.6.M4 Mauritania
Namibia, see 89.6.S6
89.6.N4 Niger
89.6.N5 Nigeria
89.6.P6 Portuguese Guinea
89.6.R5 Rio Muni
89.6.S4 Senegal
89.6.S5 Sierra Leone
89.6.S6 Southwest Africa. Namibia
89.6.T6 Togo
Upper Volta, see 89.6.B87
Zaire, see 89.6.C6

	Africa -- Continued
	Southern Africa
89.7	General works
89.8.A-Z	By country, A-Z
89.8.B6	Botswana
89.8.L4	Lesotho
89.8.M3	Malawi
89.8.N3	Namibia
89.8.R5	Rhodesia, Southern. Zimbabwe
89.8.S6	Republic of South Africa
89.8.S8	Swaziland
89.8.Z3	Zambia
	Zimbabwe, see 89.8.R5
	Indian Ocean islands
89.83	General
89.84.A-Z	Individual islands and island groups, A-Z
89.84.R48	Réunion
	Australasia. Oceania
89.9	General works
90	Australia
93	New Zealand
	Pacific islands
95	General
96.A-Z	Special, A-Z
	Hawaii, see 10.H3
96.3	Developing countries

01 America
02 Latin America
03 North America
United States
05 General works
06 Colonial period; 18th (and early 19th) century
07 19th century
08 20th century
08.5 Northeastern States
08.7 Atlantic States
10 New England
10.5 Middle Atlantic States
11 South
14 Central
17 West
18 Northwestern States
18.6 Southwestern States
19 Pacific States
25.A-W States, A-W
e.g.
Each state may be subarranged:
.x General works
.x2A-.x2Z Local (other than cities), A-Z
25.H3 Hawaii
Virginia
25.V8 General works
25.V82F3 Fairfax County
27.A-Z Cities, A-Z
28.A-Z Special artists, A-Z
Including families and firms
Ethnic groups
28.2 General works
28.3.A-Z Special, A-Z
e.g.
28.3.A35 Afro-Americans. Negroes. Blacks
28.3.A4 American Indians
For traditional art and crafts, see Classes E-F
28.3.A83 Asian Americans
Blacks, see 28.3.A35
28.3.H57 Hispanic Americans
28.3.I85 Italian Americans
28.3.L3 Latin Americans
28.3.L35 Latvian Americans
28.3.M4 Mexican Americans
(28.3.N4) Negroes
See N2 28.3.A35
Spanish Americans, see 28.3.H57
28.3.S82 Swedish Americans
29-30.3 Canada
29 General works
30.A-Z Local, A-Z
Ethnic groups
30.2 General works

	Canada
	Ethnic groups -- Continued
30.3.A-Z	Special, A-Z
30.3.G47	Germans
	Latin America, see 02
	Mexico
31	General works
32.A-Z	Local, A-Z
	Central America
33	General works
	Belize. British Honduras
35	General works
36.A-Z	Local, A-Z
	Costa Rica
37	General works
38.A-Z	Local, A-Z
	Guatemala
39	General works
40.Z-Z	Local, A-Z
	Honduras
41	General works
42.A-Z	Local, A-Z
	Nicaragua
43	General works
44.A-Z	Local, A-Z
	Panama
45.A1	General works
45.A2-Z	Local, A-Z
	El Salvador
46.A1	General works
46.A2-Z	Local, A-Z
	West Indies
47	General works
	Bahamas
49	General works
50.A-Z	Local, A-Z
	Cuba
51	General works
52.A-Z	Local, A-Z
	Haiti
53	General works
54.A-Z	Local, A-Z
	Jamaica
55	General works
56.A-Z	Local, A-Z
	Puerto Rico
57.A1	General works
57.A2-Z	Local, A-Z

Tables

West Indies -- Continued
58.A-Z Other, A-Z
Under each:
.x *General*
.x2A-.x2Z *Local, A-Z*
South America
59 General works
Argentina
61 General works
62.A-Z Local, A-Z
Bolivia
63 General works
64.A-Z Local, A-Z
Brazil
65 General works
66.A-Z Local, A-Z
Chile
67 General works
68.A-Z Local, A-Z
Colombia
69 General works
70.A-Z Local, A-Z
Ecuador
71 General works
72.A-Z Local, A-Z
Guyana (British Guiana)
73.A1 General works
73.A2-Z Local, A-Z
Surinam (Dutch Guiana)
73.2.A1 General works
73.2.A2-Z Local, A-Z
French Guiana
73.4.A1 General works
73.4.A2-Z Local, A-Z
Paraguay
75 General works
76.A-Z Local, A-Z
Peru
77 General works
78.A-Z Local, A-Z
Uruguay
79 General works
80.A-Z Local, A-Z
Venezuela
81 General works
82.A-Z Local, A-Z
Europe
83 General works
Class here general works and also works on Northern Europe, Eastern Europe, Southern Europe, etc., with no area Cutter subarrangement
Great Britain. England
85 General works

	Europe
	Great Britain. England -- Continued
87.A-Z	England. Local, A-Z
	Scotland
89	General works
90.A-Z	Local, A-Z
	Ireland
91	General works
92.A-Z	Local, A-Z
	Wales
93	General works
94.A-Z	Local, A-Z
	Austrian, German, and Swiss, see 98.6
	Austria
95	General works
96.A-Z	Local, A-Z
	France
97	General works
98.A-Z	Local, A-Z
98.A47	Alsace-Lorraine
98.6	German, Austrian, and Swiss (Collectively)
	German, Flemish, and Dutch, see 104.6
	Germany
	Including the former West Germany
99	General works
100.A-Z	Local, A-Z
	Alsace-Lorraine, see 98.A47
100.6	Former East Germany
	Greece
101	General works
102.A-Z	Local, A-Z
	Italy
103	General works
104.A-Z	Local, A-Z
104.6	Dutch, Flemish, and German (Collectively)
	Low countries
105	General works
	Holland (Netherlands)
107	General works
108.A-Z	Local, A-Z
	Belgium
109	General works
110.A-Z	Local, A-Z
	Luxembourg
110.6.A1	General works
110.6.A2-Z	Local, A-Z
	Russia in Europe. Russia (Federation)
111	General works
112.A-Z	Local, A-Z
	Class Siberia as a local here
	For Caucasian republics, see 150.A12-Z
	Scandinavia
113	General works

Tables

Europe
Scandinavia -- Continued
Denmark
115 General works
116.A-Z Local, A-Z
Iceland
117 General works
118.A-Z Local, A-Z
Norway
119 General works
120.A-Z Local, A-Z
Sweden
121 General works
122.A-Z Local, A-Z
Spain
123 General works
Class here also works on both Spain and Portugal
124.A-Z Local, A-Z
Portugal
125 General works
126.A-Z Local, A-Z
Swiss, Austrian, and German, see 98.6
Switzerland
127 General works
128.A-Z Local, A-Z
Turkey
129 General works
130.A-Z Local, A-Z
Balkan States
131 General works
Bulgaria
133 General works
134.A-Z Local, A-Z
(135) Montenegro
See N2 141.Y8
Romania
137 General works
138.A-Z Local, A-Z
(139) Serbia
See N2 141.Y8
141.A-Z Other regions or countries, A-Z
Under each:
.x *General*
.x2A-.x2Z *Local, A-Z*
141.A4 Albania
141.B34 Baltic States. Baltic Sea Region
141.B44 Belarus
141.C76 Croatia
141.C9 Czech Republic
141.E88 Estonia
141.F5 Finland
141.H8 Hungary
141.L38 Latvia

	Europe
	Other regions
	or countries, A-Z -- Continued
141.L57	Lithuania
141.M32	Macedonia (Region)
141.M35	Malta
141.M64	Moldova
141.P6	Poland
141.S54	Slovakia
141.S56	Slovenia
141.U47	Ukraine
141.Y8	Yugoslavia
142	Mediterranean Region
	Asia. The Orient
143	General works
	Southwestern Asia. Middle East
145	General works
146.A-Z	By region or country, A-Z
	Under each country:
	.x *General*
	.x2A-.x2Z *Local, A-Z*
146.A68	Arabian Peninsula
146.A7	Armenia (Historical region)
	For Armenia (Republic), see 150.A7
146.B33	Bahrain
146.C9	Cyprus
146.I7	Iraq
146.J6	Jordan
146.K8	Kuwait
146.L4	Lebanon
146.O45	Oman
146.Q36	Qatar
146.S2	Saudi Arabia
146.S9	Syria
146.U54	United Arab Emirates
146.Y4	Yemen
146.Y42	Yemen (People's Democratic Republic)
	Israel. Palestine
146.6.A1	General works
146.6.A2-Z	Local, A-Z
	Iran. Persia
147	General works
148.A-Z	Local, A-Z
	Central Asia
149	General works
	Class here also works on Russia in Asia as a whole
	For Siberia, see 112.A-Z
	Afghanistan
149.6.A1	General works
149.6.A2-Z	Local, A-Z
	Russia in Asia
	General works, see 149

Asia. The Orient
Central Asia
Russia in Asia -- Continued
150.A2-Z By republic, A-Z
Under each:
.x General
.x2A-.x2Z Local, A-Z
150.A7 Armenia (Republic)
For historical Armenia, see 146.A7
150.A9 Azerbaijan
150.D3 Daghestan
150.G4 Georgia (Republic)
150.K3 Kazakhstan
150.K5 Kirghizistan
150.T3 Tajikistan
150.T8 Turkmenistan
150.T85 Tuva
150.U9 Uzbekistan
Southern Asia
150.6 General works
India
151 General works
152.A-Z Local, A-Z
Sri Lanka. Ceylon
152.6.A1 General works
152.6.A2-Z Local, A-Z
Pakistan
153.A1 General works
153.A2-Z Local, A-Z
153.6.A-Z Other countries, A-Z
Under each country:
.x General
.x2A-.x2Z Local, A-Z
Southeastern Asia
154 General works
Burma
154.6.A1 General works
154.6.A2-Z Local, A-Z
French Indochina
155 General works
156.A-Z By country, A-Z
Under each country:
.x General
.x2A-.x2Z Local, A-Z
156.C3 Cambodia (Khmer)
156.L3 Laos
156.V5 Vietnam. South Vietnam
156.V55 Vietnam (Democratic Republic, 1946-)
Thailand. Siam
156.6.A1 General works
156.6.A2-Z Local, A-Z
Malaysia. Malaya
157 General works

Asia. The Orient
Southeastern Asia
Malaysia. Malaya -- Continued
158.A-Z Local, A-Z
Sabah, Singapore and Sarawak and Malaya are treated as locals of Malaysia here
Indonesia. Dutch East Indies
159 General works
160.A-Z Local, A-Z
Java, Sumatra, Kalimantan and West Irian are treated as locals of Indonesia here
Philippines
161 General works
162.A-Z Local, A-Z
Eastern Asia
163 General works
China
165 General works
166.A-Z Local, A-Z
Taiwan and Hong Kong are treated as locals of China in this table
Japan
167 General works
168.A-Z Local, A-Z
Korea
168.6.A1 General works
168.6.A2-Z Local, A-Z
Korea (Democratic People's Republic)
168.7.A1 General works
168.7.A2-Z Local, A-Z
172.A-Z Other countries, A-Z
Under each country:
.x General
.x2A-.x2Z Local, A-Z
Africa
173 General works
North Africa
174 General works
Algeria
174.6.A1 General works
174.6.A2-Z Local, A-Z
Libya
174.65.A1 General works
174.65.A2-Z Local, A-Z
Morocco
174.7.A1 General works
174.7.A2-Z Local, A-Z
Sudan
174.75.A1 General works
174.75.A2-Z Local, A-Z
Tunisia
174.8.A1 General works
174.8.A2-Z Local, A-Z

	Africa
	North Africa -- Continued
175	Egypt
175.3	Coptic
176.6.A-Z	Other North Africa, A-Z
176.6.I3	Ifni
176.6.S6	Spanish Sahara. Western Sahara
	Ethiopia
176.7.A1	General works
176.7.A2-Z	Local, A-Z
176.75	Sub-Saharan Africa
	Eastern Africa
176.8	General works
176.9.A-Z	By country, A-Z
	Under each country:
	.x *General*
	.x2A-.x2Z *Local, A-Z*
176.9.B8	Burundi
176.9.C6	Comoro Islands
176.9.F7	French Somaliland
176.9.K4	Kenya
176.9.M3	Madagascar
176.9.M6	Mozambique
176.9.R8	Rwanda
176.9.S6	Somali Republic
176.9.T3	Tanzania
176.9.Z3	Zanzibar
	Western Africa
177	General works
177.3	French-speaking West Africa
177.6.A-Z	By country, A-Z
	Under each:
	.x *General*
	.x2A-.x2Z *Local, A-Z*
177.6.A5	Angola
	Benin, see 177.6.D3
177.6.B87	Burkina Faso. Upper Volta
177.6.C3	Cameroon
177.6.C4	Central African Republic
177.6.C5	Chad
177.6.C6	Congo (Democratic Republic). Belgian Congo. Zaire
177.6.C7	Congo (Brazzaville)
177.6.D3	Dahomey. Benin
177.6.G25	Gabon
177.6.G3	Gambia
177.6.G5	Ghana
177.6.G8	Guinea
177.6.I8	Ivory Coast. Côte d'Ivoire
177.6.L5	Liberia
177.6.M3	Mali
177.6.M4	Mauritania
	Namibia, see 177.6.S6

	Africa
	Western Africa
	By country, A-Z -- Continued
177.6.N4	Niger
177.6.N5	Nigeria
177.6.P6	Portuguese Guinea
177.6.R5	Rio Muni
177.6.S4	Senegal
177.6.S5	Sierra Leone
177.6.S6	Southwest Africa. Namibia
177.6.T6	Togo
	Upper Volta, see 177.6.B87
	Zaire, see 177.6.C6
	Southern Africa
178	General works
178.6.A-Z	By country, A-Z
	Under each country:
	.x *General*
	.x2A-.x2Z *Local, A-Z*
178.6.B6	Botswana
178.6.L4	Lesotho
178.6.M3	Malawi
178.6.N3	Namibia
178.6.R5	Rhodesia, Southern. Zimbabwe
178.6.S6	Republic of South Africa
178.6.S8	Swaziland
178.6.Z3	Zambia
	Zimbabwe, see 178.6.R5
	Indian Ocean islands
178.83	General
178.84.A-Z	Individual islands and island groups, A-Z
	Under each:
	.x *General*
	.x2A-.x2Z *Local, A-Z*
178.84.R48	Réunion
	Australasia. Oceania
178.9	General works
	Australia
179	General works
180.A-Z	Local, A-Z
	New Zealand
181	General works
182.A-Z	Local, A-Z
	Pacific islands
183	General
184.A-Z	Special, A-Z
	Hawaii, see 25.H3
185	Developing countries

Tables

01 America
02 Latin America
03 North America
United States
05 General works
06 Colonial period; 18th (and early 19th) century
07 19th century
08 20th century
08.5 Northeastern States
08.7 Atlantic States
10 New England
10.5 Middle Atlantic States
11 South
18 Central
23 West
24 Northwestern States
24.6 Southwestern States
25 Pacific States
35.A-W States, A-W
e.g.
Each state may be subarranged:
.x General works
.x2A-.x2Z Local (other than cities), A-Z
35.H3 Hawaii
Virginia
35.V8 General works
35.V82F3 Fairfax County
38.A-Z Cities, A-Z
39.A-Z Special artists, A-Z
Including families and firms
Ethnic groups
39.2 General works
39.3.A-Z Special, A-Z
39.3.A35 Afro-Americans. Negroes. Blacks
39.3.A4 American Indians
For traditional art and crafts, see Classes E-F
39.3.A83 Asian Americans
Blacks, see 39.3.A35
39.3.H57 Hispanic Americans
39.3.I85 Italian Americans
39.3.L3 Latin Americans
39.3.L35 Latvian Americans
39.3.M4 Mexican Americans
(39.3.N4) Negroes
See N3 39.3.A35
Spanish Americans, see 39.3.H57
39.3.S82 Swedish Americans
41-43.3 Canada
Ethnic groups
43.2 General works
43.3.A-Z Special, A-Z
43.3.G47 Germans
Latin America, see 02

44-46	Mexico
	Central America
47	General works
50-52	Belize. British Honduras
53-55	Costa Rica
56-58	Guatamala
59-61	Honduras
62-64	Nicaragua
65	Panama
67	El Salvador
	West Indies
68	General works
71-73	Bahamas
74-76	Cuba
77-79	Haiti
80-82	Jamaica
83-85	Puerto Rico
86.A-Z	Other, A-Z
	South America
89	General works
92-94	Argentina
95-97	Bolivia
98-100	Brazil
101-103	Chile
104-106	Colombia
107-109	Ecuador
110	Guyana (British Guiana)
110.2	Surinam (Dutch Guiana)
110.4	French Guiana
113-115	Paraguay
116-118	Peru
119-121	Uruguay
122-124	Venezuela
	Europe
125	General works
	Class here general works and also works on Northern Europe, Eastern Europe, Southern Europe, etc. with no area Cutter subarrangement
	Great Britain. England
128	General works
131.A-Z	England. Local, A-Z
134-136	Scotland
137-139	Ireland
	Wales
140.A1	General works
140.A3A-Z	Special regions, provinces, etc., A-Z
140.A5-Z	Special cities, A-Z
142.A-Z	Special artists, A-Z
	Including individuals, families, or firms of England, Scotland, Ireland, or Wales
	Austrian, German, and Swiss, see 148.6
143-145	Austria
146-148	France

Tables

	Europe -- Continued
148.6	German, Austrian, and Swiss (Collectively)
	German, Flemish, and Dutch, see 157.6
149-151	Germany
	Including the former West Germany
	For Alsace-Lorraine, see 146-148
151.6	Former East Germany
152-154	Greece
155-157	Italy
157.6	Dutch, Flemish, and German (Collectively)
	Low countries
158	General works
161-163	Holland (Netherlands)
164-166	Belgium
166.4	Luxembourg
167-169	Russia in Europe. Russia (Federation)
	Class Siberia as a local here
	For Caucasian republics, see 225.A12-Z
	Scandinavia
170	General works
173-175	Denmark
176-178	Iceland
179-181	Norway
182-184	Sweden
185-187	Spain
185	General works
	Class here also works on both Spain and Portugal
188-190	Portugal
	Swiss, Austrian, and German, see 148.6
191-193	Switzerland
194-196	Turkey
	Balkan States
197	General works
200-202	Bulgaria
(203)	Montenegro
	See N3 212.Y8
206-208	Romania
(209)	Serbia
	See N3 212.Y8
212.A-Z	Other regions or countries, A-Z
212.A4	Albania
212.B34	Baltic States. Baltic Sea Region
212.B44	Belarus
212.C76	Croatia
212.C9	Czech Republic
212.E88	Estonia
212.F5	Finland
212.H8	Hungary
212.L38	Latvia
212.L57	Lithuania
212.M32	Macedonia (Region)
212.M35	Malta
212.M64	Moldova

Europe
Other regions or countries, A-Z -- Continued
212.P6 Poland
212.S54 Slovakia
212.S56 Slovenia
212.U47 Ukraine
212.Y8 Yugoslavia
214 Mediterranean Region
Asia. The Orient
215 General works
Southwestern Asia. Middle East
218 General works
219.A-Z By region or country, A-Z
219.A68 Arabian Peninsula
219.A7 Armenia (Historical region)
For Armenia (Republic), see 225.A7
219.B33 Bahrain
219.C9 Cyprus
219.I7 Iraq
219.J6 Jordan
219.K8 Kuwait
219.L4 Lebanon
219.O45 Oman
219.Q36 Qatar
219.S2 Saudi Arabia
219.S9 Syria
219.U54 United Arab Emirates
219.Y4 Yemen
219.Y42 Yemen (People's Democratic Republic)
220 Israel. Palestine
221-223 Iran. Persia
Central Asia
224 General works
Class here also works on Russia in Asia as a whole
For Siberia, see 167-169
224.6 Afghanistan
Russia in Asia
General works, see 224
225.A2-Z By republic, A-Z
225.A7 Armenia (Republic)
For historical Armenia, see 219.A7
225.A9 Azerbaijan
225.D3 Daghestan
225.G4 Georgia (Republic)
225.K3 Kazakhstan
225.K5 Kirghizistan
225.T3 Tajikistan
225.T8 Turkmenistan
225.T85 Tuva
225.U9 Uzbekistan
Southern Asia
226 General works

	Asia. The Orient
	Southern Asia -- Continued
227-229	India
230	Sri Lanka. Ceylon
231	Pakistan
231.6.A-Z	Other countries, A-Z
	Southeastern Asia
232	General works
232.6	Burma
	French Indochina
233	General works
234.A-Z	By country, A-Z
234.C3	Cambodia (Khmer)
234.L3	Laos
234.V5	Vietnam. South Vietnam
234.V55	Vietnam (Democratic Republic, 1946-)
235	Thailand. Siam
236-238	Malaysia. Malaya
	Sabah, Singapore and Sarawak and Malaya are treated as locals of Malaysia here
239-241	Indonesia. Dutch East Indies
	Java, Sumatra, Kalimantan and West Irian are treated as locals of Indonesia here
242-244	Philippines
	Eastern Asia
245	General works
248-250	China
	Taiwan and Hong Kong are treated as locals of China in this table
251-253	Japan
253.6	Korea
253.7	Korea (Democratic People's Republic)
259.A-Z	Other countries, A-Z
	Africa
260	General works
	North Africa
261	General works
261.6	Algeria
261.65	Libya
261.7	Morocco
261.75	Sudan
261.8	Tunisia
263-265	Egypt
263.3	Coptic
265.6.A-Z	Other North Africa, A-Z
265.6.I3	Ifni
265.6.S6	Spanish Sahara. Western Sahara
265.7	Ethiopia
265.75	Sub-Saharan Africa
	Eastern Africa
266	General works
266.6.A-Z	By country, A-Z
266.6.B8	Burundi

	Africa
	Eastern Africa
	By country, A-Z -- Continued
266.6.C6	Comoro Islands
266.6.F7	French Somaliland
266.6.K4	Kenya
266.6.M3	Madagascar
266.6.M6	Mozambique
266.6.R8	Rwanda
266.6.S6	Somali Republic
266.6.T3	Tanzania
266.6.Z3	Zanzibar
	Western Africa
267	General works
267.3	French-speaking West Africa
267.6.A-Z	By country, A-Z
267.6.A5	Angola
	Benin, see 267.6.D3
267.6.B87	Burkina Faso. Upper Volta
267.6.C3	Cameroon
267.6.C4	Central African Republic
267.6.C5	Chad
267.6.C6	Congo (Democratic Republic). Belgian Congo. Zaire
267.6.C7	Congo (Brazzaville)
267.6.D3	Dahomey. Benin
267.6.G25	Gabon
267.6.G3	Gambia
267.6.G5	Ghana
267.6.G8	Guinea
267.6.I8	Ivory Coast. Côte d'Ivoire
267.6.L5	Liberia
267.6.M3	Mali
267.6.M4	Mauritania
	Namibia, see 267.6.S6
267.6.N4	Niger
267.6.N5	Nigeria
267.6.P6	Portuguese Guinea
267.6.R5	Rio Muni
267.6.S4	Senegal
267.6.S5	Sierra Leone
267.6.S6	Southwest Africa. Namibia
267.6.T6	Togo
	Upper Volta, see 267.6.B87
	Zaire, see 267.6.C6
	Southern Africa
268	General works
268.6.A-Z	By country, A-Z
268.6.B6	Botswana
268.6.L4	Lesotho
268.6.M3	Malawi
268.6.N3	Namibia
268.6.R5	Rhodesia, Southern. Zimbabwe

	Africa
	Southern Africa
	By country, A-Z -- Continued
268.6.S6	Republic of South Africa
268.6.S8	Swaziland
268.6.Z3	Zambia
	Zimbabwe, see 268.6.R5
	Indian Ocean islands
268.83	General
268.84.A-Z	Individual islands and island groups, A-Z
268.84.R48	Réunion
	Australasia. Oceania
268.9	General works
269-271	Australia
272-274	New Zealand
	Pacific islands
275	General
276.A-Z	Special, A-Z
	Hawaii, see 35.H3
277	Developing countries

01 America
02 Latin America
03 North America
United States
05 General works
06 Colonial period; 18th (and early 19th) century
07 19th century
08 20th century
08.5 Northeastern States
08.7 Atlantic States
10 New England
10.5 Middle Atlantic States
11 South
18 Central
23 West
24 Northwestern States
24.6 Southwestern States
25 Pacific States
35.A-W States, A-W
e.g.
Each state may be subarranged:
.x General works
.x2A-.x2Z Local (other than cities), A-Z
35.H3 Hawaii
Virginia
35.V8 General works
35.V82F3 Fairfax County
38.A-Z Cities, A-Z
39.A-Z Special artists, A-Z
Including families and firms
Ethnic groups
39.2 General works
39.3.A-Z Special, A-Z
39.3.A35 Afro-Americans. Negroes. Blacks
39.3.A4 American Indians
For traditional art and crafts, see Classes E-F
39.3.A83 Asian Americans
Blacks, see 39.3.A35
39.3.H57 Hispanic Americans
39.3.I85 Italian Americans
39.3.L3 Latin Americans
39.3.L35 Latvian Americans
39.3.M4 Mexican Americans
(39.3.N4) Negroes
See N4 39.3.A35
Spanish Americans, see 39.3.H57
39.3.S82 Swedish Americans
41-43.3 Canada
Ethnic groups
43.2 General works
43.3.A-Z Special, A-Z
43.3.G47 Germans
Latin America, see 02

44-46	Mexico
	Central America
47	General works
50-52	Belize. British Honduras
53-55	Costa Rica
56-58	Guatamala
59-61	Honduras
62-64	Nicaragua
65-66	Panama
67	El Salvador
	West Indies
68	General works
71-73	Bahamas
74-76	Cuba
77-79	Haiti
80-82	Jamaica
83-85	Puerto Rico
86.A-Z	Other, A-Z
	South America
89	General works
92-94	Argentina
95-97	Bolivia
98-100	Brazil
101-103	Chile
104-106	Colombia
107-109	Ecuador
110	Guyana (British Guiana)
110.2	Surinam (Dutch Guiana)
110.4	French Guiana
113-115	Paraguay
116-118	Peru
119-121	Uruguay
122-124	Venezuela
	Europe
125	General works
	Class here general works and also works on Northern Europe, Eastern Europe, Southern Europe, etc., with no area Cutter subarrangement
	Great Britain. England
128	General works
131.A-Z	England. Local, A-Z
134-136	Scotland
137-139	Ireland
140-141	Wales
142.A-Z	Special artists, A-Z
	Including individuals, families, or firms of England, Scotland, Ireland, or Wales
	Austrian, German, and Swiss, see 150.6
143-146	Austria
147-150	France
150.6	German, Austrian, and Swiss (Collectively)
	German, Flemish, and Dutch, see 162.6

	Europe -- Continued
151-154	Germany
	Including the former West Germany
	For Alsace-Lorraine, see 147-150
154.6	Former East Germany
155-158	Greece
159-162	Italy
162.6	Dutch, Flemish, and German (Collectively)
	Low countries
163	General works
167-170	Holland (Netherlands)
171-174	Belgium
174.6	Luxembourg
175-178	Russia in Europe. Russia (Federation)
	Class Siberia as a local here
	For Caucasian republics, see 245.A12-Z
	Scandinavia
179	General works
183-186	Denmark
187-190	Iceland
191-194	Norway
195-198	Sweden
199-202	Spain
199	General works
	Class here also works on Spain and Portugal collectively
203-206	Portugal
	Swiss, Austrian, and German, see 150.6
207-210	Switzerland
211-214	Turkey
	Balkan States
215	General works
219-222	Bulgaria
(223)	Montenegro
	See N4 235.Y8
227-230	Romania
(231)	Serbia
	See N4 235.Y8
235.A-Z	Other regions or countries, A-Z
235.A4	Albania
235.B34	Baltic States. Baltic Sea Region
235.B44	Belarus
235.C76	Croatia
235.C9	Czech Republic
235.E88	Estonia
235.F5	Finland
235.H8	Hungary
235.L38	Latvia
235.L57	Lithuania
235.M32	Macedonia (Region)
235.M35	Malta
235.M64	Moldova
235.P6	Poland

Tables

Europe
Other regions
or countries, A-Z -- Continued
235.S54 Slovakia
235.S56 Slovenia
235.U47 Ukraine
235.Y8 Yugoslavia
236 Mediterranean Region
Asia. The Orient
237 General works
Southwestern Asia. Middle East
238 General works
239.A-Z By region or country, A-Z
239.A68 Arabian Peninsula
239.A7 Armenia (Historical region)
For Armenia (Republic), see 245.A7
239.B33 Bahrain
239.C9 Cyprus
239.I7 Iraq
239.J6 Jordan
239.K8 Kuwait
239.L4 Lebanon
239.O45 Oman
239.Q36 Qatar
239.S2 Saudi Arabia
239.S9 Syria
239.U54 United Arab Emirates
239.Y4 Yemen
239.Y42 Yemen (People's Democratic Republic)
240 Israel. Palestine
241-243 Iran. Persia
Central Asia
244 General works
Class here also works on Russia in Asia as a whole
For Siberia, see 175-178
244.6 Afghanistan
Russia in Asia
General works, see 244
245.A2-Z By republic, A-Z
245.A7 Armenia (Republic)
For historical Armenia, see 239.A7
245.A9 Azerbaijan
245.D3 Daghestan
245.G4 Georgia (Republic)
245.K3 Kazakhstan
245.K5 Kirghizistan
245.T3 Tajikistan
245.T8 Turkmenistan
245.T85 Tuva
245.U9 Uzbekistan
Southern Asia
246 General works
247-249 India

	Asia. The Orient
	Southern Asia -- Continued
250	Sri Lanka. Ceylon
251	Pakistan
251.6.A-Z	Other countries, A-Z
	Southeastern Asia
252	General works
252.6	Burma
	French Indochina
253	General works
254.A-Z	By country, A-Z
254.C3	Cambodia (Khmer)
254.L3	Laos
254.V5	Vietnam. South Vietnam
254.V55	Vietnam (Democratic Republic, 1946-)
255	Thailand. Siam
256-258	Malaysia. Malaya
	Sabah, Singapore and Sarawak and Malaya are treated as locals of Malaysia here
259-261	Indonesia. Dutch East Indies
	Java, Sumatra, Kalimantan and West Irian are treated as locals of Indonesia here
262-264	Philippines
	Eastern Asia
265	General works
268-270	China
	Taiwan and Hong Kong are treated as locals of China in this table
271-273	Japan
273.6	Korea
273.7	Korea (Democratic People's Republic)
279.A-Z	Other countries, A-Z
	Africa
280	General works
	North Africa
281	General works
281.6	Algeria
281.65	Libya
281.7	Morocco
281.75	Sudan
281.8	Tunisia
283-284	Egypt
283.3	Coptic
285.6.A-Z	Other North Africa, A-Z
285.6.I3	Ifni
285.6.S6	Spanish Sahara. Western Sahara
285.7	Ethiopia
285.75	Sub-Saharan Africa
	Eastern Africa
286	General works
286.6.A-Z	By country, A-Z
286.6.B8	Burundi
286.6.C6	Comoro Islands

Tables

	Africa
	Eastern Africa
	By country, A-Z -- Continued
286.6.F7	French Somaliland
286.6.K4	Kenya
286.6.M3	Madagascar
286.6.M6	Mozambique
286.6.R8	Rwanda
286.6.S6	Somali Republic
286.6.T3	Tanzania
286.6.Z3	Zanzibar
	Western Africa
287	General works
287.3	French-speaking West Africa
287.6.A-Z	By country, A-Z
287.6.A5	Angola
	Benin, see 287.6.D3
287.6.B87	Burkina Faso
287.6.C3	Cameroon
287.6.C4	Central African Republic
287.6.C5	Chad
287.6.C6	Congo (Democratic Republic). Belgian Congo. Zaire
287.6.C7	Congo (Brazzaville)
287.6.D3	Dahomey. Benin
287.6.G25	Gabon
287.6.G3	Gambia
287.6.G5	Ghana
287.6.G8	Guinea
287.6.I8	Ivory Coast. Côte d'Ivoire
287.6.L5	Liberia
287.6.M3	Mali
287.6.M4	Mauritania
	Namibia, see 287.6.S6
287.6.N4	Niger
287.6.N5	Nigeria
287.6.P6	Portuguese Guinea
287.6.R5	Rio Muni
287.6.S4	Senegal
287.6.S5	Sierra Leone
287.6.S6	Southwest Africa. Namibia
287.6.T6	Togo
	Upper Volta, see 287.6.B87
	Zaire, see 287.6.C6
	Southern Africa
288	General works
288.6.A-Z	By country, A-Z
288.6.B6	Botswana
288.6.L4	Lesotho
288.6.M3	Malawi
288.6.N3	Namibia
288.6.R5	Rhodesia, Southern. Zimbabwe
288.6.S6	Republic of South Africa

	Africa
	Southern Africa
	By country, A-Z -- Continued
288.6.S8	Swaziland
288.6.Z3	Zambia
	Zimbabwe, see 288.6.R5
	Indian Ocean islands
288.83	General
288.84.A-Z	Individual islands and island groups, A-Z
288.84.R48	Réunion
	Australasia. Oceania
288.9	General works
289-291	Australia
292	New Zealand
	Pacific islands
293	General
294.A-Z	Special, A-Z
	Hawaii, see 35.H3
294.5	Developing countries

	America
	For American Indians, see Classes E-F
01	General works
	Latin America
02	General works
02.2	Colonial period (16th-18th centuries)
02.4	19th century
02.5	20th century
03	North America
	United States
05	General works
07	Colonial period; 18th (and early 19th) century
10	19th century
12	20th century
13	Northeastern States
14	Atlantic States
15	New England
16	Appalachian region
17	Middle Atlantic States
20	South
22	Central
25	West
26	Northwestern States
27	Southwestern States
28	Pacific states
30.A-W	States, A-W
	Each state may be subarranged:
	.x General works
	.x2A-.x2Z Local (other than cities), A-Z
35.A-Z	Cities, A-Z
36	Collective biography
37.A-Z	Special artists, A-Z
37.5	Ethnic groups (Collectively)
38.A-Z	Special races and ethnic groups, A-Z
	Afro-Americans, see 38.N5
38.A4	American Indians
	For traditional art and crafts, see Classes E-F
38.A83	Asian Americans
	Blacks, see 38.N5
38.C37	Caribbean Americans
38.C48	Chinese Americans
38.C83	Cuban Americans
38.G74	Greek Americans
38.H58	Hispanic Americans
38.I8	Italian Americans
38.J4	Jews
38.K67	Korean Americans
38.L3	Latin Americans
38.M4	Mexican Americans
38.N5	Negroes. Afro-Americans. Blacks
38.S32	Scandinavian Americans
	Spanish-Americans, see 38.H58
38.S82	Swedish Americans

	America
	United States
	Special races and ethnic groups, A-Z -- Continued
38.V54	Vietnamese Americans
	Canada
40	General works
43	Before 1800 (New France)
44	19th century
45	20th century
46.A-Z	Special divisions, A-Z
47.A-Z	Special cities, A-Z
48	Collective biography
49.A-Z	Special artists, A-Z
49.3	Ethnic groups (Collectively)
49.5.A-Z	Individual races and ethnic groups, A-Z
49.5.A54	American Indians
	For traditional art and crafts, see Classes E-F
49.5.B53	Blacks
	Latin America, see 02
	Mexico
50	General works
53	Before 1800
54	19th century
55	20th century
56.A-Z	Special divisions, A-Z
57.A-Z	Special cities, A-Z
58	Collective biography
59.A-Z	Special artists, A-Z
	Central America
60	General works
	Belize. British Honduras
70	General works
71.A-Z	Local, A-Z
72.A-Z	Special artists, A-Z
	Costa Rica
73	General works
74.A-Z	Local, A-Z
75.A-Z	Special artists, A-Z
	Guatemala
76	General works
77.A-Z	Local, A-Z
78.A-Z	Special artists, A-Z
	Honduras
79	General works
80.A-Z	Local, A-Z
81.A-Z	Special artists, A-Z
	Nicaragua
82	General works
83.A-Z	Local, A-Z
84.A-Z	Special artists, A-Z
	Panama
85	General works

America
Central America
Panama -- Continued
86.A-Z Local, A-Z
87.A-Z Special artists, A-Z
El Salvador
88 General works
89.A-Z Local, A-Z
90.A-Z Special artists, A-Z
West Indies
91 General works
Bahamas
100 General works
101.A-Z Local, A-Z
102.A-Z Special artists, A-Z
Cuba
103 General works
104.A-Z Local, A-Z
105.A-Z Special artists, A-Z
Haiti
106 General works
107.A-Z Local, A-Z
108.A-Z Special artists, A-Z
Jamaica
109 General works
110.A-Z Local, A-Z
111.A-Z Special artists, A-Z
Puerto Rico
112 General works
113.A-Z Local, A-Z
114.A-Z Special artists, A-Z
115.A-Z Other, A-Z
South America
120 General works
Argentina
130 General works
133 Before 1800
134 19th century
135 20th century
136.A-Z Special divisions, A-Z
137.A-Z Special cities, A-Z
138 Collective biography
139.A-Z Special artists, A-Z
Bolivia
140 General works
143 Before 1800
144 19th century
145 20th century
146.A-Z Special divisions, A-Z
147.A-Z Special cities, A-Z
148 Collective biography
149.A-Z Special artists, A-Z
Brazil

	South America
	Brazil -- Continued
150	General works
153	Before 1800
154	19th century
155	20th century
156.A-Z	Special divisions, A-Z
157.A-Z	Special cities, A-Z
158	Collective biography
159.A-Z	Special artists, A-Z
	Chile
160	General works
163	Before 1800
164	19th century
165	20th century
166.A-Z	Special divisions, A-Z
167.A-Z	Special cities, A-Z
168	Collective biography
169.A-Z	Special artists, A-Z
	Colombia
170	General works
173	Before 1800
174	19th century
175	20th century
176.A-Z	Special divisions, A-Z
177.A-Z	Special cities, A-Z
178	Collective biography
179.A-Z	Special artists, A-Z
	Ecuador
180	General works
183	Before 1800
184	19th century
185	20th century
186.A-Z	Special divisions, A-Z
187.A-Z	Special cities, A-Z
188	Collective biography
189.A-Z	Special artists, A-Z
	Guiana
190	General works
195	Guyana (British Guiana)
196	Surinam (Dutch Guiana)
197	French Guiana
198.A-Z	Special cities, towns, etc., A-Z
199.A-Z	Special artists, A-Z
	Paraguay
200	General works
203	Before 1800
204	19th century
205	20th century
206.A-Z	Special divisions, A-Z
207.A-Z	Special cities, A-Z
208	Collective biography
209.A-Z	Special artists, A-Z

South America -- Continued
Peru
210 General works
213 Before 1800
214 19th century
215 20th century
216.A-Z Special divisions, A-Z
217.A-Z Special cities, A-Z
218 Collective biography
219.A-Z Special artists, A-Z
Uruguay
220 General works
223 Before 1800
224 19th century
225 20th century
226.A-Z Special divisions, A-Z
227.A-Z Special cities, A-Z
228 Collective biography
229.A-Z Special artists, A-Z
Venezuela
230 General works
233 Before 1800
234 19th century
235 20th century
236.A-Z Special divisions, A-Z
237.A-Z Special cities, A-Z
238 Collective biography
239.A-Z Special artists, A-Z
Europe
Class general works and also works on Northern Europe, Eastern Europe, Southern Europe, etc., in 250, or if more appropriate in 253-258, with no area Cutter arrangement
250 General works
251 Folios
Used only for NA951
(252) Ancient
See Ancient art in general period divisions, N5315-N5899, etc.
253 Medieval
Used only for NA5453
In other cases, see the general period divisions
Modern
254 General works
255 Renaissance
Used only for NA5455
In other cases, see the general period divisions
256 17th-18th centuries
257 19th century
258 20th century
Special countries
Great Britain. England
261 General works

Europe
Special countries
Great Britain. England -- Continued
262 Ancient
263 Anglo-Saxon. Gothic. Medieval
In Class NA, includes general architectural antiquities
Modern
264 General works
265 14th-16th centuries
Including the Renaissance, Tudor, Elizabethian periods
266 17th-18th centuries
Including the Stuart, Caroline, Georgian periods
267 19th century
Including the Regency, Victorian, Edwardian periods
268 20th century
England - Local
269.A-Z English counties, A-Z
For a list of English counties, see Table N8
270 London
271.A-Z Other English cities, A-Z
Scotland
272 General works
273 Ancient
274 Medieval
In Class NA includes general architectural antiquities
Modern
275 General works
276 14th-16th centuries
277 17th-18th centuries
278 19th century
279 20th century
280.A-Z Special counties, A-Z
281.A-Z Special cities, A-Z
Ireland
282 General works
283 Ancient
284 Medieval
In Class NA, includes general architectural antiquities
Modern
285 General works
286 14th-16th centuries
287 17th-18th centuries
288 19th century
289 20th century
290.A-Z Special counties, A-Z
291.A-Z Special cities, A-Z
Wales

Tables

Europe
Special countries
Great Britain. England
Wales -- Continued
292 General works
Modern
292.6 19th century
292.7 20th century
293.A-Z Special counties, A-Z
294.A-Z Special cities, A-Z
295.A-Z Other local, A-Z
e.g.
295.W6 Isle of Wight
296 Collective biography. British artists
297.A-Z Special artists, A-Z
Austrian, German, and Swiss, see 359
Austria
Including the former Austro-Hungarian empire
301 General works
302 Ancient
303 Medieval. Gothic. Romanesque
Modern
304 General works
305 14th-16th centuries. Renaissance
306 17th-18th centuries
307 19th century
308 20th century
309.A-Z Special divisions of Austria, A-Z
310.A-Z Special cities of Austria, A-Z
311 Collective biography
311.5.A-Z Special artists, A-Z
311.6.A-Z Special works, by name (artists unknown), A-Z
Hungary
312 General works
314 Ancient
315 Medieval. Gothic. Romanesque
Modern
316 General works
317 14th-16th centuries
318 17th-18th centuries
319 19th century
320 20th century
321.A-Z Special divisions, A-Z
321.5.A-Z Special cities of Hungary, A-Z
322 Collective biography
322.5.A-Z Special artists, A-Z
322.6.A-Z Special works, by name (artists unknown), A-Z
Czechoslovakia. Czech Republic
323 General works
325 Ancient
326 Medieval. Gothic. Romanesque
Modern
327 General works

Europe
Special countries
Czechoslovakia.
Czech Republic
Modern -- Continued
328 14th-16th centuries
329 17th-18th centuries
330 19th century
331 20th century
332.A-Z Special divisions, A-Z
333.A-Z Special cities of the Czech Republic, A-Z
334 Collective biography
334.5.A-Z Special artists, A-Z
Special cities of Austria-Hungary
(335) Vienna
(336.A-Z) Others, A-Z
(337) Collective Austro-Hungarian biography
(338.A-Z) Special artists of Austria-Hungary, A-Z
France
341 General works
342 Ancient
343 Medieval. Gothic. Romanesque
Modern
344 General works
345 14th-16th centuries
346 17th-18th centuries
347 19th century
348 20th century
349.A-Z Special divisions, A-Z
e.g.
349.A4 Alsace-Lorraine
350 Paris
351.A-Z Other special cities, A-Z
352 Collective biography
353.A-Z Special artists, A-Z
353.3.A-Z Special works. By name (artists unknown), A-Z
359 German, Austrian and Swiss (Collectively)
German, Flemish, and Dutch, see 425
Germany
Including the former West Germany
361 General works
362 Ancient
363 Medieval. Gothic. Romanesque
Modern
364 General works
365 14th-16th centuries
366 17th-18th centuries
367 19th century
368 20th century

Europe
Special countries
Germany -- Continued
Special divisions
Including divisions of Germany considered as a whole, divisions of Germany before 1949 and after 1990, and divisions of West Germany, 1949-1990
369 A - Als
(370) Alsace-Lorraine
See N5 349.A4
371 Als - Bad
372 Baden
Including Baden-Württemberg
372.5 Baltic Sea Region
373 Bavaria
374 Bav - Hes
375 Hesse
376 Hes - Pr
377 Prussia
378 Pr - Rh
379 Rhine provinces
Including Rhine Valley, North Rhine-Westphalia
380 Rho - Sax
381 Saxony
382 Sax - Wu
383 Württemburg
384 Wu - Z
(384.5) Democratic Republic, 1949-1990
See N5 389
385 Berlin
386.A-Z Other cities, A-Z
387 Collective biography
388.A-Z Special artists, A-Z
388.3.A-Z Special works. By name (artists unknown), A-Z
East Germany
389 General works
(389.2) Local
See N5 369-384
Berlin, see 385
(389.4) Collective biography
See N5 387
(389.5.A-Z) Special artists, A-Z
See N5 388
Greece
391 General works
392 Ancient
393 Medieval. Gothic. Romanesque
Modern
394 General works
395 14th-16th centuries
396 17th-18th centuries
397 19th century

	Europe
	Special countries
	Greece
	Modern -- Continued
398	20th century
399.A-Z	Special divisions, A-Z
400	Athens
401.A-Z	Other special cities, A-Z
402	Collective biography
403.A-Z	Special artists, A-Z
403.3.A-Z	Special works. By name (artists unknown), A-Z
	Italy
411	General works
412	Ancient
413	Medieval. Gothic. Romanesque
	Modern
414	General works
415	14th-16th centuries
416	17th-18th centuries
417	19th century
418	20th century
419.A-Z	Special divisions, A-Z
420	Rome
421.A-Z	Other special cities, A-Z
422	Collective biography
423.A-Z	Special artists, A-Z
423.3.A-Z	Special works. By name (artists unknown), A-Z
425	Dutch, Flemish, and German (Collectively)
	Low countries
	Including the historic region of Flanders
431	General works
432	Ancient
433	Medieval. Gothic. Romanesque
	Modern
434	General works
435	14th-16th centuries
436	17th-18th centuries
437	19th century
438	20th century
	Holland (Netherlands)
441	General works
442	Ancient
443	Medieval. Gothic. Romanesque
	Modern
444	General works
445	14th-16th centuries
446	17th-18th centuries
447	19th century
448	20th century
449.A-Z	Special divisions, A-Z
450	Amsterdam
451.A-Z	Other special cities, A-Z
452	Collective biography

	Europe
	Special countries
	Low countries
	Holland (Netherlands) -- Continued
453.A-Z	Special artists, A-Z
453.3.A-Z	Special works. By name (artists unknown), A-Z
	Belgium
461	General works
462	Ancient
463	Medieval. Gothic. Romanesque
	Modern
464	General works
465	14th-16th centuries
466	17th-18th centuries
467	19th century
468	20th century
469.A-Z	Special divisions, A-Z
	e.g.
469.F5	Flanders
469.W3	Wallonia
470	Brussels
471.A-Z	Other special cities, A-Z
472	Collective biography
473.A-Z	Special artists, A-Z
473.3.A-Z	Special works. By name (artists unknown), A-Z
	Luxembourg
474	General
474.2.A-Z	Local, A-Z
474.3.A-Z	Special artists, A-Z
476	Slavic art. General works
	Russia
481	General works
482	Ancient
483	Medieval. Gothic. Romanesque
	Modern
484	General works
485	14th-16th centuries
486	17th-18th centuries
487	19th century
488	20th century
	Special divisions of European Russia
(491)	Poland. Polish art
	See N5 755.P6
(493)	Finland. Finnish art
	See N5 755.F5
495.A-Z	Other, A-Z
	Caucasus, see 792.4
	Special cities
496	Leningrad. St. Petersburg
497.A-Z	Other cities, A-Z
498	Collective biography
499.A-Z	Special artists, A-Z
	Scandinavia

Europe
Special countries
Scandinavia -- Continued
501 General works
502 Ancient
503 Medieval. Gothic. Romanesque
Modern
504 General works
505 14th-16th centuries
506 17th-18th centuries
507 19th century
508 20th century
509 Collective biography
Denmark
511 General works
512 Ancient
513 Medieval. Gothic. Romanesque
Modern
514 General works
515 14th-16th centuries
516 17th-18th centuries
517 19th century
518 20th century
519.A-Z Special divisions, A-Z
520 Copenhagen
521.A-Z Other special cities, A-Z
522 Collective biography
523.A-Z Special artists, A-Z
523.3.A-Z Special works. By name (artists unknown), A-Z
Iceland
541 General works
542 Ancient
543 Medieval. Gothic. Romanesque
Modern
544 General works
545 14th-16th centuries
546 17th-18th centuries
547 19th century
548 20th century
549.A-Z Special divisions, A-Z
550 Reykjavik
551.A-Z Other special cities, A-Z
552 Collective biography
553.A-Z Special artists, A-Z
553.3.A-Z Special works. By name (artists unknown), A-Z
Norway
561 General works
562 Ancient
563 Medieval. Gothic. Romanesque
Modern
564 General works
565 14th-16th centuries
566 17th-18th centuries

Tables

Europe
Special countries
Scandinavia
Norway
Modern -- Continued
567 19th century
568 20th century
569.A-Z Special divisions, A-Z
570 Oslo
571.A-Z Other special cities, A-Z
572 Collective biography
573.A-Z Special artists, A-Z
573.3.A-Z Special works. By name (artists unknown), A-Z
Sweden
581 General works
582 Ancient
583 Medieval. Gothic. Romanesque
Modern
584 General works
585 14th-16th centuries
586 17th-18th centuries
587 19th century
588 20th century
589.A-Z Special divisions, A-Z
590 Stockholm
591.A-Z Other special cities, A-Z
592 Collective biography
593.A-Z Special artists, A-Z
593.3.A-Z Special works. By name (artists unknown), A-Z
Spain and Portugal. Spain
For Moorish architecture, see NA385, NA387
For Moorish art, see N6270, N6271
For Moorish decorative arts, see NK725, and NK1275
601 General works
602 Ancient
603 Medieval. Gothic. Romanesque
Modern
604 General works
605 14th-16th centuries
606 17th-18th centuries
607 19th century
608 20th century
609.A-Z Special divisions, A-Z
610 Madrid
611.A-Z Other special cities, A-Z
612 Collective biography
613.A-Z Special artists, A-Z
613.3.A-Z Special works. By name (artists unknown), A-Z
Portugal
621 General works
622 Ancient
623 Medieval. Gothic. Romanesque

Europe
Special countries
Spain and Portugal. Spain
Portugal -- Continued
Modern
624 General works
625 14th-16th centuries
626 17th-18th centuries
627 19th century
628 20th century
629.A-Z Special divisions, A-Z
630 Lisbon
631.A-Z Other special cities, A-Z
632 Collective biography
633.A-Z Special artists, A-Z
633.3.A-Z Special works. By name (artists unknown), A-Z
Swiss, German, and Austrian, see 359
Switzerland
641 General works
642 Ancient
643 Medieval. Gothic. Romanesque
Modern
644 General works
645 14th-16th centuries
646 17th-18th centuries
647 19th century
648 20th century
649.A-Z Special divisions, A-Z
650 Bern
651.A-Z Other special cities, A-Z
652 Collective biography
653.A-Z Special artists, A-Z
653.3.A-Z Special works. By name (artists unknown), A-Z
Turkey
661 General works
662 Ancient
663 Medieval. Gothic. Romanesque
Modern
664 General works
665 14th-16th centuries
666 17th-18th centuries
667 19th century
668 20th century
669.A-Z Special divisions, A-Z
670 Istanbul
671.A-Z Other special cities, A-Z
672 Collective biography
673.A-Z Special artists, A-Z
673.3.A-Z Special works. By name (artists unknown), A-Z
675 Other Balkan states
Bulgaria
681 General works
682 Ancient

Tables

Europe
Special countries
Other Balkan states
Bulgaria -- Continued

683 Medieval. Gothic. Romanesque
Modern
684 General works
685 14th-16th centuries
686 17th-18th centuries
687 19th century
688 20th century
689.A-Z Special divisions, A-Z
690 Sofia
691.A-Z Other special cities, A-Z
692 Collective biography
693.A-Z Special artists, A-Z
693.3.A-Z Special works. By name (artists unknown), A-Z
(701-713.3) Montenegro
See N5 749, and N5 751
Romania
721-723.3 General works
722 Ancient
723 Medieval. Gothic. Romanesque
Modern
724 General works
725 14th-16th centuries
726 17th-18th centuries
727 19th century
728 20th century
729.A-Z Special divisions, A-Z
730 Bucharest
731.A-Z Other special cities, A-Z
732 Collective biography
733.A-Z Special artists, A-Z
733.3.A-Z Special works. By name (artists unknown), A-Z
Yugoslavia
741 General works
742 Ancient
743 Medieval. Gothic. Romanesque
Modern
744 General works
745 14th-16th centuries
746 17th-18th centuries
747 19th century
748 20th century
749.A-Z Special divisions, A-Z
750 Belgrade
751.A-Z Other special cities, A-Z
752 Collective biography
753.A-Z Special artists, A-Z
753.3.A-Z Special works. By name (artists unknown), A-Z

Europe
Special countries -- Continued
755.A-Z Other regions or countries, A-Z
Under each country:
.x General works
.x2A-.x2Z Local, A-Z
.x3A-.x3Z Special artists, A-Z
755.A4 Albania
755.B44 Belarus
755.C76 Croatia
755.E8 Estonia
755.F5 Finland
755.L37 Latvia
755.L54 Liechtenstein
755.L57 Lithuania
755.M3 Malta
755.P6 Poland
755.S54 Slovakia
755.S56 Slovenia
755.U47 Ukraine
758 Mediterranean Region
Asia. The Orient
760 General works
762 Collections. Catalogs. Exhibitions
Southwestern Asia. Middle East
765 General works
Arab countries
765.3 General works
765.5 Arabian peninsula
Iraq. Mesopotamia
767 General works
768.A-Z Local, A-Z
769.A-Z Special artists, A-Z
Saudi Arabia
770 General works
771.A-Z Local, A-Z
772.A-Z Special artists, A-Z
Bahrain
772.2 General works
772.3.A-Z Local, A-Z
772.4.A-Z Special artists, A-Z
Kuwait
772.5 General works
772.6.A-Z Local, A-Z
772.7.A-Z Special artists, A-Z
United Arab Emirates
773 General works
773.2.A-Z Local, A-Z
773.3.A-Z Special artists, A-Z
Qatar
773.5 General works
773.6.A-Z Local, A-Z
773.7.A-Z Special artists, A-Z

	Asia. The Orient
	Southwestern Asia. Middle East -- Continued
	Armenia
	Class here works on art produced in the historic kingdom and region of Armenia as a whole
	For works on art produced in the territories incorporated after 1920 into other countries, see Armenia (Republic) or Turkey
774	General works
775.A-Z	Local, A-Z
776.A-Z	Special artists, A-Z
	Lebanon
776.6	General works
776.7.A-Z	Local, A-Z
776.8.A-Z	Special artists, A-Z
	Israel. Palestine
777	General works
778.A-Z	Local, A-Z
778.5	Collective biography
779.A-Z	Special artists, A-Z
	Jordan
779.6	General works
779.7.A-Z	Local, A-Z
779.8.A-Z	Special artists, A-Z
	Iran. Persia
780	General works
783	Before 1800
784	19th century
785	20th century
786.A-Z	Special divisions, A-Z
787.A-Z	Special cities, A-Z
788	Collective biography
789.A-Z	Special artists, A-Z
	Syria
789.6	General works
789.7.A-Z	Local, A-Z
789.8.A-Z	Special artists, A-Z
790.A-Z	Other divisions, A-Z
	e.g.
	Under each country:
	.x *General works*
	.x2A-.x2Z *Local, A-Z*
	.x3A-.x3Z *Special artists, A-Z*
	Cyprus
790.C9	General works
790.C92A-Z	Local, A-Z
790.C93A-Z	Special artists, A-Z
	Central Asia
791	General works
	Afghanistan
792	General works
792.2.A-Z	Local, A-Z

	Asia. The Orient
	Central Asia
	Afghanistan -- Continued
792.3.A-Z	Special artists, A-Z
	Russia in Asia
	For Russia in Asia as a whole, see 791
792.4	Caucasus
792.5	Abkhasia
792.6	Armenia (Republic)
	For historical Armenia, see 774-776
792.7	Azerbaijan
792.8	Daghestan
792.9	Georgia
793	Kazakhstan
794	Kirghizistan
795	Tajikistan
796	Turkmenistan
797	Uzbekistan
797.5.A-Z	Special regions, A-Z
798.A-Z	Special cities, A-Z
799.A-Z	Special artists, A-Z
	Southern Asia
800	General
	India. Indic art
801	General works
802	Before 1800
803	19th century
804	20th century
807.A-Z	Special regions, A-Z
808.A-Z	Special cities, A-Z
809	Collective biography
810.A-Z	Special artists, A-Z
810.3.A-Z	Special works. By name (artists unknown), A-Z
	Sri Lanka. Ceylon
810.6	General
810.62.A-Z	Local, A-Z
810.63.A-Z	Special artists, A-Z
	Pakistan
810.7	General
810.72.A-Z	Local, A-Z
810.73.A-Z	Special artists, A-Z
810.8.A-Z	Other regions or countries, A-Z
	e.g.
	Under each country:
	.x *General works*
	.x2A-.x2Z *Local, A-Z*
	.x3A-.x3Z *Special artists, A-Z*
	Nepal
810.8.N4	General works
810.8.N42A-Z	Local, A-Z
810.8.N43A-Z	Special artists, A-Z
	Southeastern Asia
811	General works

Tables

Asia. The Orient
Southeastern Asia -- Continued
Burma
812 General
812.2.A-Z Local, A-Z
812.3.A-Z Special artists, A-Z
French Indochina
813 General works
Vietnam. South Vietnam
814 General
814.2.A-Z Local, A-Z
814.3.A-Z Special artists, A-Z
Vietnam (Democratic Republic, 1946-)
814.6 General
814.62.A-Z Local, A-Z
814.63.A-Z Special artists, A-Z
Cambodia. Khmer art
815 General
815.2.A-Z Local, A-Z
815.3.A-Z Special artists, A-Z
Laos
816 General
816.2.A-Z Local, A-Z
816.3.A-Z Special artists, A-Z
Thailand. Siam
821 General
822.A-Z Local, A-Z
823.A-Z Special artists, A-Z
Malaysia
825 General works
825.6.A-Z Local, A-Z
825.7 Collective biography
825.8.A-Z Special artists, A-Z
Indonesia. Dutch East Indies
826 General works
826.6.A-Z Local, A-Z
Including Bali, Java, Kalimantan, and Sumatra
826.7 Collective biography
826.8.A-Z Special artists, A-Z
Philippines
827 General
828.A-Z Local, A-Z
829.A-Z Special artists, A-Z
830.A-Z Other divisions, A-Z
Under each country:
.x General works
.x2A-.x2Z Local, A-Z
.x3A-.x3Z Special artists, A-Z
832.A-Z Special artists, A-Z
Eastern Asia. China, Japan, etc.
836 Collections. Catalogs. Exhibitions (not A-Z)
837 General works
China

Asia. The Orient
Eastern Asia.
China, Japan, etc.
China -- Continued
840 General works
842 Collections. Catalogs. Exhibitions (not A-Z)
Prefer classification by period
Before 1800
843 General works
Pre-T'ang
843.2 General works
843.22 Early through Chou dynasty (To 221 B.C.)
843.23 Ch'in-Han dynasties (221 B.C.-220 A.D.)
843.24 Three kingdoms, six dynasties-Sui dynasty (220-618)
843.3 T'ang-Five dynasties (618-960)
843.4 Sung-Yüan dynasties (960-1368)
843.5 Ming-Ch'ing dynasties (1368-1912)
844 19th century
845 20th century
846.A-Z Special divisions, A-Z
e.g.
846.M2 Manchuria
846.T5 Tibet
847.A-Z Special cities, A-Z
848 Collective biography
849.A-Z Special artists, A-Z
849.6.A-Z Special works. By name (artists unknown), A-Z
849.7 Outer Mongolia. Mongolian People's Republic
849.75 Macao
Taiwan. Formosa
849.8 General works
849.82.A-Z Local, A-Z
849.825 Collective biography
849.83.A-Z Special artists, A-Z
Japan
For Formosa, see 849.8-83
850 General works
852 Collections. Catalogs. Exhibitions (not A-Z)
Prefer classification by period
Early to 1868
853 General works
To 1600
853.12 General works
853.2 Early through 794 A.D.
853.3 Fujiwara (Heian) period (794-1185)
853.4 Kamakura-Momoyama periods (1185-1600)
853.5 Tokugawa (Edo) period (1600-1868)
19th century
854 General works
854.5 Meiji period (1868-1912)
20th century
855 General works

Tables

Asia. The Orient
Eastern Asia.
China, Japan, etc.
Japan
20th century -- Continued
855.3 Taisho period (1912-1926)
855.4 Showa period (1926-1989)
856.A-Z Special divisions, A-Z
857.A-Z Special cities, A-Z
858 Collective biography
859.A-Z Special artists, A-Z
859.6.A-Z Special works. By name (artists unknown), A-Z
Korea. South Korea
860 General works
862 Collections. Catalogs. Exhibitions (not A-Z)
Before 1900
863 General works
863.2 Earliest to 935
Including Silla Kingdom, etc.
863.3 Koryo (Koryu) period, 935-1392
I (Yi) dynasty, 1392-1910
863.4 General works
863.8 18th century
864 19th century
865 20th century
866.A-Z Special divisions, A-Z
867.A-Z Special cities, A-Z
868 Collective biography
869.A-Z Special artists, A-Z
869.6.A-Z Special works. By name (artists unknown), A-Z
North Korea
870 General works
870.2.A-Z Local, A-Z
870.3.A-Z Special artists, A-Z
Northern Asia
For Russia in Central Asia, see 792.4-799
For Siberia, see N5 495
Africa
880 General
880.5 Collections. Catalogs. Exhibitions. By author or title
Egypt
881 General works
Modern
881.6 19th century
881.7 20th century
882 Coptic art
883 Cairo
884.A-Z Other local, A-Z
885.A-Z Special artists, A-Z
885.3.A-Z Special peoples, A-Z
885.3.A97 Ayyubids
Copts, see 882

Africa
Egypt
Special peoples, A-Z -- Continued
885.3.M35 Mamelukes
Ethiopia
886 General works
886.2.A-Z Local, A-Z
886.3.A-Z Special artists, A-Z
North Africa
887 General works
Algeria
888 General works
888.2.A-Z Local, A-Z
888.3.A-Z Special artists, A-Z
Libya
889 General works
889.2.A-Z Local, A-Z
889.3.A-Z Special artists, A-Z
Morocco
890 General works
890.2.A-Z Local, A-Z
890.3.A-Z Special artists, A-Z
Tunisia
891 General works
891.2.A-Z Local, A-Z
891.3.A-Z Special artists, A-Z
891.6.A-Z Other, A-Z
Under each country:
.x General works
.x2A-.x2Z Local, A-Z
.x3A-.x3Z Special artists, A-Z
891.65 Sub-Saharan Africa. Central Africa
Southern Africa
891.7 General works
Republic of South Africa
892 General works
894.A-Z Special divisions, A-Z
895.A-Z Special cities, A-Z
895.6 Collective biography
896.A-Z Special artists, A-Z
896.6.A-Z Other countries, A-Z
Botswana
896.6.B6 General works
896.6.B62A-Z Local, A-Z
896.6.B63A-Z Special artists, A-Z
Lesotho
896.6.L4 General works
896.6.L42A-Z Local, A-Z
896.6.L43A-Z Special artists, A-Z
Malawi
896.6.M3 General works
896.6.M32A-Z Local, A-Z
896.6.M33A-Z Special artists, A-Z

Tables

	Africa
	Southern Africa
	Other countries, A-Z -- Continued
	Namibia
896.6.N35	General works
896.6.N352A-Z	Local, A-Z
896.6.N353A-Z	Special artists, A-Z
	Rhodesia, Southern. Zimbabwe
896.6.R5	General works
896.6.R52A-Z	Local, A-Z
896.6.R53A-Z	Special artists, A-Z
	Swaziland
896.6.S8	General works
896.6.S82A-Z	Local, A-Z
896.6.S83A-Z	Special artists, A-Z
	Zambia
896.6.Z3	General works
896.6.Z32A-Z	Local, A-Z
896.6.Z33A-Z	Special artists, A-Z
	Zimbabwe, see 896.6.R5-R53
	Eastern Africa
897	General works
897.6.A-Z	By country, A-Z
	Burundi
897.6.B8	General works
897.6.B82A-Z	Local, A-Z
897.6.B83A-Z	Special artists, A-Z
	Comoro Islands
897.6.C6	General works
897.6.C62A-Z	Local, A-Z
897.6.C63A-Z	Special artists, A-Z
	French Somaliland
897.6.F7	General works
897.6.F72A-Z	Local, A-Z
897.6.F73A-Z	Special artists, A-Z
	Kenya
897.6.K4	General works
897.6.K42A-Z	Local, A-Z
897.6.K43A-Z	Special artists, A-Z
	Madagascar
897.6.M3	General works
897.6.M32A-Z	Local, A-Z
897.6.M33A-Z	Special artists, A-Z
	Mozambique
897.6.M6	General works
897.6.M62A-Z	Local, A-Z
897.6.M63A-Z	Special artists, A-Z
	Rwanda
897.6.R8	General works
897.6.R82A-Z	Local, A-Z
897.6.R83A-Z	Special artists, A-Z
	Somali Republic
897.6.S6	General works

	Africa
	Eastern Africa
	By country, A-Z
	Somali Republic -- Continued
897.6.S62A-Z	Local, A-Z
897.6.S63A-Z	Special artists, A-Z
	Sudan
897.6.S73	General works
897.6.S732A-Z	Local, A-Z
897.6.S733A-Z	Special artists, A-Z
	Tanzania
897.6.T3	General works
897.6.T32A-Z	Local, A-Z
897.6.T33A-Z	Special artists, A-Z
	Zanzibar
897.6.Z3	General works
897.6.Z32A-Z	Local, A-Z
897.6.Z33A-Z	Special artists, A-Z
	Western Africa
898	General works
899.A-Z	By country, A-Z
	Angola
899.A5	General works
899.A52A-Z	Local, A-Z
899.A53A-Z	Special artists, A-Z
	Benin, see 899.D3-D33
	Burkina Faso
899.B87	General works
899.B872A-Z	Local, A-Z
899.B873A-Z	Special artists, A-Z
	Cameroon
899.C3	General works
899.C32A-Z	Local, A-Z
899.C33A-Z	Special artists, A-Z
	Central African Republic
899.C4	General works
899.C42A-Z	Local, A-Z
899.C43A-Z	Special artists, A-Z
	Chad
899.C5	General works
899.C52A-Z	Local, A-Z
899.C53A-Z	Special artists, A-Z
	Congo (Democratic Republic). Belgian Congo. Zaire
899.C6	General works
899.C62A-Z	Local, A-Z
899.C63A-Z	Special artists, A-Z
	Congo (Brazzaville)
899.C7	General works
899.C72A-Z	Local, A-Z
899.C73A-Z	Special artists, A-Z
899.C76	Cross River Region (Cameroon and Nigeria)
	Dahomey. Benin

Tables

Africa
Western Africa
By country, A-Z
Dahomey. Benin -- Continued

899.D3 General works
899.D32A-Z Local, A-Z
899.D33A-Z Special artists, A-Z

Equatorial Guinea

899.E68 General works
899.E682A-Z Local, A-Z
899.E683A-Z Special artists, A-Z

Gabon

899.G25 General works
899.G252A-Z Local, A-Z
899.G253A-Z Special artists, A-Z

Gambia

899.G3 General works
899.G32A-Z Local, A-Z
899.G33A-Z Special artists, A-Z

Ghana

899.G5 General works
899.G52A-Z Local, A-Z
899.G53A-Z Special artists, A-Z

Guinea

899.G8 General works
899.G82A-Z Local, A-Z
899.G83A-Z Special artists, A-Z

Guinea-Bissau, see 899.P6-P63

Ivory Coast

899.I8 General works
899.I82A-Z Local, A-Z
899.I83A-Z Special artists, A-Z

Liberia

899.L4 General works
899.L42A-Z Local, A-Z
899.L43A-Z Special artists, A-Z

Mali

899.M3 General works
899.M32A-Z Local, A-Z
899.M33A-Z Special artists, A-Z

Mauritania

899.M4 General works
899.M42A-Z Local, A-Z
899.M43A-Z Special artists, A-Z

Niger

899.N4 General works
899.N42A-Z Local, A-Z
899.N43A-Z Special artists, A-Z

Nigeria

899.N5 General works
899.N52A-Z Local, A-Z
899.N53A-Z Special artists, A-Z

Portuguese Guinea. Guinea-Bissau

Africa
Western Africa
By country, A-Z
Portuguese Guinea. Guinea-Bissau -- Continued

899.P6	General works
899.P62A-Z	Local, A-Z
899.P63A-Z	Special artists, A-Z
(899.R5)	Rio Muni See N5 899.E68
	Senegal
899.S4	General works
899.S42A-Z	Local, A-Z
899.S43A-Z	Special artists, A-Z
	Sierra Leone
899.S5	General works
899.S52A-Z	Local, A-Z
899.S53A-Z	Special artists, A-Z
	Southwest Africa
899.S6	General works
899.S62A-Z	Local, A-Z
899.S63A-Z	Special artists, A-Z
	Togo
899.T6	General works
899.T62A-Z	Local, A-Z
899.T63A-Z	Special artists, A-Z
	Upper Volta, see 899.B87-B873
	Zaire, see 899.C6-C63
	Indian Ocean islands
899.4	General
899.5.A-Z	Individual islands, A-Z *Under each island:* *.x General works* *.x2A-.x2Z Local, A-Z* *.x3A-.x3Z Special artists, A-Z*
	Mauritius
899.5.M38	General works
899.5.M382A-M382Z	Local, A-Z
	Réunion
899.5.R48	General works
899.5.R482A-R482Z	Local, A-Z
899.5.R483A-R483Z	Special artists, A-Z
899.6	Southern Hemisphere
	Australasia. Oceania
899.7	General works
	Australia
900	General
900.14	Colonial
900.15	19th century
900.2	20th century
901	Native art
902.A-Z	Special divisions, A-Z e.g.

Tables

Australasia. Oceania
Australia
Special divisions, A-Z -- Continued
902.T2 Tasmania
903.A-Z Special cities, A-Z
904 Collective biography
905.A-Z Special artists, A-Z
Including aboriginal artists, firms, etc.
905.3 Ethnic groups (Collectively)
New Zealand
906 General
Modern
906.3 19th century
906.5 20th century
907.A-Z Local, A-Z
907.5 Collective biography
908.A-Z Special artists, A-Z
Oceania. Pacific islands
Including Melanesia, Micronesia, Polynesia
See N5 30-35, for Hawaiian Islands
910 General
911.A-Z Special, A-Z
912.A-Z Special cities, A-Z
913.A-Z Special artists, A-Z
914 Developing countries

Use Tables N6 and N7 to subarrange works by and about individual artists throughout the schedule

Use Table N6 for classes reading "Special artists, A-Z" with first Cutter designating the artist, e.g. ND623.L5, Leonardo da Vinci

.xA2	Autobiography. By date
.xA3	Letters. By date
.xA35	Speeches, essays, interviews, etc. of the artist. By date
.xA4	Reproductions (Collections). By date Including exhibition catalogs
.xA6-.xA79	Individual works of art. Alphabetically by title of work of art and date
.xA8-.xZ	Biography and criticism

Tables

Use Tables N6 and N7 to subarrange works by and about individual artists throughout the schedule

Use Table N7 for classes in which a three Cutter span is assigned for geographical areas, the third Cutter representing special artists, e.g., ND955.P6A233-ND955.P6239, (Poland - Aberdam, Alfred - Biography and criticism

x Autobiography, letters, speeches, essays, interviews, etc. By date

x2 Reproductions. By date

Including collections, individual works of art, exhibition catalogs

x3-.x39 Biography and criticism. Alphabetically by author

This table generally represents the counties before the 1974 reorganization

.B4	Bedfordshire
.B5	Berkshire
.B9	Buckinghamshire
.C2	Cambridgeshire
.C5	Cheshire
.C7	Cornwall
.C9	Cumberland
.D4	Derbyshire
.D5	Devonshire
.D7	Dorsetshire
.D9	Durham
.E8	Essex
.G5	Gloucestershire
.H2	Hampshire
.H5	Herefordshire
.H6	Hertfordshire
.H7	Huntingdonshire
.K3	Kent
.L2	Lancashire
.L5	Leicestershire
.L7	Lincolnshire
.M6	Middlesex
.N5	Norfolk
.N6	Northamptonshire
.N7	Northumberland
.N8	Nottinghamshire
.O9	Oxfordshire
.R9	Rutlandshire
.S3	Shropshire
.S5	Somerset
.S52	South Yorkshire
.S6	Staffordshire
.S7	Suffolk
.S8	Surrey
.S9	Sussex
.W3	Warwickshire
.W5	Westmorland
.W7	Wiltshire
.W9	Worcestershire
.Y5	Yorkshire

Tables

Use Table N9 to subarrange works by and/or about individual museums

.A1-.A4 Reports

.A5-.A7 Catalogs

Subarranged by title

History and description

Including biographies of individual museum personnel associated with only a single museum

.A8-.A89 Cataloged under name of museum

.A9-.Z9 Cataloged under author other than the museum

Use Table N10 to subarrange works by and/or about international exhibitions

.A1-.A4 Official reports

.A5-.A7 Official catalogs

.A8-.Z9 Non-official (by author)

Tables

.A1	Periodicals and societies
.A2	Collections. Congresses
.A3A-Z	Exhibitions. By city, A-Z
.A4	General works
	History
.A5	General works
.A6-.Z9	By region or country, A-Z

.x1	Periodicals and societies
.x2	Collections. Congresses
.x3A-Z	Exhibitions. By city, A-Z
.x4	General works
	History
.x5	General works
.x6A-Z	By region or country, A-Z

.A2	General works
	Including collective biography
.A3	Technique
.A4A-Z	Special styles, A-Z
.A5-.Z5	Special artists, A-Z
.Z6A-Z	Special works, by name (artists unknown)

.x	General works
	Including collective biography
.x3	Techniques
.x4A-Z	Special styles, A-Z
.x5A-Z	Special artists, A-Z
.x6A-Z	Special works, by name (artists unknown)

INDEX

NUMERALS

A

INDEX

INDEX

INDEX

INDEX

INDEX

INDEX

INDEX

INDEX

C

INDEX

INDEX

INDEX

Index

INDEX

F

INDEX

INDEX

Index

K

M

INDEX

P

INDEX

Index

S

Index

W